MW00781330

SAP PRESS e-books

Print or e-book, Kindle or iPad, workplace or airplane: Choose where and how to read your SAP PRESS books! You can now get all our titles as e-books, too:

- ▶ By download and online access
- ▶ For all popular devices
- ▶ And, of course, DRM-free

Convinced? Then go to www.sap-press.com and get your e-book today.

Financial Accounting in SAP®: Business User Guide

 PRESS

SAP PRESS is a joint initiative of SAP and Rheinwerk Publishing. The know-how offered by SAP specialists combined with the expertise of Rheinwerk Publishing offers the reader expert books in the field. SAP PRESS features first-hand information and expert advice, and provides useful skills for professional decision-making.

SAP PRESS offers a variety of books on technical and business-related topics for the SAP user. For further information, please visit our website: *www.sap-press.com*.

Jens Krüger
SAP S/4HANA Finance: An Introduction (2nd Edition)
2016, 411 pages, hardcover and e-book
www.sap-press.com/4122

Kathrin Schmalzing
Configuring Controlling in SAP ERP
2016, 526 pages, hardcover and e-book
www.sap-press.com/3887

Narayanan Veeriah
Configuring Financial Accounting in SAP (2nd Edition)
2015, 907 pages, hardcover and e-book
www.sap-press.com/3665

Janet Salmon
Controlling with SAP: Practical Guide (2nd Edition)
2014, 700 pages, hardcover and e-book
www.sap-press.com/3625

David Burns

Financial Accounting in SAP®:
Business User Guide

Rheinwerk®
Publishing

Bonn • Boston

Editor Hareem Shafi
Acquisitions Editor Emily Nicholls
Copyeditor Melinda Rankin
Cover Design Graham Geary
Photo Credit iStockphoto.com: 14443978/© blackred; 20657041/© tashka2000;
  12786483/© blackred
Layout Design Vera Brauner
Production Graham Geary
Typesetting III-satz, Husby (Germany)
Printed and bound in the United States of America, on paper from sustainable sources

ISBN 978-1-4932-1314-6
© 2016 by Rheinwerk Publishing, Inc., Boston (MA)
1st edition 2016

Library of Congress Cataloging-in-Publication Data
Names: Burns, David, (Financial accounting specialist)
Title: Financial account in SAP-practical guide / David Burns.
Description: 1st Edition. | Boston : Rheinwerk Publishing, 2016. | Includes index.
Identifiers: LCCN 2016010835| ISBN 9781493213146 (print : alk. paper) | ISBN 9781493213153 (ebook) | ISBN 9781493213160 (print and ebook : alk. paper)
Subjects: LCSH: SAP ERP. | Accounting--Computer programs. | Accounting--Data processing.
Classification: LCC HF5679 .B837 2016 | DDC 657.0285/53--dc23 LC record available at http://lccn.loc.gov/2016010835

All rights reserved. Neither this publication nor any part of it may be copied or reproduced in any form or by any means or translated into another language, without the prior consent of Rheinwerk Publishing, 2 Heritage Drive, Suite 305, Quincy, MA 02171.

Rheinwerk Publishing makes no warranties or representations with respect to the content hereof and specifically disclaims any implied warranties of merchantability or fitness for any particular purpose. Rheinwerk Publishing assumes no responsibility for any errors that may appear in this publication.

"Rheinwerk Publishing" and the Rheinwerk Publishing logo are registered trademarks of Rheinwerk Verlag GmbH, Bonn, Germany. SAP PRESS is an imprint of Rheinwerk Verlag GmbH and Rheinwerk Publishing, Inc.

All of the screenshots and graphics reproduced in this book are subject to copyright © SAP SE, Dietmar-Hopp-Allee 16, 69190 Walldorf, Germany.

SAP, the SAP logo, ABAP, Ariba, ASAP, Duet, hybris, SAP Adaptive Server Enterprise, SAP Advantage Database Server, SAP Afaria, SAP ArchiveLink, SAP Business ByDesign, SAP Business Explorer (SAP BEx), SAP BusinessObjects, SAP Business-Objects Web Intelligence, SAP Business One, SAP Business-Objects Explorer, SAP Business Workflow, SAP Crystal Reports, SAP d-code, SAP EarlyWatch, SAP Fiori, SAP Ganges, SAP Global Trade Services (SAP GTS), SAP GoingLive, SAP HANA, SAP Jam, SAP Lumira, SAP MaxAttention, SAP MaxDB, SAP NetWeaver, SAP PartnerEdge, SAPPHIRE NOW, SAP PowerBuilder, SAP PowerDesigner, SAP R/2, SAP R/3, SAP Replication Server, SAP SI, SAP SQL Anywhere, SAP Strategic Enterprise Management (SAP SEM), SAP StreamWork, SuccessFactors, Sybase, TwoGo by SAP, and The Best-Run Businesses Run SAP are registered or unregistered trademarks of SAP SE, Walldorf, Germany.

All other products mentioned in this book are registered or unregistered trademarks of their respective companies.

Contents at a Glance

Dear Reader,

As a financial professional, you know what it means to want to close the books accurately and quickly. As an editor, so do I.

Well, okay; I'm talking about the type of book you're holding right now, and you're thinking of the accounting process. But when you think about it, there are a lot of similarities!

Financial accounting is about understanding and accounting for the financial resources of a business. You need to be able to document the movement of money inside and outside a company, handle financial assets, interface with banks, and more. At the end of the day, it's important that you are able to understand your company's finances and relay that information accurately and efficiently to the people or agencies that need it.

As an editor, the assets I handle are books, and it's my job to make sure that everything adds up before a book prints. Is the information presented accurate? Is it clear and concise? Is it easy-to-understand? Above all, is it helpful to the people who need it?

While I have yet to find a comprehensive book that will guide me through the editorial process, you need look no further in your search for *the* book on SAP ERP Financial Accounting. David Burns has brought together his considerable expertise, his incredible writing talents, and his tireless dedication to create a book that is everything you need to become a veritable FI expert.

So, dear reader, I close the books on *Financial Accounting in SAP: Business User Guide* and hand it off to you. What did you think about this book? Your comments and suggestions are the most useful tools to help us make our books the best they can be. Please feel free to contact me and share any praise or criticism you may have.

Thank you for purchasing a book from SAP PRESS!

Hareem Shafi
Editor, SAP PRESS

Rheinwerk Publishing
Boston, MA

hareems@rheinwerk-publishing.com
www.sap-press.com

Contents

In this chapter, we cover some basic concepts and terms that make up the backbone of Financial Accounting in SAP. Specifically, we cover the definition and assignment of business units, as represented in the SAP enterprise structure.

1 Introduction to Financial Accounting

Financial Accounting in SAP ERP consists of several essential system accounting functions, such as General Ledger (G/L), Accounts Receivable (A/R), Accounts Payable (A/P), Banking, and Fixed Assets. To achieve a full understanding of Financial Accounting (FI), first you need to grasp the concept of the system enterprise structure. In SAP, the *enterprise structure* is the definition of specific organizational units that together represent your company's business units and divisions. Enterprise structures are the building blocks upon which additional configuration hinges. They also represent the relationships between the organizational units in your company and enable integration and the exchange of data.

For most SAP users, the majority of time in SAP is spent creating transactions and running reports. Behind the scenes, however, an enterprise structure enables the execution of transactions and reports and facilitates the exchange of data between SAP modules. The enterprise structure is the backbone of SAP system design. When an SAP system is first designed for use in FI, the enterprise structure is defined. Getting this structure right is critical to the remainder of the system setup and configuration.

Regardless of your company's size, industry, or geography, you must define an enterprise structure. When an SAP system is configured, your company structure is reflected in organizational units defined in modules for accounting, logistics, human resources, and more. The assignment of these organizational units to one another is what enables integration between the modules.

As a practical guide to FI, the content in this book focuses on business scenarios and transactions. However, by giving you an understanding of enterprise structures, this chapter empowers you with a better overall understanding of FI and the necessary building blocks that influence specific parts of your business processes.

Let's start our discussion by talking about company, company code, and other FI enterprise structures in the next section.

1.1 Defining the Organizational Structure

The organizational structure of your company (i.e., business units and divisions) is defined in the SAP Customizing Implementation Guide (IMG). The organizational structures as a whole make up your enterprise structure and are created in the IMG. IMG activities are considered configuration, and it is not the intent here to teach how to configure the enterprise structure. However, it is important for you to have an understanding of the underlying structure of FI. Moreover, when creating financial transactions it is important for the end user to be aware of the enterprise structure in order to ensure transactions are posted properly. It is also important to know when and how financial transactions impact business processes and areas within the company.

To access the IMG, enter "SPRO" in the COMMAND field (as shown in Figure 1.1) and press Enter.

Figure 1.1 SPRO in Command Field

The CUSTOMIZING: EXECUTE PROJECT screen will appear (Figure 1.2).

Click on the SAP REFERENCE IMG button shown in Figure 1.2, and the DISPLAY IMG screen will appear (Figure 1.3).

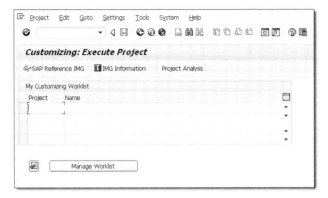

Figure 1.2 Transaction SPRO, Customizing: Execute Project Screen

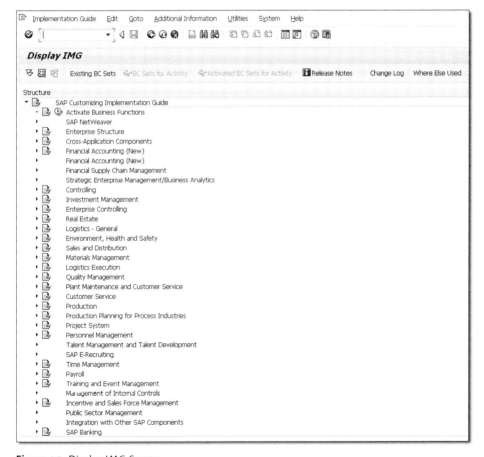

Figure 1.3 Display IMG Screen

To define the enterprise structure for FI, follow the IMG menu path ENTERPRISE STRUCTURE • DEFINITION • FINANCIAL ACCOUNTING, as shown in Figure 1.4.

Figure 1.4 IMG Define Enterprise Structure Menu Path for Financial Accounting

The IMG menu path shown in Figure 1.4 points to where you create FI enterprise structures. These enterprise structures include company, credit control crea, company code, business area, functional area, consolidation business area, financial management area, and segment and profit center. All of these structures are discussed in the sections that follow.

1.1.1 Company

According to SAP, a *company* is an organizational unit in accounting that represents a business organization according to the requirements of commercial law in a particular country. Consolidation functions in FI are based on companies. One or more company codes can be assigned to a company. It is important to note that all company codes assigned to a company must use the same operational chart of accounts and fiscal year, but the currencies used can be different.

Figure 1.5 shows an example of a company defined in the IMG. The six-character COMPANY field contains the company ID. In its entirety, the company definition consists of the company ID, company name, and detailed information such as address, country, language, and currency.

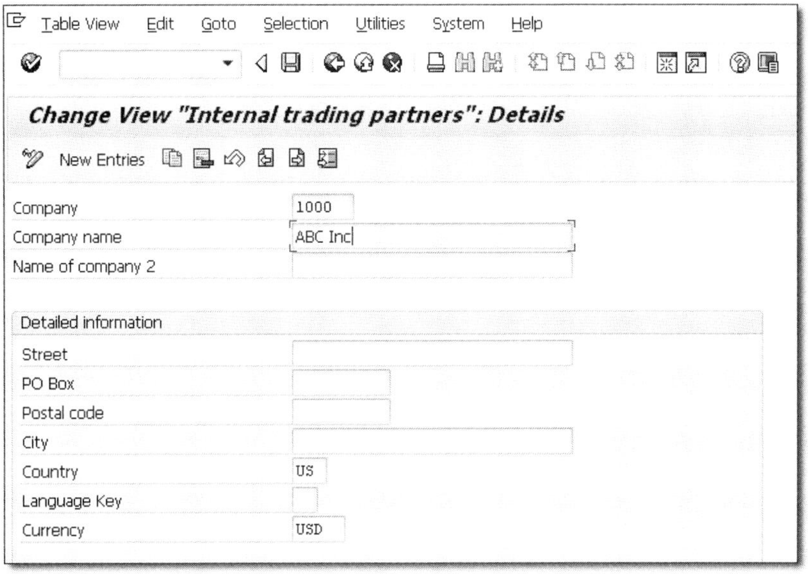

Figure 1.5 Display Company

1.1.2   Company Code

Typically, a *company code* is a legally independent company. The company code may also represent a legally dependent operating unit based abroad if there are external reporting requirements for the operating unit. You must define at least one company code to use FI, because the company code is the central organizational unit for financial transactions and is necessary to configure business processes and to create master data. According to SAP, you should create a company code according to tax law, commercial law, and other financial accounting criteria.

All financial postings require a company code specification. It serves as a central link to many posting functions, including field status control, posting periods, workflows, G/L accounts, and many additional processing parameters. The company code also serves as a link to other SAP modules to enable FI integration with

Sales and Distributions (SD), Materials Management (MM), Controlling (CO), Funds Management (FM), and more.

Figure 1.6 shows an example of a company code. COMPANY CODE is a four-character field. Within a company code, you can set many essential specifications, including a chart of accounts, fiscal year variant, posting period variant, and workflow variant. The company code is a fundamental enterprise structure in FI, with numerous ACCOUNTING ORGANIZATION settings and PROCESSING PARAMETERS linked to it that influence and control financial postings.

Figure 1.6 Example Company Code

Note that while the IMG node EDIT, COPY, DELETE, CHECK COMPANY CODE (Figure 1.4) is used to initially create your company code, the functional characteristics of the company code aren't specified until FI is configured. These settings are made using Transaction OBY6.

1.1.3 Credit Control Area

The *credit control area* is an FI organizational unit that specifies and checks a credit limit for customers. In essence, the credit control area is where customer credit is given and monitored. A credit control area can be assigned to more than one company code, but each company code can only be assigned to one credit control area.

Figure 1.7 shows an example of a credit control area defined in the IMG. CRED.CONTR.AREA is a four-character field within which a credit limit is specified based upon a risk category and/or group. In addition, the UPDATE field specifies when value checks take place for sales orders, deliveries, and billing documents.

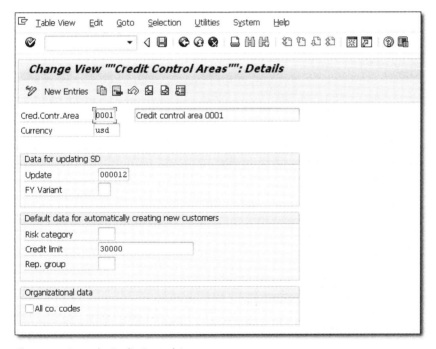

Figure 1.7 Example Credit Control Area

Let's discuss a few other important points about the credit control area. It is used for credit management in both accounts receivable, and sales and distributions. The CRED.CONTR.AREA field (Figure 1.7) is also referred to as the *credit control key*.

A simple approach to the credit control area is to create one area for each company code. This is referred to as the *decentralized credit management* approach. In other words, credit is awarded and monitored based on a singular relationship between credit control area, company code, sales organization, and currency.

However, when you have the same customer created in multiple company codes, you have a unique challenge. That challenge is that credit management for each customer is determined by the credit control area assigned to the company code. Yet, if a customer is created in multiple company codes and each company code is assigned to the same credit control area, then the cross-company customers are managed by the same credit management settings in a common credit control area. This is referred to as the *central credit management* approach. With it, customer credit management across company codes is combined.

As a final note on credit control areas, it is possible for a company code to have a different local currency from the one specified in the credit control area. In this case, the system converts receivable amounts (such as, open sales orders, deliveries, and bills) into the currency of the credit control area. In other words, credit limits and monitoring in done in the credit control area currency.

1.1.4 Segment

A *segment* is a division of a company for which you can create financial statements for external reporting. Accounting principles in US GAAP and IFRS necessitate companies to perform segment reporting. US GAAP and IFRS require a complete balance sheet at the segment level. In accounting terms, this is referred to as *segment reporting*. The segment dimension was introduced by SAP in the New G/L (see Appendix A) to fulfill this requirement.

You can enter a segment in the master record of a profit center, and then the segment is derived from the assigned profit center during posting. You can also enter a segment manually in FI transactions.

Figure 1.8 shows an example of a segment defined in the IMG. SEGMENT is a ten-character field with a fifty-character DESCRIPTION field. A segment has no other fields, parameters, or control settings.

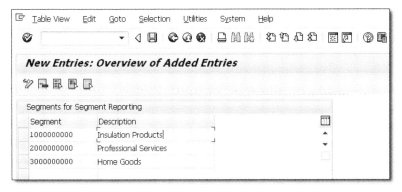

Figure 1.8 Example Segment

Throughout this book, the segment characteristic is presented and discussed numerous times. It is a very important concept for financial managers and accountants to understand. Therefore, we won't shy away from repeated discussions about it.

In summary, a segment is a subarea of a company with significant enough expenses, revenues, and operating results (according to accounting rules) to warrant separate financial statements.

1.1.5   Profit Center

A *profit center* is a management-oriented organizational unit used for internal control purposes. Dividing your company into profit centers allows you to analyze areas of responsibility and delegate responsibility to decentralized units. Before defining a profit center, you must create a controlling (CO) area and a standard hierarchy.

Figure 1.9 shows an example profit center. PROFIT CENTER is a ten-character field. Notice that in the GENERAL DATA screen a PROFIT CENTER is assigned to a CONTROLLING AREA and has a VALIDITY PERIOD.

Figure 1.9 shows profit center tabs for BASIC DATA, INDICATORS, COMPANY CODES, ADDRESS, COMMUNICATION, and HISTORY. It is beyond the scope of this book to cover each of these tabs in detail. However, you should become familiar with these tabs and settings if you use profit centers.

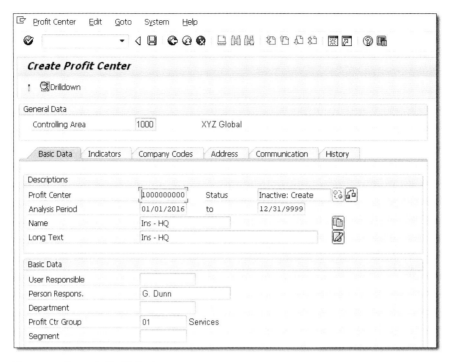

Figure 1.9 Example Profit Center

It's important to know that profit centers were integrated into FI with the New G/L. For more information, see Appendix A.

1.1.6 Business Area

A *business area* is an optional FI organizational unit. It defines organizational units within accounting that represent separate areas of operations or responsibilities. Financial statements can be created by business area for internal purposes. For the most part, companies have transitioned away from the use of business areas with the introduction of segments and the New G/L.

Figure 1.10 shows an example of a business area. BUSINESS AREA is a four-character field with a thirty-character DESCRIPTION field. A business area has no other fields, parameters, or control settings.

Before moving on, let's discuss the distinction between business areas, segments, and profit centers. There is often confusion about when and how to use each object. We want to make this distinction to ensure you are clear about how to use the business area.

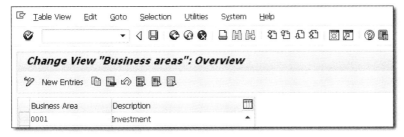

Figure 1.10 Example Business Area

Today, SAP defines a business area as a separate area of responsibility or operations. However, in the past, it was also referred to as a separate segment of the business. With the introduction of New G/L and the segment dimension, segment—not business area—should be used to fulfill accounting requirements for segment reporting.

Profit centers, on the other hand, are management-oriented organizational units used for internal controlling purposes.

On a final point, we should note that in Figure 1.4 there is a node called MAINTAIN CONSOLIDATION BUSINESS AREA. This activity allows you to create consolidation business areas to represent central business segments. Because of the variability in the use of business areas, this topic is not addressed in this section. Moreover, with the introduction of the segment dimension, the applicability of business areas and consolidated business areas is in flux.

1.1.7 Functional Area

A *functional area* is an organizational unit in FI that classifies expenses according to function. It was originally designed for use in cost-of-sales accounting. SAP lists possible functional classifications as administration, sales, marketing, production, and research and development. In traditional application, functional areas can be used to create profit and loss statements using cost-of-sales accounting. Since its original creation, the functional area has also been used in Funds Management for government accounting, in which it represents government functions, such as public safety.

Figure 1.11 shows an example of a functional area. FUNCTIONAL AREA is a sixteen-character field with a twenty-five-character DESCRIPTION field. A functional area has no other fields, parameters, or control settings.

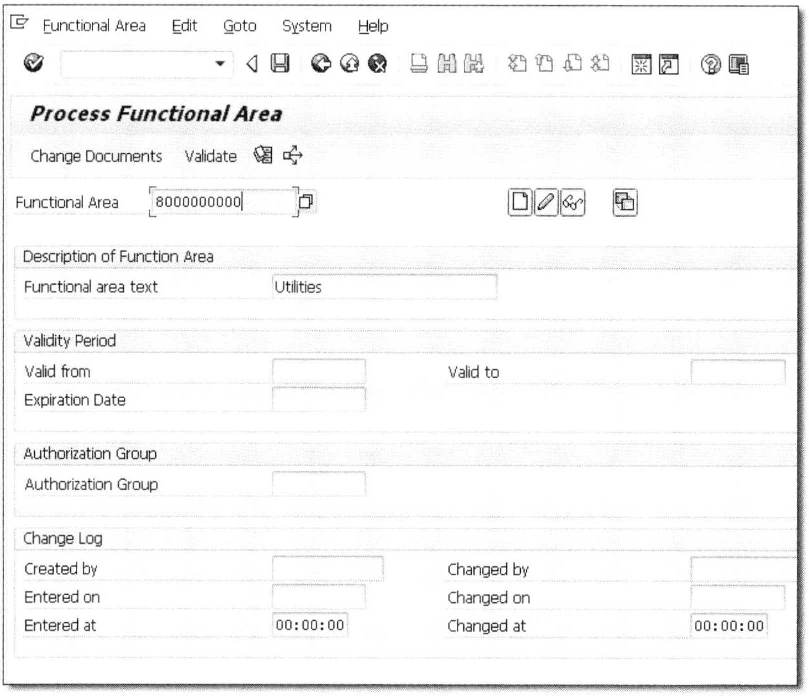

Figure 1.11 Example Functional Area

1.1.8 Financial Management Area

The *financial management* (FM) *area* is an organizational unit in FI that structures the business organization from the perspective of Cash Budget Management and Funds Management. The system derives the FM area from the company code when you assign the company code to an FM area. Several company codes can be assigned to an FM area.

Figure 1.12 shows an example of an FM area defined in the IMG. FM AREA is a four-character field with a twenty-five-character description. It also has a currency assigned.

Now that we have discussed the definition of enterprise structures in FI, let's move on to discuss the assignment of specific structures to one another—much like putting together the pieces of a puzzle. Organizational structures are linked in the IMG to establish relationships and enable system integration.

Figure 1.12 Example Funds Management Area

1.2 Assigning Organizational Structures

In Section 1.1 we covered the topic of defining organizational structures in FI. This is referred to as the definition of the enterprise structure. The next step after defining these structures is to assign them to one another—in other words, to build the references between the organizational units that you have defined. Once these assignments are complete, the organizational framework is, for the most part, complete, active, and ready for data integration between modules.

To assign organizational structures for your company (i.e., business units and divisions), use the IMG. To access the IMG, enter "SPRO" in the COMMAND field (as shown in Figure 1.13) and press [Enter].

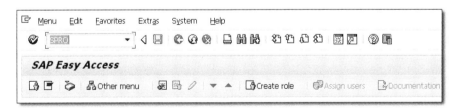

Figure 1.13 SPRO in Command Field

The CUSTOMIZING: EXECUTE PROJECT screen will appear (Figure 1.14).

Click on the SAP REFERENCE IMG button shown in Figure 1.14, and the DISPLAY IMG screen will appear (Figure 1.15).

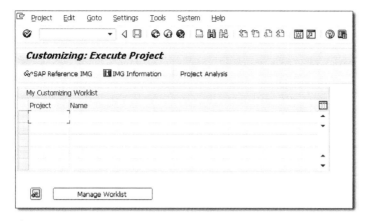

Figure 1.14 Transaction SPRO, Customizing: Execute Project Screen

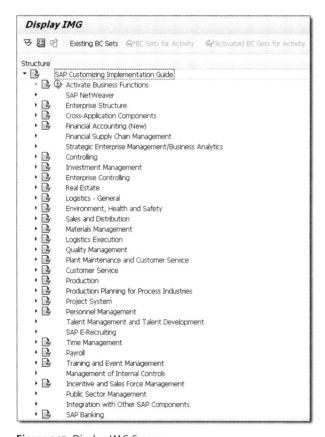

Figure 1.15 Display IMG Screen

To assign the enterprise structure for FI, follow IMG menu path ENTERPRISE STRUCTURE • ASSIGNMENT • FINANCIAL ACCOUNTING, as shown in Figure 1.16.

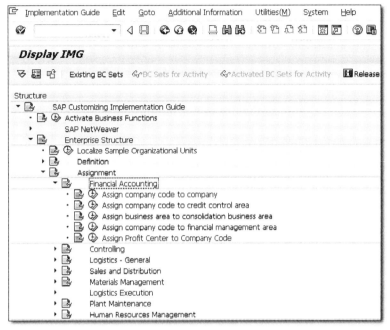

Figure 1.16 IMG Assign Enterprise Structure Menu Path for Financial Accounting

The IMG menu path shown in Figure 1.16 points to where you assign FI enterprise structures.

1.2.1 Company Code to Company

Assigning a company code to a company establishes a relationship between these objects. Consolidation functions in FI are built upon the company object. A company can comprise one or more company codes.

When assigning organizational units, it is important to know that they have dependencies and limitations. In the case of company code to company assignment, all company codes assigned to the same company must use the same operational chart of accounts and fiscal year.

Figure 1.17 shows an example of a company code assignment (COCD) to a company.

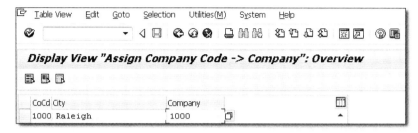

Figure 1.17 Example Company Code to Company Assignment

1.2.2 Company Code to Credit Control Area

Assigning a company code to a credit control area enables you to specify and check a credit limit for customers. A credit control area can include one or more company codes, but it is not possible to assign a company code to more than one credit control area.

Figure 1.18 shows an example of a company code assignment to a credit control area (CCAr).

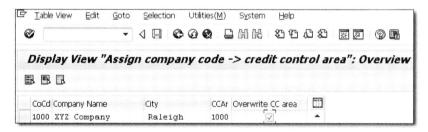

Figure 1.18 Example Company Code Assigned to Credit Control Area

Note the OVERWRITE CC AREA checkbox in Figure 1.18. If this indicator is checked, you can overwrite the credit control area defaulted from the company code while posting a financial transaction. However, this capability only exists during document creation; it does not work when changing a document.

1.2.3 Company Code to Financial Management Area

In this activity, you assign each company code that is relevant to Cash Budget Management or Funds Management to an FM area. You can assign multiple company codes to an FM area, but you cannot assign a single company code to multiple FM areas.

Figure 1.19 shows an example of company code assignment to an FM area.

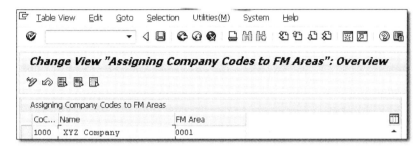

Figure 1.19 Example Company Code to FM Area Assignment

In making enterprise structure assignments, you must be aware of irreversible links. When assigning a company code to an FM area, the assignment is irreversible once Cash Budget Management or Funds Management is active or after actual data has been posted. Posting actual data includes posting commitment items to any of the G/L accounts in a company code.

1.2.4 Profit Centers to Company Code

In this activity, you assign one or more profit centers to a company code. If no assignment is made, the system will assign the profit center to all company codes in the CO area by default.

Figure 1.20 shows an example of profit centers assigned to a company code.

As you can see in Figure 1.20, assignment options are based on the profit center STANDARD HIERARCHY or PROFIT CENTER GRP (i.e., profit center group). From this screen, you can also enter a range of company codes or a single value. An assignment is made by checking the box next to a profit center.

Now that we have looked at enterprise structure assignments within FI, let's discuss some relationships between FI and organizational structures in other modules.

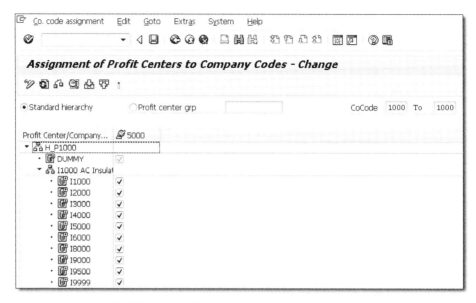

Figure 1.20 Example Profit Centers to Company Code Assignment

1.3   Making Cross-Modular Assignments

In Section 1.1 and Section 1.2, we discussed the definition of enterprise structures in FI and the assignment of these structures to one another within FI. In this section, we broaden our reach by discussing the links between FI enterprise structures and organizational structures in other modules. In other words, we discuss several specific assignments of FI enterprise structures to other enterprise structures in other modules. This broader association of enterprise structures is what enables cross-modular integration and data exchange.

The assignments discussed in this section do not include a complete list of the structure assignments available for enterprise objects in FI. Rather, this section provides some of the more common assignments used to enable integration of FI, SAP Sales and Distribution (SD), SAP Controlling (CO), and SAP Human Capital Management (HCM). This book focuses on FI and integration scenarios between FI, SD, CO, and MM. Therefore, the relationships between these enterprise structures are emphasized.

1.3.1 Company Code to Controlling Area

The assignment of a company code to a CO area is the link that integrates the FI and CO modules.

The CO area is an organizational unit for cost accounting purposes. A CO area is assigned to one or more company codes. The relationship can be one-to-one, but, more often than not, it is one-to-many (one CO area to many company codes) in order to enable cost accounting across company codes. This one-to-many relationship between a CO area and company codes is a common practice. Internal management reporting is usually a global function. While Corporate Controllers usually exist at the local level, a Chief or Global Controller is centrally responsible for controlling functions overall for an enterprise. Therefore, management accounting data needs to be integrated and available across company codes.

To assign a company code to a CO area, use the IMG. To access the IMG, enter "SPRO" in the COMMAND field (as shown in Figure 1.21) and press [Enter].

Figure 1.21 SPRO in Command Field

The CUSTOMIZING: EXECUTE PROJECT screen will appear (Figure 1.22).

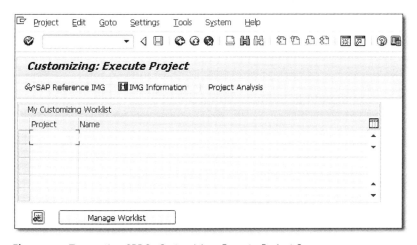

Figure 1.22 Transaction SPRO, Customizing: Execute Project Screen

Click on the SAP Reference IMG button shown in Figure 1.22, and the Display IMG screen will appear (Figure 1.23).

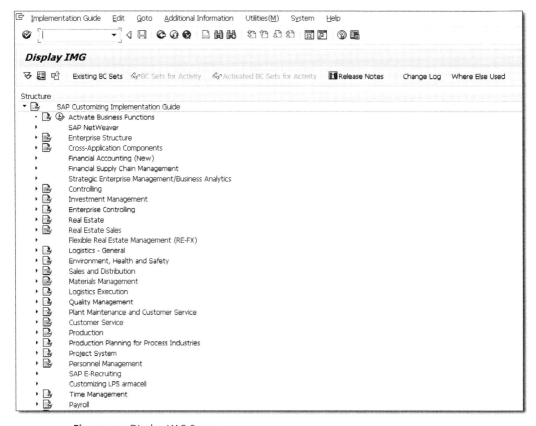

Figure 1.23 Display IMG Screen

To assign the enterprise structures for Controlling, follow IMG menu path Enterprise Structure • Assignment • Controlling, as shown in Figure 1.24.

The IMG menu path shown in Figure 1.24 points to where you assign company codes to controlling areas. Figure 1.25 shows an example company code to CO area assignment.

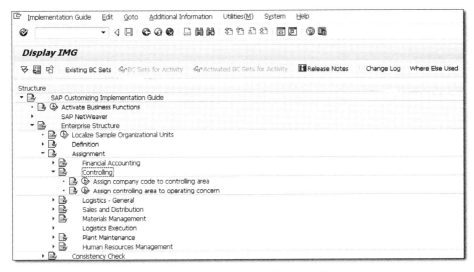

Figure 1.24 IMG Assign Enterprise Structure Menu Path for Controlling

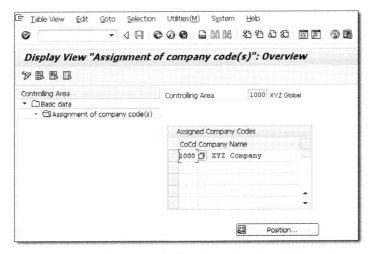

Figure 1.25 Example Company Code to Controlling Area Assignment

1.3.2 Plants to Company Code

A *plant* is an enterprise structure in SAP Logistics. It represents a physical location where materials are produced or goods or services provided. The plant is an organizational unit in logistics that divides an enterprise according to key logistical functions, such as production, procurement, maintenance, and materials planning.

A plant can only be assigned to one company code. Typically, a plant should only be assigned to a company code in the same country—but exceptions do exist.

To assign the enterprise structures for logistics, follow IMG menu path ENTERPRISE STRUCTURE • ASSIGNMENT • LOGISTICS—GENERAL, as shown in Figure 1.26.

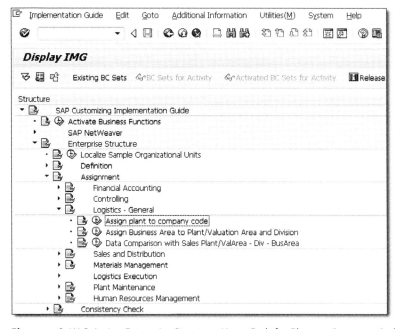

Figure 1.26 IMG Assign Enterprise Structure Menu Path for Plant to Company Code

The IMG menu path shown in Figure 1.26 points to where you assign plants to company codes. Figure 1.27 shows an example plant to company code assignment.

Figure 1.27 Example Plant to Company Code Assignment

1.3.3 Sales Organization to Company Code

A *sales organization* is an organizational unit in the SD module responsible for the sale and distribution of goods and services. A sales organization can only be linked to one company code. This linkage is the key integration between the FI and SD modules. To assign the enterprise structure for SD, follow IMG menu path ENTERPRISE STRUCTURE • ASSIGNMENT • SALES AND DISTRIBUTION, as shown in Figure 1.28.

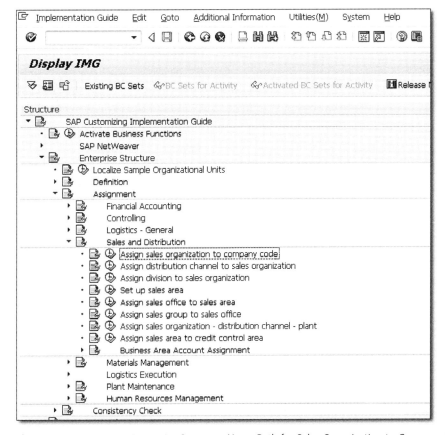

Figure 1.28 IMG Assign Enterprise Structure Menu Path for Sales Organization to Company Code

The IMG menu path shown in Figure 1.28 points to where you assign sales organizations to company codes. Figure 1.29 shows an example sales organization to company code assignment.

Figure 1.29 Example Sales Organization to Company Code Assignment

1.3.4   Purchasing Organization to Company Code

The purchasing organization is an enterprise structure in the Materials Management (MM) module. A *purchasing organization* is an organizational unit responsible for purchasing activities, such as purchasing requisitions and purchase orders.

If corporate purchasing is centralized, the purchasing organization to company code assignment may be one-to-many, but it can also be a one-to-one relationship if purchasing is a company code–specific function. A purchasing organization can also exist without being assigned to a company code. Because each plant must be assigned to a company code, the company code can be derived from the plant during a procurement transaction. To assign the enterprise structure for MM, follow IMG menu path ENTERPRISE STRUCTURE • ASSIGNMENT • MATERIALS MANAGEMENT, as shown in Figure 1.30.

The IMG menu path shown in Figure 1.30 points to where you assign purchasing organizations to company codes. Figure 1.31 shows an example purchasing organization to company code assignment.

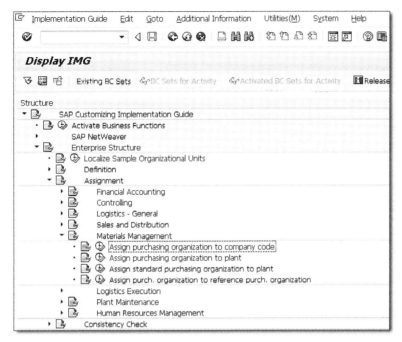

Figure 1.30 IMG Assign Enterprise Structure Menu Path for Purchasing Organization to Company Code

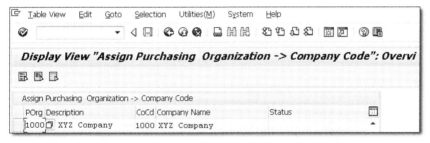

Figure 1.31 Example Purchasing Organization to Company Code Assignment

1.3.5 Personnel Area to Company Code

A *personnel area* is an organizational unit in the HR module that represents a specific area of the enterprise according to aspects of personnel, time management, and payroll. A personnel area is assigned to one company code.

To assign the enterprise structure for Human Resources Management, follow IMG menu path ENTERPRISE STRUCTURE • ASSIGNMENT • HUMAN RESOURCES MANAGEMENT, as shown in Figure 1.32.

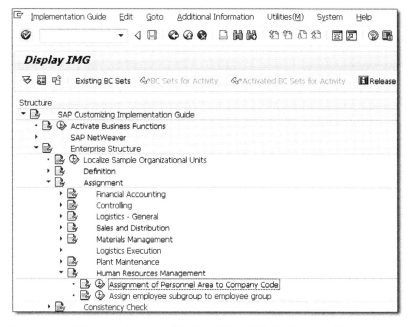

Figure 1.32 IMG Assign Enterprise Structure Menu Path for Personnel Area to Company Code

The IMG menu path shown in Figure 1.32 points to where you assign personnel areas to company codes. Figure 1.33 shows an example personnel area to company code assignment.

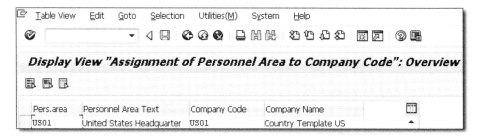

Figure 1.33 Example Personnel Area to Company Code Assignment

1.4   Summary

This chapter laid the foundation for learning in the remainder of the book by detailing the essential elements of defining and assigning an enterprise structure. Although the remainder of this book presents specific FI business processes and transactions, you will be better prepared to comprehend the material, having learned about the underlying structure of your organization, as represented in SAP.

Each module in SAP has its own enterprise structures. In FI, these structures include company, company code, credit control area, segment, business area, consolidation business area, functional area, profit center, and financial management area. Once these enterprise structures are defined and activated in the IMG, many of them are assigned to other structures, as appropriate, to accurately reflect your company's business units and divisions. It is these assignments that provide the basis for FI integration.

Modules outside of FI also require the definition and assignment of enterprise structures. In this chapter, we reviewed some of these modules, touching on the integration between FI and other non-FI modules, including SD, Logistics, MM, CO, and Human Resource Management. We discussed assigning company codes to controlling areas, plants, sales organizations, purchasing organizations, and personnel areas.

Defining enterprise structures and their relationships, inside and outside of FI, is important to your understanding of financial integration and data flows within your SAP system. These structures provide constraints and capabilities for posting financial transactions and reporting. Becoming aware of your own enterprise structure is an important first step in broadening your understanding of SAP FI.

Now that you understand enterprise structures, we'll move on to discuss FI master data in the next chapter. Understanding master data is important and relevant to business processes, particularly understanding how specific master data settings influence transactions.

In this chapter, we provide an introduction to FI master data, including an overview of G/L accounts, vendor accounts, customer accounts, banks, and fixed assets.

2   Financial Accounting Master Data

SAP defines *master data* as data that remains unchanged over a long period of time. It contains information that is needed again and again in the same way. In FI, primary master data includes G/L accounts, vendor accounts, customer accounts, banks, and fixed assets. Each type of master data is important in its own way to specific business processes. In this chapter, we will cover these individual pieces of master data at a high level and then describe their structure and relevance to business processes in detail.

Before delving into the details, let's take a few minutes to understand the concept of master data more fully. Master data plays an essential role in all SAP business processes. It is defined as data that remains unchanged over a long period of time because it is required to fulfill business requirements and to execute transactions. G/L accounts, for example, are used to record financial entries. In addition, G/L accounts are required to produce financial statements. Over time, additional G/L accounts may be added, but the basic structure of your G/L accounts, as reflected in the chart of accounts, is likely to change very little. In addition, within G/L accounts, specific settings indicate when and how a G/L account is used.

Another important point of master data is that, although the data is created individually in separate modules, it can be referenced and used across modules. For example, a fixed asset master record is created in asset accounting, but can be specified in purchase orders and FI transactions.

Now that you understand the basic concept of SAP master data, let's explore specific FI master data structures in the sections that follow.

2.1   General Ledger Accounts

General ledger accounts are considered fundamental master data in FI as they are essential to capturing accounting details and financial reporting. They are used for recording financial transactions and tracking account balances to fulfill external financial reporting requirements, legal or otherwise. In SAP, G/L accounts are assigned to a chart of accounts; they are used in all accounting transactions and are entered either manually or derived through *account determination*, a procedure which uses predetermined G/L accounts.

Before getting into the specifics of the G/L account master data structure, it's important that you understand the value of a clean, well-organized *chart of accounts*. For those of you not familiar with the term chart of accounts, it is simply a complete collection of every G/L account in your system. In SAP, a chart of accounts is defined and assigned to a company code.

When FI is first set up, one of the most important steps is to determine the structure for your chart of accounts. Over the decades, various G/L account approaches have been used. As a general rule, a simple structure is best to easily understand and maintain your chart of accounts and the G/L accounts in it. You also want a structure that provides a solid basis for financial reporting. Table 2.1 below is an example of a G/L account structure commonly used today.

Account Type	Beginning Number Range	Ending Number Range
Assets	100000	199999
Liabilities	200000	299999
Equity	300000	399999
Expenses	500000	599999
Revenues	600000	699999

Table 2.1 Sample Chart of Accounts

The good news is that in addition to distinguishing G/L accounts by number range, SAP provides the ability to designate each as balance sheet or profit and loss accounts, to subdivide G/L accounts further into account groups, and make individual settings within each G/L account for added control.

Now that you have a better understanding of the overall structure and importance of G/L accounts, let's look at the specific elements of the master data structure.

The G/L account itself is made up of two distinct parts: general data and company code data. In the remainder of this section, we will describe the chart of accounts, G/L account general data, and G/L account company code data.

2.1.1   Chart of Accounts

In the previous section, we described the chart of accounts at a high level. It's an important concept, so here we will go into greater detail. SAP defines a *chart of accounts* as a classification scheme consisting of a group of G/L accounts that provides a framework for recording values to ensure an orderly rendering of accounting data. If you think that's a mouthful, you are not alone. Put more simply, a chart of accounts is collection of G/L accounts used in a company code to record financial transactions and balances. Therefore, all the G/L accounts that a company code needs are contained in the chart of accounts. It's always important to keep in mind that financial reporting is based off G/L account transaction details and balances.

In SAP, there are three different chart of account types. The first is the *operative chart of accounts*, used for your day-to-day operations and accounting entries. The second is the *group chart of accounts*, used for consolidation purposes. The third is the *country chart of accounts*, which is used to meet a country's specific legal and tax requirements.

Let's discuss each of these chart of account types in more detail, starting with the operative chart of accounts. The operative chart of accounts is also referred to as the *operating chart of accounts*. It is assigned to a company code using Transaction OBY6 and is used in the daily recording of accounting entries. In addition, both the FI and CO modules use this chart of accounts. For the CO module, this means that the operative chart of accounts expense and revenue accounts are also cost or revenue elements in CO.

If the operative chart of accounts doesn't meet country-specific legal and tax reporting requirements, then a country chart of accounts can be used. In other words, the country chart of accounts is the G/L account structure prescribed under national regulations. The assignment of a country chart of accounts to a company code is optional from a system configuration perspective. Like the operative chart of accounts, the country chart of accounts is assigned to a company code using Transaction OBY6. The need for a country specific chart of accounts is typical in multinational companies, which have separate company codes for each country.

The group chart of accounts contains the G/L accounts that are used by the entire corporation for group reporting. It is optional.

Now that you have a solid understanding of the chart of accounts concept, let's move on and discuss the specific parts of a G/L account master record. Bear in mind as you read through the remainder of this chapter and book, that references to "chart of accounts" refers to the operative chart of accounts, unless otherwise specified.

2.1.2   G/L General Data

G/L accounts are created and maintained in the application menu path ACCOUNTING • FINANCIAL ACCOUNTING • GENERAL LEDGER • MASTER RECORDS • G/L ACCOUNTS, as seen in Figure 2.1.

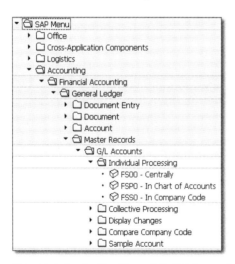

Figure 2.1 Application Menu Path G/L Accounts

G/L accounts can be managed individually or collectively. G/L accounts must be created with basic data relevant to a chart of accounts using Transaction FSP0. Once the basic data is created, it is reused to create the same G/L account in multiple company codes using Transaction FSS0. In other words, the basic data of a G/L account is not specific to a company code. It is specific only to a chart of accounts.

Figure 2.2 shows an example G/L account screen displayed using Transaction FSP0 and containing the following three tabs: Type/Description, Key word/ translation, and Information.

The Type/Description tab contains a section called Control in chart of accounts, which is where the most important settings are made. The Account Group dropdown lets you choose and assign an account group, which determines the permitted G/L account number interval and also specifies G/L master data fields as required, optional, or suppressed.

In the Control in chart of accounts section, you designate each G/L account as a profit and loss (P&L) account or a balance sheet account. Your account groups should be aligned as P&L or balance sheet accounts, so there is no chance of incorrectly assigning G/L account types to the wrong number range.

In the Description section of the master record, you specify G/L account Short Text and long text (G/L Acct Long Text).

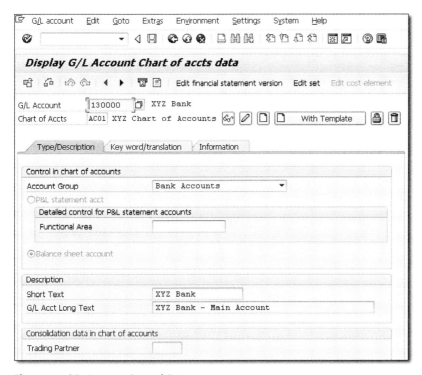

Figure 2.2 G/L Account General Data

The KEY WORD/TRANSLATION tab allows you to designate keywords for the account in the chart of accounts and to designate the language in which to display, enter, and print text.

The INFORMATION tab displays when and who created the account and provides access to change documents.

As mentioned earlier, once basic data for a G/L account is created, it can be used for multiple company codes. For example, if your company has two SAP company codes that use the same chart of accounts, the basic data only needs to be created once. However, each company code will each have its own set of company code data for each G/L account created using Transaction FSS0.

2.1.3   G/L Company Code Data

Company code data in the master record is the most complex part of the G/L master data. Without it, a company code cannot post financial transactions with the G/L account. This section of master data must be completed using Transaction FSS0 for each company code assigned to the chart of accounts.

Figure 2.3 shows an example G/L company code data screen, containing the following three tabs: CONTROL DATA, CREATE/BANK/INTEREST, and INFORMATION. The CONTROL DATA tab includes a section called ACCOUNT CONTROL IN COMPANY CODE. The fields in this section determine account settings for currency, exchange rates, taxes, and reconciliation account types (i.e., assets, customers, and vendors). The ALTERNATIVE ACCOUNT NO. field allows you to designate an account number for a country chart of accounts.

In the ACCOUNT MANAGEMENT IN COMPANY CODE section, you set G/L accounts as open item managed or not. Selecting the OPEN ITEM MANAGEMENT checkbox turns on the open item managed function. Open item management is relevant to any business process in which a G/L line item needs to be cleared via a subsequent step (e.g., bank reconciliation).

Open item management is an important concept. Its relevant to many processes, including bank reconciliation, goods receipt/invoice receipt, accounts payable, and accounts receivable. The basic concept is that an accounting entry posted to a G/L account is expected to be offset (i.e., cleared) in the future and zeroed out in the G/L account. Each accounting entry in a G/L clearing account has a status of OPEN or CLEARED.

Another important concept in G/L account master data is line item display. If you wish to display individual line items in an account, you must set the LINE ITEM DISPLAY flag. Doing so permits you to see individual line items that make up the G/L account balance. When determining this setting, be careful not to set the Indicator unless it makes sense. For example, seeing individual line items in most P&L accounts is important. However, for reconciliation accounts (e.g., accounts payable), it is not, because the line item detail is available via subledgers (e.g., vendor accounts).

The last field we will cover on this screen is SORT KEY. This field provides the layout rule for the ALLOCATION field in the document line item, which is significant for bank and other specific accounts.

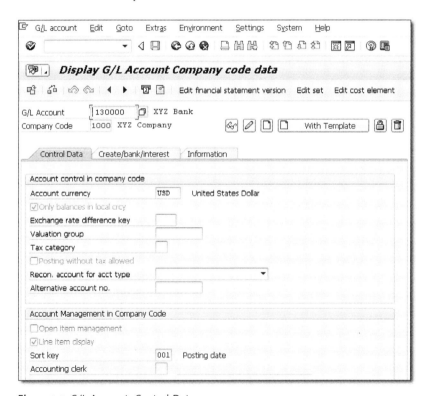

Figure 2.3 G/L Account: Control Data

Figure 2.4 shows the CREATE/BANK/INTEREST screen, which includes the CONTROL OF DOCUMENT CREATION IN COMPANY CODE section. These field control settings are used during document creation. The FIELD STATUS GROUP determines the screen layout for document entry and specifies document line item fields that are optional, required, or suppressed. If checked, the POST AUTOMATICALLY ONLY option indicates that the account can only be posted to through account determination and therefore cannot be manually entered in a transaction. If checked, the SUPPLEMENT AUTO. POSTINGS option allows the account to be used for automatic system-generated line items (e.g., bank charges).

The BANK/FINANCIAL DETAILS IN COMPANY CODE section is relevant to cash management. These settings are made for bank accounts and accounts relevant to cash position and liquidity forecasting.

The INTEREST CALCULATION INFORMATION IN COMPANY CODE section is relevant to G/L accounts that use automatic interest calculation.

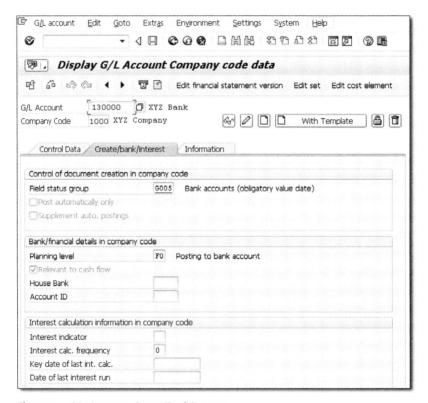

Figure 2.4 G/L Account: Create/Bank/Interest

The INFORMATION tab displays who created the account and when and provides access to change documents.

Now that you have learned about G/L account master data, we will discuss vendor account master data. Vendor master data provides our first exposure into the important subledger concept in SAP. Essentially, a subledger is where individual transaction details are managed for each master record separately, and collectively their balances roll up to a single G/L account referred to as a vendor reconciliation account.

2.2 Vendor Accounts

Vendors are your suppliers of goods and services. Vendor master records contain all the pertinent data needed to place orders, post invoices, and issue payments. Each individual vendor master record is considered a subledger. As stated in the previous section, the subledger concept means that individual vendor transaction details are maintained within the vendor master record itself. Collectively, the balances of all vendor master records roll up into a single G/L account known as an *accounts payable reconciliation account*.

Vendor master records are created and maintained in the application menu path ACCOUNTING • FINANCIAL ACCOUNTING • ACCOUNTS PAYABLE • MASTER RECORDS, as seen in Figure 2.5.

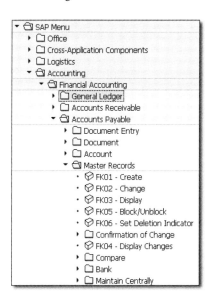

Figure 2.5 Application Menu Path Vendor Master Records

Vendor master data is made up of three distinct parts: general data, company code data, and purchasing organization data. Because the focus of this book is FI, we will not go into detail on purchasing organization data, which is created and maintained in MM-Purchasing. Instead, this section covers vendor master data as it pertains to accounts payable. In the remainder of this section, we will describe vendor general data and company code data.

2.2.1 Vendor General Data

Figure 2.6 shows the DISPLAY VENDOR selection screen (Transaction FK03). To see GENERAL DATA, you only need to enter a VENDOR. On this screen, enter a VENDOR and check the boxes under GENERAL DATA that you wish to view. When all your selections are made, press Enter or click the green checkmark ✅.

Figure 2.6 Display Vendor: Selection Screen for General Data

The DISPLAY VENDOR: ADDRESS screen will open (Figure 2.7). You will see the NAME of the vendor, along with pertinent address and communication fields. In the SEARCH TERM 1/2 fields, two separate values can be entered for use when searching for vendors. The two fields are used independently of one another.

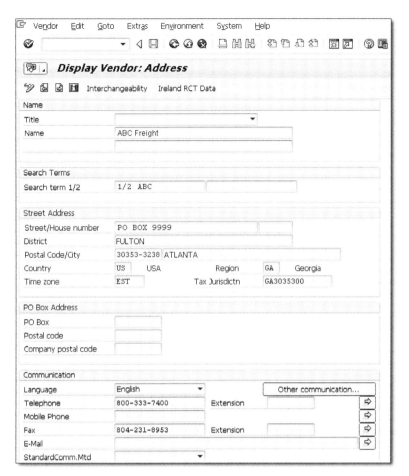

Figure 2.7 Display Vendor: Address

Figure 2.8 shows the general data control screen. In the Account Control section, grouping functions are enabled. For example, if a vendor is also a customer, you can enter the correct customer number in the Customer field. Doing so allows for joint management of a business partner and provides the ability to offset payables with receivables during automatic payment.

In the Tax information section, tax identification numbers, jurisdiction codes, and other tax-related information for the vendor is specified. If the vendor is an individual, you can enter withholding tax information at the bottom of the screen in the Person Subject to Withholding Tax section.

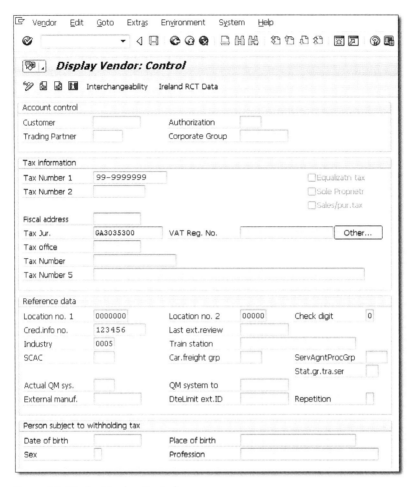

Figure 2.8 Display Vendor: Control

In the REFERENCE DATA section, you can specify external reference numbers and indicators as applicable. For example, if you report on vendors within a specific industry, you can assign a code in the INDUSTRY field.

Figure 2.9 shows the DISPLAY VENDOR: PAYMENT TRANSACTIONS screen. In the BANK DETAILS section, you can enter a vendor's bank details.

The PAYMENT TRANSACTIONS section largely consists of country-specific settings. However, in the ALTERNATE PAYEE field, you can enter a different vendor number if payment is to be made to vendor different than the one to whom the payable is owed. To specify an alternate payee in the document, adjust the settings in the ALTERNATE PAYEE IN DOCUMENT section.

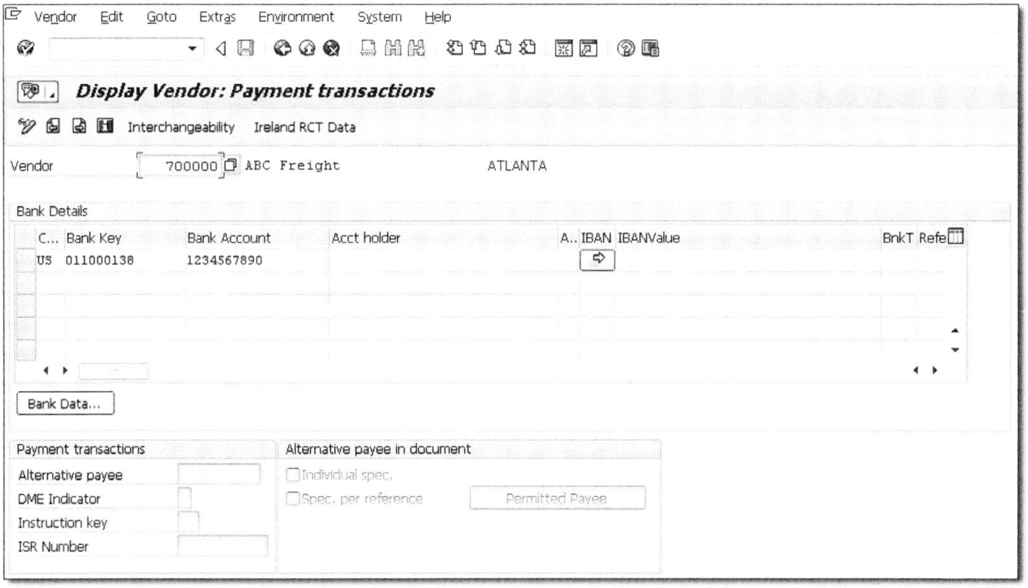

Figure 2.9 Display Vendor: Payment Transactions

2.2.2 Vendor Company Code Data

Figure 2.10 shows the DISPLAY VENDOR selection screen (Transaction FK03). To display COMPANY CODE DATA, enter a VENDOR and COMPANY CODE, and then check the boxes under COMPANY CODE DATA that you wish to view.

Note that WITHHOLDING TAX is only available when extended withholding tax is relevant.

When all your selections are made, press [Enter] or click the green check mark ✔ . The DISPLAY VENDOR: ACCOUNTING INFORMATION ACCOUNTING screen shown in Figure 2.11 will open, corresponding to the first checkbox selected in Figure 2.10. The most important field on this screen is the RECON. ACCOUNT field in the ACCOUNTING INFORMATION section. This field lists the reconciliation account that is the G/L account updated in parallel to the vendor subledger account for normal postings. Special postings (e.g., down payments) post to different G/L accounts, as designated in configuration.

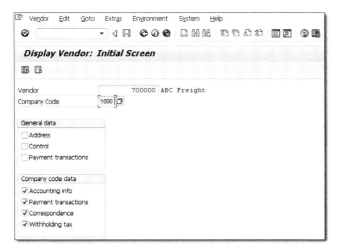

Figure 2.10 Display Vendor: Selection Screen for Company Code Data

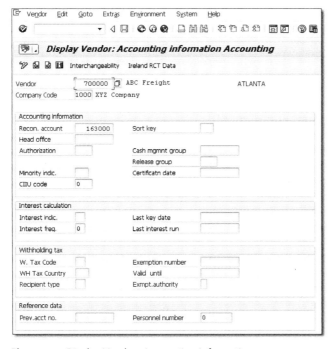

Figure 2.11 Display Vendor: Accounting Information

The Accounting Information screen of the vendor master data also contains values for interest calculations, withholding taxes, and reference data.

Click on the next page icon ☒ to open the DISPLAY VENDOR: PAYMENT TRANSAC-
TIONS ACCOUNTING screen (Figure 2.12). This screen contains payment terms
(PAYT TERMS field), which default from vendor master data into invoices during
the document creation process. Also noteworthy in the PAYMENT DATA section are
the TOLERANCE GROUP field and the CHK DOUBLE INV. checkbox. Tolerances affect
cash discounts and allowable payment differences. Selecting the CHK DOUBLE INV.
checkbox searches for duplicate invoices during document creation, based on
vendor, currency, company code, gross invoice amount, reference document
number, and invoice date. This option provides a safeguard to avoid the risk of
entering the same invoice more than once.

The AUTOMATIC PAYMENT TRANSACTIONS section contains important information
relevant to the use of the automated payment program (Transaction F110). You
should be familiar with all of these fields; they can, and often do, impact the output of your automatic payment runs.

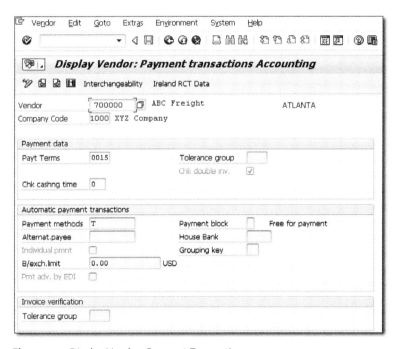

Figure 2.12 Display Vendor: Payment Transactions

Click on the next page icon ☒ to open the DISPLAY VENDOR: CORRESPONDENCE
ACCOUNTING screen (Figure 2.13). This screen contains specifications for dunning
and correspondence with a vendor.

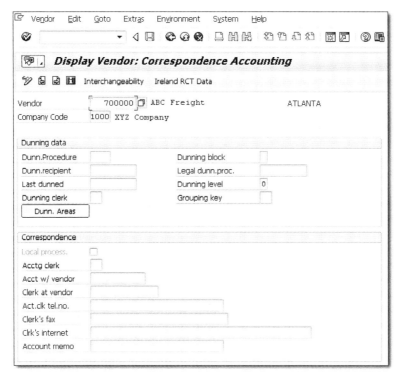

Figure 2.13 Display Vendor: Correspondence Accounting

Now that you have learned about vendor account master data, we will discuss customer account master data. Like vendor master data, customer master data uses the subledger concept in SAP, meaning that individual transaction details are managed for each individual master record separately and their balances collectively roll up to a single G/L account.

2.3 Customer Accounts

Customer master records contain all the pertinent data needed to receive orders, post invoices, and receive payments. Each individual customer master record is considered a subledger. The subledger concept is the same for vendor and customer accounts. For both, individual transaction details are maintained within the subledger. Collectively, the balances of all customer master records roll up into a single G/L account known as an *accounts receivable reconciliation account*.

Customer master records are created and maintained in the application menu path ACCOUNTING • FINANCIAL ACCOUNTING • ACCOUNTS RECEIVABLE • MASTER RECORDS, as seen in Figure 2.14.

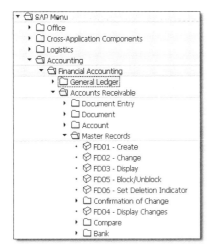

Figure 2.14 Application Menu Path for Customer Master Records

Like vendor master data, customer master data is made up of three separate parts. For customer master records these include: general data, company code data, and sales area data. We won't go into the details of sales area data, which is created and maintained in SD, and therefore beyond the scope of this book. Instead, we will discuss customer master data in relation to accounts receivable. In the remainder of this section, we will describe customer general data and company code data.

2.3.1 Customer General Data

Figure 2.15 shows the DISPLAY CUSTOMER: GENERAL DATA screen (Transaction FD03). On the ADDRESS tab, you can see the NAME of the customer, along with address fields. In the SEARCH TERM 1/2 fields, two separate values can be entered to search for customers. The two fields are used independently of one another.

Click on the next page icon 🗎 to open the CONTROL DATA screen (Figure 2.16). In the ACCOUNT CONTROL section, grouping functions are enabled. For example, if a customer is also a vendor, you can enter the correct vendor number in the VENDOR field. Doing so allows for joint management of a business partner and provides the ability to offset payables with receivables during automatic payment.

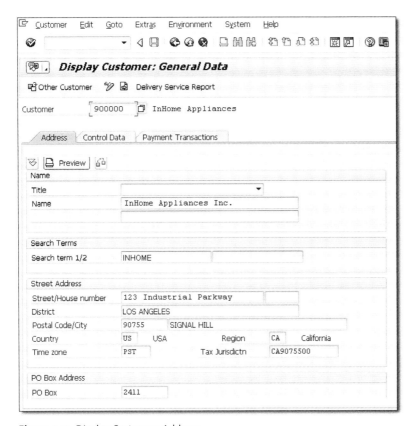

Figure 2.15 Display Customer: Address

In the TAX INFORMATION section, you can enter tax identification numbers, county codes, and other tax-related information for a customer. In the REFERENCE DATA/ AREA section, specify external reference numbers and indicators as applicable. For example, if you report on customers within a specific industry, you can assign a code in the INDUSTRY field.

Click on the next page icon 🗐 to open the PAYMENT TRANSACTIONS screen (Figure 2.17). In the BANK DETAILS section, enter the customer's bank details. The PAYMENT TRANSACTIONS section of the screen provides the ALTERNATE PAYEE field, in which you can enter a different customer number if payment is to be received from a customer different from the one who owns payable. To specify an alternate payee in the document, adjust the settings in the ALTERNATE PAYEE IN DOCUMENT section.

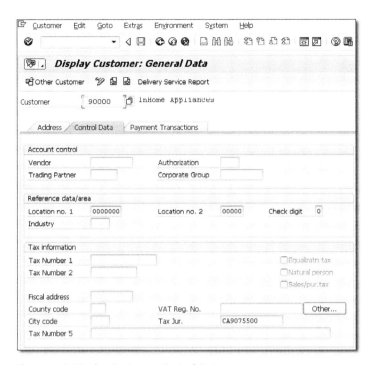

Figure 2.16 Display Customer: Control Data

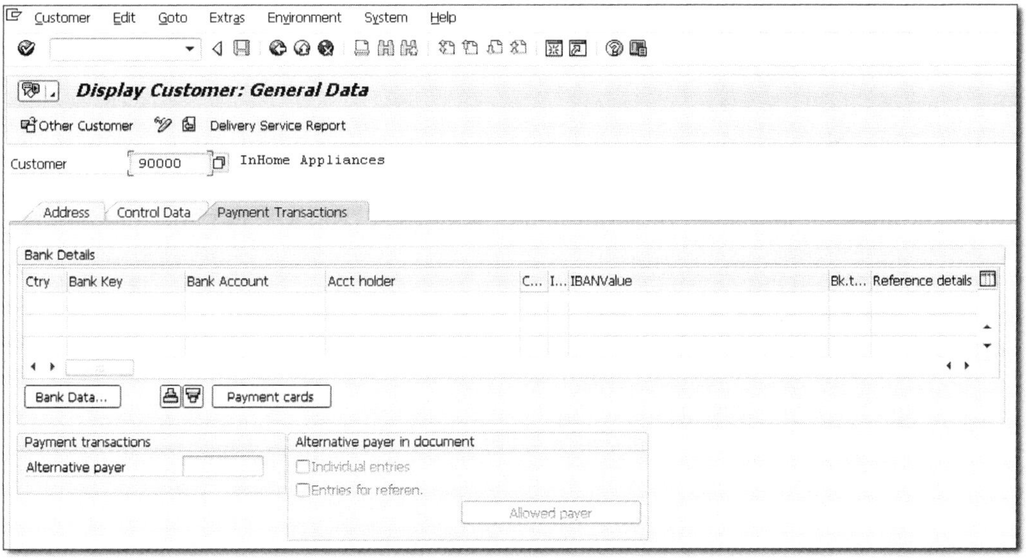

Figure 2.17 Display Customer: Payment Transactions

2.3.2 Customer Company Code Data

Figure 2.18 shows the Account Management screen. The most important field is Recon. account, which indicates the reconciliation account that is the G/L account updated in parallel to the customer subledger account for normal postings. Special postings (e.g., down payments) post to different G/L accounts, as designated in configuration.

The Account Management tab also contains values for interest calculations, withholding taxes, and reference data.

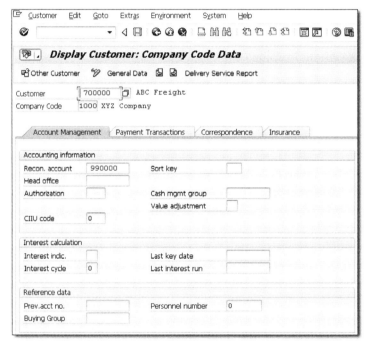

Figure 2.18 Display Customer: Account Management

Next is the Payment Transactions screen (Figure 2.19). Most importantly, this screen contains the Terms of Payment field, which defaults from the customer master record into invoices during document creation.

Figure 2.20 shows the Correspondence screen. This screen contains specifications for dunning and correspondence with a customer. Checkboxes in the Payment Notices To section indicate the customer or internal department to which a payment notice is to be sent.

Figure 2.19 Display Customer: Payment Transactions

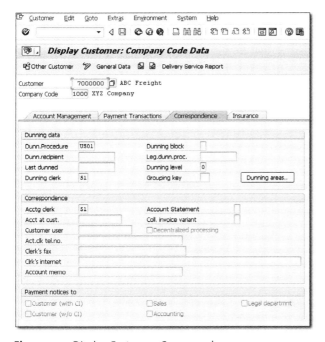

Figure 2.20 Display Customer: Correspondence

The last tab in the customer master record is INSURANCE, where you can fill in the customer's insurance information (Figure 2.21).

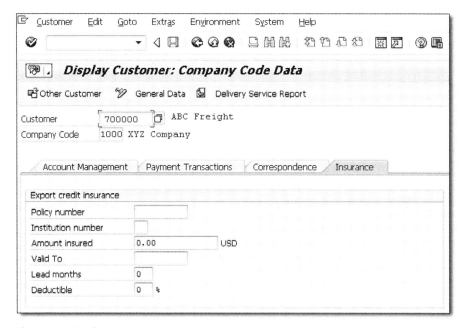

Figure 2.21 Display Customer: Insurance

Now that you have learned about customer account master data, we will discuss fixed asset master data. Like vendor and customer master data, fixed asset master records use the subledger concept in SAP, meaning that individual transaction details are managed for each individual master record separately and their balances rolled up collectively to a single G/L account.

2.4 Fixed Assets

Fixed assets are structured according to asset classes for balance sheet reporting and depreciation. Each fixed asset master record is assigned to an asset class and company code. Asset classes determine, among other things, asset number ranges and screen layout rules.

The subledger concept that we've discussed several times already in this chapter is also applicable to fixed assets. Each individual asset master record is considered a subledger, meaning that individual transaction details are maintained within the asset master record and fixed asset ledger. Collectively, the balances of all asset master records roll up into a G/L account known as an *asset reconciliation account*.

Fixed asset master records are created and maintained in the application menu path ACCOUNTING • FINANCIAL ACCOUNTING • FIXED ASSETS • ASSET, as seen in Figure 2.22.

Figure 2.22 Application Menu Path Fixed Asset Master Records

Figure 2.23 shows an example asset master record (Transaction AS03), consisting of several different tabs. In this section, we will cover some of the important tabs and fields within the asset master record, but asset accountants should become familiar with the complete asset master record.

In the GENERAL DATA section of the GENERAL tab, you will find basic information about the asset. The DESCRIPTION and ASSET MAIN NO. TEXT fields describe the asset. The ACCT DETERMINATION field specifies the reconciliation account and offsetting accounts during certain business transactions. Other important fields on this screen include SERIAL NUMBER, INVENTORY NUMBER, and QUANTITY.

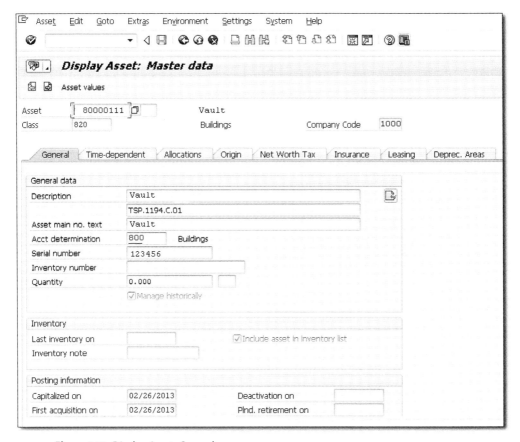

Figure 2.23 Display Asset: General

Click on the next page icon to open the TIME-DEPENDENT tab (Figure 2.24), which displays an asset's association with other objects. Some of the most important links are to the COST CENTER and PLANT. Additional associations may be necessary depending upon your business processes. For example, if you are using Plant Maintenance, a maintenance order may be assigned.

Now that you have learned about asset master records, we will discuss bank master data and learn about its relevance to vendors, customers, and bank-related business processes.

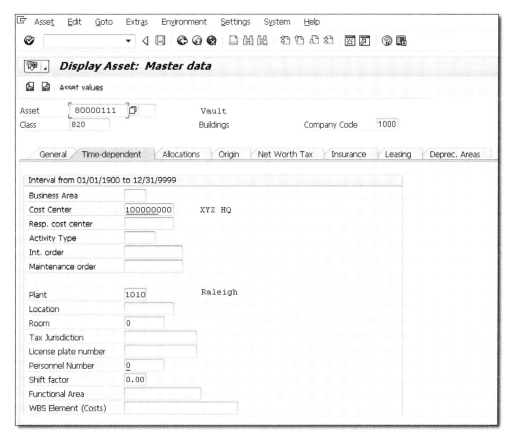

Figure 2.24 Display Asset: Time-Dependent

2.5 Banks

There are two types of banks in SAP: The house bank is used for automatic payments, and there also are banks associated with customers and vendors. In this section, we will discuss the latter category. See Chapter 15 for more details on bank master data and the specifics on setting up house banks.

Figure 2.25 shows an example bank master record. To view a bank master record using Transaction FI03, a BANK COUNTY and BANK KEY must be specified. The use of the BANK KEY differs between countries. In the United States, the bank key is the American Bankers Association (ABA) number, commonly known as the routing transit number (RTN).

The ADDRESS section contains the name of the bank, address, and branch. The CONTROL DATA section contains important information such as a SWIFT/BIC code, BANK GROUP, and BANK NUMBER.

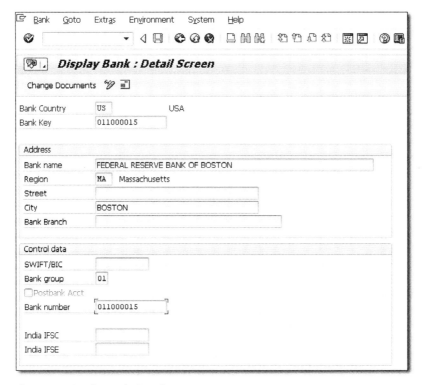

Figure 2.25 Display Bank: Detail

Once created, bank master data can be assigned for use in vendor and customer master records.

2.6 Summary

In FI, master data includes G/L accounts, vendors, customers, fixed assets, and banks. Other modules have their own master data, and the cross-modular relationships between master data are important to consider to understand end-to-end business processes.

G/L accounts are relevant to all accounting transactions. G/L master data is assigned to a chart of accounts and consists of general data and company code data. G/L accounts are designated as balance sheet or P&L accounts in the master record, and the account groups should be aligned to avoid any chance of assigning the wrong account number for a specific G/L account type.

The concept of subledgers is discussed throughout this chapter. A subledger is where individual financial transaction detail is managed in a separate ledger and roll-up to reflect overall balances in a central set of G/L accounts. Subledgers are relevant to vendors, customers, and fixed assets. Subledger accounts in FI always link to a G/L reconciliation account that is updated in parallel with a subledger. Because line item detail is maintained within the subledger, G/L reconciliation accounts should not be set to display line item detail. For each type of subledger, different G/L reconciliation account types exist and is specified for the master data. These reconciliation account types include vendor reconciliation accounts, customer reconciliation accounts, and asset reconciliation accounts.

Specific bank master data was also discussed in this chapter. In FI, there is a distinction between a house bank and bank master data. House banks are configurations used by a company code to make automatic payments. House banks are covered in detail in Chapter 15. Bank master data, on the other hand, is data pertaining to the bank accounts of your business partners. Within customer and vendor master records, you can assign bank master records. Vendor bank accounts are used to transfer payments for goods and services received. Customer bank accounts are used to receive payments for goods and services rendered.

Master data is a key element to your business processes. In this chapter, we provided an overview of FI master data to give you a foundation for the remainder of the book. In summary, master data plays an essential role in all SAP business processes. It is defined as data that remains unchanged over a long period of time and is required to fulfill business requirements and to execute transactions. As an accountant or financial manager, understanding the basic structure of FI master data is essential.

In this chapter you learned what master data is, how it is used, and the basic structures of master data in FI. In the next chapter you will receive your first glimpse of how master data is used in our discussion of G/L account transactions.

In this chapter, we cover G/L transactions in detail. These transactions consist of accounting line items without a subledger entry and are created directly in the G/L module. This chapter also covers associated G/L concepts and transactions, such as credit memos, reversals, parking, and G/L document maintenance functions.

3 General Ledger Transactions

This chapter covers G/L account transactions that originate in the G/L module. The most common G/L transaction is the entry of a G/L accounting document, using Transaction FB50. This chapter covers not only the creation of a G/L document but also associated G/L functions, such as document display, change, reverse, park, and more.

Creating a G/L accounting document is straightforward, but it is only one of many associated tasks that have to be completed in the G/L module by the accounting department. Posting credit memos, making document corrections, clearing accounts, and reconciling balances are just some of the additional functions that have to be performed by accountants in SAP G/L.

This chapter begins by covering the basics of creating a G/L accounting document. We then dive into each associated function of the G/L module.

Some of the transactions covered in this chapter, such as the creation of accounting documents, are tasks you are likely to perform on a daily basis. Other transactions, such as document reverse, are executed less frequently. This chapter can be revisited repeatedly as a reference point for less frequently used transactions and can provide you with an overall refresher on the G/L module. Our goal is to provide you with the full gamut of SAP G/L capabilities so that you can choose the right tool for the task at hand.

3.1 Journal Vouchers

This section covers the G/L document creation process, which includes document entry, park, post, save as complete, and hold tasks. It also covers the Transaction FB50 tree display, screen variants, account assignment templates, editing options, and the post with reference task, all of which provide valuable insights to help you be more productive and organized in the G/L module.

Let's start by discussing why this section is titled "Journal Vouchers." *Journal vouchers* are accounting documents that consist of line items without a subledger entry (i.e., customer, vendor, or asset) that are created directly in the G/L module. In SAP terms, a journal voucher refers to G/L accounting documents entered via Transaction FB50.

To create a journal voucher in SAP using Transaction FB50, you must enter document header details (e.g., posting date) and at least two line items that net to a balance of zero. This seems straightforward, right? In fact, it is. However, small complications can get in the way of your ability to perform such a simple task. For example, in the middle of entering an accounting document, you might be whisked away to a meeting by your boss, or while entering a document line item, you might notice that a field you need to enter is not on the entry screen. This section gives you the tools you need to deal with these and other challenges and provides you with the knowledge to enter G/L accounting transactions more efficiently.

3.1.1 Document Entry

To enter a G/L account document, use Transaction FB50 or application menu path ACCOUNTING • FINANCIAL ACCOUNTING • GENERAL LEDGER • DOCUMENT ENTRY • FB50—ENTER G/L ACCOUNT DOCUMENT, as shown in Figure 3.1.

Double-click FB50—ENTER G/L ACCOUNT DOCUMENT from the menu path, or enter "FB50" in the COMMAND field (as shown in Figure 3.2) and press Enter .

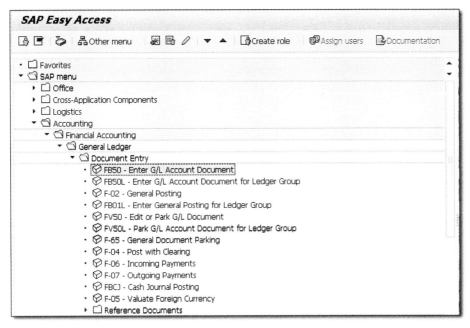

Figure 3.1 Transaction FB50 Menu Path

Figure 3.2 FB50 in Command Field

The ENTER G/L ACCOUNT DOCUMENT entry screen will appear (Figure 3.3). The fields that appear on the header with prepopulated values may vary depending upon your system configuration and editing options. In this example, the DOCUMENT DATE field was manually entered, whereas field values defaulted for the CURRENCY, POSTING DATE, DOCUMENT TYPE, andCOMPANY CODE fields. Document type configuration determines if field entry is required in the REFERENCE and DOC.HEADER TEXT fields. In this example, these fields are not required for document type SA.

Figure 3.3 Transaction FB50 Entry Screen

After entering header details, the next step is to enter at least two line items, as shown in Figure 3.4.

Here, the line items make up a cash movement between petty cash and a bank account. Because both G/L accounts are balance sheet accounts, only the G/L Account, Debit/Credit Indicator, and Amount fields require input. However, your SAP system may have additional field entry requirements.

After entering document line items, click the Simulate button in the top center of the Enter G/L Account Document entry screen to initiate simulation of the G/L document posting logic in order to determine if the document can be properly posted. If the simulation is unsuccessful, an error message will appear. If successful, the Document Overview screen appears, as shown in Figure 3.5.

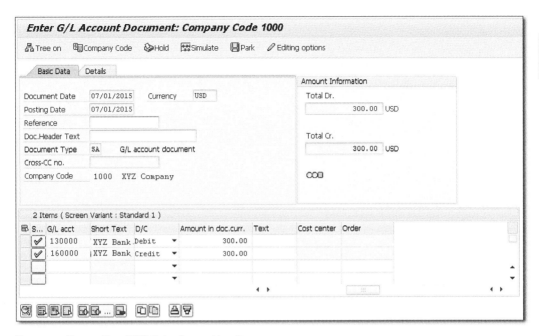

Figure 3.4 Transaction FB50 Entry Screen Line Items

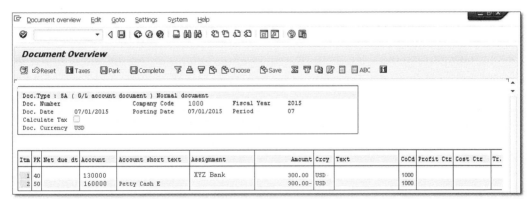

Figure 3.5 Transaction FB50 Document Overview Screen

Once simulation is complete, click the POST button 🖫 to the right of the command field in the upper-left-hand corner of the screen. This will post the journal voucher, and a message will appear with the new document number, as shown at the bottom of Figure 3.6.

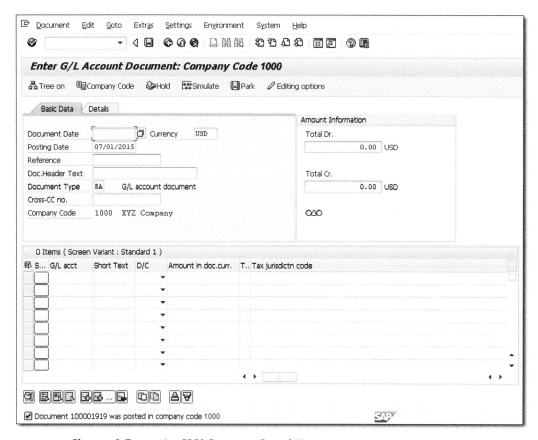

Figure 3.6 Transaction FB50 Document Posted Message

3.1.2 Post, Park, Save as Complete, and Hold

This section describes the different ways to create G/L accounting documents: post, park, save as complete, and hold. All are universal concepts in FI and therefore are not unique to journal vouchers and Transaction FB50. However, the discussion of their use is confined to journal vouchers in this section.

Post

Posting a journal voucher was covered in its entirety in Section 3.1.1. A posted document is a G/L document that is considered complete, produces a G/L accounting document number, and updates the G/L account balances.

Once a document is posted, the only way to reverse its impact on the G/L account balance is to reverse the document. Reversing G/L documents is covered in Section 3.4.

Park

Document parking is a function that allows you to save a G/L document without impacting G/L account balances. This may be necessary if the document is incomplete or if further edits, data validation, or document approval is required prior to posting.

Because parked documents are considered incomplete, they can be changed or deleted. When parked, these G/L documents do not update transaction figures and G/L balances. Moreover, a parked document does not go through the extensive entry checks performed on posted documents. Parking only checks whether data exists.

To enter and park a G/L accounting document, use Transaction FV50 or follow application menu path ACCOUNTING • FINANCIAL ACCOUNTING • GENERAL LEDGER • DOCUMENT ENTRY • FV50—EDIT OR PARK G/L DOCUMENT, as shown in Figure 3.7.

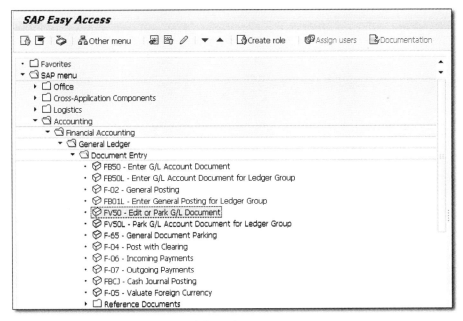

Figure 3.7 Transaction FV50 Menu Path for Park Document

Double-click FV50—EDIT OR PARK G/L DOCUMENT from the menu path, or enter "FV50" in the COMMAND field (as shown in Figure 3.8) and press ⌐Enter⌐.

Figure 3.8 FV50 in Command Field

The PARK G/L ACCOUNT DOCUMENT entry screen now will open (Figure 3.9). The fields that appear on the header with prepopulated values may vary depending upon your system configuration and editing options. In this example, the DOCU-MENT DATE field was manually entered, whereas field values defaulted for the CURRENCY, POSTING DATE, DOCUMENT TYPE, and COMPANY CODE fields.

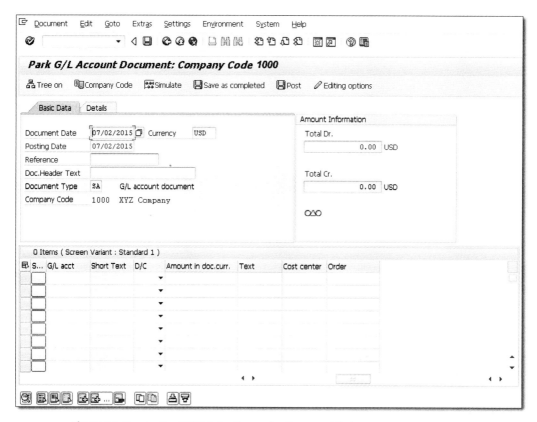

Figure 3.9 Transaction FV50 Entry Screen for Document Park

After inputting values on the header screen, enter at least two line items, as shown in Figure 3.10.

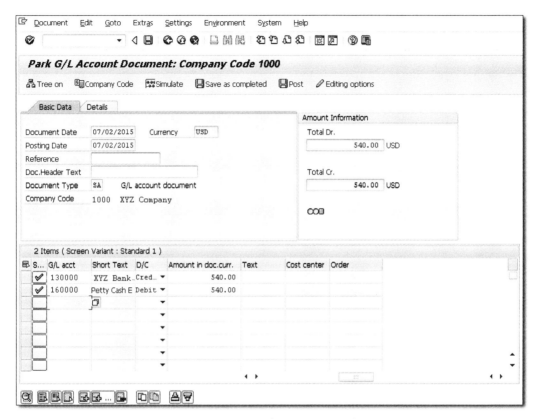

Figure 3.10 Transaction FV50 Entry Screen Line Items for Document Park

Next, click the PARK button 🖫 to the right of the COMMAND field in the upper-left-hand portion of the screen. This will park the journal voucher, and a message will appear with the new parked document number, as shown at the bottom of Figure 3.11.

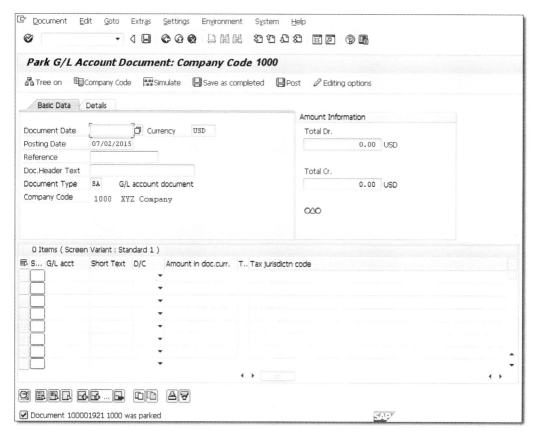

Figure 3.11 Transaction FV50 Document Parked Message

Save as Completed

The *save as completed* function is similar to document parking, but with some key distinctions. When you save a document as completed, that document goes through more extensive document check logic, just as if the document were being posted. Like parked documents, however, documents that are saved as completed can be edited and changed prior to posting.

Although the park and save as completed functions are similar, save as completed generally should be used when you are sure the document is accurate and complete and only needs final approval before being posted.

To save a G/L accounting document as completed, use Transaction FV50 or follow application menu path ACCOUNTING • FINANCIAL ACCOUNTING • GENERAL LEDGER • DOCUMENT ENTRY • FV50—EDIT OR PARK G/L DOCUMENT, as shown in Figure 3.12.

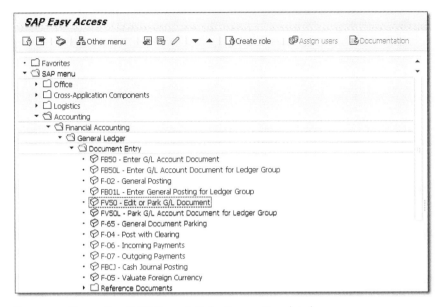

Figure 3.12 Transaction FV50 Menu Path for Save as Completed

Double-click FV50—EDIT OR PARK G/L DOCUMENT from the menu path, or enter "FV50" in the Command Field (as shown in Figure 3.13) and press Enter.

Figure 3.13 FV50 in Command Field

The PARK G/L ACCOUNT DOCUMENT entry screen will open (Figure 3.14). The fields that appear on the header with prepopulated values may vary depending upon your system configuration and editing options. In this example, the DOCUMENT DATE field was manually entered, whereas field values defaulted for the CURRENCY, POSTING DATE, DOCUMENT TYPE, andCOMPANY CODE fields.

After inputting values on the PARK G/L ACCOUNT DOCUMENT header screen, enter at least two line items, as shown in Figure 3.15.

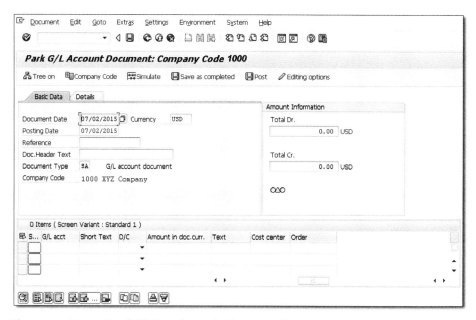

Figure 3.14 Transaction FV50 Entry Screen for Document Save as Completed

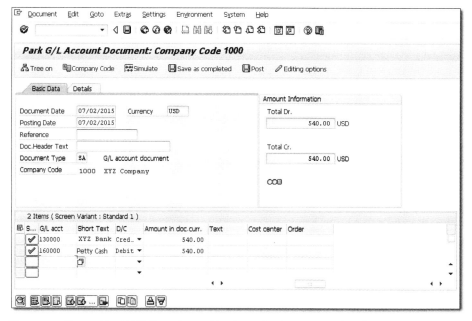

Figure 3.15 Transaction FV50 Entry Screen Line Items for Save as Completed Document

Now, click the SAVE AS COMPLETED button at the top-center portion of the screen. This will save the journal voucher as completed, and a message will appear with the new document number, as shown in Figure 3.16.

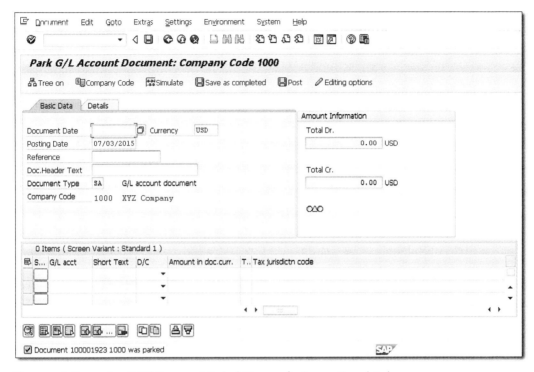

Figure 3.16 Transaction FV50 Document Parked Message for Save as Completed

Hold

Document hold is a function that temporarily saves your data. It is most useful when interrupted during document creation (if your boss needs you to be at a last-minute meeting, for example). Because held documents are temporary, they do not update G/L transactions and balances. Furthermore, in subsequent processing they can be edited, deleted, parked, or posted. Unlike post, park, and save as completed, the hold function produces no permanent document number until the document is parked or posted.

To hold a G/L accounting document, use Transaction FB50 or application menu path ACCOUNTING • FINANCIAL ACCOUNTING • GENERAL LEDGER • DOCUMENT ENTRY • FB50—ENTER G/L ACCOUNT DOCUMENT, as shown in Figure 3.17.

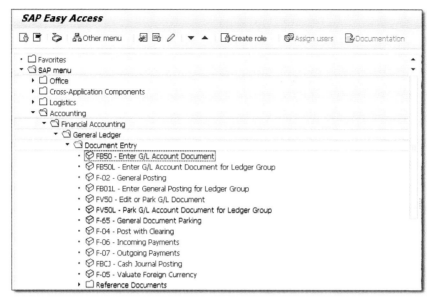

Figure 3.17 Transaction FB50 Menu Path for Document Hold

Double-click FB50—ENTER G/L ACCOUNT DOCUMENT from the menu path shown in Figure 3.17, or enter "FB50" in the COMMAND field (as shown in Figure 3.18) and press [Enter].

Figure 3.18 FB50 in Command Field

You can use the hold function at any point in Transaction FB50. You can do so regardless of how much or little information has been entered, because no system checks take place in holding document.

In the example shown in Figure 3.19, the DOCUMENT DATE field has been entered, along with one complete line item. In the screen header, field values were pre-populated for the CURRENCY, POSTING DATE, DOCUMENT TYPE, andCOMPANY CODE fields.

At any point, you can hold a document by pressing [F5] or selecting DOCUMENT • HOLD from the dropdown menu path, as shown in Figure 3.20.

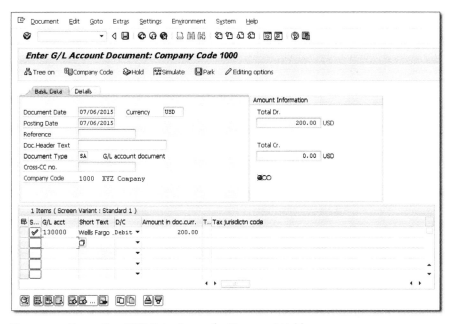

Figure 3.19 Transaction FB50 Entry Screen for Document Hold

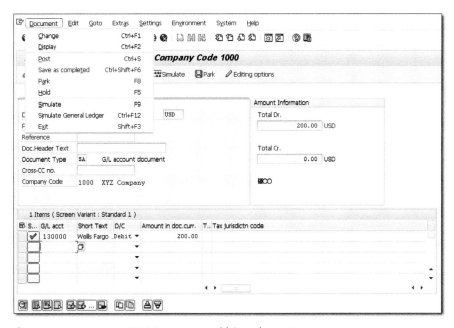

Figure 3.20 Transaction FB50 Document Hold Dropdown Menu

A dialogue box will open (Figure 3.21) and prompt you to enter a ten-character preliminary temporary document number, which can contain numbers, letters, and/or special characters. A permanent number is assigned when the document is posted, parked, or saved as complete.

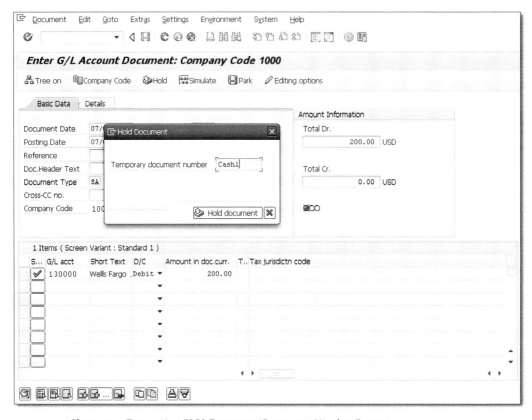

Figure 3.21 Transaction FB50 Temporary Document Number Prompt

After entering a temporary document number, press ⌈Enter⌉ or click the HOLD DOCUMENT button. As a result, a temporary accounting document will be created and a message will appear with the held document number, as shown in Figure 3.22.

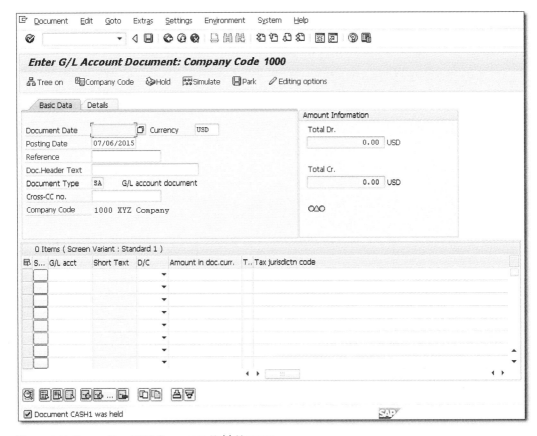

Figure 3.22 Transaction FB50 Document Held Message

3.1.3 Tree Display

The *tree display* provides an easy-to-use visual display for several functions that can also be accessed from the dropdown menu in Transaction FB50. The tree display is a universal concept, or shortcut, for accessing accounting documents and document entry tools in FI. In this section, we will confine the discussion of the tree display to Transaction FB50 and Transaction FV50, but take note that this capability can be used in any financial transaction in which the tree display appears.

The tree display is a toggle function, meaning that it can be turned on (i.e., made visible) or turned off (i.e., made invisible) by the click of a button or keyboard combination.

Figure 3.23 shows Transaction FB50 with the tree display on.

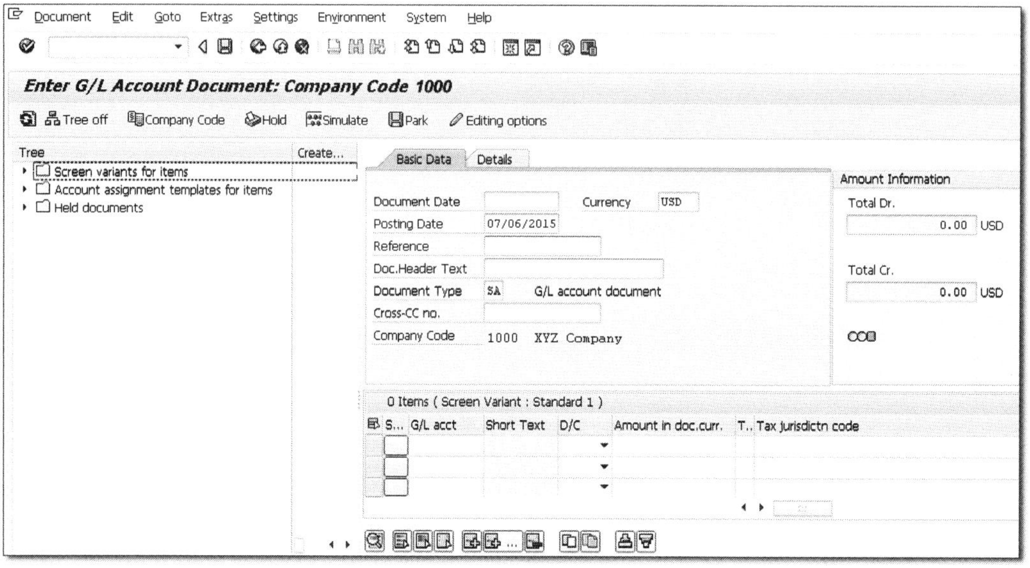

Figure 3.23 Transaction FB50 with Tree Display On

Note that with the tree display on, a panel that lists folders will be visible on the left. The folders that appear in the display vary by transaction code. In Transaction FB50, you will see the following folders:

- SCREEN VARIANTS FOR ITEMS
- ACCOUNT ASSIGNMENT TEMPLATES FOR ITEMS
- HELD DOCUMENTS

Screen variants and account assignment templates are covered in detail in Section 3.1.4. For now, know that screen variants and account assignment templates are accessible from the tree display.

In Section 3.1.2, you learned how to hold a G/L document. Held documents can be shown in the tree display by clicking the triangle to the left of the HELD DOCUMENTS folder. This action opens the folder and displays all the held documents created by the user. Moreover, if you double-click a held document in the tree display, the details appear in the G/L document entry screen (as shown in Figure 3.24), which allows you to resume entering the document.

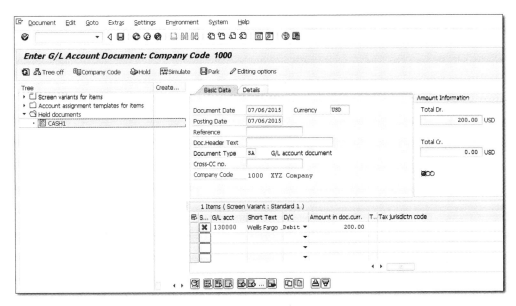

Figure 3.24 Transaction FB50 Held Document in Tree Display

The tree display function in Transaction FV50 is the same as in Transaction FB50. It has the same toggle capability, meaning that it can be turned on (i.e., made visible) or turned off (i.e., hidden) by the click of a button or by a keyboard combination.

Figure 3.25 shows Transaction FV50 with the tree display on.

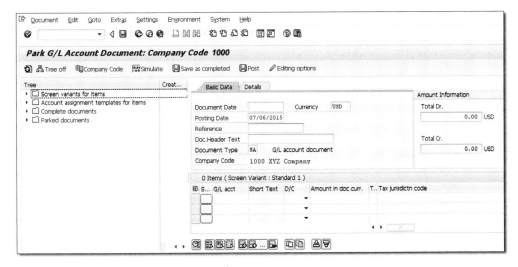

Figure 3.25 Transaction FV50 with Tree Display On

In Transaction FV50, you will see the following folders:

- ▶ SCREEN VARIANTS FOR ITEMS
- ▶ ACCOUNT ASSIGNMENT TEMPLATES FOR ITEMS
- ▶ COMPLETE DOCUMENTS
- ▶ PARKED DOCUMENTS

In Transaction FV50's tree display, folders for screen variants and account assignment templates appear at the top, as they did in Transaction FB50. The display also includes folders for complete and parked documents, which did not appear in the Transaction FB50 tree display. Finally, the folder for held documents, which appeared in Transaction FB50, does not appear in Transaction FV50. As you can see, the tree display default folders will vary depending on the purpose of the transaction.

3.1.4 Using Screen Variants and Account Assignment Templates

Screen variants and *account assignment templates* are tools available in FI to simplify entry of G/L documents. They are not unique to Transaction FB50, but in this section we will confine our discussion of these tools to this transaction. Note that both screen variants and account assignment templates can be accessed and maintained from the tree display in Transaction FB50 and from the dropdown menu. In this section, we will focus on using the tree display, which is the most user-friendly and frequently used method of access.

Use of Screen Variants

A screen variant sets the columns in the line item entry portion of Transaction FB50 (Figure 3.26). In other words, it controls the fields displayed on the screen and the order in which they appear.

A well-developed screen variant reduces the data entry time and the number of data entry errors. In essence, your goal is to have only the fields you need to enter visible on the screen.

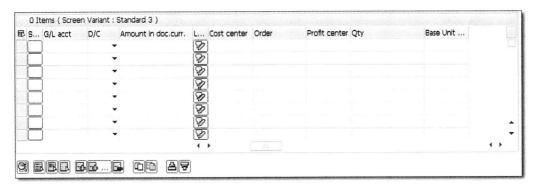

Figure 3.26 Transaction FB50 Line Entry Screen

Transaction FB50 has a default screen variant assigned, which is displayed each time you execute the transaction. However, the default may not be your preferred line item entry screen, or you may prefer different screen variants depending on the type of journal voucher you are creating. Through the tree display or the dropdown menu in Transaction FB50, you can select different screen variants at any point in time.

Let's look at screen variants in action. Go to Transaction FB50 and make sure the tree display is on (see Section 3.1.3). Click the triangle next to the SCREEN VARIANTS FOR ITEMS folder to open a list of available variants to choose from (Figure 3.27).

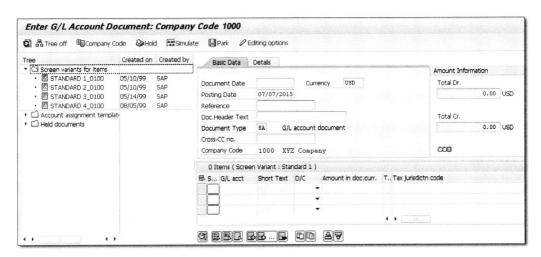

Figure 3.27 Transaction FB50 Screen Variant List

Double-click the screen variant you want to use (Figure 3.28), and the line layout at the bottom right of the screen will change.

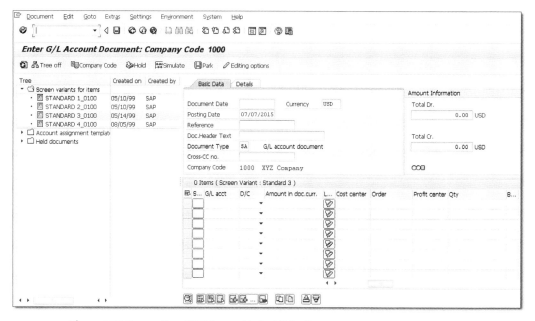

Figure 3.28 Transaction FB50 Screen Variant Selection

Discussion of the creation and maintenance of screen variants is beyond the scope of this book. It is important to note, however, that screen variants are considered *cross-client dependent*, meaning that if a screen variant change is made in one client, the change is reflected in every other client within that instance of SAP. For this reason, screen variant creation and maintenance is a function usually restricted to an SAP support team.

Use of Account Assignment Templates

Account assignment templates are line layouts in Transaction FB50 with prepopulated field values. They are useful for reducing data entry requirements for journal vouchers, which are frequent and consistent in their makeup. These templates allow you to quickly enter journal vouchers without the hassle of reentering all the necessary field values each time you create a new entry.

The next time you find yourself entering a journal voucher from scratch that you have created repeatedly in the past, consider creating an account assignment template for it. You might simply your life by doing so, especially for journal vouchers with a large number of line items.

Let's take a look. Go to Transaction FB50 and make sure the tree display is on (see Section 3.1.3). Click the triangle next to the ACCOUNT ASSIGNMENT TEMPLATE FOR ITEMS folder to open a list of available templates to choose from (Figure 3.29).

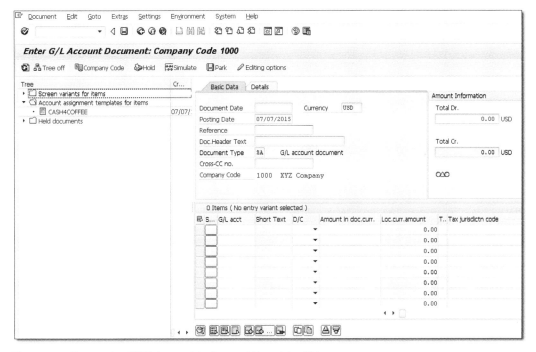

Figure 3.29 Transaction FB50 Account Assignment Templates List

Double-click the template you want to use (Figure 3.30), and the line layout in the line item entry screen will change based on the prepopulated values contained in the template. Note that at this point you can add or edit the field values.

As you see in our example, account assignment template CASH4COFFEE contains prepopulated values for the G/L ACCOUNT, DEBIT/CREDIT INDICATOR, TEXT, and PROFIT CENTER fields. With all other fields for the transaction prepopulated, you simply need to enter values in the AMOUNT fields to complete the document entry (Figure 3.31).

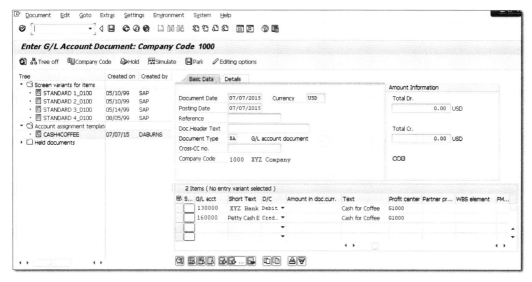

Figure 3.30 Transaction FB50 Account Assignment Template Selection

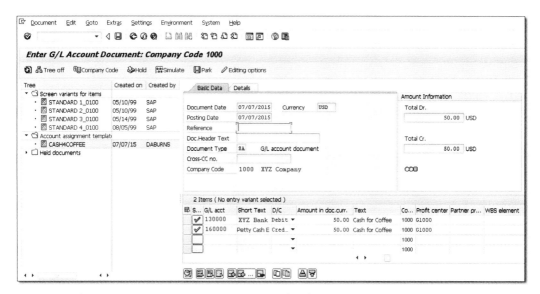

Figure 3.31 Transaction FB50 Amount Entered with Account Assignment Template

With document entry complete, you can post, park, or save this G/L journal voucher as completed. For the current example, we posted the document (Figure 3.32).

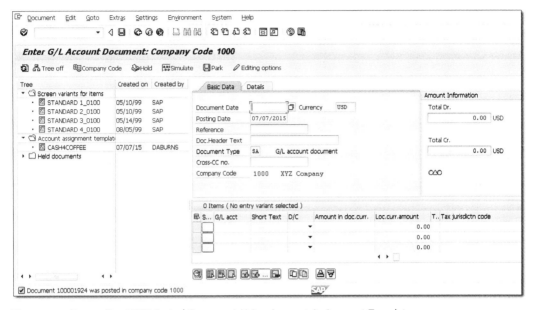

Figure 3.32 Transaction FB50 Posted Document Using Account Assignment Template

3.1.5 Controlling Document Entry with Editing Options

Controlling document entry with editing options allows you to make user-specific settings for transactions in accounting. Editing options give you some level of field control over the entry screen, what is displayed, and values that are defaulted, and they determine the interpretation of certain field entry values.

Editing options are a universal concept in FI, but discussion in this section is limited to their use in Transaction FB50. However, note that the settings you make are user-specific, not transaction-specific; therefore, once you have set an editing option in Transaction FB50, it will also apply to other accounting transactions, such as Transactions FB60 and FB70.

In this section, we will discuss some of the most commonly used settings and provide a complete list of all editing options and their descriptions (Table 3.1).

To access editing options from Transaction FB50 (Figure 3.33), click the EDITING OPTIONS button in the top center of the ENTER G/L ACCOUNT DOCUMENT screen or press `Shift`+`F4`.

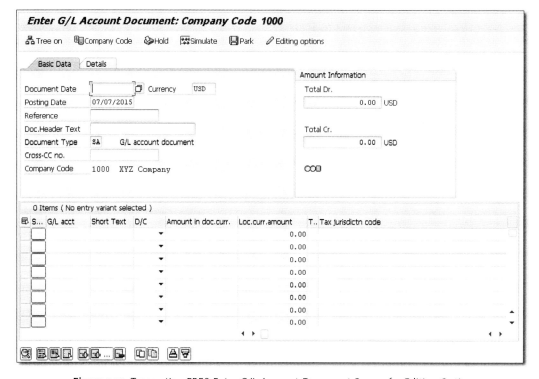

Figure 3.33 Transaction FB50 Enter G/L Account Document Screen for Editing Options

The ACCOUNTING EDITING OPTIONS screen will open (Figure 3.34). Editing options fall into four general categories, each with its own section of the screen:

▶ GENERAL ENTRY OPTIONS

▶ SPECIAL OPTIONS FOR SINGLE SCREEN TRANSACTIONS

▶ DEFAULT DOCUMENT CURRENCY

▶ DEFAULT COMPANY CODE

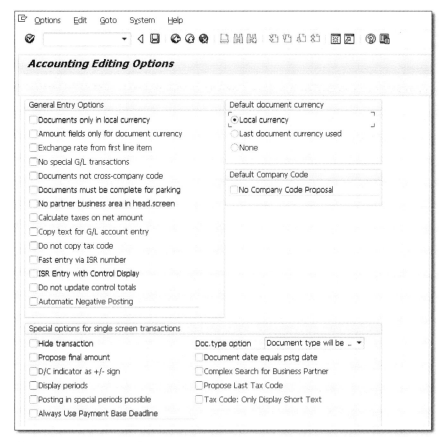

Figure 3.34 Accounting Editing Options Screen

In the upper-right-hand corner of Figure 3.34, you can see that the LOCAL CUR-RENCY radio button is selected in the DEFAULT DOCUMENT CURRENCY section. With this setting, the local currency of the company code to which the user is assigned will default into Transaction FB50.

For this example, we will change DEFAULT DOCUMENT CURRENCY to NONE (Figure 3.35). This might be necessary if you process most of your accounting entries in different currencies, as may be the case if you work for a multinational company with central accounting functions.

Once your selection is made, click the SAVE button 🖫 or press Ctrl+S.

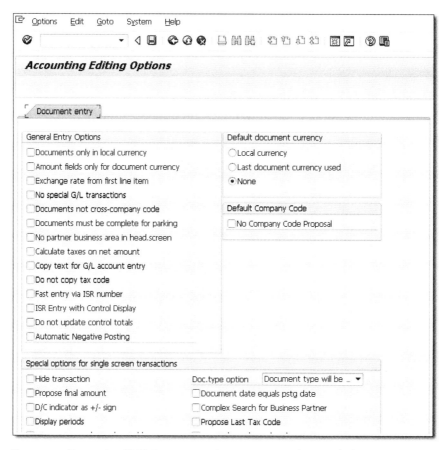

Figure 3.35 Transaction FB50 Accounting Editing Options with No Default Currency

Now, return to Transaction FB50 and you will see that the CURRENCY field in the header is blank (Figure 3.36), meaning that no value defaulted into the CURRENCY field.

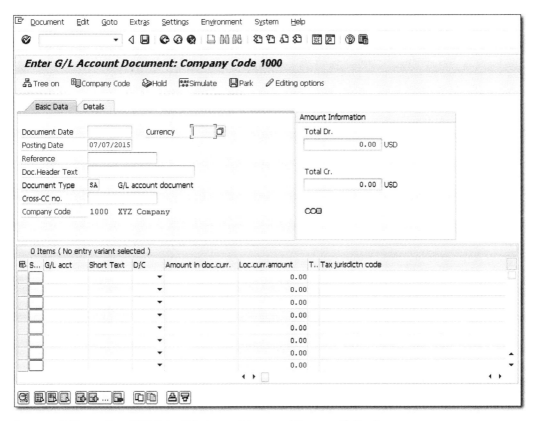

Figure 3.36 Transaction FB50 Enter G/L Account Document Screen with No Currency

Similarly, you can use editing options to change the transaction entry screen so that no company code is proposed. This might be desirable if you enter transactions frequently using different company codes. If your accounting department manages financial transactions across the globe, this is likely the case. It is common for those working in a centralized accounting or finance department for a global company to use this setting.

For this example, select the checkbox next to the NO COMPANY CODE PROPOSAL field in the ACCOUNTING EDITING OPTIONS screen (Figure 3.37). Then, click the SAVE button 🖫 or press Ctrl + S .

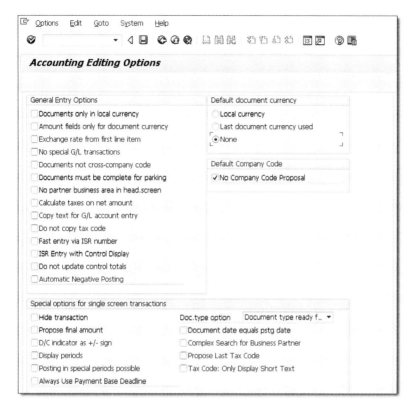

Figure 3.37 Transaction FB50 Accounting Editing Options with No Company Code Proposed

Now, return to Transaction FB50; you are immediately prompted to enter a COM-PANY CODE (Figure 3.38).

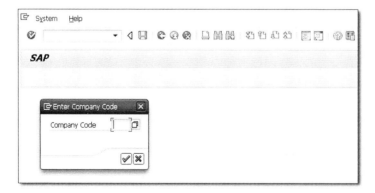

Figure 3.38 Transaction FB50 Prompt for Company Code

Another common use of editing options is to change the document type setting. For this example, change the DOC.TYPE OPTION field to DOCUMENT TYPE HIDDEN (Figure 3.39). Then, click the SAVE button 💾 or press Ctrl+S.

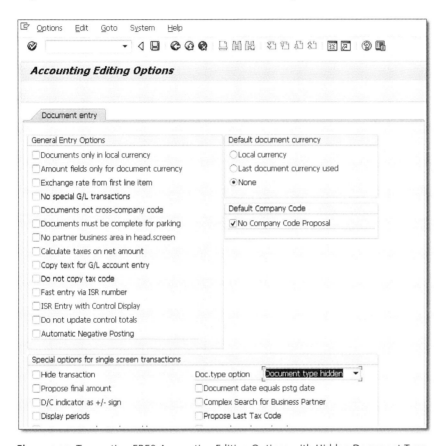

Figure 3.39 Transaction FB50 Accounting Editing Options with Hidden Document Type

Now, return to Transaction FB50, and you will see that the DOCUMENT TYPE field is hidden from view (Figure 3.40). As a result, you can no longer change the document type used in this transaction. This is a control feature, forcing users to use only one document type.

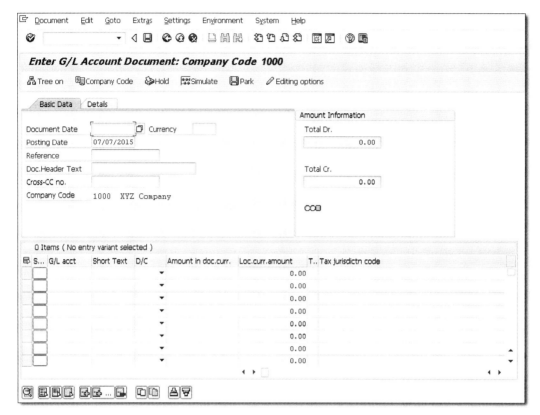

Figure 3.40 Transaction FB50 Enter G/L Account Document Screen with Hidden Document Type

Table 3.1 provides a complete list of editing options for controlling document entry, along with their descriptions.

Editing Option	Description
DOCUMENTS ONLY IN LOCAL CURRENCY	Only allows entry of documents in local currency.
AMOUNT FIELDS ONLY FOR DOCUMENT CURRENCY	Only allows entry amounts in foreign currency when entering documents in foreign currency.
EXCHANGE RATE FROM FIRST LINE ITEM	When posting foreign currency documents, the exchange rate in the document header is corrected automatically using the amounts in the first line item.

Table 3.1 Editing Options and Descriptions

Editing Option	Description
NO SPECIAL G/L TRANSACTIONS	Prevent entry of special G/L transactions.
DOCUMENTS NOT CROSS-COMPANY CODE	Cross-company code entries are prevented.
DOCUMENTS MUST BE COMPLETE FOR PARKING	Prevents incomplete documents from being parked.
NO PARTNER BUSINESS AREA IN HEADER SCREEN	Default partner business area cannot be entered in document header.
CALCULATE TAXES ON NET AMOUNT	Indicates the G/L account amounts entered are net of taxes.
COPY TEXT FOR G/L ACCOUNT ENTRY	Automatically copy text from last G/L line item to subsequent line items.
DO NOT COPY TAX CODE	Deactivates the setting that the last tax code entered is automatically copied to G/L account line items.
FAST ENTRY VIA ISR NUMBER	Enables the fast entry of incoming invoices using the ISR subscriber number.
ISR ENTRY WITH CONTROL DISPLAY	Provides the ability to enter an alternative vendor number in cases in which several vendors may have the same ISR number.
DO NOT UPDATE CONTROL TOTALS	Control totals are not updated.
AUTOMATIC NEGATIVE POSTING	When the negative postings indicator is set for at least one manually entered line, also makes any automatically generated lines negative postings.
DEFAULT DOCUMENT CURRENCY	1. Default local currency used in header currency field. 2. Default last currency used in header currency field. 3. Defaults no currency in the header currency field.
DEFAULT COMPANY CODE	When the NO COMPANY CODE PROPOSAL indicator is checked, you must manually select the company code to be used.
HIDE TRANSACTION	Hides the TRANSACTION field on the entry screen.
PROPOSE FINAL AMOUNT	System proposes the final invoice amount in the customer or vendor line, after a G/L line has been entered.
D/C INDICATOR AS +/- SIGN	Allows the entry of +/- sign with amounts, and the debit/credit indicator is thus derived.

Table 3.1 Editing Options and Descriptions (Cont.)

Editing Option	Description
DISPLAY PERIODS	Enables the display of periods on the entry screen under basic data.
POSTING IN SPECIAL PERIODS POSSIBLE	Enables the period field for data input.
ALWAYS USE PAYMENT BASE DEADLINE	Only permit payment deadline calculation based on the baseline date.
DOCUMENT TYPE OPTION	1. Display document type in header.
	2. Document type is ready for input.
	3. Display document type using short name.
	4. Document type is ready for input using short name.
	5. Document type is hidden.
DOCUMENT DATE EQUALS POSTING DATE	Defaults the document date from the posting date.
COMPLEX SEARCH FOR BUSINESS PARTNER	Specifies if a complex search is possible for the number of the trading partner when entering a vendor invoice.
PROPOSE LAST TAX CODE	Proposes the last tax code used the next time the transaction is called.
TAX CODE: ONLY DISPLAY SHORT TEXT	Changes the tax code dropdown list in the transaction to only display the short text of the tax code.

Table 3.1 Editing Options and Descriptions (Cont.)

3.1.6 Post with Reference

Post with reference is a quick and easy way to create a new G/L document by replicating all or most of the accounting data from a document that has already been posted. It allows you to quickly create a new G/L account document based upon an existing, previously posted document, with little to no data entry.

In many ways, this option works much like a document copy function, except that SAP provides several flow control indicators that allow you to select specific actions in the process. For example, there is a DO NOT PROPOSE AMOUNTS flow control indicator. When this indicator is selected, you must enter document line item amounts manually. Without this indicator, you could only use the post with reference function to post a new document with the exact same amount as the reference document.

Post with reference is a universal concept in FI, but the scope of our discussion in this section is limited to its use in Transaction FB50. We will demonstrate its use with a simple example and then provide complete list of flow control options and their descriptions (Table 3.2 later in this section).

Post with reference can be used when you enter a G/L accounting document via Transaction FB50 or application menu path ACCOUNTING • FINANCIAL ACCOUNTING • GENERAL LEDGER • DOCUMENT ENTRY • FB50—ENTER G/L ACCOUNT DOCUMENT (see Figure 3.41).

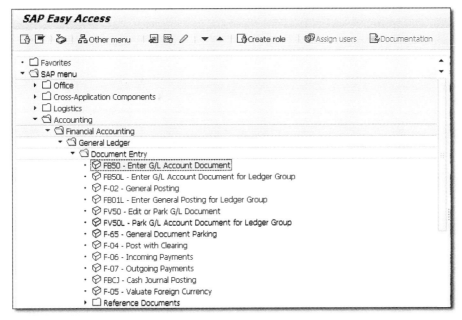

Figure 3.41 Menu Path for Post with Reference

Double-click FB50—ENTER G/L ACCOUNT DOCUMENT from the menu path shown in Figure 3.42 or enter "FB50" in the COMMAND field (as shown in Figure 3.42) and press ⌷Enter⌷.

Figure 3.42 FB50 in Command Field

From the ENTER G/L ACCOUNT DOCUMENT entry screen (Figure 3.43), choose the GOTO • POST WITH REFERENCE dropdown menu option or press Shift+F9 (Figure 3.43).

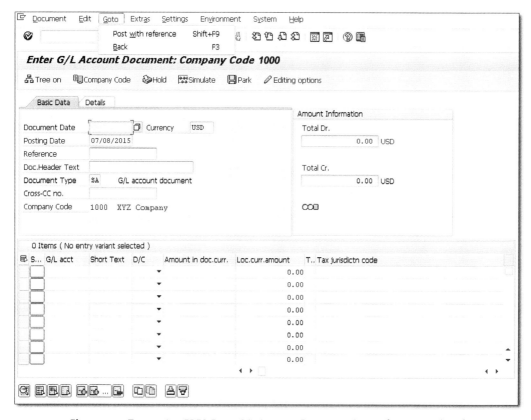

Figure 3.43 Transaction FB50 Enter G/L Account Document Screen for Post with Reference

The post with reference POST DOCUMENT: HEADER DATA selection screen will open (Figure 3.44). Here, complete the DOCUMENT NUMBER, COMPANY CODE, and FISCAL YEAR fields in the REFERENCE section. For this example, also select the DO NOT PROPOSE AMOUNTS indicator in the FLOW CONTROL section.

Once the relevant fields are populated in the POST DOCUMENT: HEADER DATA screen, press Enter to move to the first screen of the new G/L document creation process (Figure 3.45). The header data contains the field values copied from the reference document, including the DOCUMENT DATE and POSTING DATE fields from the reference transaction. Note that at this point you can edit many field values.

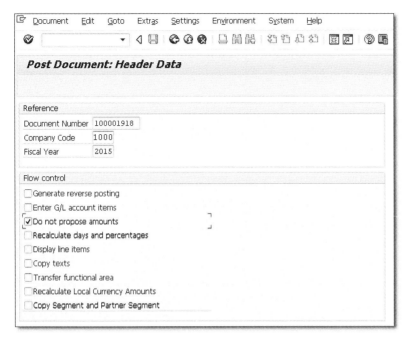

Figure 3.44 Post with Reference Header Selection Screen

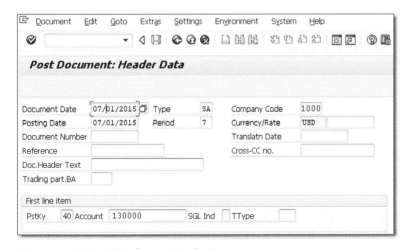

Figure 3.45 Post with Reference Header Screen

For this example, we changed both the DOCUMENT DATE and POSTING DATE fields (Figure 3.46).

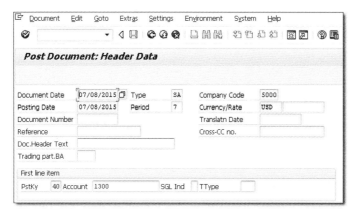

Figure 3.46 Post with Reference Header Screen with Date Change

Once you have edited any header fields that you want to change, press ⌈Enter⌉ and the POST DOCUMENT ADD G/L ACCOUNT ITEM screen will appear (Figure 3.47). Notice that the amount field is blank in Figure 3.47. This is because we selected the DO NOT PROPOSE AMOUNTS indicator in FLOW CONTROL (Figure 3.44) when we initiated the post with reference transaction.

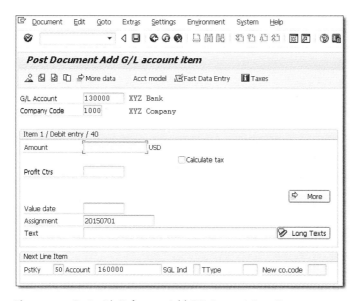

Figure 3.47 Post with Reference Add G/L Account Item Screen

For this example, enter "100" in the AMOUNT field (Figure 3.48).

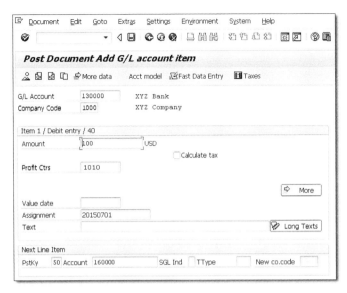

Figure 3.48 Post with Reference Add G/L Account Item Screen with Amount Change

Now, press ⏎Enter and a second POST DOCUMENT ADD G/L ACCOUNT ITEM screen will open (Figure 3.49). You will see that the AMOUNT field is blank here as well.

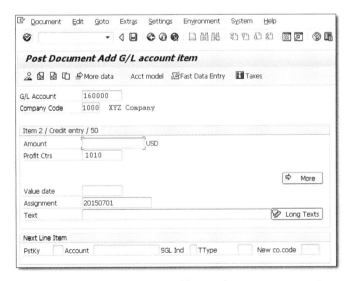

Figure 3.49 Post with Reference Add Second G/L Account Item Screen with Amount Blank

For this example, enter "100" again in the AMOUNT field (Figure 3.50).

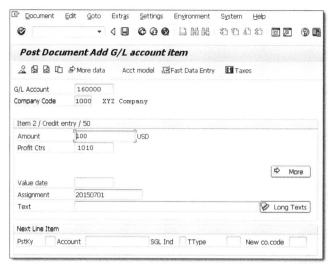

Figure 3.50 Post with Reference Add Second G/L Account Item Screen with Amount Change

After entering G/L account line items is complete, click the Post button ▣ or press [Ctrl]+[S] to post the G/L document (Figure 3.51). A message will pop up with the new G/L document number.

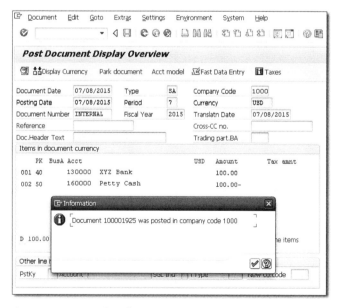

Figure 3.51 Post with Reference Document Created Message

As you can see, post with reference is a great time-saving tool, which allows you to quickly create a new G/L account document based upon an existing, previously posted document, with little to no data entry.

Table 3.2 provides a complete list of flow control options and their descriptions (Figure 3.44).

Flow Control Indicator	Description
GENERATE REVERSE POSTING	Automatically generate reverse debit/credit indicators to offset the reference document.
ENTER G/L ACCOUNT ITEMS	Line items are transferred to the fast entry screen for G/L accounts so that several line items can be displayed and processed from one screen.
DO NOT PROPOSE AMOUNTS	Line item amounts must be manually entered in the new document.
RECALCULATE DAYS AND PERCENTAGES	Days and percentages from payment terms will be recalculated.
DISPLAY LINE ITEMS	Displays each individual line item separately so default field values can be changed if necessary.
COPY TEXTS	Copies long texts from the reference document to the new document.
TRANSFER FUNCTIONAL AREA	The functional area is normally derived; therefore, this option transfers the reference functional area instead of rederiving it.
RECALCULATE LOCAL CURRENCY AMOUNTS	Recalculates local currency amounts to account for changes in exchange rates.
COPY SEGMENT AND PARTNER SEGMENT	These fields are normally derived; therefore, this option transfers them instead of rederiving their values.

Table 3.2 Flow Control Options and Descriptions

Post with reference in essence allows you to copy an existing document, but note that it is an SAP best practice to allow derived field values to be rederived with each new posting. For example, if you derive the SEGMENT field from the profit center, you should allow the program to automatically rederive the field instead of entering it manually into the transaction.

Now that we have covered post with reference, let's discuss post with clearing. This is an important function in many business processes, including electronic bank statements, A/R, A/P, and GR/IR.

3.2   Post with Clearing

Post with clearing is a concept in FI that enables you to select and offset a G/L open item. With this transaction, you enter one line item in a G/L accounting document and then select a G/L open item to clear. When you select an open item, the clearing program automatically produces an opposing G/L line item, netting the G/L account balance of the line items to zero.

There are several examples of accounting business processes that perform post with clearing. The most notable examples are posting incoming payments in accounts receivable and posting outgoing payments in accounts payable. In the G/L module, the most common example is clearing open items in bank accounts, which we will focus on for the remainder of this section.

In the G/L module, post with clearing is performed using Transaction F-04 or via application menu path ACCOUNTING • FINANCIAL ACCOUNTING • GENERAL LEDGER • DOCUMENT ENTRY • F-04—POST WITH CLEARING, as shown in Figure 3.52.

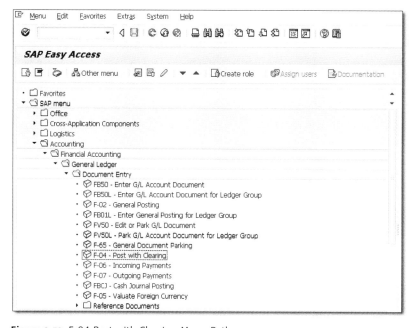

Figure 3.52 F-04 Post with Clearing Menu Path

Double-click F-04—POST WITH CLEARING from the menu path shown in Figure 3.52, or enter "F-04" in the COMMAND field (as shown in Figure 3.53) and press ⌈Enter⌋.

Figure 3.53 F-04 in the Command Field

The POST WITH CLEARING: HEADER DATA screen will appear (Figure 3.54). On this screen, enter a value for the DOCUMENT DATE field and any other fields that are required, but do not default a value. For this example, select TRANSFER POSTING WITH CLEARING in the TRANSACTION TO BE PROCESSED section. At the bottom of the screen, you need to enter values for the POSTING KEY and ACCOUNT fields for the first line item of the G/L document.

With your field entries complete, press Enter.

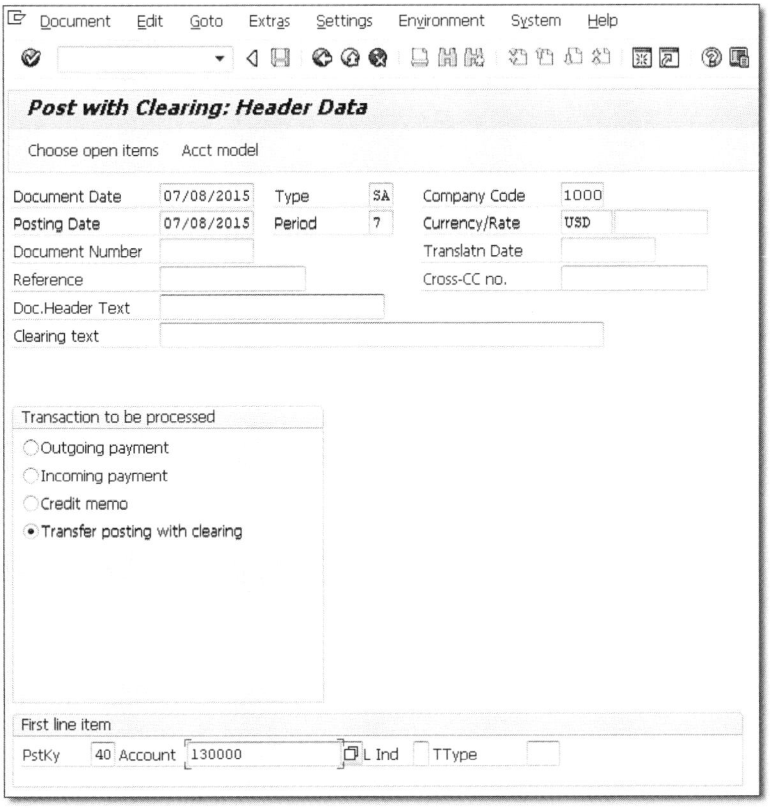

Figure 3.54 Transaction F-04 Post with Clearing Header Data Screen

The POST WITH CLEARING ADD G/L ACCOUNT ITEM screen will open (Figure 3.55). For this example, enter a value in the AMOUNT field (we entered "4991.83" here) and click on the CHOOSE OPEN ITEMS button.

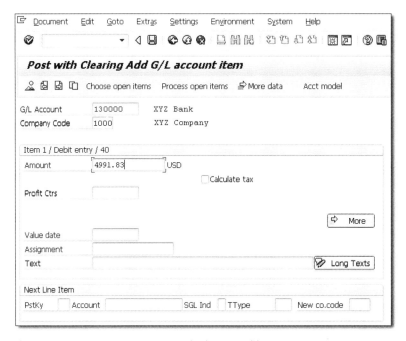

Figure 3.55 Transaction F-04 Post with Clearing Add G/L Account Item Screen

The POST WITH CLEARING SELECT OPEN ITEMS screen will open (Figure 3.56). In this example, values defaulted for the COMPANY CODE and ACCOUNT TYPE fields, and we manually entered a value into the ACCOUNT field (here, "1311"). The ACCOUNT field must be filled with the G/L account containing the open item to be cleared.

In the ADDITIONAL SELECTIONS section, select a field relevant to the search for open items. For this example, select the AMOUNT field.

At this point, the program has all the information it needs to search for and select open items. Click on the PROCESS OPEN ITEMS button.

The POST WITH CLEARING ENTER SELECTION CRITERIA screen will open (Figure 3.57). Here, enter a dollar amount in the FROM AMOUNT field. Then, click the PROCESS OPEN ITEMS button.

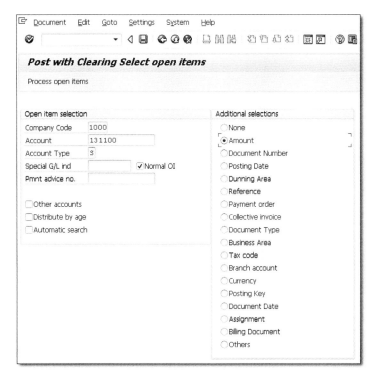

Figure 3.56 F-04 Post with Clearing Select Open Items Screen

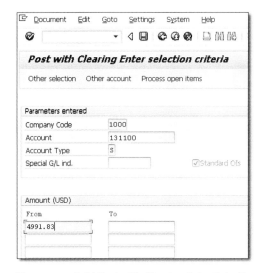

Figure 3.57 F-04 Post with Clearing Enter Selection Criteria Screen

The Post with Clearing Process Open Items screen will open, with one line item selected for clearing (Figure 3.58).

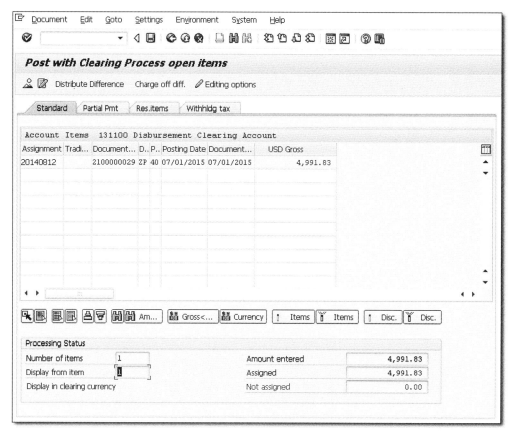

Figure 3.58 F-04 Post with Clearing Process Open Items Screen

Click the Post button 🖫 or press `Ctrl`+`S` to post the G/L document. A message will pop up with the new G/L document number (Figure 3.59).

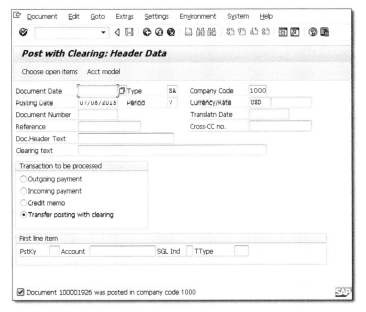

Figure 3.59 F-04 Post with Clearing Document Created Message

Now that we've covered post with clearing, let's move on to the topic of resetting and reversing G/L documents.

3.3 Resetting and Reversing Documents

Reversing documents is a common occurrence in a day in the life of an accountant. It needs to happen when some error occurred in the posting of the original document, such as when a document posts with the wrong date or, as frequently occurs, an error arose in the line of accounting.

The most important factor to know before attempting to reverse an SAP accounting document, is what type of document you are working with. For reversal purposes, accounting documents can be classified as either clearing or nonclearing documents.

Clearing documents are those produced through a post with clearing transaction, such as Transaction F-04 (see Section 3.2). These documents have two technical components: First, a clearing document contains complete header data and at least two completed line items with debit/credit amounts netting to zero. The second component of a clearing document is the account clearing. Through the clearing process, a G/L open item was selected and its status changed from open to cleared when the document was posted.

A *nonclearing accounting document* has the same attributes as a clearing document, but it does not clear a G/L open item. Therefore, a nonclearing document has not changed the status of a G/L line item from open to cleared. Nonclearing documents are by far the simplest to reverse.

To reverse a single G/L accounting document, use Transaction FB08 or application menu path ACCOUNTING • FINANCIAL ACCOUNTING • GENERAL LEDGER • DOCUMENT • REVERSE • FB08—INDIVIDUAL REVERSAL, as seen in Figure 3.60.

Figure 3.60 FB08 Menu Path

Double-click FB08—INDIVIDUAL REVERSAL from the menu path, or enter "FB08" in the COMMAND field (as shown in Figure 3.61) and press ⌞Enter⌝.

Figure 3.61 FB08 in the Command Field

The REVERSE DOCUMENT: HEADER DATA screen appears (Figure 3.62). At a minimum, the DOCUMENT NUMBER, COMPANY CODE, FISCAL YEAR, and REVERSAL REASON fields are required.

The REVERSAL REASON field is noted in the reversed document, and it determines if an alternative posting date is allowed or if the reversal can be created from a negative posting. In this example, the REVERSAL REASON field is populated with a value of 01, signifying that the reversal will take place in the current period.

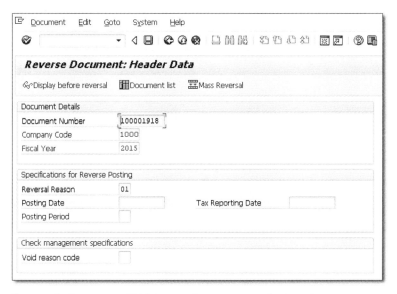

Figure 3.62 Transaction FB08 Reverse Document: Header Data Screen

When all the required fields are entered, click the POST icon 💾 or press Ctrl+S to post the G/L reversal document. A message will pop up with the new G/L document number (Figure 3.63).

If you have more than one nonclearing document to reverse, use Transaction F.80 or application menu path ACCOUNTING • FINANCIAL ACCOUNTING • GENERAL LEDGER • DOCUMENT • REVERSE • F.80—MASS REVERSAL, as shown in Figure 3.64.

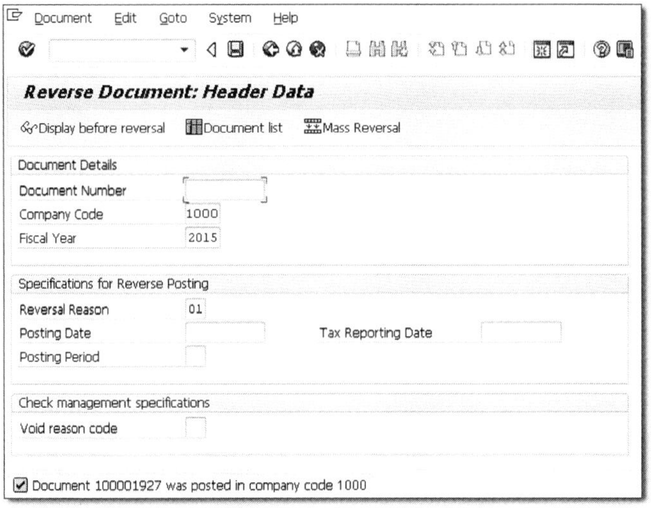

Figure 3.63 Transaction FB08 Reversal Document Created Message

Figure 3.64 F.80 Menu Path

Double-click F.80—Mass Reversal from the menu path shown in Figure 3.64, or enter "F.80" in the Command field (as shown in Figure 3.65) and press ⌜Enter⌝.

Figure 3.65 F.80 in Command Field

The Mass Reversal of Documents: Initial Screen screen appears (Figure 3.66). As in Transaction FB08, the Company Code, Document Number, Fiscal Year, and Reversal Reason fields are required. Note that in Transaction F.80 you can enter a range of values for these fields, whereas in Transaction FB08 you can only enter a single value for each. Transaction F.80 also provides a Ledger field, which in most cases will refer to your primary ledger.

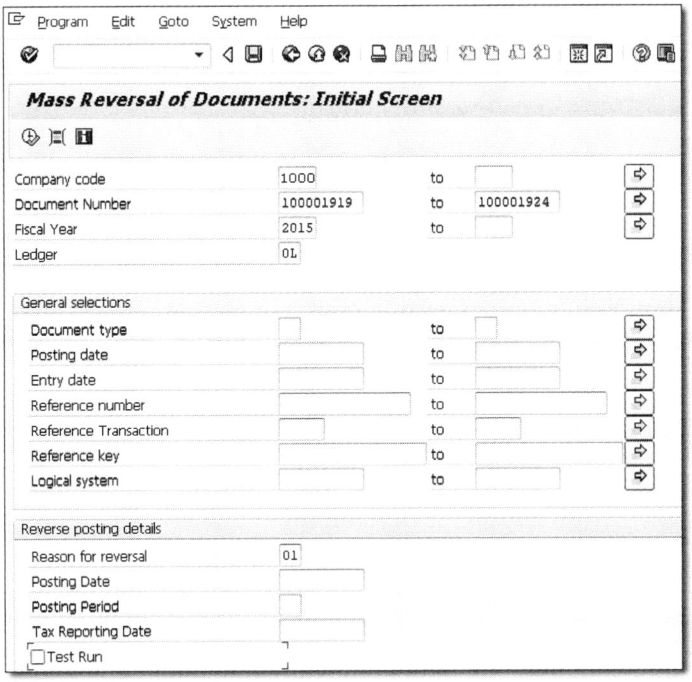

Figure 3.66 F.80 Mass Reversal Documents Screen

Transaction F.80 has some other additional features. Under General Selections there are several input fields that may be useful. In addition, in the Reverse

Posting Details section there is a Test Run button. For mass reversals, it is always a good idea to run the program in test mode first.

When all the required fields are entered, click the Execute button ⊕ or press F8 to post the G/L reversal documents.

Detailed results are provided on the Mass Reversal of Documents output screen (Figure 3.67).

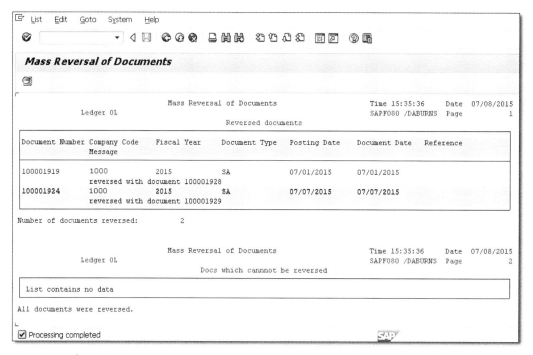

Figure 3.67 Transaction F.80 Mass Reversal of Documents Output Screen

Now that we have discussed reversing individual and multiple nonclearing documents, let's move on to the process for reversing clearing documents.

To reverse a G/L clearing document, use Transaction FBRA or application menu path Accounting • Financial Accounting • General Ledger • Document • FBRA—Reset Cleared Items, as shown in Figure 3.68.

Double-click FBRA—Reset Cleared Items from the menu path shown in Figure 3.68, or enter "FBRA" in the Command field (as shown in Figure 3.69) and press Enter.

Figure 3.68 Transaction FBRA Menu Path

Figure 3.69 FBRA in Command Field

The RESET CLEARED ITEMS screen will open (Figure 3.70). The CLEARING DOCUMENT, COMPANY CODE, and FISCAL YEAR fields are all required.

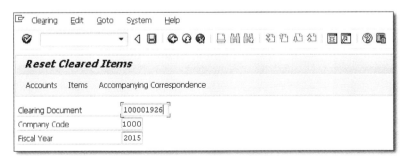

Figure 3.70 FBRA Reset Cleared Items Screen

After entering the required screen elements, click the RESET CLEARED ITEMS button or press $\boxed{\text{Ctrl}}$+$\boxed{\text{S}}$. This will bring up the REVERSAL OF CLEARING DOCUMENT dialog box (Figure 3.71), in which you must choose one of three options: ONLY RESETTING, RESETTING AND REVERS, or CANCEL.

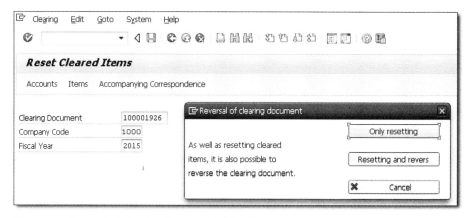

Figure 3.71 Reversal of Clearing Document Dialog Box

The ONLY RESETTING option does not reverse the clearing document. Rather, it breaks the link between a clearing document and the G/L item it cleared and changes the status of the cleared G/L item back to open. Only use this option when the G/L item selected for clearing was the wrong line item. The clearing document thus becomes an open item and can be reassigned to clear the correct G/L open item.

The RESETTING AND REVERS option not only resets the cleared item back to open status, but also reverses the clearing document. For this example, select the RESETTING AND REVERS option; the REVERSAL DATA dialogue box will open (Figure 3.72).

The CANCEL button closes the REVERSAL OF CLEARING DOCUMENT box without taking any further action and returns you to the RESET CLEARED ITEMS screen.

The REVERSAL REASON field is noted in the reversed document. It also determines if an alternative posting date is allowed or if the reversal can be created from a negative posting. In this example, the REVERSAL REASON field is populated with a value of 01, signifying that the reversal will take place in the current period.

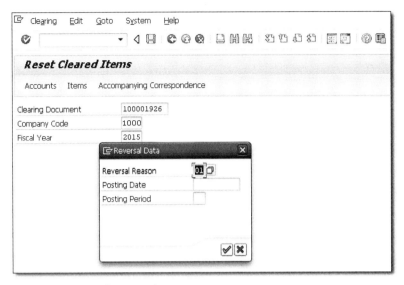

Figure 3.72 Reversal Data Dialog Box

Click the CONTINUE button ✔ or press Enter. Two subsequent information dialogue boxes will appear: The first, shown in Figure 3.73, states that the clearing document was reset; the second, shown in Figure 3.74, provides the number of a new document that has been posted, which is the document that reversed the clearing document.

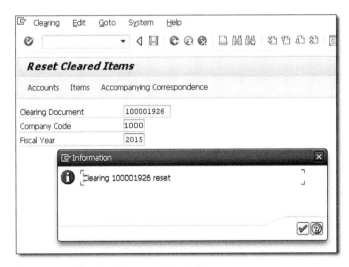

Figure 3.73 Clearing Document Reset Message

Figure 3.74 Reversal Document Posted Message

Now you know how to reverse G/L accounting documents. Next, let's take a look at how to change and display accounting documents.

3.4 Changing and Displaying Documents

This section covers the change and display capabilities for G/L accounting documents. The scope of this section is limited to Transaction FB50.

Rules for changing field values in SAP accounting documents is defined in configuration. Separate rules are defined for header and line item fields. Note, however, that SAP will never allow you to change fields considered central to the principle of orderly accounting. In other words, fields that are material to G/L account balances, posting dates, and integration cannot be changed after a G/L accounting document has been posted. These include not only the POSTING DATE, DEBIT/CREDIT INDICATOR, and AMOUNT fields, but also update objects (i.e., cost center). If a G/L accounting document contains an incorrect value that falls into one of these categories, the document should be reversed using Transaction FB08 or Transaction FBRA.

To change a G/L document, use Transaction FB02 or application menu path ACCOUNTING • FINANCIAL ACCOUNTING • GENERAL LEDGER • DOCUMENT • FB02—CHANGE, as shown in Figure 3.75.

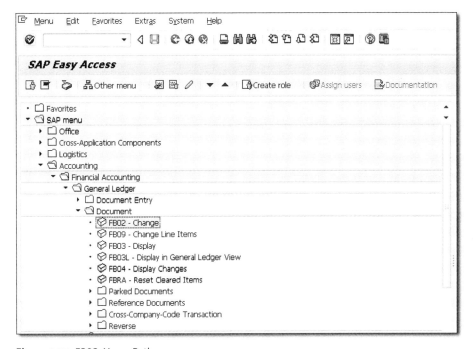

Figure 3.75 FB02 Menu Path

Double-click FB02—CHANGE from the menu path shown in Figure 3.75, or enter "FB02" in the COMMAND field (as shown in Figure 3.76) and press [Enter].

Figure 3.76 FB02 in Command Field

The CHANGE DOCUMENT: INITIAL SCREEN screen will open (Figure 3.77). The DOCUMENT NUMBER, COMPANY CODE, and FISCAL YEAR fields are required.

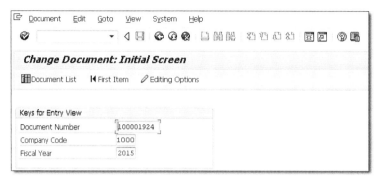

Figure 3.77 Transaction FB02 Change Document Screen

After entering all field values, press Enter. The CHANGE DOCUMENT: DATA ENTRY VIEW screen appears (Figure 3.78).

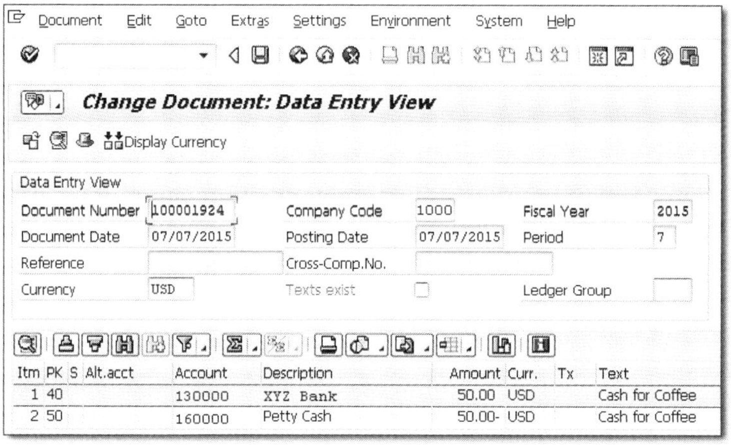

Figure 3.78 Transaction FB02 Change Document: Data Entry View Screen

To change a header field, click on the top hat icon, and the document header dialogue box will open (Figure 3.79). Fields that cannot be changed are greyed out (e.g., DOCUMENT TYPE). Fields that can be changed are white and are ready for field values to be entered or changed (e.g, REFERENCE).

From the CHANGE DOCUMENT: DATA ENTRY VIEW screen (Figure 3.78), you can change line item fields by double-clicking a line to open the CHANGE DOCUMENT: LINE ITEM screen (Figure 3.80).

Figure 3.79 Transaction FB02 Document Header Dialogue Box

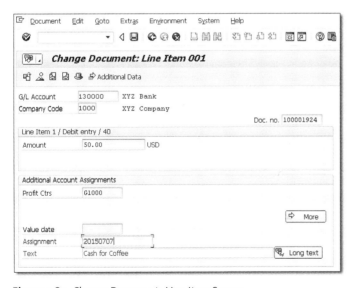

Figure 3.80 Change Document: Line Item Screen

As before, fields that cannot be changed are greyed out. Those that can are white and are ready for field values to be entered or changed. For this example, change the TEXT field (Figure 3.81).

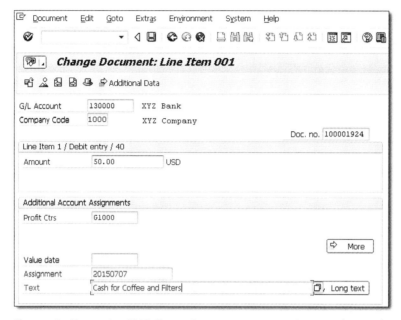

Figure 3.81 Transaction FB02 Change Document: Line Item Screen with Text Change

After changing field values, click the SAVE button 🖫 or press ⌈Ctrl⌉+⌈S⌉. A message will indicate that the document changes have been saved (Figure 3.82).

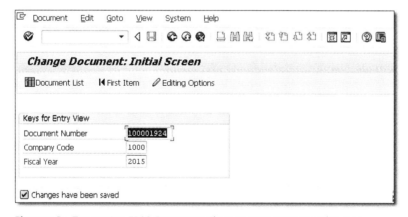

Figure 3.82 Transaction FB02 Document Changes Have Been Saved Screen

To display a G/L accounting document, use Transaction FB03 or application menu path Accounting • Financial Accounting • General Ledger • Document • FB03 — Display, as shown in Figure 3.83.

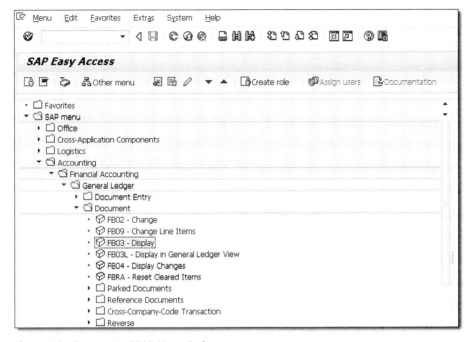

Figure 3.83 Transaction FB03 Menu Path

Double-click FB03 — Display from the menu path shown in Figure 3.83, or enter "FB03" in the Command field (as shown in Figure 3.84) and press ⟨Enter⟩.

Figure 3.84 FB03 in Command Field

The Document Display: Initial Screen screen will open (Figure 3.85). The Document Number, Company Code, and Fiscal Year fields are required.

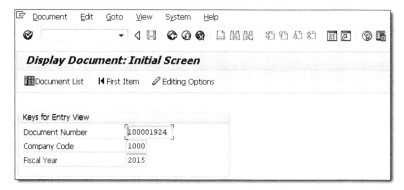

Figure 3.85 Transaction FB03 Document Display: Initial Screen

After entering field values, press [Enter]. The DISPLAY DOCUMENT: DATA ENTRY VIEW screen will open (Figure 3.86).

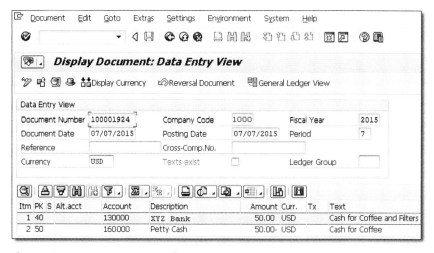

Figure 3.86 Transaction FB03 Display Document: Data Entry View Screen

From this screen, you can double-click a line to view line item details or click on the top hat icon 🔲 to view header details.

Now that you have learned how to display and change accounting documents, let's discuss viewing associated documents using the Document Relationship Browser.

3.5 Relationship Browser

In SAP, the *Document Relationship Browser* provides the ability to view within all documents associated with an accounting document via tree display. The Relationship Browser is a universal concept in FI, but in this section our discussion is limited to its application in Transaction FB50.

The Relationship Browser is a document tie point. By tying associated documents together in one view, it becomes simpler to understand business steps and business process flow. This browser is a useful tool for troubleshooting accounting problems. Most importantly, the Relationship Browser allows you, the user, to easily see follow-on documents. It alleviates time-consuming efforts associated with manually reconciling accounts and associating documents in a business process.

To view the Relationship Browser from Transaction FB50, use the dropdown menu path ENVIRONMENT • DOCUMENT ENVIRONMENT • RELATIONSHIP BROWSER, as shown in Figure 3.87.

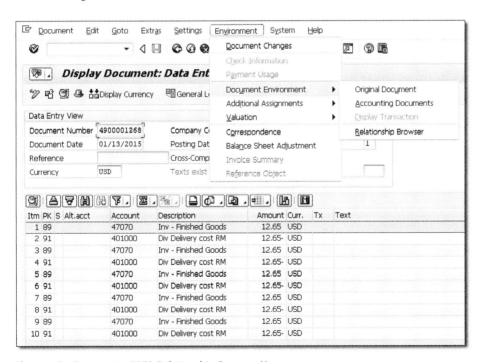

Figure 3.87 Transaction FB50 Relationship Browser Menu

The DOCUMENT RELATIONSHIP BROWSER screen will open (Figure 3.88).

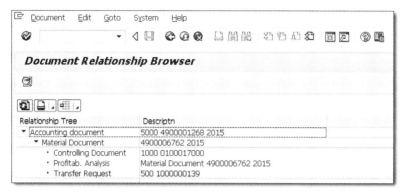

Figure 3.88 Document Relationship Browser

From this view, you can double-click any document in the RELATIONSHIP TREE, or you can click an item and then click the magnifying glass icon 🔍 (DETAILS). The Document Relationship Browser not only provides a document tie point view, but also permits document drilldown capability.

This concludes our discussion of the Relationship Browser in G/L. Yet, it is an important tool that will be discussed in a number of chapters throughout this book. In some cases, like in MM-Purchasing, document relationships are tied together in what's called a document follow-on function. Although the terminology may change slightly from module to module, the concept is the same, which is to see all the reference documents associated with a central document in one place. These document associations are updated real-time and present a huge time savings to end users.

3.6 Reference Documents

In addition to the other G/L functions and transactions covered previously in this chapter, SAP provides some additional nifty tools called *Reference Documents*. These include the account assignment model, recurring documents, and sample document. The application menu path to access them is shown in Figure 3.89.

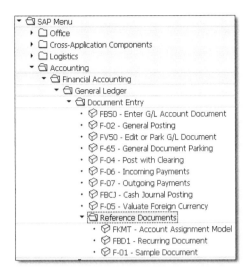

Figure 3.89 Application Menu Path G/L Reference Documents

3.6.1   Account Assignment Models

An *account assignment model* is a reference for document entry that provides default values for posting accounting transactions. It contains G/L account items that can be changed or supplemented at any time. The accounting lines entered in the account assignment model need not be complete. During document entry, the account assignment model serves as a starting reference point for the accounting transaction, but field values can be added, changed, and deleted.

To create, change, or delete an account assignment model, use Transaction FKMT. In Figure 3.90, you can see an example model. The ACCT ASSIGNMENT MODEL field is for the name of the model and is a 10-character field. In the ATTRIBUTES section, CURRENCY and CHART OF ACCOUNTS are required fields. In this example, SAMPLE TEXT was also added, but is not necessary.

Notice also in Figure 3.90 that the EQUIVALENCE TO box is selected. This is a special feature of account assignment models. Amounts can be entered directly into account assignment models, or distributed based on an equivalency entry and calculation.

With the account assignment model header information entered, press $\boxed{\text{Shift}}$ + $\boxed{\text{F8}}$.

Figure 3.90 Create Account Assignment Model: Header

The Account Assignment Model: Change Line Items screen appears (Figure 3.91). Enter line items and click the Save icon 🖫 .

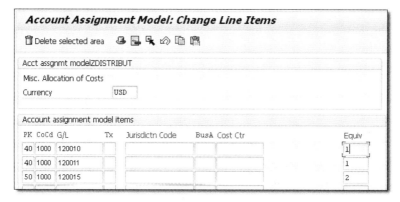

Figure 3.91 Create Account Assignment Model: Line Items

To use your account assignment model in a transaction, go to Transaction FB50. Enter a Posting Date and then press F6 . The FB50 Display Overview screen will appear (Figure 3.92).

Press F7 and the Select Account Assignment Model pop-up box will appear (Figure 3.93). Enter your account assignment model and press Enter .

Figure 3.92 FB50 Document Display Overview Screen

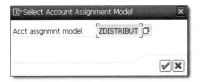

Figure 3.93 Select Account Assignment Model

The ACCOUNT ASSIGNMENT MODEL: ENTRY FOR POSTING screen appears (Figure 3.94). Notice the fields for DEBIT DISTRIBUTION and CREDIT DISTRIBUTION. Enter amounts in each and press Enter.

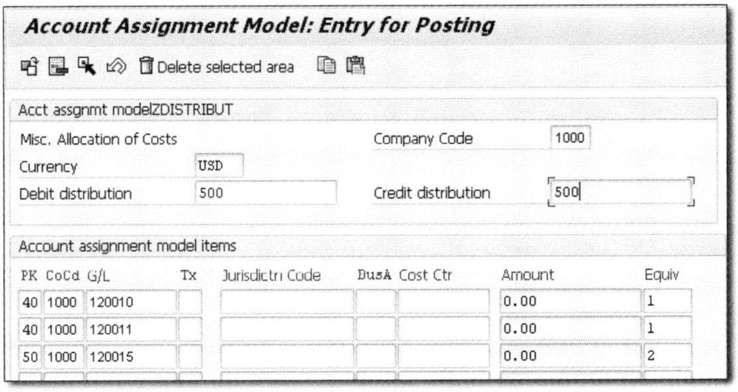

Figure 3.94 Account Assignment Entry for Posting Screen

The amounts are then distributed to line items, as shown in Figure 3.95.

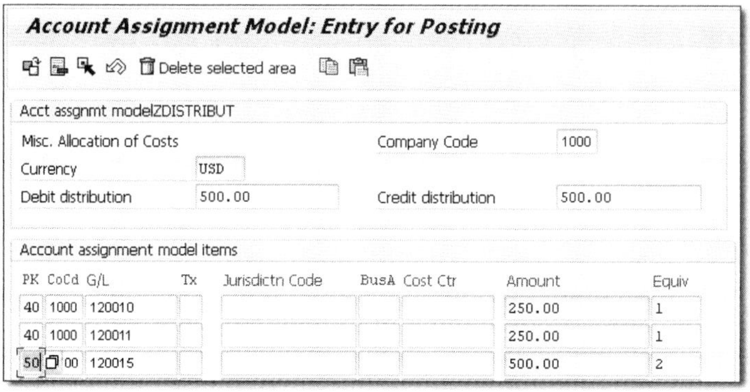

Figure 3.95 Account Assignment Entry for Posting Amount Distributions

Press the SAVE icon ⊟ and a new document will be posted referencing the account assignment model.

Account assignment models have been around for a long time and are not as widely used now as in years past. Their use has largely been filled by the use of account assignment templates (see Section 3.1.4).

3.6.2 Recurring Documents

Recurring documents are accounting transactions that are repeated at regular intervals, usually monthly or quarterly. In other words, recurring documents are used to capture information on accounting transactions with a fixed payment date and amount, such as rent or insurance. However, the run schedule can be configured to provide variability in the exact payment date.

Specific recurring data is entered into a recurring entry document.This document does not create accounting entries or update the G/L. Rather, the data in a recurring entry document is used for reference purposes for the recurring entry program, which in turn creates accounting documents.

To post recurring entry documents in your company codes, you have to set up the X1 number range. The recurring entry original document numbers are assigned according to this number range.

To create an original recurring entry document, use Transaction FBD1. The ENTER RECURRING ENTRY: HEADER DATA screen appears (Figure 3.96). Enter a COMPANY

CODE. The RECURRING ENTRY RUN parameters must be entered to indicate the start and end validity dates, intervals, etc. Of particular note here is that you can enter a specific RUN DATE if the accounting entry is also to be created with a specific posting date in mind. If there is some variability in the posting date, a RUN SCHEDULE can be configured and specified.

DOCUMENT HEADER INFORMATION is entered and is used and transferred to accounting documents that are created.

At the bottom of the screen, you begin to enter line items by entering a posting key, account, and, if applicable, a special G/L indicator or transaction type.

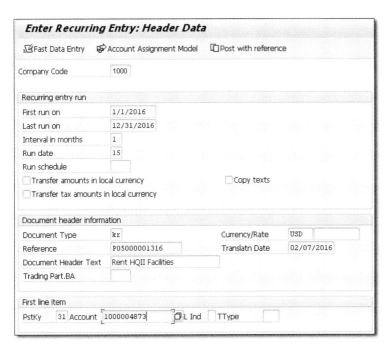

Figure 3.96 Transaction FBD1 Enter Recurring Entry Document Header

With header details filled out, press ⟨Enter⟩. In this example, the ENTER RECURRING ENTRY ADD VENDOR ITEM screen appears (Figure 3.97).

After inputting vendor line item details and a posting key and account for the second line item at the bottom of the screen, press ⟨Enter⟩. The ENTER RECURRING ENTRY ADD G/L ACCOUNT ITEM screen appears Figure 3.98. Enter an amount and any other field values you require.

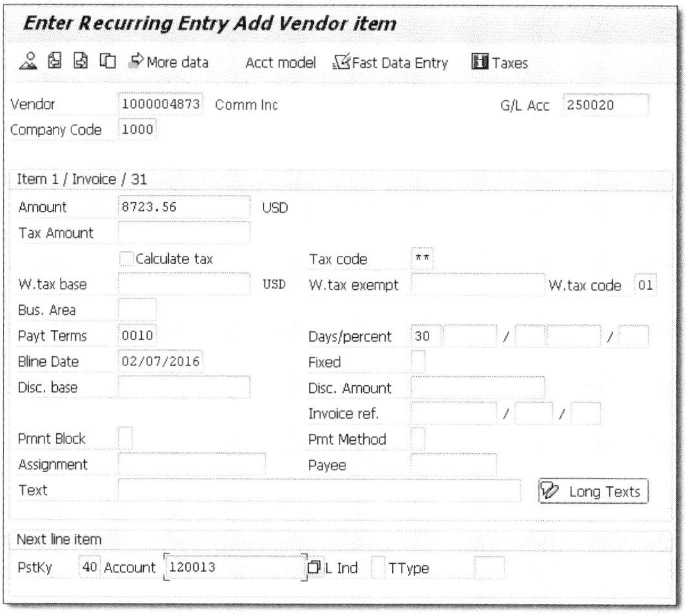

Figure 3.97 Transaction FBD1 Add Vendor Line Item

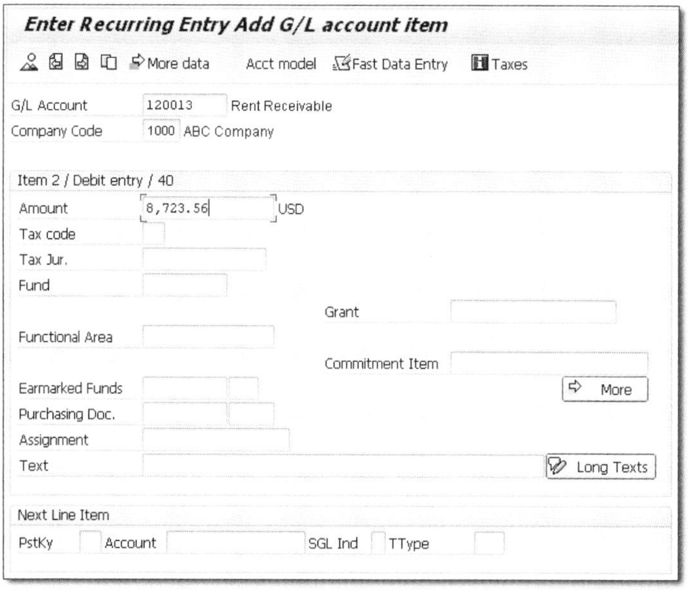

Figure 3.98 Transaction FBD1 Add G/L Account Item

With the second line item of the original recurring entry document complete, click the Post icon 🖫 . As shown in Figure 3.99, a message appears at the bottom of the screen saying that the document has been stored.

Enter Recurring Entry: Header Data

🖫Fast Data Entry   🖫Account Assignment Model   🗋Post with reference

Company Code   1000 🗇

Recurring entry run

First run on
Last run on
Interval in months
Run date
Run schedule
☐ Transfer amounts in local currency   ☐ Copy texts
☐ Transfer tax amounts in local currency

Document header information

Document Type   ☑   Currency/Rate   USD
Reference   Translatn Date 02/07/2016
Document Header Text
Trading Part.BA

First line item

PstKy   Account   SGL Ind   TType

☑ Document 1000314 was stored in company code 1000

Figure 3.99 Transaction FBD1 Recurring Entry Document Stored

After an original recurring entry document has been created, it can be displayed using Transaction FBD3. Figure 3.100 shows the Display Recurring Document: Initial Screen where you enter the Document Number, Company Code, and Fiscal Year. After inputting these field values, press Enter.

Display Recurring Document: Initial Screen

🖫Document List |◀ First Item   ✐ Editing Options

Keys for Entry View

Document Number   1000314
Company Code   1000
Fiscal Year   2016

Figure 3.100 Transaction FBD3 Display Recurring Document Initial Screen

The Display Recurring Document: Overview screen appears (Figure 3.101).

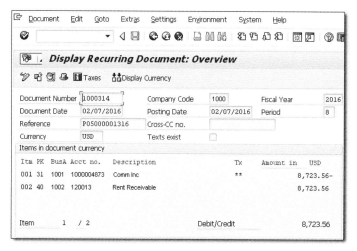

Figure 3.101 Transaction FBD3 Display Recurring Document Overview Screen

To display the document header details, click on the top-hat icon ⚓ (Figure 3.102) or press F5.

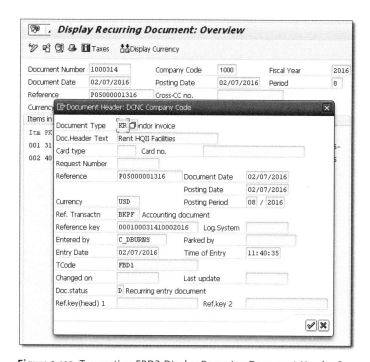

Figure 3.102 Transaction FBD3 Display Recurring Document Header Screen

Cancel out of the document header and press F7 to display the recurring entry data of the document (Figure 3.103).

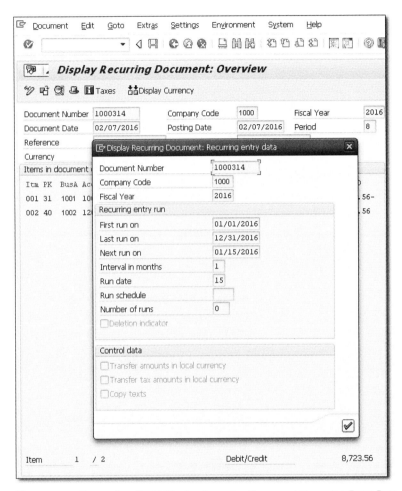

Figure 3.103 Transaction FBD3 Display Recurring Document Recurring Entry Data

This concludes our discussion, for now, of recurring entry documents. In this section we presented the creation and display of original recurring entry documents. See Chapter 16, Section 16.4 for further discussion on how to create posting documents from recurring entry documents.

3.6.3 Sample Documents

The final type of reference document is the *sample document*. A sample document is way to create a reference document for use when posting accounting documents. To create sample documents, you have to set up the X2 number range. The sample document numbers are assigned by this number range. This document does not create account entries or update the G/L. Rather, the data in a sample document is used for reference purposes.

Since sample documents serve only as a data source, they present some advantages over posting with reference with a normal accounting document. Mainly, they can be changed or enhanced when creating postings.

Transaction F-01 is used to create a sample document. Figure 3.104 displays the ENTER SAMPLE DOCUMENT: HEADER DATA screen. Enter all the relevant fields in the header, as well as a posting key and account in the FIRST LINE ITEM at the bottom of the screen. Then press Enter.

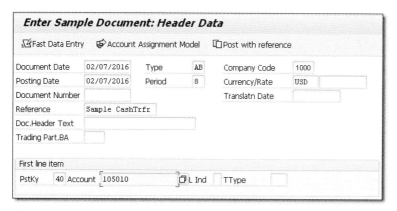

Figure 3.104 Transaction F-01 Enter Sample Document Header Data

The ENTER SAMPLE DOCUMENT ADD G/L ACCOUNT ITEM screen appears (Figure 3.105). For the first line item, be sure to enter an amount or the line will be ignored. Also enter any additional field values and a posting key and account in the NEXT LINE ITEM section at the bottom of the screen, before pressing Enter.

In the next screen you will the amount and field values for the second G/L line item (Figure 3.106). Once this is done, click on the Post icon 🖫 .

Enter Sample Document Add G/L account item
More data
Acct model
Fast Data Entry
Taxes
G/L Account 105010
Company Code 1000 XYZ Inc.
Item 1 / Debit entry / 40
Amount 1500 USD
Calculate tax
Fund
Grant
Functional Area
Funds Center
Commitment Item
More
Value Date 02/07/2016
Assignment
Text
Long Texts
Next Line Item
PstKy 50 Account 105000
L Ind
TType

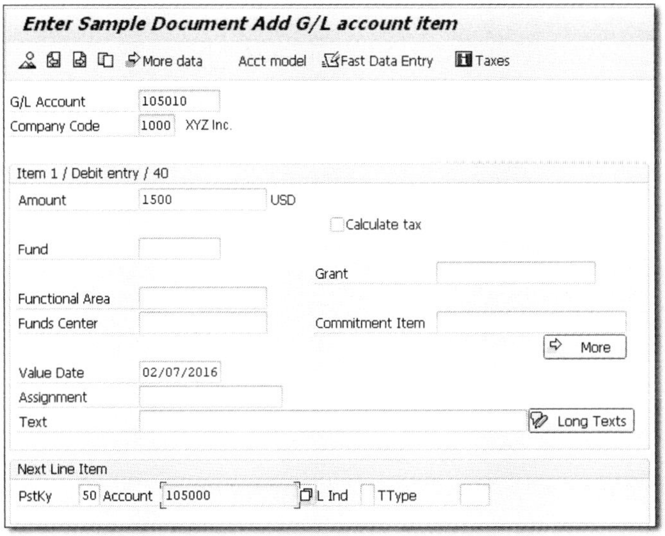

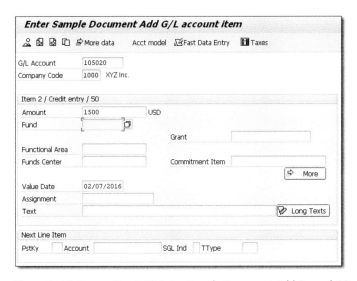

Figure 3.105 Transaction F-01 Enter Sample Document Add G/L Account Item

Enter Sample Document Add G/L account item
More data
Acct model
Fast Data Entry
Taxes
G/L Account 105020
Company Code 1000 XYZ Inc.
Item 2 / Credit entry / 50
Amount 1500 USD
Fund
Grant
Functional Area
Funds Center
Commitment Item
More
Value Date 02/07/2016
Assignment
Text
Long Texts
Next Line Item
PstKy
Account
SGL Ind
TType

Figure 3.106 Transaction F-01 Enter Sample Document Add Second G/L Account Item

A message will appear saying that the sample document number has been stored (Figure 3.107). Once again, this indicates that the document information was saved to be used for reference when creating accounting entries. However, no updates have been made to the general ledger or to transaction figures.

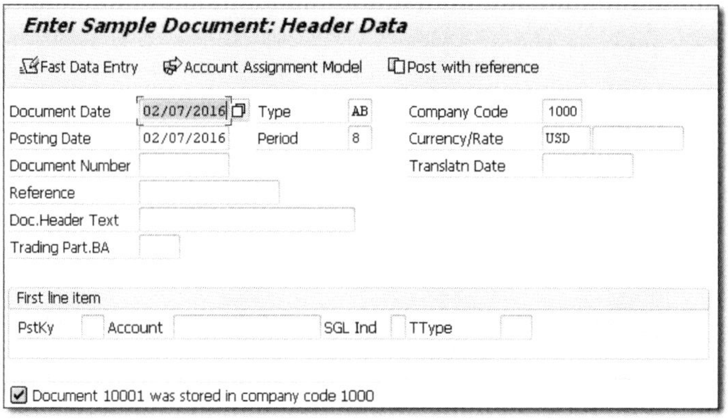

Enter Sample Document: Header Data

🖉 Fast Data Entry   🖘 Account Assignment Model   📋 Post with reference

Document Date	02/07/2016 📇	Type	AB	Company Code	1000	
Posting Date	02/07/2016	Period	8	Currency/Rate	USD	
Document Number				Translatn Date		
Reference						
Doc.Header Text						
Trading Part.BA						

First line item

PstKy ___ Account _____ SGL Ind ___ TType ___

☑ Document 10001 was stored in company code 1000

Figure 3.107 Transaction F-01 Sample Document Stored Message

To use a sample document as a reference when creating a G/L document, use Transaction FB50. Use Shift + F9 to enter the transaction, or use the dropdown menu GOTO • POST WITH REFERENCE. The POST DOCUMENT: HEADER DATA screen will appear (Figure 3.108). Enter the sample document number, company code, fiscal year, and any relevant flow control indicators, and then press Enter.

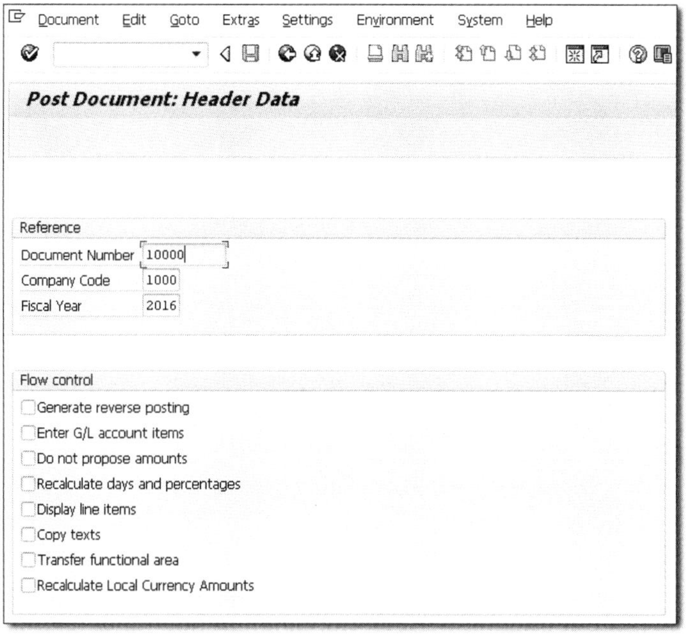

🖙 Document   Edit   Goto   Extras   Settings   Environment   System   Help

Post Document: Header Data

Reference

Document Number	10000
Company Code	1000
Fiscal Year	2016

Flow control

☐ Generate reverse posting
☐ Enter G/L account items
☐ Do not propose amounts
☐ Recalculate days and percentages
☐ Display line items
☐ Copy texts
☐ Transfer functional area
☐ Recalculate Local Currency Amounts

Figure 3.108 Post with Reference Sample Document

The Post Document: Header Data screen appears with sample document data entered as a reference (Figure 3.109). From here, simply walk through each line item of the transaction, changing field values as you wish, and post the document when done.

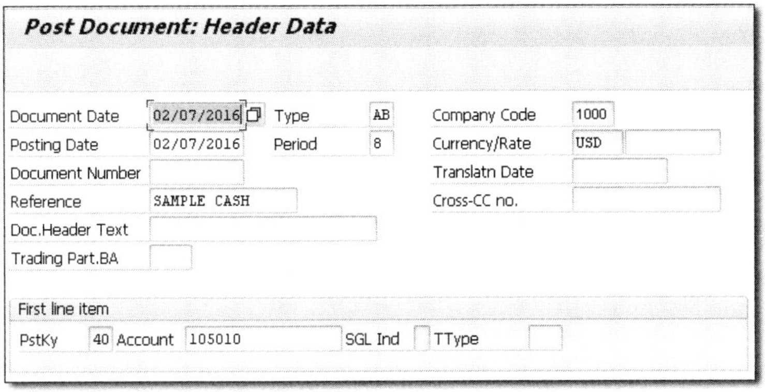

Figure 3.109 Post with Reference Sample Document Header Data

This completes our discussion of sample documents.

3.7 Summary

In this chapter, we covered G/L account transactions originating in the General Ledger module. The most common G/L transaction is the entry of a G/L accounting document using Transaction FB50. This chapter covered not only the creation of a G/L document but also associated G/L functions, such as document display, change, reverse, park, and more.

In addition, we also discussed functions associated with Transaction FB50, such as the tree display, screen variants, account assignment templates, editing options, and post with reference, all of which provide valuable insights to help you be more productive and organized in the G/L module. All of these are universal concepts in FI. Consider what you learned about them in this chapter as your first introduction to them. In future chapters we will revisit these topics and discuss them in relation to other types of transactions in FI.

In this chapter, you learned the differences between document posting, parking, save as completed, and hold. A posted document is a G/L document that is complete, produces a G/L accounting document number, and updates the G/L account balances. Parking a G/L document allows you to save an accounting document without impacting G/L account balances. This process may be necessary if the document is incomplete or if further edits, data validation, or document approval is required prior to posting. The save as completed function is similar to document parking, but the document undergoes more extensive document check logic, as though it was being posted. A document hold is a function to temporarily save your data. It is most useful when you are interrupted during document creation. The hold function produces no permanent document number until the document is parked or posted. Once again, these concepts are not unique to G/L. They are also applicable to A/P, A/R, and other accounting transactions. We will revisit these topics for each module in which they are applicable.

Other G/L concepts discussed in this chapter include the relationship browser, account assignment templates, recurring documents, and sample documents. These all are tools to make your job easier and to improve your efficiency in creating and managing financial and accounting transactions.

Now that you have learned about creating and managing G/L transactions, the next chapter will teach you how to perform inquiries in the G/L module.

In Chapter 3, we covered transactions in the G/L that you will use on a daily basis. Now, in this chapter, we explore transactions and reports you can use to troubleshoot G/L account problems.

4   General Ledger Account Inquiries

This chapter discusses G/L account inquiry and maintenance functions that can help you research individual transactions, find account balances, display account transaction details, and run reports and queries.

G/L account inquiry and validation are essential job functions of an accounting clerk or supervisor. Often, you can use these functions to uncover data entry and other posting errors. Knowing how to perform the transactions in this chapter will provide you with essential skills needed in the day-to-day operations of an accounting department. To use a sports analogy, these transactions are the "blocking" and "tackling" of FI; that is, they are basic tasks practitioners must be able to perform quickly and routinely.

Account inquiries are important for several reasons. In particular, validation for month-end and year-end reporting must take place to ensure that accounting entries are accurate and complete. Furthermore, as a regular course of doing business errors are found often and must be corrected. These errors could be as simple as accounting documents posted on the wrong date—but regardless of the reason for the error, this chapter will enable you to better navigate the G/L module and analyze your accounting transactions.

Let's get started by learning how to view G/L account displays.

4.1   Account Displays

G/L account displays allow you to view individual or collective G/L account balances and transaction details (i.e., individual accounting line items). Transaction FAGLB03 is used for G/L account balances, and Transaction FAGLL03 is for G/L account line items. In addition, from Transaction FAGLB03 you can double-click a number and drill down to the line item detail in Transaction FAGLL03.

The selection screens available via these transactions give you the flexibility to filter data by company code, posting date, and more. These selection options can be saved as *variants*, making them reusable. In addition, the output screen allows for further filtering, searching, sorting, and more. The output can be downloaded into various file formats (e.g., Excel), making further analysis outside SAP possible when needed.

Let's take a closer look at G/L account balance displays.

4.1.1   Account Balance

The G/L account balance display shows a G/L account balance (or range of accounts) by period for the fiscal year specified. The resulting output is organized by period, debit balances, credit balances, net balances, and cumulative balances. This structure is particularly useful for reconciling G/L accounts with financial reports.

To display G/L account balances, use Transaction FAGLB03 or application menu path Accounting • Financial Accounting • General Ledger • Account • FAGLB03—Display Balances (New), as shown in Figure 4.1.

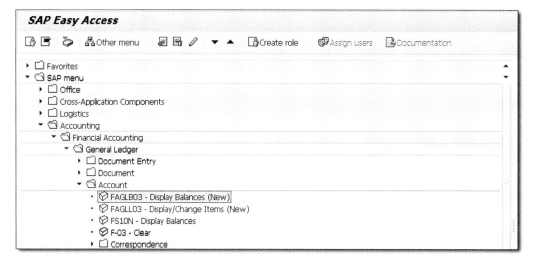

Figure 4.1 FAGLB03 Menu Path

Double-click FAGLB03 — DISPLAY BALANCES (NEW) from the menu path shown in Figure 4.1, or enter "FAGLB03" in the COMMAND field (as shown in Figure 4.2) and press Enter.

Figure 4.2 FAGLB03 in Command Field

In the Transaction FAGLB03 selection screen (Figure 4.3), enter values in the fields ACCOUNT NUMBER, COMPANY CODE, and FISCAL YEAR. Notice that in the LEDGER field, the leading ledger defaults into the selection screen, but you can select a nonleading ledger by clicking the CHOOSE LEDGER button (see Figure 4.3) and selecting the ledger of your choice.

On the selection screen (Figure 4.3), you can enter individual values or ranges. If you click the MULTIPLE SELECTION icon (i.e., the yellow arrow) to the right of a field, you can enter multiple individual values or ranges, or exclude values and ranges.

G/L Account Balance Display

Activate Worklist   Choose Ledger

Account Number	300000	to		⇨
Company Code	1000	to		⇨
Fiscal Year	2015			
Ledger	0L			

Figure 4.3 FAGLB03 Selection Screen

After inputting values on the selection screen, click the EXECUTE icon ⊕. The output is shown in Figure 4.4.

The resulting output is organized by period, debit balances, credit balances, net balances, and cumulative balances.

Now that you are familiar with the display of G/L account balances, let's take a look at G/L account line item displays. In essence, G/L line item displays are individual accounting lines from a financial document.

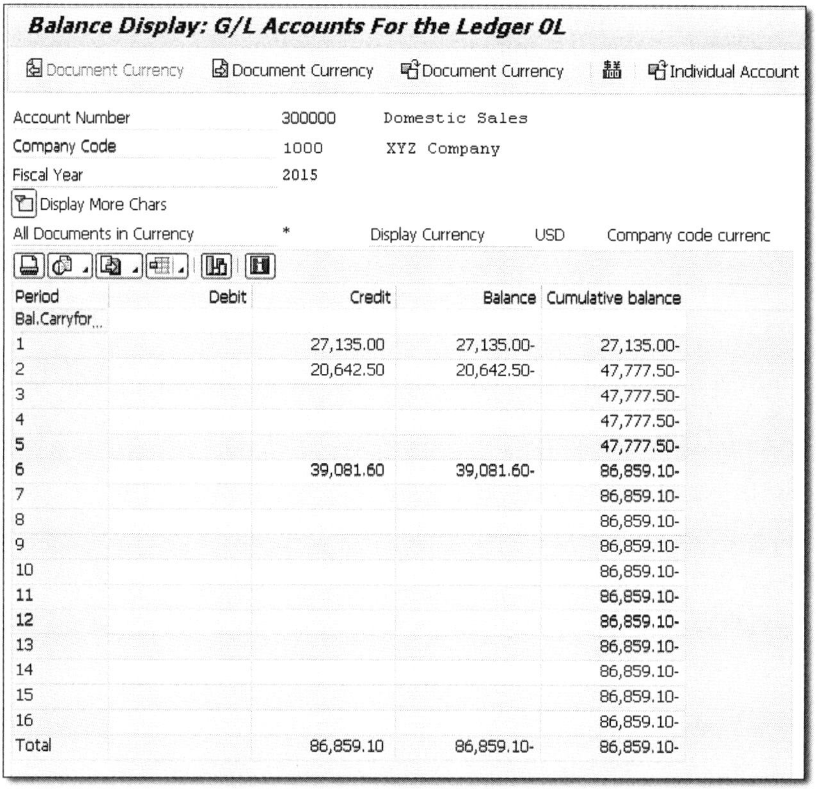

Balance Display: G/L Accounts For the Ledger 0L

Document Currency | Document Currency | Document Currency | Individual Account

Account Number 300000 Domestic Sales

Company Code 1000 XYZ Company

Fiscal Year 2015

Display More Chars

All Documents in Currency * Display Currency USD Company code currenc

Period	Debit	Credit	Balance	Cumulative balance
Bal.Carryfor...				
1		27,135.00	27,135.00-	27,135.00-
2		20,642.50	20,642.50-	47,777.50-
3				47,777.50-
4				47,777.50-
5				47,777.50-
6		39,081.60	39,081.60-	86,859.10-
7				86,859.10-
8				86,859.10-
9				86,859.10-
10				86,859.10-
11				86,859.10-
12				86,859.10-
13				86,859.10-
14				86,859.10-
15				86,859.10-
16				86,859.10-
Total		86,859.10	86,859.10-	86,859.10-

Figure 4.4 FAGLB03 Output Screen

4.1.2 Account Line Items

The *G/L account line item display* shows G/L account transaction details. Here, *details* means all the individual line item transactions that go into the G/L account balance. This transaction is particularly useful in sorting out discrepancies and suspected errors in G/L account balances and reports.

Viewing line item displays is essential in reconciling back to account totals. The balance of a G/L account is the sum of the parts. The parts, in this instance, are individual accounting transactions. Viewing the G/L account detail allows you to not only reconcile the totals but also track back to the original source of the entry. Being able to do so quickly and accurately is an important skill.

To display G/L account balances, use Transaction FAGLL03 or application menu path Accounting • Financial Accounting • General Ledger • Account • FAGLL03 — Display/Change Items (New), as shown in Figure 4.5.

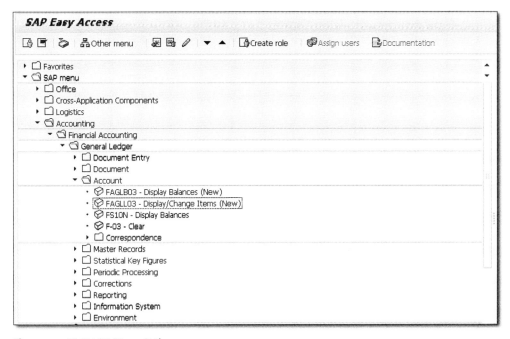

Figure 4.5 FAGLL03 Menu Path

Double-click FAGLL03 — Display/Change Items (New) from the menu path shown in Figure 4.5, or enter "FAGLL03" in the Command field (as shown in Figure 4.6) and press Enter.

Figure 4.6 FAGLL03 in Command Field

On the FAGLL03 selection screen (Figure 4.7), enter parameters for G/L Account, Company Code, and Line Item Selection • Status. The Status section requires you to choose one of three options:

- ▶ OPEN ITEMS
- ▶ CLEARED ITEMS
- ▶ ALL ITEMS

Each option contains date parameters, which will select relevant items without a date restriction if left blank. Notice that in the LEDGER field the leading ledger defaults into the selection screen, but you can select a nonleading ledger by clicking the CHOOSE LEDGER button (see Figure 4.7) and selecting the ledger of your choice.

On the selection screen (Figure 4.7), you can enter individual values or ranges. If you click the MULTIPLE SELECTION icon (i.e., the yellow arrow) to the right of a field, you can enter multiple individual values or ranges, or exclude values and ranges.

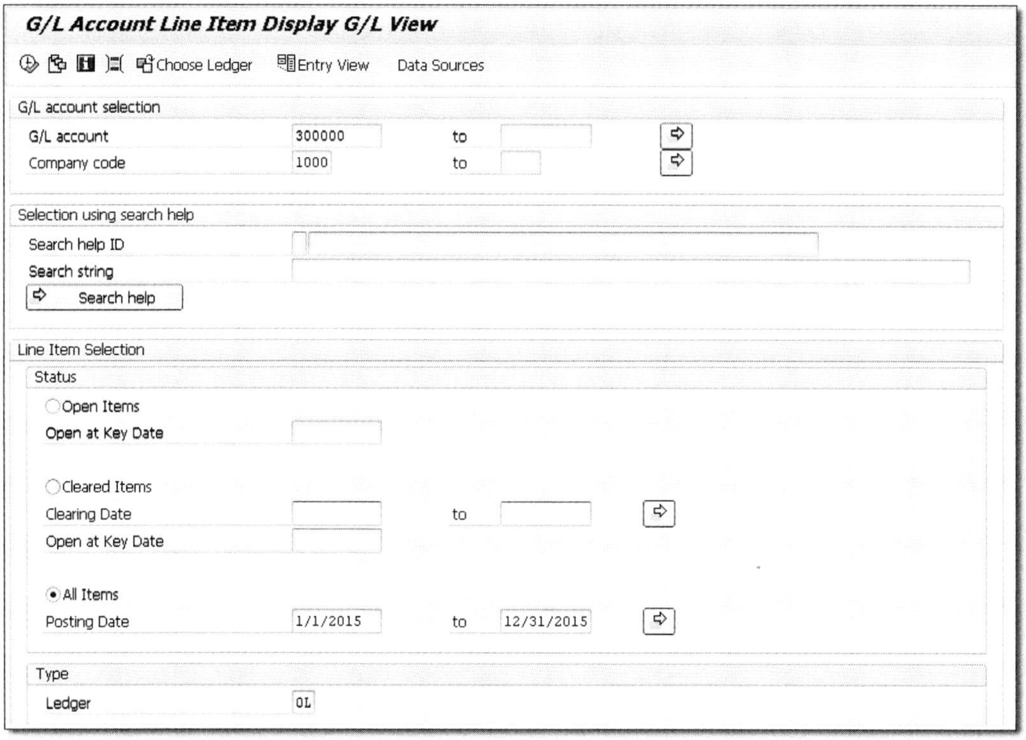

Figure 4.7 FAGLL03 Selection Screen

After inputting values on the selection screen, click the EXECUTE icon ⊕. The output is shown in Figure 4.8.

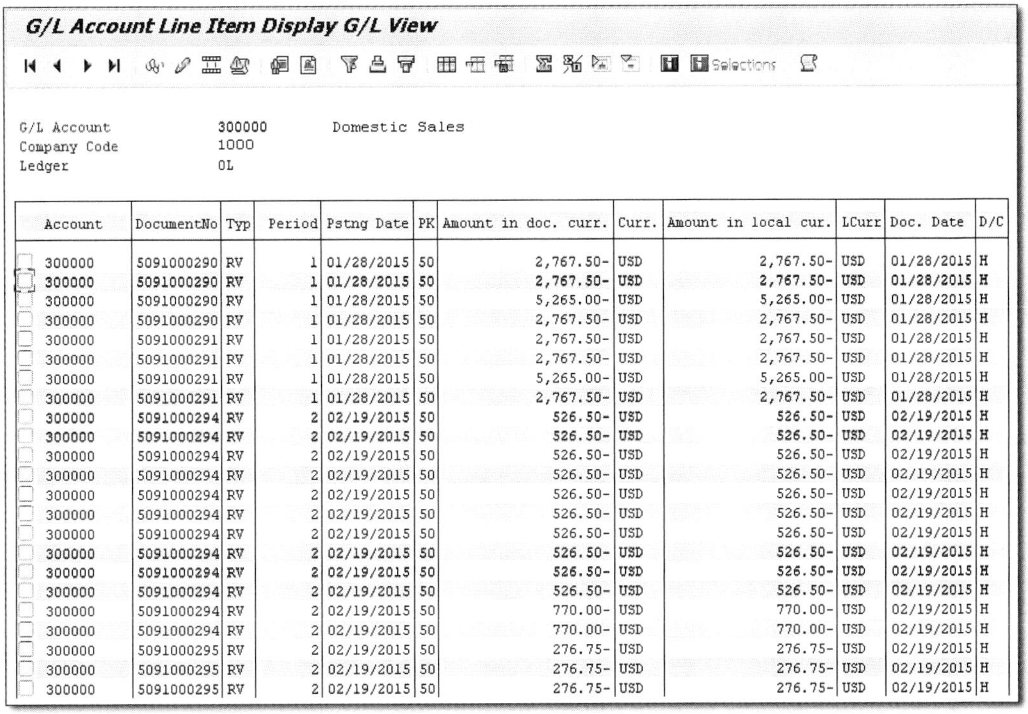

G/L Account Line Item Display G/L View

Account	DocumentNo	Typ	Period	Pstng Date	PK	Amount in doc. curr.	Curr.	Amount in local cur.	LCurr	Doc. Date	D/C
300000	5091000290	RV	1	01/28/2015	50	2,767.50-	USD	2,767.50-	USD	01/28/2015	H
300000	5091000290	RV	1	01/28/2015	50	2,767.50-	USD	2,767.50-	USD	01/28/2015	H
300000	5091000290	RV	1	01/28/2015	50	5,265.00-	USD	5,265.00-	USD	01/28/2015	H
300000	5091000290	RV	1	01/28/2015	50	2,767.50-	USD	2,767.50-	USD	01/28/2015	H
300000	5091000291	RV	1	01/28/2015	50	2,767.50-	USD	2,767.50-	USD	01/28/2015	H
300000	5091000291	RV	1	01/28/2015	50	2,767.50-	USD	2,767.50-	USD	01/28/2015	H
300000	5091000291	RV	1	01/28/2015	50	5,265.00-	USD	5,265.00-	USD	01/28/2015	H
300000	5091000291	RV	1	01/28/2015	50	2,767.50-	USD	2,767.50-	USD	01/28/2015	H
300000	5091000294	RV	2	02/19/2015	50	526.50-	USD	526.50-	USD	02/19/2015	H
300000	5091000294	RV	2	02/19/2015	50	526.50-	USD	526.50-	USD	02/19/2015	H
300000	5091000294	RV	2	02/19/2015	50	526.50-	USD	526.50-	USD	02/19/2015	H
300000	5091000294	RV	2	02/19/2015	50	526.50-	USD	526.50-	USD	02/19/2015	H
300000	5091000294	RV	2	02/19/2015	50	526.50-	USD	526.50-	USD	02/19/2015	H
300000	5091000294	RV	2	02/19/2015	50	526.50-	USD	526.50-	USD	02/19/2015	H
300000	5091000294	RV	2	02/19/2015	50	526.50-	USD	526.50-	USD	02/19/2015	H
300000	5091000294	RV	2	02/19/2015	50	526.50-	USD	526.50-	USD	02/19/2015	H
300000	5091000294	RV	2	02/19/2015	50	770.00-	USD	770.00-	USD	02/19/2015	H
300000	5091000294	RV	2	02/19/2015	50	770.00-	USD	770.00-	USD	02/19/2015	H
300000	5091000295	RV	2	02/19/2015	50	276.75-	USD	276.75-	USD	02/19/2015	H
300000	5091000295	RV	2	02/19/2015	50	276.75-	USD	276.75-	USD	02/19/2015	H
300000	5091000295	RV	2	02/19/2015	50	276.75-	USD	276.75-	USD	02/19/2015	H

G/L Account 300000 Domestic Sales
Company Code 1000
Ledger 0L

Figure 4.8 FAGLL03 Output Screen

The resulting output shows the detail of a G/L account balance. From this screen, you can sort, filter, total, and subtotal the output, and converted it to external file formats (e.g., Excel). In addition, you can create and save screen layouts.

Some people today do all they can to eliminate spreadsheets. In accounting and finance departments, however, spreadsheets are alive and well. In fact, it is more common today than ever before to begin with a G/L line item query, like that shown in Figure 4.8, and then filter, sort, reorder data elements, and save to a spreadsheet for further analysis.

Now that you have seen how to display G/L account balances and line item detail, let's take a look at a few standard SAP reports as an alternative means of obtaining this information.

4.2   Reports and Queries

Section 4.1 covered Transaction FABLB03 and Transaction FABLL03 were discussed in detail. For validating account balances and transaction details, these transactions are beneficial particularly because they provide drilldown capability all the way to accounting documents. However, other tools do exist to view G/L account balances and transaction detail. In this section, we will show you where to find these alternatives in G/L reports and queries.

Standard reports are SAP delivered and are universally found in the INFORMATION SYSTEM folder of the application menu. The most useful general-purpose G/L account balance reports can be accessed via the following application menu path: ACCOUNTING • FINANCIAL ACCOUNTING • GENERAL LEDGER • INFORMATION SYSTEM • GENERAL LEDGER REPORTS (NEW) • ACCOUNT BALANCES • GENERAL (see Figure 4.9).

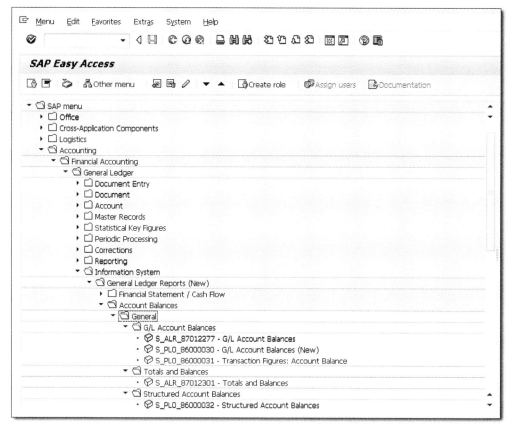

Figure 4.9 G/L Account Balances Reports

The most useful non-financial-statement reports (i.e., general G/L account balance inquiry reports) are in the G/L ACCOUNT BALANCES and TOTALS AND BALANCES folders.

Let's look at an example. In the G/L ACCOUNT BALANCES folder (Figure 4.10), you will see a listing for Report S_PLO_86000030: S_PLO_86000030 — G/L ACCOUNT BALANCES (NEW).

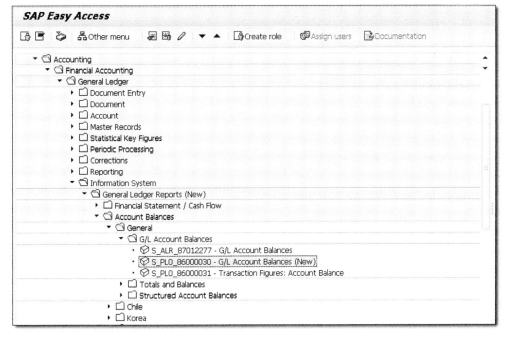

Figure 4.10 G/L Account Balances (New) Report Transaction Code

Double-click the report link to open the selection screen. The top portion (Figure 4.11) consists of general selections. A powerful feature of this report is its ability to filter data upfront using a myriad of field selections. In Figure 4.11, we have added values in the CURRENCY TYPE (i.e., 10 for company code currency), COMPANY CODE, ACCOUNT NUMBER, and SEGMENT fields.

At the bottom of the selection screen, after GENERAL SELECTIONS, additional selection options are listed (Figure 4.12). Here, we have added values in the LEDGER, FISCAL YEAR, FROM PERIOD, and TO PERIOD fields. We selected GRAPHICAL REPORT OUTPUT under OUTPUT TYPE; avoid using the CLASSIC DRILLDOWN REPORT option, which is an outdated report view.

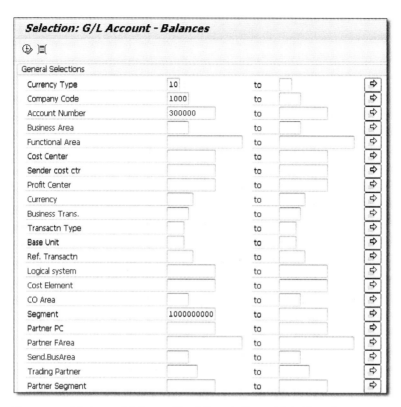

Figure 4.11 G/L Account Balances (New) Report: General Selections Screen

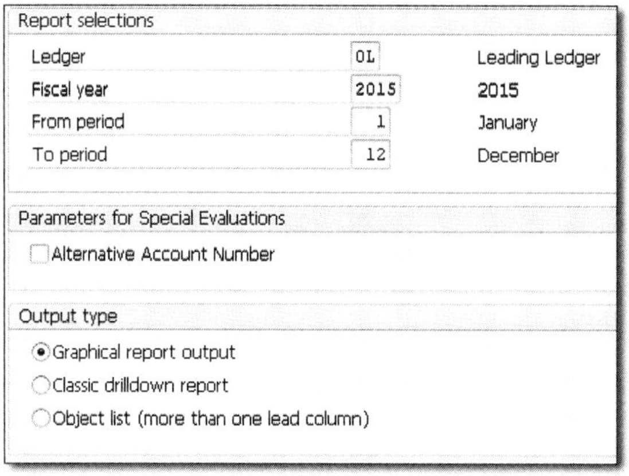

Figure 4.12 G/L Account Balances (New) Report: Additional Selections

After inputting values on the selection screen, click the EXECUTE icon ⊕. The output is shown in Figure 4.13.

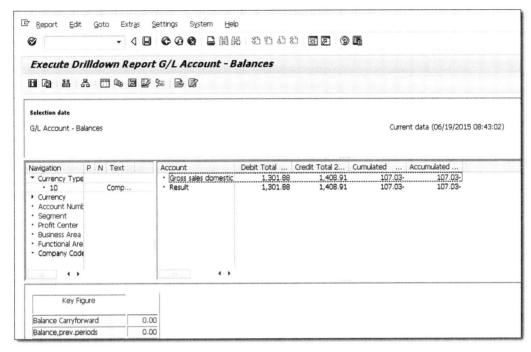

Figure 4.13 G/L Account Balances (New) Report Output

There are pros and cons to using standard finance reports rather than Transaction FAGLB03 and Transaction FAGLL03. On the pro side, reports generally have more choices to filter data on the field selection screen, and the output screen provides a NAVIGATION pane (shown in Figure 4.13), which provides built-in filtering capability.

On the con side, reports typically do not have drilldown capability. This is certainly not always the case, so you should test each report you use so that you know one way or another. Moreover, reports typically do not provide the sorting and ad hoc, multidimensional filtering of, for example, Transaction FAGLL03.

In addition to SAP standard reports, there are several methods to create custom reports and queries. These include custom ABAP reports, queries, Report Writer/Painter, and SAP BW/BI. You should check within your organization to ensure you have access to any useful custom reports and queries.

4.3 Summary

In this chapter, we covered some of the most essential tools for G/L account inquiries. These tools include the G/L account balances transaction (Transaction FAGLB03), the G/L account line item display transaction (Transaction FAGLL03), and standard G/L reports. Use of these transactions and reports often is essential to understanding the activity posting to the G/L.

This chapter approached inquiries from two perspectives: G/L account totals (i.e., balances) and line item details. Both are important. You need account balances for numerous reasons, including financial reporting. Line item details are important to reconcile back to account totals and to manage specific account details. Being able to perform these tasks quickly and accurately is an essential skill.

Just as a carpenter cannot build a house with only one tool, so too may you need multiple tools to complete your G/L account inquiries. Use these tools to narrow down account discrepancies by company code, posting date, and other relevant selection criteria. All the relevant accounting data is easily accessible. Your job is to know how to quickly and easily get to this data like the back of your hand, using the transactions and reports covered in this chapter.

Now that we have completed our discussion of G/L transactions and account queries, let's explore the topic of Accounts Payable transactions in the next chapter.

In this chapter, we discuss A/P business processes. The steps that make up the procurement of goods and services are not isolated to the A/P module, but rather reach back into transactions in MM and other modules.

5 Accounts Payable Processes

Accounts Payable (A/P) is the SAP module used for managing vendor accounts and issuing payments for goods and services your company procures. Specific A/P transactions are covered in Chapter 6. The intent of this chapter, however, is broaden your perspective so that you learn to think of A/P as steps in a business process, not as isolated transactions.

Thinking in terms of business processes instead of individual transaction codes is important. It helps you grasp the bigger picture and to be more effective as an accountant or financial manager working in SAP. At times, it's uncomfortable because doing so forces you to think outside the box and coordinate more closely with other departments. In the end, however, it's the only way to grasp the concept of real-time SAP integration. In addition, understanding end-to-end business processes is very useful in executing tasks such as financial close.

There are several A/P related business processes. In this chapter, we will focus on one core process: procure-to-pay. Using this process as the topic for discussion, you will see the integration between Materials Management (MM) and Accounts Payable (A/P) in a complete procure-to-pay scenario. In addition, we will discuss some variations of the process. Variations may exist depending on your industry, business practices, and SAP modules implemented.

A typical procure-to-pay business process consists of the following steps:

1. Create purchase requisition

2. Create purchase order or convert purchase requisition to purchase order

3. Create inbound delivery

4. Post goods receipt

5. Peform invoice verification

6. Issue outgoing payment

Let's begin our discussion with the front end of the procure-to-pay process in the MM-Purchasing module.

5.1 Logistics

Before getting into specific procurement transactions, let's put the MM-Purchasing module into perspective. It fits within the broader category of logistics. Logistics functionality in SAP covers a broad spectrum of capabilities. Figure 5.1 shows the application menu path for LOGISTICS, which includes MATERIALS MANAGEMENT, SALES AND DISTRIBUTION, PRODUCTION, PLANT MAINTENANCE, and more.

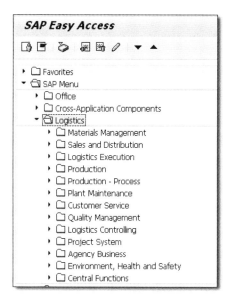

Figure 5.1 Application Menu Path Logistics

The front-end procurement transactions exist in Materials Management. It is here that we will begin our discussions, with the purchase requisition transaction.

5.1.1 Create Purchase Requisition

The first transaction in the procure-to-pay business process is the creation of a *purchase requisition*. SAP defines a purchase requisition as a request or instruction to a purchasing department to procure a certain quantity of a material or a service so that it is available at a certain point in time. In other words, purchase requisitions are internal requests for purchasing actions. They are not orders to directly procure goods or services from a particular vendor.

Most often, companies with centralized procurement use purchase requisitions. Purchase requisitions are particularly relevant when purchasing departments are responsible for making sourcing decisions. In some companies, purchase requisitions are not used at all. In others, they are used only for certain types of procurements.

Even before a purchase requisition is created, the procurement process begins by identifying the need for a good or service. There are several functions in SAP to help you plan for these needs, particularly if you work for a manufacturing company. Some of the options for creating purchase requisitions include the following:

▸ Creating them automatically from Material Requirements Planning (MRP).

▸ Creating them automatically from APO runs.

▸ Creating them indirectly from modules such as PP, SD, PM, and PS.

▸ Creating them from shopping carts in SRM.

▸ Creating them manually, by an end user.

5.1.2 Purchase Orders

While a purchase requisition is a request, a *purchase order* is a specific procurement action. In other words, a purchase order is a formal request from a purchasing organization to a vendor, and asks the vendor to supply or provide a certain quantity of goods or services. Purchase orders are not dependent upon purchase requisitions; however, if a purchase requisition is created, it can be referenced during purchase order creation, and the purchase order will adopt many details from the purchase requisition.

Figure 5.2 shows an example purchase order displayed using Transaction ME23N. A PO consists of three parts: header, item overview, and item details.

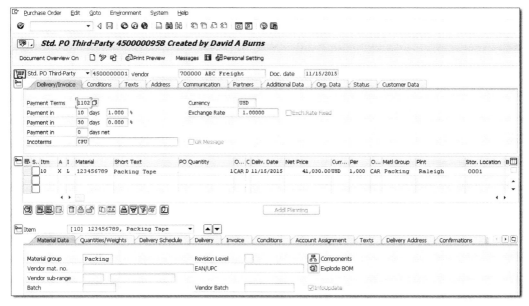

Figure 5.2 Display Purchase Order Screen

5.1.3 Inbound Delivery/Post Goods Receipt/Invoice Receipt

Once you create a purchase order and schedule an inbound delivery, the next step is to receive the goods and services. You can create a goods receipt using Transaction MIGO and referencing the purchase order. Once a goods receipt exists, the purchase order will display a PURCHASE ORDER HISTORY tab in the ITEM DETAILS section of the purchase order (Figure 5.3), with the material document number displayed.

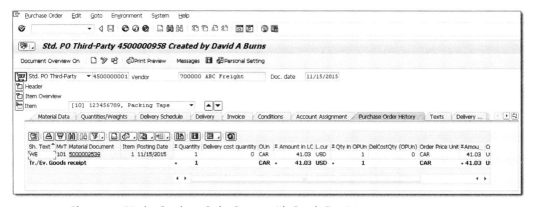

Figure 5.3 Display Purchase Order Screen with Goods Receipt

Click on the material document number to be taken directly into the material document (Figure 5.4). Note the FI DOCUMENTS button in the center of the screen, which indicates that FI documents were automatically created from the goods receipt transaction.

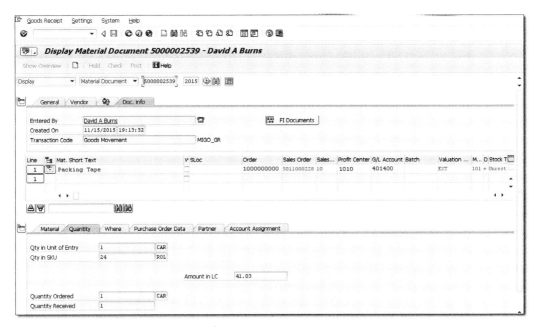

Figure 5.4 Display Goods Receipt Material Document

In this example, clicking on the FI DOCUMENTS button opens the LIST OF DOCUMENTS IN ACCOUNTING dialogue box (Figure 5.5), which lists one accounting document and one controlling document.

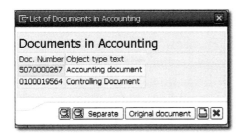

Figure 5.5 List of Documents in Accounting from Goods Receipt

Double-click the accounting document number (Figure 5.5) to open the financial document (Figure 5.6), which reveals that the goods receipt transaction created a goods movement to update the G/L. Note that the document number highlighted in Figure 5.5 is the same document number in the header of Figure 5.6.

Goods movements are configured in MM, with account determination settings that specify which G/L accounts are used in G/L postings. *Account determinations are configured settings that determine what G/L accounts will be posted to.* Account determinations are beyond the scope of this book, but it is important to obtain your company's posting models, which should lay out all the accounting entries by transaction type and their associated account determination configuration settings.

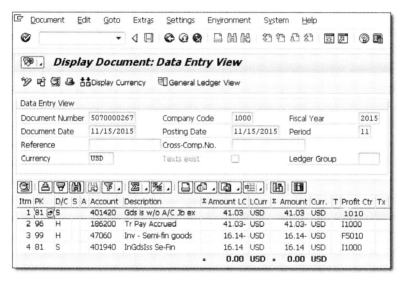

Figure 5.6 Display Accounting Document from Goods Receipt

Creating an invoice receipt document typically follows the creation of the goods receipt. SAP provides configuration settings to determine if a goods receipt must precede the posting of an invoice receipt. SAP also provides functionality called Evaluated Receipt Settlement (ERS), via which invoices do not need to be posted; instead, invoices post automatically on the basis of the PO and goods receipt. It is important to know which process your company follows.

You can create an invoice receipt document using Transaction MIRO, referencing the PO. When you create an invoice receipt, the PO will display a PURCHASE

ORDER HISTORY tab in the ITEM DETAILS section of the PO (Figure 5.7), with the material document number displayed.

> **Note**
>
> Posting invoice receipts in MM with reference to a purchase order is referred to as *Logistics Invoice Verification (LIV)*. This differs from posting an A/P invoice in FI using Transaction FB60.

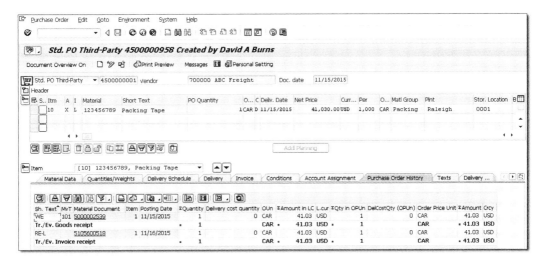

Figure 5.7 Display Purchase Order with Invoice Receipt

5.1.4 Automatic Creation of Accounting Invoice

The invoice receipt document created using Transaction MIRO creates two documents: a material document and an A/P invoice—and this is where things become a little tricky. Both documents can have the same document number, which is typically the case for most SAP customers. SAP has a configuration setting that allows you to keep the MM and A/P document numbers the same or allows them to be different.

Let's take a look at an invoice document using the example from Figure 5.7. If you click on the invoice receipt document shown in Figure 5.7, the display material invoice document will open (Figure 5.8). You know that these are the same document because the invoice receipt document number in Figure 5.7 is the same as the document number shown in the top center of Figure 5.8.

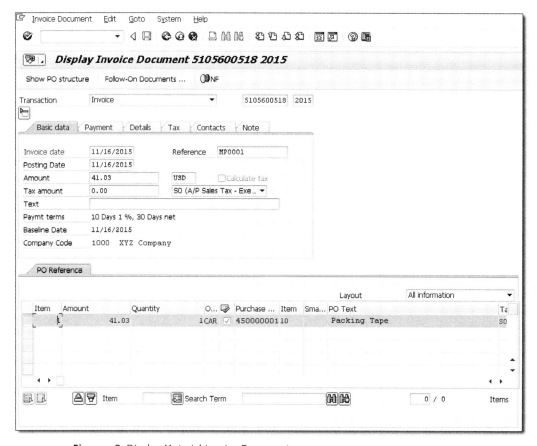

Figure 5.8 Display Material Invoice Document

Now, bear in mind that you have two invoice documents: a material document in MM and another in A/P. The invoice shown in Figure 5.8 is the MM document; you can view the corresponding A/P invoice by clicking the FOLLOW-ON DOCU-MENTS button shown in Figure 5.8. When you do so, the A/P invoice will open (Figure 5.9). It is this A/P invoice that triggers the open vendor payable. In other words, the A/P invoice updates the G/L and vendor account with the expense and payable amounts, and it is the document that is cleared through the payment process.

Now that you have seen the procure-to-pay process all the way through to the creation of an A/P invoice using MM-LIV, let's take a look at how to create an invoice directly in A/P.

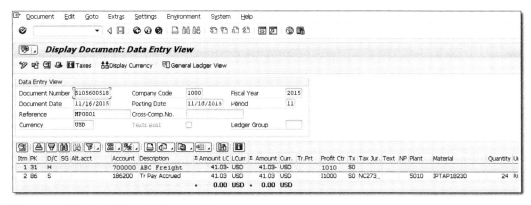

Figure 5.9 Display A/P Invoice Document

5.2 Create Direct Invoices

Direct invoices is a term often used to refer to A/P invoices created using Transaction FB60. These are A/P invoices created directly in the A/P module rather than in MM.

There are a few distinguishing features of direct invoices. First, they have no corresponding material invoice number; material invoice documents are only created using Transaction MIRO in MM-LIV. A few other differences exist and are illustrated in Figure 5.10. The standard document type for direct A/P invoices is KR, whereas those from MM-LIV are document type RE. The document number ranges also differ, because number ranges are assigned to document types.

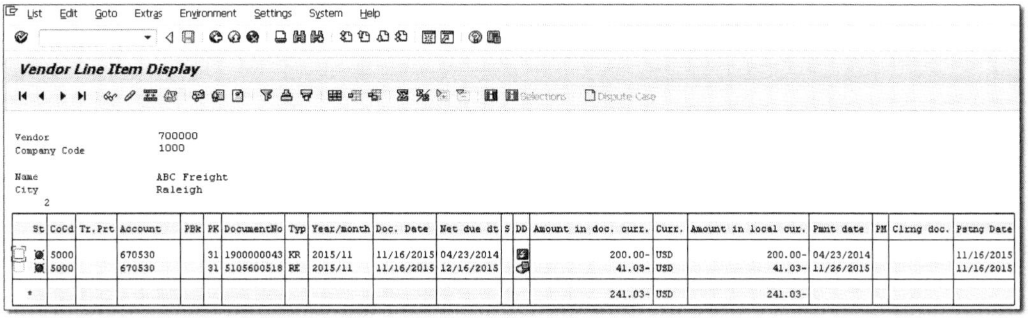

Figure 5.10 FBL1N Vendor Line Item Display Screen

For more information on direct A/P invoices, see Chapter 6, Section 6.1.1.

Now that we have stepped through all the preceding steps in the procure-to-pay process, let's discuss outgoing payments.

5.3 Issue Outgoing Payments

Whether an A/P invoice is created as a follow-on document from MM-LIV, or created as a direct invoice using Transaction FB60, the last step in the procure-to-pay process is to issue payment to the vendor. This is the physical transfer of money from your company to the vendor that supplied the goods or services.

There are two ways to issue outgoing payments in SAP. The first and most commonly used way is to use automatic payments, via Transaction F110 (covered in detail in Chapter 7). The other way to issue payments is referred to as *manual payments*. Two transaction codes are used for manual payments: Transaction F-53 and Transaction F-58. The main difference between the two is that Transaction F-58 prints payment output forms (i.e., checks), and Transaction F-53 only does not. Both create a payment document, which clears open A/P invoices and updates the G/L. In the remainder of this section, we will focus on Transaction F-53.

To enter an A/P outgoing payment, follow application menu path ACCOUNTING • FINANCIAL ACCOUNTING • ACCOUNTS PAYABLE • DOCUMENT ENTRY • OUTGOING PAYMENT • F-53—POST, as shown in Figure 5.11.

Double-click F-53—POST and the POST OUTGOING PAYMENTS: HEADER DATA screen will open (Figure 5.12). The fields that appear on the header with prepopulated values may vary depending upon your system configuration and editing options. In this example, values defaulted into the POSTING DATE, PERIOD, DOCUMENT TYPE, CURRENCY, and COMPANY CODE fields, whereas we entered values into the DOCUMENT DATE and REFERENCE fields.

In the BANK DATA section, we entered a bank G/L account number into the ACCOUNT field; the AMOUNT field was populated with the A/P invoice amount.

In the OPEN ITEM SELECTION area, we entered the vendor number in the ACCOUNT field, and in ADDITIONAL SELECTIONS, we selected the AMOUNT radio button.

With all field values entered, click the PROCESS OPEN ITEMS button at the top left of the screen.

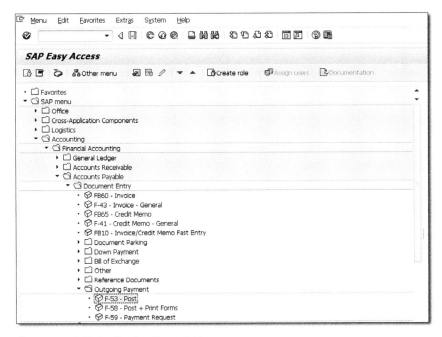

Figure 5.11 F-53 Application Menu Path

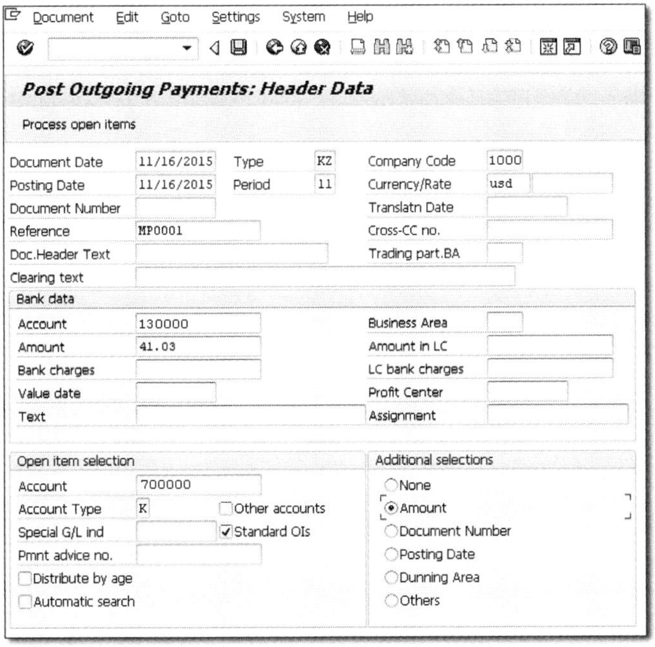

Figure 5.12 Post Outgoing Payments: Header Data

The POST OUTGOING PAYMENTS ENTER SELECTION CRITERIA screen now will open (Figure 5.13). In this example, we entered the A/P invoice amount in the FROM and To fields. When ready, click the PROCESS OPEN ITEMS button.

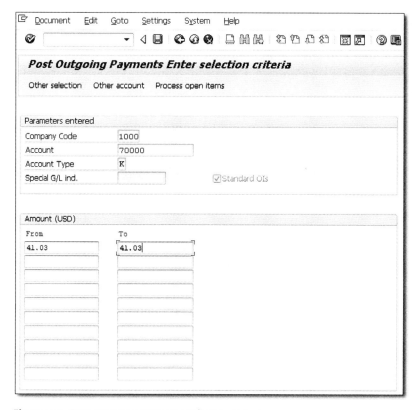

Figure 5.13 Post Outgoing Payments Selection Criteria

The POST OUTGOING PAYMENTS PROCESS OPEN ITEMS screen now will open (Figure 5.14). With the A/P invoice selected, click the SAVE icon 💾 .

The system creates a clearing document, and the status of the invoice changes from open to cleared.

Now that we have discussed on the procure-to-pay process, let's look into a few scenarios that require additional process steps.

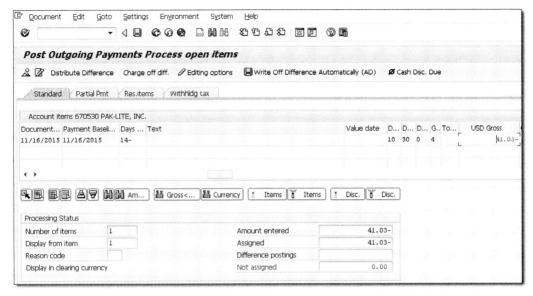

Figure 5.14 Process Open Items Screen

5.4 Process Exceptions

Throughout business processes, exceptions happen. Goods may arrive damaged and need to be returned. An invoice may contain an incorrect amount or quantity. Documents may be posted with incorrect information. In this chapter, we will not attempt to identify all the possible exceptions that can occur. Instead, we will examine three transactions in FI that users frequently use to correct errors or to make adjustments.

5.4.1 Credit Memos

You might create a credit memo because of a defective good, an overcharge, or another adjustment needed to a vendor account. Credit memos net against amounts at the time of payment to ensure a vendor is not overpaid.

There are two ways to create credit memos. The first is in the A/P module, using Transaction FB65 (see Chapter 6, Section 6.2). Transaction FB65 should be used for general vendor account adjustments and overcharges not specific to purchasing transactions originating in MM. However, when you require a credit memo for a transaction that originated in MM, the best approach is to create the credit memo via Transaction MIRO.

Figure 5.15 shows the TRANSACTION dropdown box in Transaction MIRO, with the CREDIT MEMO selection option highlighted.

Figure 5.15 Transaction Dropdown Selection

Once you have created a credit memo, the purchase order referenced in the credit memo displays the credit memo document number on the PURCHASE ORDER HISTORY tab. In the example shown in Figure 5.16, the invoice receipt line showing a quantity of -1 is a credit memo document.

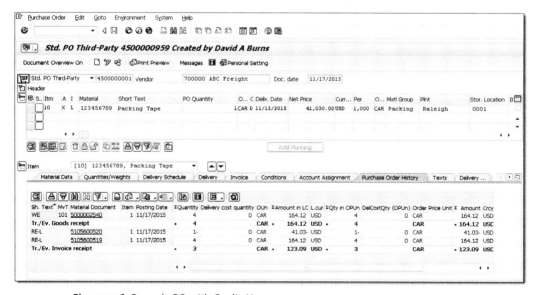

Figure 5.16 Example PO with Credit Memo

You can confirm the credit memo in the A/P module via Transaction FBL1N (Figure 5.17).

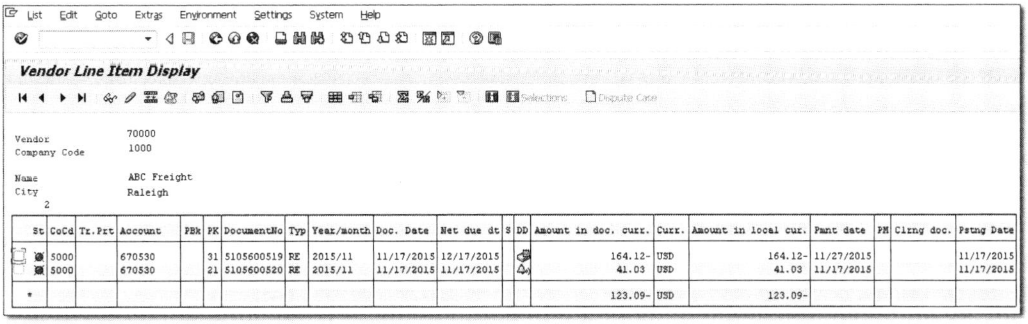

Figure 5.17 Transaction FBL1N with Credit Memo

5.4.2 Document Reversals

The need to reverse documents is universal across SAP modules. However, as you have seen throughout this chapter, not all financial documents were originally created in FI. Therefore, it is an SAP best practice to reverse documents from within the module from which they originated. This is an important concept for keeping modules in sync.

In Chapter 6, Section 6.4, we discussed resetting and reversing A/P documents in detail. However, for documents that originated in MM, document reversals should be completed in MM. One such transaction is ME21N which is used to create a purchase order. To cancel a purchase order, you must unrelease it if you use release strategies. Then, use the purchase order change transaction (ME22N) to delete each line in the purchase order ME22N. Any change to a purchase order should be made by the procurement department. An AP clerk or supervisor may request that a change be made to a purchase order, but that individual should not make the change directly unless it is part of his or her job responsibilities and he or she has been trained. This holds true for returning goods as well, which offsets a goods receipt.

As shown in Figure 5.18, Transaction MIGO has a dropdown box from which you can select an action. Two of the dropdown selections are Return Delivery and Subsequent Adjustment. When products are defective or the wrong product was shipped, the Return Delivery option is used. If an adjustment needs to be made to quantity or price, Subsequent Adjustment is selected.

Figure 5.18 Executable Action Dropdown Selection

Finally, on the topic of document reversals, any A/P invoice created automatically using Transaction MIRO should not be reversed in FI using Transaction FB08 or F.80. Instead, use Transaction MR8M to reverse the material invoice document, which in turn reverses the A/P invoice in FI.

5.4.3 Change Posted Documents

The need to change documents is universal across SAP modules. However, as you have seen throughout this chapter, not all financial documents originate in FI. An SAP best practice is to change posted documents in the module in which they were created. This concept is important for keeping modules in sync. There is an exception to this rule, however, with the A/P invoice. We will discuss this exception towards the end of this section.

Earlier, we discussed three MM transactions. The first, Transaction ME21N, creates a purchase order. Purchase orders s can be cancelled, and it's line items can be deleted and added. The transaction to change a purchase order is Transaction ME22N. Any change to a purchase order should be made by the procurement department. An AP clerk or supervisor may request that a change be made to a purchase order, but that individuals should not make the change directly unless it is part of their job responsibilities and they have been trained.

The second MM transaction discussed is the goods receipt, Transaction MIGO. To make a subsequent adjustment to a goods receipt, see Section 5.4.2.

The last transaction is the invoice receipt, created using Transaction MIRO. You cannot change a LIV invoice after posting it. In the case of an A/P invoice, you need to make any change directly in the A/P invoice in FI, which was created as a follow-on document for Transaction MIRO. The FI transaction to change the A/P invoice is Transaction FB02.

One of the more common fields to change in an A/P invoice is the baseline date. You may also need to change the payment terms or the payment method assigned in the document. These are simple changes that cause no reconciliation problems between A/P and MM. However, if the change needed in the invoice is more complex (e.g., to a cost object), then you should reverse it using Transaction MR8M and repost.

5.5   Summary

Accounts Payable (A/P) is the SAP module used for managing vendor accounts and issuing payments for the goods and services your company procures. The content presented in this chapter broadened your perspective to help you think of A/P as a series of steps in a business process, not as isolated transactions. Thinking in terms of business processes instead of individual transaction codes is important and makes you more effective in executing tasks, such as financial close.

In this chapter, the primary focus was the procure-to-pay business process. Using this process as the topic for discussion, you learned about fundamental integration between Materials Management (MM) and Accounts Payable (A/P).

Integration between MM and FI is important. A complete procure-to-pay business process is not complete without the two, and the procurement process makes up an important part of any business.

Purchase requisitions and purchase orders start the procurement process in MM-Purchasing. After goods are procured, delivery must be scheduled and the goods received, inspected, and accepted. Receiving the goods is an important process step in itself. It involves delivery receipt, inspection, and verification that what was delivered is in fact what was ordered. Within MM-Purchasing, a goods receipt document is created and linked to the purchase order's history.

A goods receipt document references a purchase order. It is in this step that the power of SAP ERP demonstrates itself in the procure-to-pay business process. Once posted, the goods receipt document is displayed in purchase order history. Linking documents to a purchase order makes the management of the procure-to-pay process streamlined and efficient.

The creation of an invoice typically follows goods receipt. In MM-LIV, this transaction is called *invoice receipt*. The result of an invoice receipt is the creation of an MM material document, which is linked to an A/P invoice. This A/P invoice is referred to as a *follow-on document*. With each invoice receipt posted, at least two documents are created: one material document and one A/P invoice document.

It is an SAP best practice to change or reverse a document in the module in which it was created. Both purchase orders and goods receipts can be changed in MM-Purchasing. Purchase orders cannot be reversed, but they can be cancelled by deleting all their line items and un-releasing them, if releases are used. Goods receipts are not reversed, but goods returns create the same effect.

Invoice receipts can be reversed in MM-LIV, but invoice receipt documents cannot be changed. To change something such as payment terms, change the A/P invoice directly in FI. For more complex changes, such as to a cost object, the invoice document should be reversed in MM-LIV and reposted.

By using transactions from both MM and FI, you can complete the procure-to-pay process. In this chapter, you learned about each step in the process, integration points, and the importance of when and how to reverse or change documents.

Now that you have learned about A/P integration and the procure-to-pay business process, let's move on to discuss A/P transactions in detail in the next chapter.

In this chapter, we cover A/P transactions in detail. These include transactions such as vendor invoices and credit memos, which create vendor subledger entries.

6 Accounts Payable Transactions

This chapter covers Accounts Payable (A/P) transactions that originate in the A/P module. This may seem like a basic concept, but as you saw in Chapter 5, it is possible to create A/P invoices and credit memos in MM-Purchasing. A/P processes, such as procure-to-pay, span multiple modules. That's why it's important to understand A/P integration as well as A/P-specific transactions.

The most common A/P transaction is the entry of a vendor invoice document using Transaction FB60. This chapter covers not only the creation of an A/P vendor invoice, but also associated A/P functions, such as document display, change, reverse, park, and more. These associated functions are also covered for G/L transactions in Chapter 3 and for A/R transactions in Chapter 10. These functions work the same in all cases, yet it's important to address them independently in each chapter to ensure you grasp their relevance to unique business scenarios.

In essence, A/P exists to pay the bills. This is the tail end of the procure-to-pay business process, addressed in detail in Chapter 5. Prior to paying a vendor, a vendor invoice is created. Subsequently the outgoing payment is issued using either the manual method (see Section 6.6) or the automatic payment program (see Chapter 7).

This seemingly straightforward process of creating and paying a vendor invoice can take many twists and turns. Posting credit memos, making down payments, clearing accounts, making document corrections, and reconciling balances are just some of the additional functions that have to be performed by accountants in the A/P department. Vendor account maintenance and tracking is an important part of the job function.

In this chapter, we will begin by covering the basics of creating an A/P invoice before diving into each associated function of the A/P module. Some of the transactions covered in this chapter are tasks you likely need to perform on a daily basis. Others, such as document reversals, are executed less frequently. This chapter can serve as a useful reference guide in the future for less frequently used transactions, and it can provide you with an overall refresher on the A/P module.

6.1 Vendor Invoices

This section covers the A/P invoice creation process, which includes document entry, park, post, save as complete, and hold. It also covers the Transaction FB60 tree display, screen variants, account assignment templates, editing options, and post with reference, all of which provide valuable insights to help you be more productive and organized in the A/P module.

To create a vendor invoice in SAP using Transaction FB60, you must enter document header details (e.g., posting date) and at least one non-vendor line item that nets the document balance to zero. Creating a vendor invoice is a relatively simple transaction. With the vendor number, proper G/L account numbers, and lines of accounting, you can enter and post this transaction with little difficulty. Yet you need to be prepared to handle interruptions, such as calls from vendors that may require you to step away in the middle of entering a vendor invoice or document. This section gives you the tools you need to deal with these and other challenges and provides you with the knowledge to enter A/P transactions more efficiently.

6.1.1 Document Entry

To enter an A/P invoice document, use Transaction FB60 or application menu path ACCOUNTING • FINANCIAL ACCOUNTING • ACCOUNTS PAYABLE • DOCUMENT ENTRY • FB60—INVOICE, as shown in Figure 6.1.

Figure 6.1 Transaction FB60 Application Menu Path

Double-click FB60—INVOICE from the menu path, or enter "FB60" in the COM-MAND field (as shown in Figure 6.2) and press ⌈Enter⌉.

Figure 6.2 FB60 in Command Field

The ENTER VENDOR INVOICE entry screen will open (Figure 6.3). The fields that appear on the header with prepopulated values may vary depending upon your system configuration and editing options. In this example, values defaulted into the INVOICE DATE, POSTING DATE, DOCUMENT TYPE, CURRENCY, and COMPANY CODE fields, whereas we entered values in the VENDOR, REFERENCE, and AMOUNT fields.

It is a best practice to input the vendor's invoice number in the REFERENCE field. In addition, special note should be made of the INVOICE DATE field. The invoice date is the start date for the due date calculation. In other words, if the payment terms are net 30, then the clock starts ticking based on the date in the INVOICE DATE field, not the POSTING DATE field.

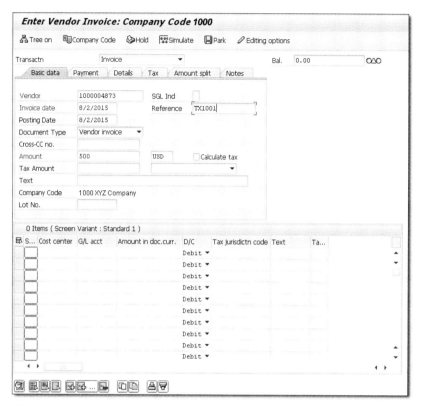

Figure 6.3 Transaction FB60 Entry Screen

After entering header details, the next step is to enter at least one line item, as shown in Figure 6.4.

Here, the line item entered is a debit to an expense account. For an expense line item, you are required to enter a G/L ACCOUNT, DEBIT/CREDIT INDICATOR, AMOUNT, and a cost object, at minimum. Here, we entered a COST CENTER as the cost object. You may also select INTERNAL ORDER or WBS ELEMENT, based on your business requirements. Additionally, your SAP system may have additional field entry requirements, based upon your configuration and field status settings.

After entering your document line items, click the SIMULATE button in the top center of the entry screen. This initiates simulation of the vendor invoice posting logic in order to determine if the document can be properly posted. If the simulation is unsuccessful, an error message will appear. If successful, the document overview screen will open, as shown in Figure 6.5.

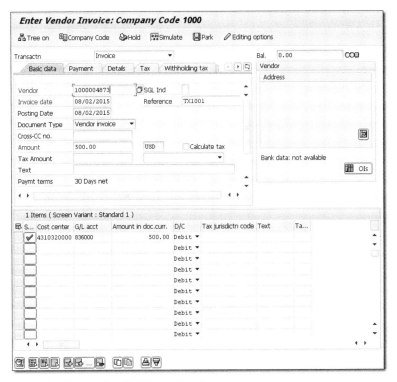

Figure 6.4 Transaciton FB60 Enter Line Items

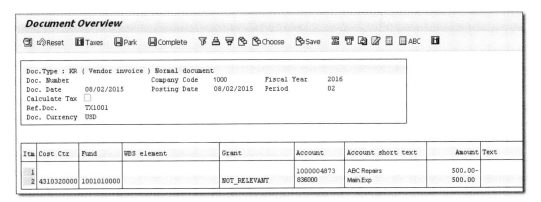

Figure 6.5 Transaction FB60 Document Overview Screen

Once simulation is complete, click the POST icon 🖫 to the right of the COMMAND field in the upper-left-hand corner of the screen to post the vendor invoice. A message will appear with the new document number, as shown in Figure 6.6.

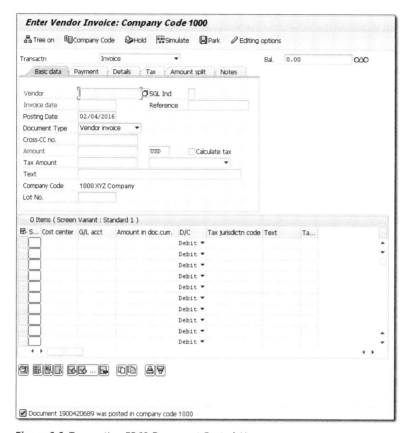

Figure 6.6 Transaction FB60 Document Posted Message

6.1.2 Post, Park, Save as Complete, and Hold

This section describes the different ways to create vendor invoice documents: post, park, save as complete, and hold. These universal concepts within FI are not unique to vendor invoices and Transaction FB60, but here we will focus on their use in vendor invoices.

Post

Posting a vendor invoice is covered in its entirety in Section 6.1.1. A *posted document* is a vendor invoice that is considered complete, produces an accounting document number, and updates the vendor and G/L account balances.

Once a document is posted, the only way to reverse its impact on the vendor and G/L account balance is to reverse the document. Reversing G/L documents is covered in Section 6.4.

A vendor invoice cannot be paid until it is posted.

Park

Document parking allows you to save a vendor invoice document without impacting vendor and G/L account balances. This may be necessary if the document is incomplete, or if further edits, data validation, or document approval is required prior to posting.

Because parked documents are considered incomplete, they can be changed or deleted. When parked, these vendor documents do not update transaction figures and account balances. Moreover, a parked document does not go through the extensive entry checks performed when documents are posted.

Another important point about parked vendor invoices is that they cannot be paid. This means that the automated payment program (Transaction F110) will not select the item when the payment proposal is created (see Chapter 7 for details on running the automatic payment program). Parked items also cannot be paid using Transaction F-53 and Transaction F-58 (manual payments).

To park a vendor invoice document, use Transaction FV60 or follow application menu path ACCOUNTING • FINANCIAL ACCOUNTING • ACCOUNTS PAYABLE • DOCUMENT ENTRY • DOCUMENT PARKING • FV60—PARK OR EDIT INVOICE, as shown in Figure 6.7.

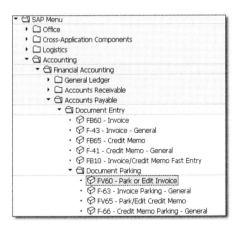

Figure 6.7 Transaction FV60 Application Menu Path for Document Park

Double-click on FV60—PARK OR EDIT INVOICE from the menu path shown in Figure 6.7, or enter "FV60" in the COMMAND field (as shown in Figure 6.8) and press Enter.

Figure 6.8 FV60 in Command Field for Park Vendor Invoice

The PARK VENDOR INVOICE entry screen will open (Figure 6.9). The fields that default values into the document header will vary depending upon your system configuration and editing options. In this example, we manually entered values for the VENDOR, INVOICE DATE, REFERENCE, and AMOUNT fields, whereas values defaulted for the POSTING DATE, DOCUMENT TYPE, CURRENCY, and COMPANY CODE fields.

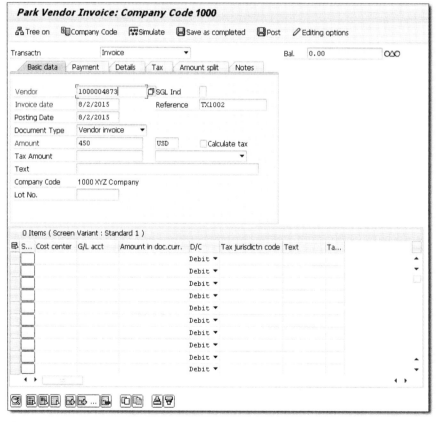

Figure 6.9 Transaction FV60 Park Vendor Invoice Screen

After inputting field values on the header screen, enter at least one line item, as shown in Figure 6.10.

Figure 6.10 Transaction FV60 Entry Screen for Line Items

Once the line items are entered, click the Park icon 🖫 to the right of the Command field in the upper left hand portion of the screen. This will park the vendor invoice, and a message will appear with the new parked document number, as shown in Figure 6.11.

Figure 6.11 Transaction FV60 Document Parked Message

Save as Completed

The *save as completed* function is similar to document parking, but with some key distinctions. When you save a document as completed, the program goes through more extensive document check logic, just as if the document were being posted. Like parked documents, however, documents that are saved as completed can be edited and changed prior to posting.

Although the park and save as completed functions are similar, the latter generally should only be used when you are sure the document is accurate and complete and only needs final approval before being posted.

Note

Like parked documents, documents that are saved as completed cannot be paid.

To save a vendor invoice as complete, use Transaction FV60 or follow application menu path ACCOUNTING • FINANCIAL ACCOUNTING • ACCOUNTS PAYABLE • DOCUMENT ENTRY • DOCUMENT PARKING • FV60—PARK OR EDIT INVOICE, as shown in Figure 6.12.

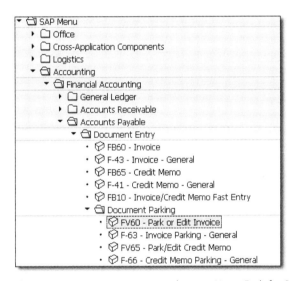

Figure 6.12 Transaction FV60 Application Menu Path for Save as Complete

Double-click FV60—PARK OR EDIT INVOICE from the menu path shown in Figure 6.12, or enter "FV60" in the COMMAND field (as shown in Figure 6.13) and press `Enter`.

Figure 6.13 FV60 in Command Field

The Park Vendor Invoice entry screen will appear (Figure 6.14). The fields that appear in the header with prepopulated values may vary, depending upon your system configuration and editing options. In this example, we manually entered values for the Vendor, Invoice Date, Reference, and Amount fields, whereas values defaulted for the Posting Date, Document Type, Currency, and Company Code fields.

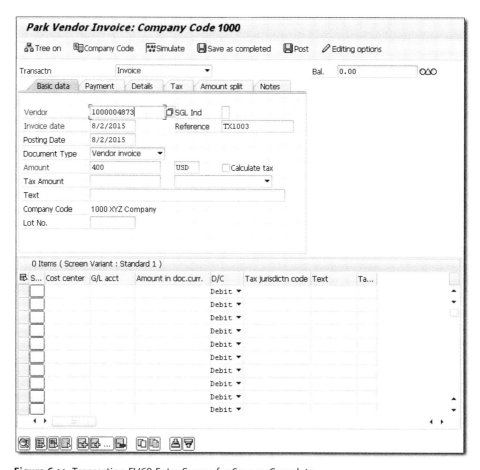

Figure 6.14 Transaction FV60 Entry Screen for Save as Complete

After the PARK VENDOR INVOICE header screen is complete, enter at least one line item, as shown in Figure 6.15.

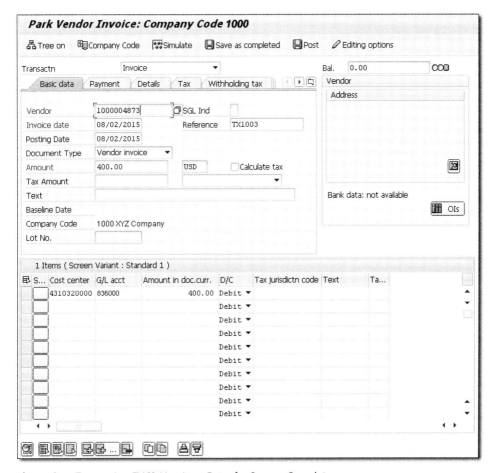

Figure 6.15 Transaction FV60 Line Item Entry for Save as Complete

After entering line items, click the SAVE AS COMPLETED icon in the top-center portion of the screen. This will save the vendor invoice as completed, and a message will appear with the new document number, as shown in Figure 6.16.

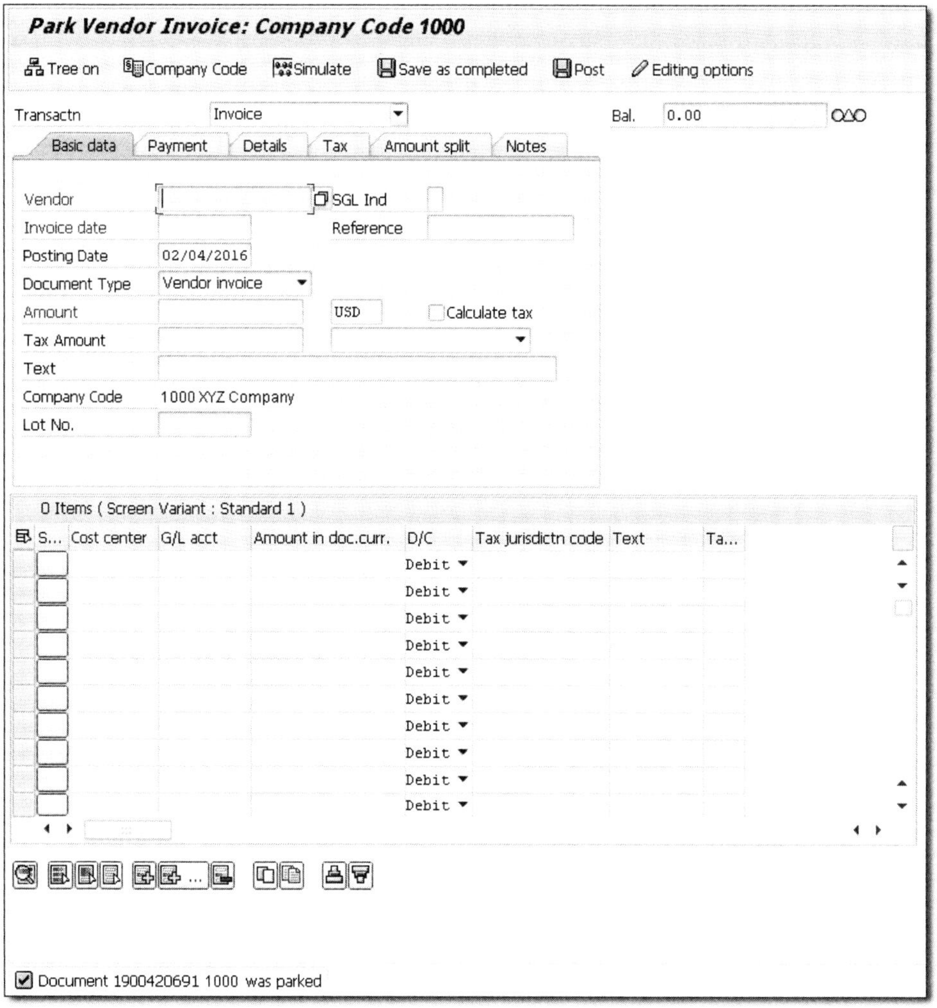

Figure 6.16 Transaction FV60 Document Created Message for Save as Completed

Hold

Document hold allows you to temporarily save your data. It is most useful when you are interrupted during document entry. Because held documents are temporary, they do not update A/P and G/L transactions and balances. Subsequent to holding a document, you can edit, delete, park, or post it. Unlike post, park, and save as completed, the hold function produces no permanent document number until the document is parked or posted.

To hold an A/P accounting document, use Transaction FB60 or application menu path ACCOUNTING • FINANCIAL ACCOUNTING • ACCOUNTS PAYABLE • DOCUMENT ENTRY • FB60–INVOICE, as shown in Figure 6.17.

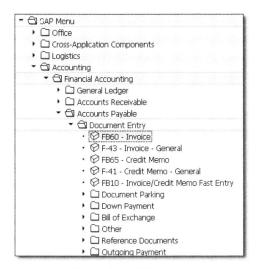

Figure 6.17 Transaction FB60 Menu Path for Document Hold

Double-click FB60—INVOICE from the menu path shown in Figure 6.17, or enter "FB60" in the COMMAND field (as shown in Figure 6.18) and press Enter .

Figure 6.18 FB60 in Command Field

You can use the hold function at any point during Transaction FB60 regardless of how much or little information you have entered, because no system checks take place when you hold an A/P document.

In the example shown in Figure 6.19, the VENDOR, INVOICE DATE, REFERENCE, and AMOUNT fields have been entered, along with one partially complete line item. In the screen header, field values were prepopulated for the CURRENCY, POSTING DATE, DOCUMENT TYPE, and COMPANY CODE fields.

At any point, the document can be held by pressing F5 or selecting DOCUMENT • HOLD from the dropdown menu path, as shown in Figure 6.20.

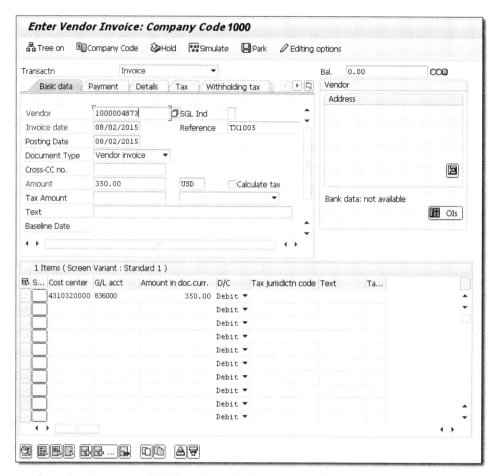

Figure 6.19 Transaction FB60 Entry Screen for Document Hold

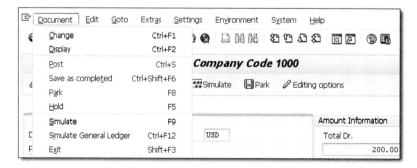

Figure 6.20 Transaction FB60 Document Hold Dropdown Menu

A dialogue box (Figure 6.21) will prompt you to enter a temporary document number, a ten-character preliminary document number that can contain numbers, letters, or special characters. This temporary document number will no longer be valid when a permanent number is assigned, such as when the document is posted, parked, or saved as complete.

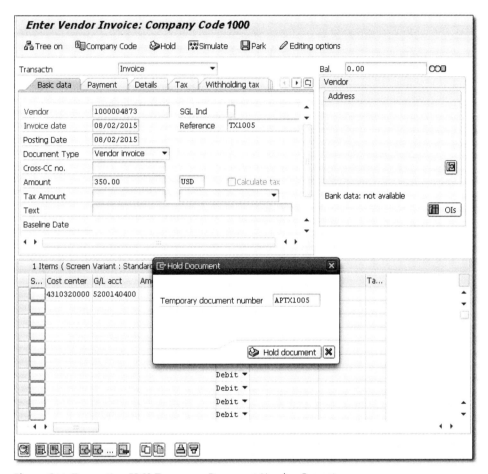

Figure 6.21 Transaction FB60 Temporary Document Number Prompt

After entering a temporary document number, press ⟨Enter⟩ or click the HOLD DOCUMENT button. As a result, a temporary accounting document will be created, and a message will appear with the held document number, as shown in Figure 6.22.

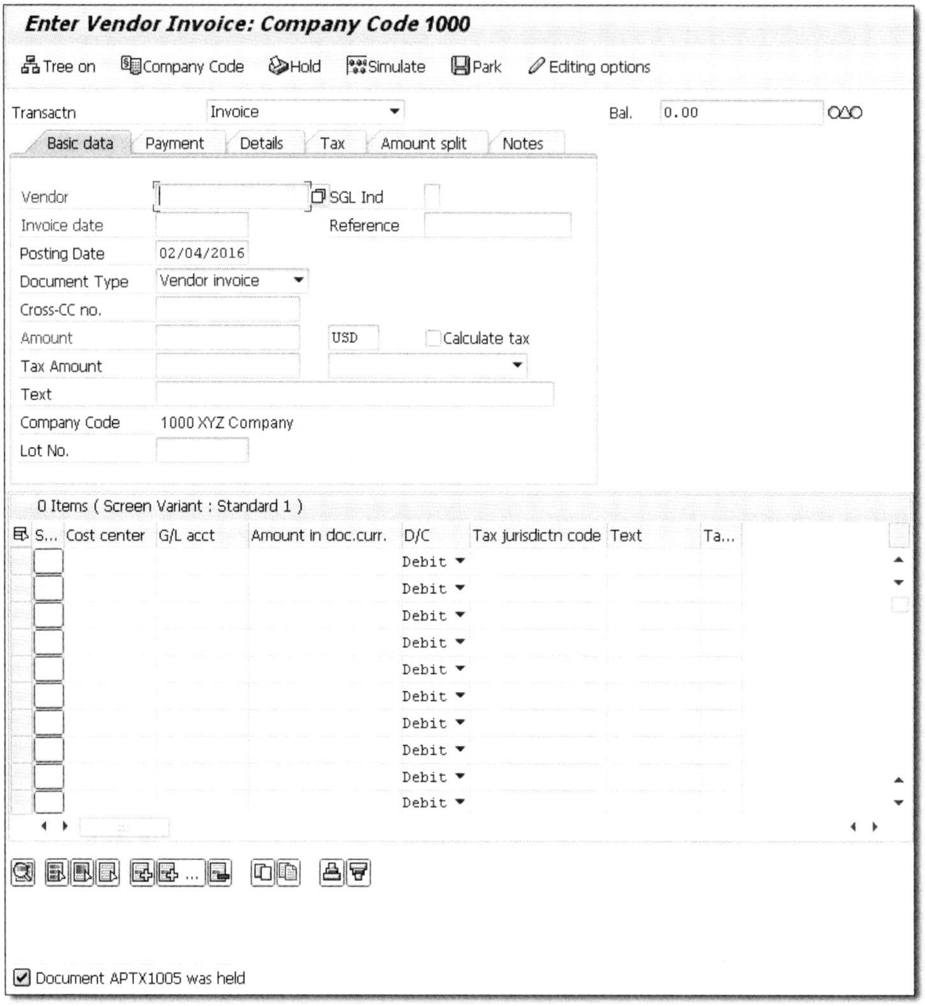

Figure 6.22 Transaction FB60 Document Held Message

6.1.3 Tree Display

The tree display provides an easy-to-use visual display for several functions that can also be accessed from the dropdown menu in Transaction FB60. The tree display is a universal concept, or shortcut, for accessing accounting documents and document entry tools in FI. In this section, we will confine the discussion of the tree display to Transaction FB60 and Transaction FV60, but this capability can be used in any financial transaction for which the tree display is available, such as Transactions FB50 and FB70.

The tree display is a toggle function, meaning that it can be turned on (i.e., made visible) or turned off (i.e., made invisible) by the click of a button or keyboard combination.

Figure 6.23 shows Transaction FB60 with the tree display on, visible as a panel on the left-hand side of the transaction screen.

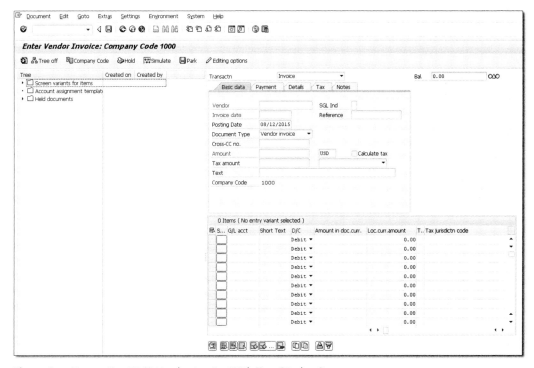

Figure 6.23 Transaction FB60 Vendor Invoice With Tree Display On

Note that with the tree display on, a panel with folders is visible on the left. The folders that appear in the display vary by transaction code. In Transaction FB60, we see the following folders:

- ▸ SCREEN VARIANTS FOR ITEMS
- ▸ ACCOUNT ASSIGNMENT TEMPLATES FOR ITEMS
- ▸ HELD DOCUMENTS

Screen variants and account assignment templates are covered in detail in Section 6.1.4.

In Section 6.1.2, you learned how to hold a vendor invoice document. Held documents can be viewed in the tree display by clicking on the triangle to the left of the HELD DOCUMENTS folder. This action opens the folder and displays all the held documents created by the user.

When you double-click a held document in the tree display, the details appear in the vendor invoice document entry screen, as shown in Figure 6.24. Once displayed, held document details can be edited, parked, or posted.

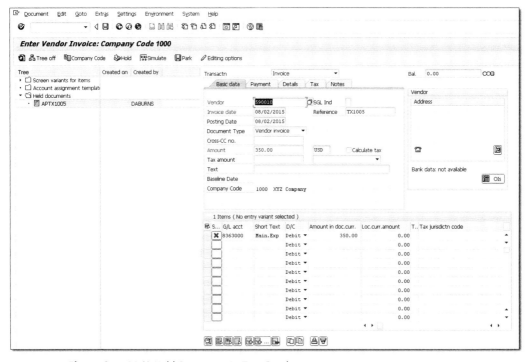

Figure 6.24 FB60 Held Document in Tree Display

The tree display function in Transaction FV60 is the same as in Transaction FB60 and has the same toggle capability.

Figure 6.25 shows the tree display turned on in Transaction FV60.

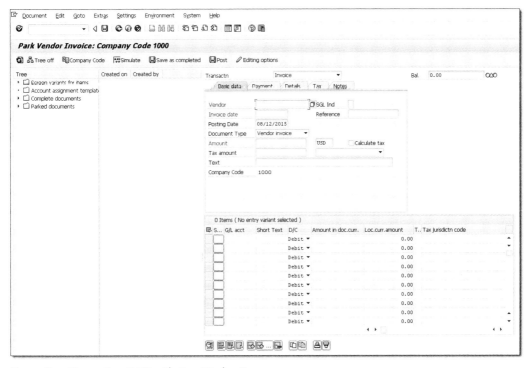

Figure 6.25 Transaction FV60 with Tree Display On

In Transaction FV60, you can see the following folders in the tree display:

▶ SCREEN VARIANTS FOR ITEMS

▶ ACCOUNT ASSIGNMENT TEMPLATES FOR ITEMS

▶ COMPLETE DOCUMENTS

▶ PARKED DOCUMENTS

In Transaction FV60's tree display, folders for screen variants and account assignment templates appear at the top, as they did in Transaction FB60. However, folders for complete and parked documents, which appear in Transaction FV60, are not present in the Transaction FB60 tree display. Finally, a folder for held documents, which appeared in Transaction FB60's tree display, does not appear in Transaction FV60. As you can see, the tree display default folders will vary by transaction.

6.1.4 Using Screen Variants and Account Assignment Templates

Screen variants and *account assignment templates* are tools available in FI that simplify entry of vendor documents. They are not unique to Transaction FB60, but in this section we will confine our discussion to this transaction. Note that both screen variants and account assignment templates can be accessed and maintained from both the tree display in Transaction FB60 and the dropdown menu. In this section, we will focus on using the tree display, which is the most user-friendly and frequently used method.

Use of Screen Variants

A screen variant sets the columns for display and entry in the line item entry portion of Transaction FB60 (Figure 6.26). In other words, it controls the fields displayed on the screen and the order in which they appear.

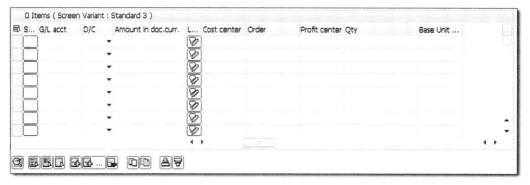

Figure 6.26 Transaction FB60 Line Entry Screen

A well-developed screen variant reduces data entry time and the number of data entry errors. In essence, your goal is to have only the fields you need to enter or display appear on the screen. Specific screen variants for A/P, for instance, will have the cost center, internal order, and WBS element fields prominently placed for easy data entry.

Transaction FB60 has a default screen variant assigned, which is displayed each time you execute the transaction. However, the assigned default may not be your preferred line item entry screen, and you may prefer different screen variants depending on the type of vendor invoice you are creating. In fact, it's quite common to have several screen variants for different types of vendor invoices.

The tree display and the dropdown menu in Transaction FB60 give you the ability to select different screen variants at any point in time.

Let's see screen variant selection in action. Go to Transaction FB60, and make sure the tree display is on (see Section 6.1.3). Click on the triangle next to the Screen Variants for Items folder to see a list of available variants to choose from (Figure 6.27).

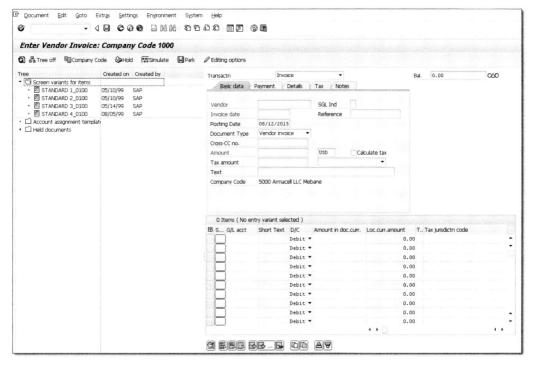

Figure 6.27 Transaction FB60 Screen Variant List

Double-click the screen variant you wish to use (Figure 6.28), and the line layout in the bottom right of the screen will change accordingly.

The creation and maintenance of screen variants is beyond the scope of this book because users do not typically have the permissions required to create or change them. These functions are usually restricted to an SAP support team or system administrator.

Figure 6.28 Transaction FB60 Screen Variant Selection

Note

Screen variants are cross-client dependent, meaning that if a screen variant is created or changed in one SAP client, the change is reflected in every other client within that same SAP instance.

Use of Account Assignment Templates

Account assignment templates in Transaction FB60 are prepopulated field values in document line items. These templates allow you to reduce data entry requirements for vendor invoices, which are frequent and consistent in their makeup. They allow you to expedite the creation of a vendor invoice without the hassle of reentering all the necessary field values each time you create a new document.

Account assignment templates get a lot of use in A/P. Most often they are used to prepopulate G/L accounts and cost objects that are frequently posted. They not only ease data entry, but also ensure consistency.

The next time you find yourself entering a vendor invoice from scratch that you have created repeatedly in the past, consider creating an account assignment template for it. Doing so may simplify your life—especially for vendor invoices with multiple line items.

Let's take a closer look. Go to Transaction FB60 and make sure the tree display is on (see Section 6.1.3). Click on the triangle next to the ACCOUNT ASSIGNMENT TEMPLATE FOR ITEMS folder to see a list of available templates to choose from (Figure 6.29).

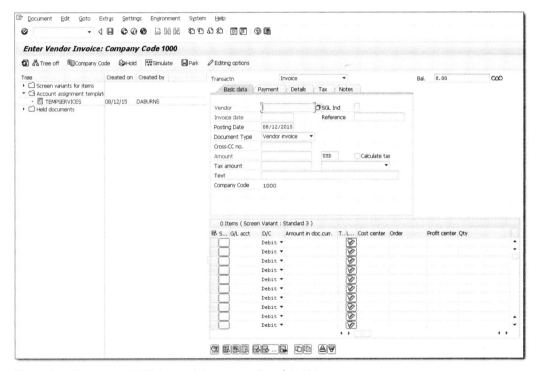

Figure 6.29 Transaction FB60 Account Assignment Template List

Double-click the template you wish to use (Figure 6.30). When you do so, the line layout in the line item entry screen will change based on the prepopulated values contained in the template. Note that you can add to or edit these field values at this point.

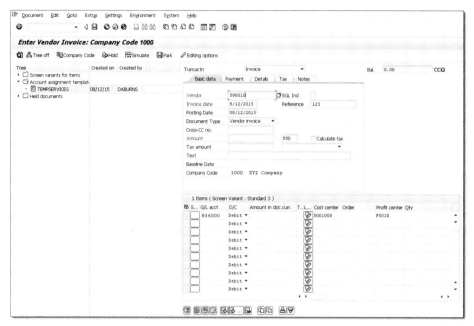

Figure 6.30 FB60 Account Assignment Template Selection

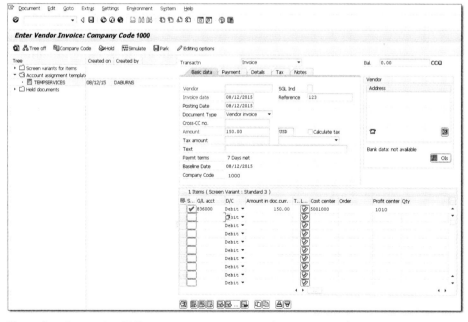

Figure 6.31 Transaction FB60 Account Assignment Template Entry Complete

In this example, account assignment template TEMPSERVICES contains prepopulated values for the G/L ACCOUNT, DEBIT/CREDIT INDICATOR, COST CENTER, and PROFIT CENTER fields. In the header, we entered the VENDOR, REFERENCE, and INVOICE DATE fields manually. With all the required fields populated, you simply need to enter a value in the AMOUNT field to complete the document entry (Figure 6.31).

With document entry complete, you can post, park, or save this vendor invoice as completed. In this example, we posted the document (Figure 6.32).

Figure 6.32 Transaction FB60 Posted Document Using Account Assignment Template

6.1.5   Controlling Document Entry with Editing Options

Controlling document entry with editing options allows you to make user-specific settings for transactions in accounting. Editing options are useful tools that gives you some level of field control over the entry screen, what fields are displayed, and values that are defaulted, and that let you determine the interpretation of certain field entry values.

Editing options are available throughout FI. The discussion in this section, however, is limited to their use in Transaction FB60. The editing options selected are user-specific, not transaction-specific; therefore, editing options set in Transaction FB60 will also apply to other accounting transactions, such as Transaction FB50 and Transaction FB70.

In an A/P department, some of the editing options set will depend upon your role. For example, if you work for a global company and your job function is to create vendor invoices for multiple company codes, you need the company code field available in Transaction FB60. If your job function is localized and you only create vendor invoices for one company code, you do not need the company code field.

In this section, we will demonstrate some of the most commonly used settings and then provide a complete list of all editing options and their descriptions (Table 6.1). Throughout this section, we will also point out editing options that are of particular interest in A/P.

To access editing options from Transaction FB60 (Figure 6.33), click the EDITING OPTIONS button in the top center of the ENTER VENDOR INVOICE screen, or press Shift + F4 .

The ACCOUNTING EDITING OPTIONS screen will open (Figure 6.34). Editing options are divided into four general categories, each with its own section of the screen:

▶ GENERAL ENTRY OPTIONS
▶ SPECIAL OPTIONS FOR SINGLE SCREEN TRANSACTIONS

▸ Default Document Currency

▸ Default Company Code

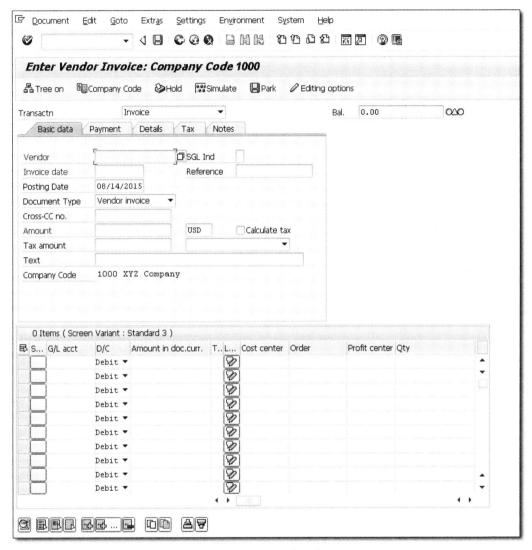

Figure 6.33 Transaction FB60 Enter Vendor Invoice Screen for Editing Options

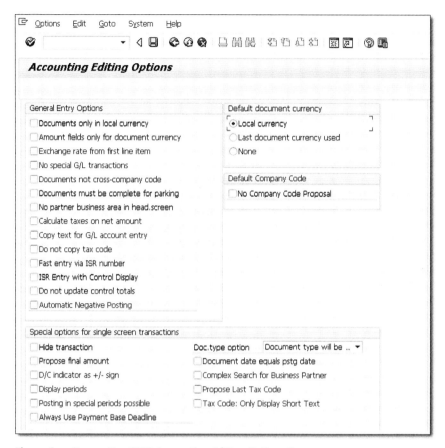

Figure 6.34 Transaction FB60 Accounting Editing Options Screen

In the upper-right-hand corner of Figure 6.34, you can see that the LOCAL CURRENCY push button is selected in the DEFAULT DOCUMENT CURRENCY section. With this setting, the local currency of the company code to which the user is assigned will default into Transaction FB60.

If you are an A/P clerk or accounting supervisor creating A/P transactions for multiple regions using multiple currencies, this setting may be useful. In addition, there may be times, such as at month-end, when you repeatedly need to make entries in a foreign currency. Since editing options are user specific, you can turn them on and off as needed to perform your job function.

For this example, change the DEFAULT DOCUMENT CURRENCY to NONE (Figure 6.35), then click the SAVE icon ⊟ or press ⌃Ctrl⌄+⌃S⌄.

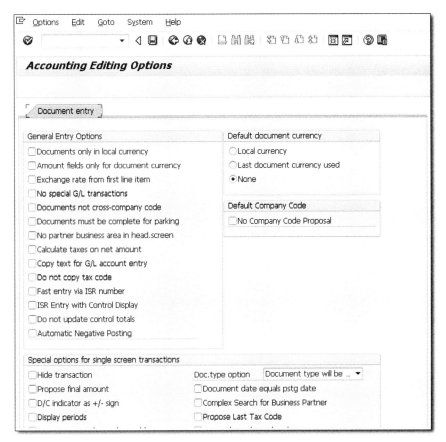

Figure 6.35 Transaction FB60 Accounting Editing Options with No Default Currency

Once the editing options are saved, return to Transaction FB60 to find that the CURRENCY field in the header is now blank (Figure 6.36), meaning that no value defaulted into the CURRENCY field. As you see, this is useful to an A/P clerk who needs to select a foreign currency. It's also a reminder to ensure that you enter a vendor invoice with the proper currency, instead of inadvertently posting it in your local currency.

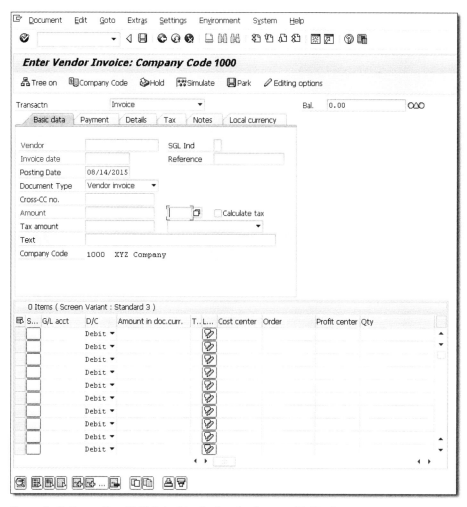

Figure 6.36 Transaction FB60 Enter Vendor Invoice Screen with No Currency

Similarly, you can use editing options to change the transaction entry screen so that no company code is proposed. For this example, do so by selecting the checkbox next to NO COMPANY CODE PROPOSAL field in the ACCOUNTING EDITING OPTIONS screen (Figure 6.37). Once this selection is made, click the SAVE icon 🖫 or press Ctrl+S.

Once the editing options are saved, return to Transaction FB60; you are immediately prompted to enter a COMPANY CODE (Figure 6.38). This is a useful feature for an A/P clerk or accounting supervisor responsible for multiple regions.

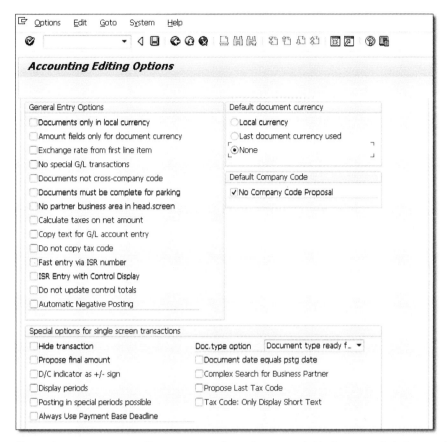

Figure 6.37 Transaction FB60 Accounting Editing Options with No Company Code Proposed

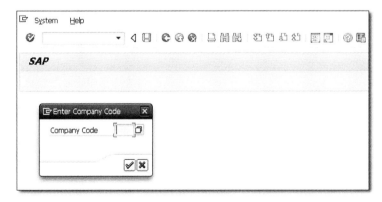

Figure 6.38 FB60 Prompt for Company Code

Another common use of EDITING OPTIONS is to change the document type setting. For this example, change the DOC.TYPE OPTION field to DOCUMENT TYPE HIDDEN (Figure 6.39).

Once this selection is made, click the SAVE icon 🖫 or press ⌈Ctrl⌉+⌈S⌉.

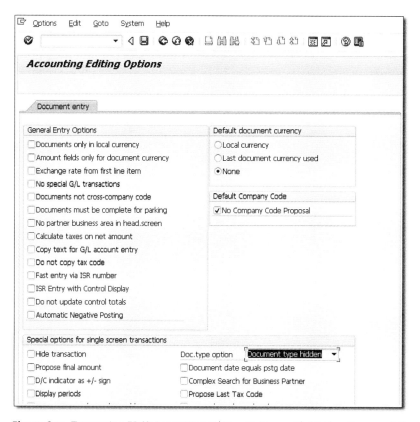

Figure 6.39 Transaction FB60 Accounting Editing Options with Hidden Document Type

Once the editing options are saved, return to Transaction FB60 and see that the DOCUMENT TYPE field is now hidden from view (Figure 6.40).

In A/P, the applicability of this setting depends upon the number of document types created for vendor invoices. The standard delivered SAP document type is KR, but you may have additional custom document types as well. Be mindful of what A/P document types exist in your system (whether standard delivered by SAP or custom document types) and when to use them.

Figure 6.40 Transaction FB60 Enter G/L Account Document Screen with Hidden Document Type

Now that you've seen a few examples of changing editing options, let's take a look at the SAP descriptions for the all the options available. These are provided in Table 6.1.

Editing Option	Description
DOCUMENTS ONLY IN LOCAL CURRENCY	Only allows entry of documents in local currency.
AMOUNT FIELDS ONLY FOR DOCUMENT CURRENCY	Only allows entry amounts in foreign currency when entering documents in foreign currency.

Table 6.1 Editing Options and Descriptions

Editing Option	Description
EXCHANGE RATE FROM FIRST LINE ITEM	When posting foreign currency documents, the exchange rate in the document header is corrected automatically using the amounts in the first line item.
NO SPECIAL G/L TRANSACTIONS	Prevents entry of special G/L transactions.
DOCUMENTS NOT CROSS-COMPANY CODE	Cross-company code entries are prevented.
DOCUMENTS MUST BE COMPLETE FOR PARKING	Prevents incomplete documents from being parked.
NO PARTNER BUSINESS AREA IN HEAD.SCREEN	Default partner business area cannot be entered in document header.
CALCULATE TAXES ON NET AMOUNT	Indicates the G/L account amounts entered are net of taxes.
COPY TEXT FOR G/L ACCOUNT ENTRY	Automatically copies text from last G/L line item to subsequent line items.
DO NOT COPY TAX CODE	Deactivates automatically copying the last tax code entered to G/L account line items.
FAST ENTRY VIA ISR NUMBER	Enables the fast entry of incoming invoices using the ISR subscriber number.
ISR ENTRY WITH CONTROL DISPLAY	Provides the ability to enter an alternative vendor number in cases in which several vendors may have the same ISR number.
DO NOT UPDATE CONTROL TOTALS	Control totals are not updated.
AUTOMATIC NEGATIVE POSTING	When the negative postings indicator is set for at least one manually entered line, also makes any automatically generated lines negative postings.
DEFAULT DOCUMENT CURRENCY	1. Default local currency used in header currency field. 2. Default last currency used in header currency field. 3. Defaults no currency in the header currency field.
DEFAULT COMPANY CODE	When the NO COMPANY CODE PROPOSAL indicator is checked, you must manually select the company code to be used.
HIDE TRANSACTION	Hides the TRANSACTION field on the entry screen.
PROPOSE FINAL AMOUNT	The system proposes the final invoice amount in the customer or vendor line after a G/L line has been entered.

Table 6.1 Editing Options and Descriptions (Cont.)

Editing Option	Description
D/C INDICATOR AS +/- SIGN	Allows the entry of +/- sign with amounts; the debit/credit indicator is thus derived.
DISPLAY PERIODS	Enables the display of periods on the entry screen under basic data.
POSTING IN SPECIAL PERIODS POSSIBLE	Enables the period field for data input.
ALWAYS USE PAYMENT BASE DEADLINE	Only permits payment deadline calculation based on the baseline date.
DOC.TYPE OPTION	1. Displays document type in header. 2. Document type is ready for input. 3. Display document type using short name. 4. Document type is ready for input using short name. 5. Document type is hidden.
DOCUMENT DATE EQUALS PSTG DATE	Defaults the document date from the posting date.
COMPLEX SEARCH FOR BUSINESS PARTNER	Specifies when entering a vendor invoice if a complex search is possible for the number of the trading partner.
PROPOSE LAST TAX CODE	Propose the last tax code used the next time the transaction is called.
TAX CODE: ONLY DISPLAY SHORT TEXT	Changes the tax code drop-down list in the transaction to only display the short text of the tax code.

Table 6.1 Editing Options and Descriptions (Cont.)

As you read through Table 6.1, consider the applicability of each to your job function in A/P.

6.1.6 Post with Reference

Post with reference is a quick and easy way to create a new vendor invoice by replicating all or most of the accounting data from a document that has already been posted. In many ways, it is much like a document copy function, except that SAP provides several *flow control indicators*, which allow you to select specific actions to control in the process. For example, there is a flow control indicator DO NOT PROPOSE AMOUNTS. When this indicator is selected, you must enter document line item amounts.

Post with reference is a universal concept in FI, but the scope of our discussion in this section is limited to its use in Transaction FB60. You must be cautious while using this functionality in A/P. It's often tempting to use post with reference as an easy way to replicate large documents. But if you aren't careful, it can lead to a posting error. In particular, you need to make sure your posting date, reference number, amounts, and lines of accounting are all changed properly.

In this section, we will demonstrate the use of post with reference with a simple example and then provide a complete list of flow control options and their descriptions (Table 6.2).

In the example that follows we demonstrate how to use post with reference to create a new vendor invoice document using Transaction FB60 or application menu path Accounting • Financial Accounting • Accounts Payable • Document Entry • FB60—Invoice, as shown in Figure 6.41.

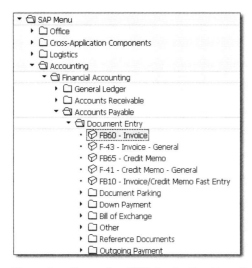

Figure 6.41 Transaction FB60 Application Menu Path for Post with Reference

Double-click FB60—Invoice from the menu path, or enter "FB60" in the Command field (as shown in Figure 6.42) and press Enter.

Figure 6.42 FB60 in Command Field

From the Enter Vendor Invoice entry screen (Figure 6.43), initiate the post with reference function from the dropdown menu options Goto • Post with Reference (Figure 6.43), or press [Shift]+[F9].

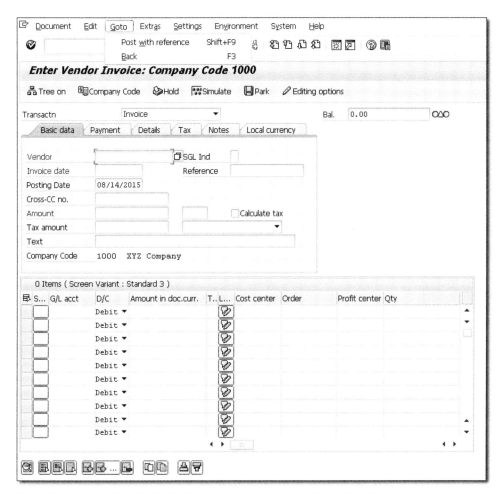

Figure 6.43 Transaction FB60 Enter Vendor Invoice Screen for Post with Reference

The post with reference Post Document: Header Data selection screen will open (Figure 6.44). On this screen, enter values for the Document Number, Company Code, and Fiscal Year fields in the Reference section. In this example, we selected the Do Not Propose Amounts indicator in the Flow Control section.

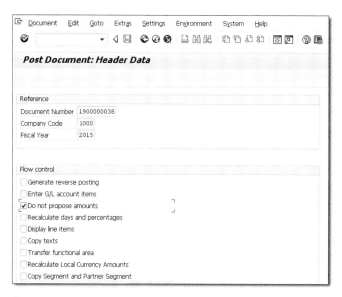

Figure 6.44 Transaction FB60 Post with Reference Header Selection Screen

Once the relevant fields are populated in the POST DOCUMENT: HEADER DATA screen, press [Enter] to open the first screen of the new vendor invoice document creation process (Figure 6.45). Header data in this new document contains the field values copied from the reference document, including the DOCUMENT DATE, POSTING DATE, and REFERENCE fields. Note that you can edit many field values at this point.

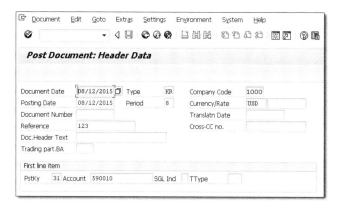

Figure 6.45 Transaction FB60 Post with Reference Header Screen

In this example, we changed the DOCUMENT DATE, POSTING DATE, and REFERENCE fields (Figure 6.46).

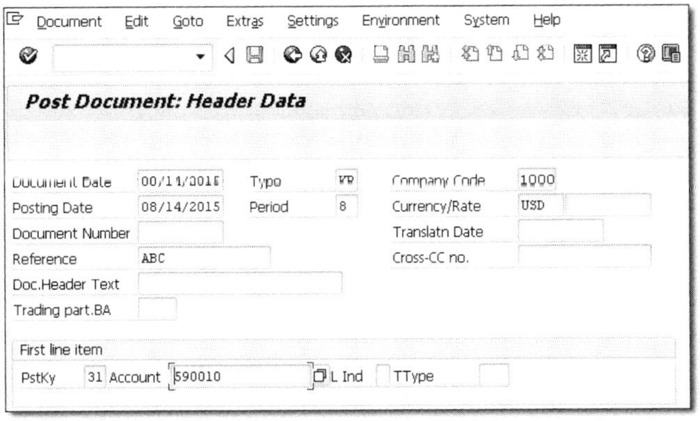

Figure 6.46 Transaction FB60 Post with Reference Header Screen with Changes

Once you have changed any header fields you want to change, press [Enter], and the POST DOCUMENT ADD VENDOR ITEM screen will appear (Figure 6.47). You will note that the AMOUNT field is blank. This is because you selected the DO NOT PROPOSE AMOUNTS indicator in FLOW CONTROL (Figure 6.44) when you initiated the post with reference transaction.

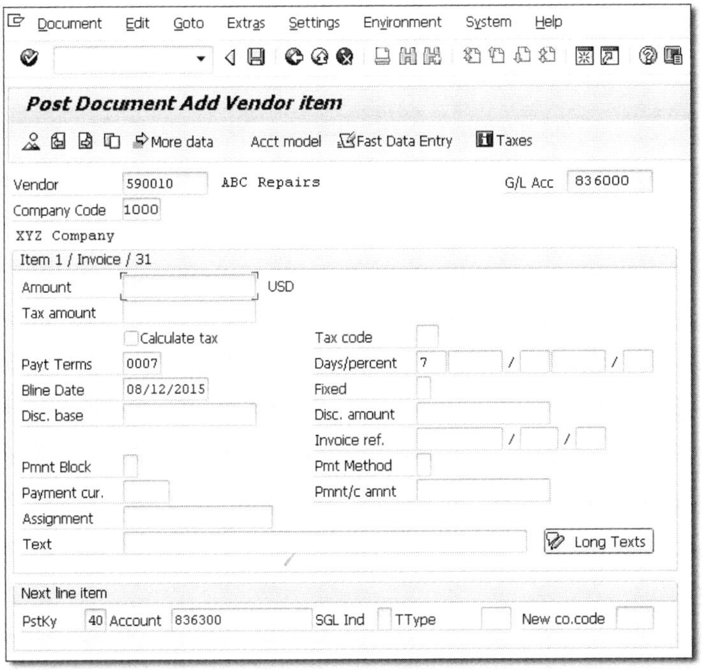

Figure 6.47 Post with Reference Add Vendor Item Screen

In this example, we entered "1000" in the AMOUNT field (Figure 6.48).

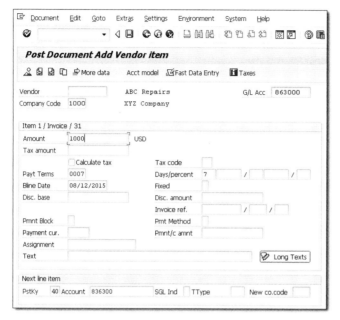

Figure 6.48 Post with Reference Add Vendor Item Screen with Amount Change

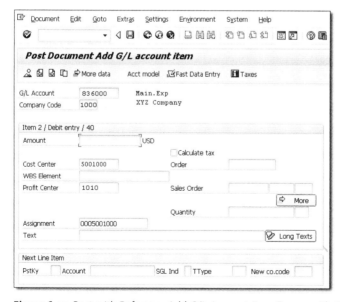

Figure 6.49 Post with Reference Add G/L Account Item Screen with Amount Blank

Once the AMOUNT field is entered, press $\boxed{\texttt{Enter}}$, and a second POST DOCUMENT ADD G/L ACCOUNT ITEM screen will open (Figure 6.49). Notice in Figure 6.49 that the AMOUNT field is blank again.

Again, we entered "1000" in the AMOUNT field (Figure 6.50).

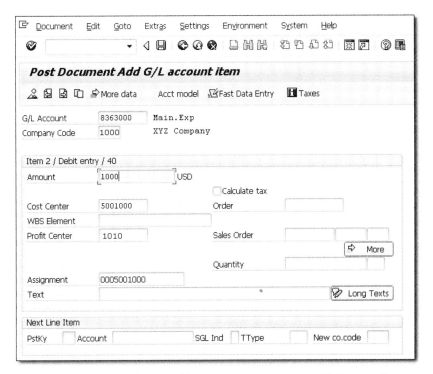

Figure 6.50 Post with Reference Add G/L Account Item Screen with Amount Change

After entering all G/L account line items, click the POST icon 🖫 or press $\boxed{\texttt{Ctrl}}+\boxed{\texttt{S}}$ to post the vendor invoice document (Figure 6.51). A message appears with the new vendor invoice document number.

Now that you've seen a simple example of post with reference, let's take a look at all the flow control indicator options, listed in Table 6.2. As you read through them, think about their relevance to specific A/P transactions, such as vendor invoices and credit memos.

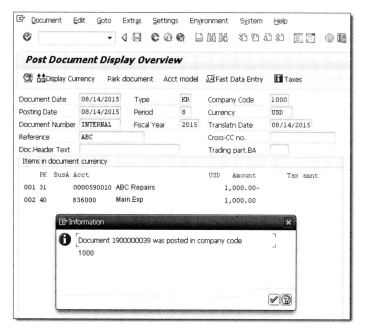

Figure 6.51 Post with Reference Document Created Message

Flow Control Indicator	Description
GENERATE REVERSE POSTING	Automatically generates reverse debit/credit indicators to offset the reference document.
ENTER G/L ACCOUNT ITEMS	Line items are transferred to the fast entry screen for G/L accounts so that several line items can be displayed and processed from one screen.
DO NOT PROPOSE AMOUNTS	Line item amounts must be manually entered in the new document.
RECALCULATE DAYS AND PERCENTAGES	Days and percentages from payment terms will be recalculated.
DISPLAY LINE ITEMS	Displays each individual line item separately so that default field values can be changed if necessary.
COPY TEXTS	Copies long texts from reference document to the new document.
TRANSFER FUNCTIONAL AREA	Functional area is normally derived; therefore, this option transfers the reference functional area instead of rederiving it.

Table 6.2 Flow Control Indicators and Descriptions

Flow Control Indicator	Description
RECALCULATE LOCAL CURRENCY AMOUNTS	Recalculates local currency amounts to account for changes in exchange rates.
COPY SEGMENT AND PARTNER SEGMENT	These fields are normally derived; therefore, this option transfers them instead of rederiving their values.

Table 6.2 Flow Control Indicators and Descriptions (Cont.)

On a final note, post with reference allows you to copy an existing document, but it is an SAP best practice to allow derived field values to rederive with each new document posting.

6.2 Credit Memos

Vendor invoices are amounts you owe to a vendor for goods or services purchased. *Credit memos*, on the other hand, are credits back to you on the vendor account. A credit may be due for any number of reasons, including overpayment, damaged goods, additional discounts, and erroneous bill amounts.

Credit memos allow you to correct erroneous vendor balances and to offset outgoing payment balances. In other words, the amount paid to a vendor is the open invoice amounts less any credit memos posted to the vendor's account.

In the A/P module, you post a credit memo via Transaction FB65 or application menu path ACCOUNTING • FINANCIAL ACCOUNTING • ACCOUNTS PAYABLE • DOCUMENT ENTRY • FB65—CREDIT MEMO, as shown in Figure 6.52.

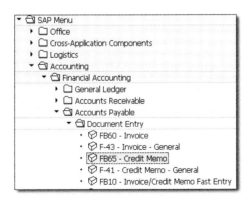

Figure 6.52 Transaction FB65 Application Menu Path

Double-click FB65—Credit Memo from the menu path shown in Figure 6.52, or enter "FB65" in the Command field (as shown in Figure 6.53) and press Enter.

Figure 6.53 FB65 in Command Field

The Enter Vendor Credit Memo screen will open (Figure 6.54). In the document header, enter values for the Vendor, Document Date, and Amount fields and any other fields that are required, but do not prepopulate a system value. In this example, values are prepopulated in the Posting Date and Currency fields.

Figure 6.54 Transaction FB65 Enter Vendor Credit Memo Screen

With header entry complete, enter at least one G/L line item (Figure 6.55). In this example, the line item is an offset (i.e., credit) to an expense account. Here, we manually entered line item values for the G/L ACCT, D/C (i.e., debit/credit indicator), AMOUNT, and COST CENTER fields.

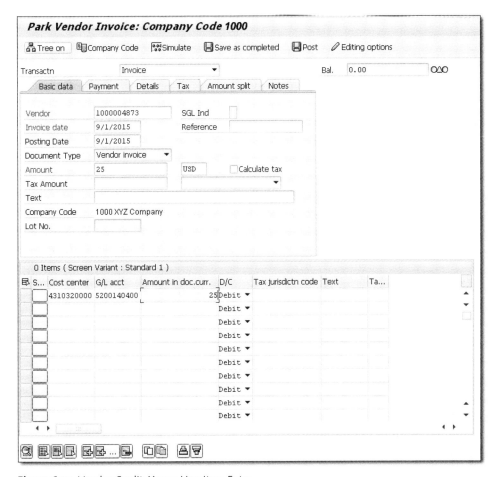

Figure 6.55 Vendor Credit Memo Line Item Entry

After entering document line items, click the SIMULATE button in the top center of the ENTER VENDOR CREDIT MEMO screen to initiate simulation of the vendor credit memo posting logic, which will determine if the document can be properly posted. If the simulation is unsuccessful, an error message will appear. If successful, the DOCUMENT OVERVIEW screen appears, as show in Figure 6.56.

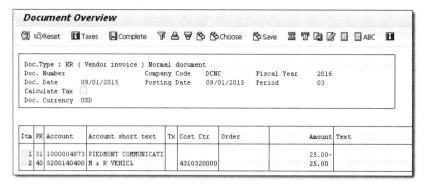

Figure 6.56 Enter Vendor Credit Memo Overview Screen

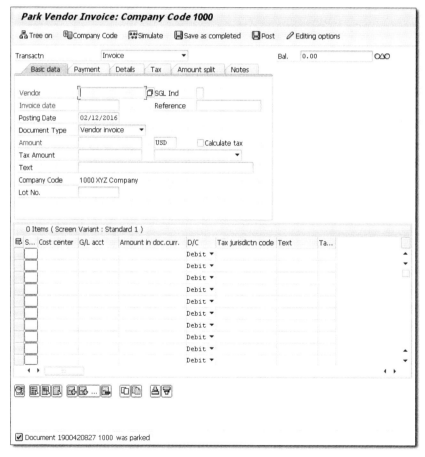

Figure 6.57 Transaction FB65 Vendor Credit Memo Posted Message

Once simulation is complete, click the POST icon 🖫 to the right of the COMMAND field in the upper-left-hand corner of the screen. This will post the vendor credit memo, and a message will appear with the new document number, as shown in Figure 6.57.

Credit memos are an important function in managing vendor accounts. Now that you have seen an example and understand the role credit memos play in A/P, let's discuss the vendor down payment transaction.

6.3 Down Payments Sent

Down payments sent are prepayments to vendors in advance of receiving goods or services. A down payment may be requested by a vendor as a sign of good faith or required in order to reserve a product.

The starting point for the down payment process in A/P is the *down payment request.* You enter a vendor down payment request in order to make a down payment automatically via the payment program. Note that down payment requests are *noted items* in FI, meaning that G/L account balances are not updated. In other words, down payment requests are not reflected in either the transaction figures or the balance displays. They can only be viewed in line item displays by specifying that you want to see noted items.

To enter a vendor down payment request in the A/P module, use Transaction F-47 or application menu path ACCOUNTING • FINANCIAL ACCOUNTING • ACCOUNTS PAYABLE • DOCUMENT ENTRY • DOWN PAYMENT • F-47 — REQUEST, as shown in Figure 6.58.

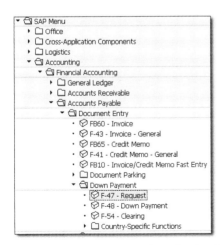

Figure 6.58 Transaction F-47 Application Menu Path

Double-click F-47—REQUEST from the menu path, or enter "F-47" in the COM-
MAND field (as shown in Figure 6.59) and press Enter.

Figure 6.59 F-47 in Command Field

The DOWN PAYMENT REQUEST: HEADER DATA screen will open (Figure 6.60). In the
document header, enter a value in DOCUMENT DATE and any other fields that are
required, but do not default a value. In this example, field values defaulted for
POSTING DATE, TYPE (i.e., document type), PERIOD, COMPANY CODE, and CUR-
RENCY.

In the VENDOR section at the bottom of the screen, you must also enter an
ACCOUNT and special G/L indicator (in the TRG.SP.G/L IND. field).

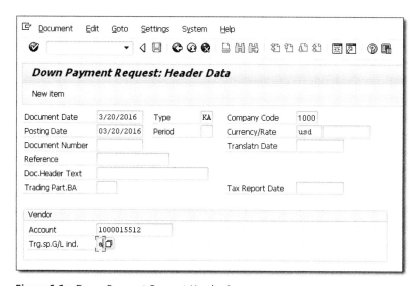

Figure 6.60 Down Payment Request Header Screen

With header data complete, click the NEW ITEM button. The DOWN PAYMENT
REQUEST ADD VENDOR ITEM screen will open (Figure 6.61). Here, enter values for
the AMOUNT, DUE ON, and any other required fields.

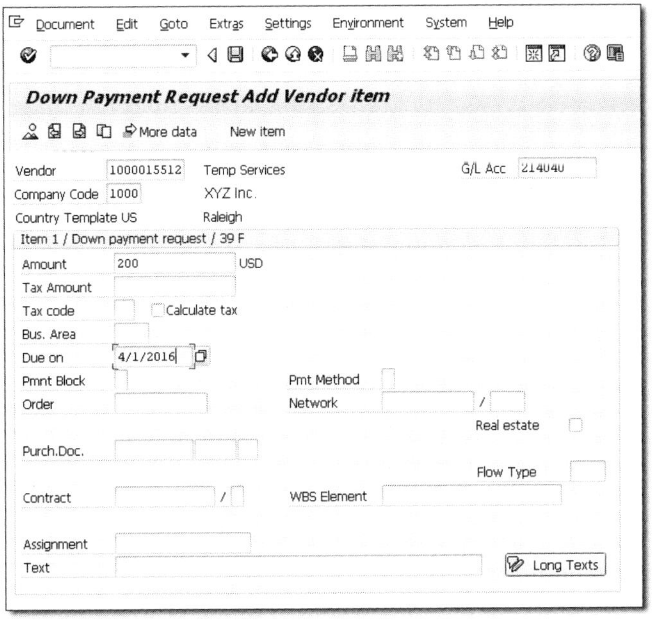

Figure 6.61 Add Vendor Item to Down Payment Request Screen

After entering the vendor line items, click the SAVE icon 🖫 at the top of the entry screen, to the right of the COMMAND field. This will post the vendor down payment request, and a message will appear with the new document number, as shown in Figure 6.62.

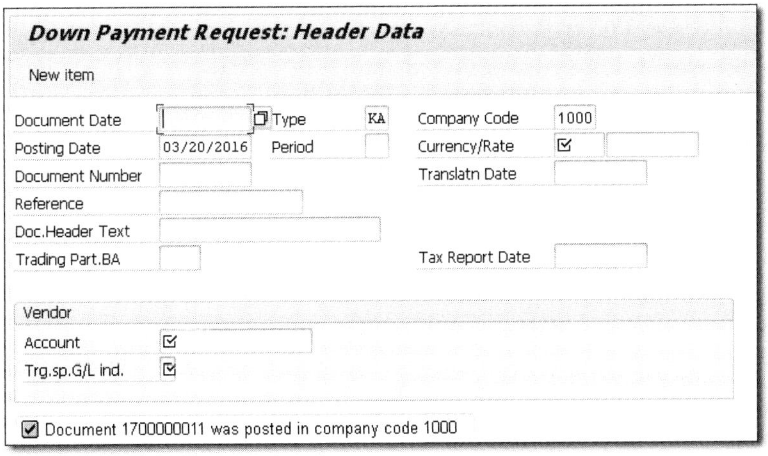

Figure 6.62 Down Payment Request Posted Message

The down payment request is now ready to be paid to the vendor via the A/P payment program (i.e., Transaction F110). See Chapter 7 for details on the automated payment program.

6.4   Resetting and Reversing Documents

Before attempting to reverse an A/P document, you need to know what type of document it is. Is it a vendor invoice, credit memo, or other transaction type? In addition, you need to know if the document to be reversed is a clearing document or not, and what this means.

Let's begin with a discussion of clearing versus nonclearing documents. *Clearing documents* are those produced through a post with clearing transaction, such as Transaction F-04 (see Chapter 3, Section 3.2), or through the payment program. A clearing document has two technical components: First, it contains complete header data and at least two completed line items with debit/credit amounts netting to zero. Second is the account clearing component. Through the clearing process, a vendor open item is selected and its status changed from open to cleared when the clearing document is posted.

A *nonclearing accounting document* has the same attributes as a clearing document, except that it does not clear an open vendor line item. Therefore, in posting a nonclearing document, it does not select a vendor open item and change its status from open to cleared.

Now that you understand the difference between clearing and nonclearing documents, let's walk through some examples of document reversals. We'll begin with nonclearing documents, since they are the simplest to reverse.

To reverse a single A/P document, use Transaction FB08 or application menu path ACCOUNTING • FINANCIAL ACCOUNTING • ACCOUNTS PAYABLE • DOCUMENT • REVERSE • FB08 — INDIVIDUAL REVERSAL, as shown in Figure 6.63.

Double-click FB08 — INDIVIDUAL REVERSAL from the menu path shown in Figure 6.63, or enter "FB08" in the COMMAND field (as shown in Figure 6.64) and press Enter.

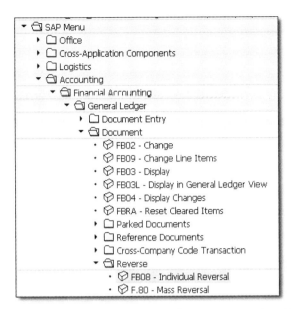

Figure 6.63 Transaction FB08 Application Menu Path in A/P

Figure 6.64 FB08 in the Command Field

The REVERSE DOCUMENT: HEADER DATA screen will open (Figure 6.65). At a minimum, the DOCUMENT NUMBER, COMPANY CODE, FISCAL YEAR, and REVERSAL REASON fields are required.

The REVERSAL REASON field is noted in the reversed document. Beyond indicating why a document is reversed, the reversal reason also determines if an alternative posting date is allowed and if the reversal can be created from a negative posting. In this example, the REVERSAL REASON field is populated with a value of 01, signifying that the reversal will take place in the current period.

When all the required fields are entered, click the POST icon 💾 or press Ctrl + S to post the A/P reversal document. A message will appear with the reverse document number (Figure 6.66).

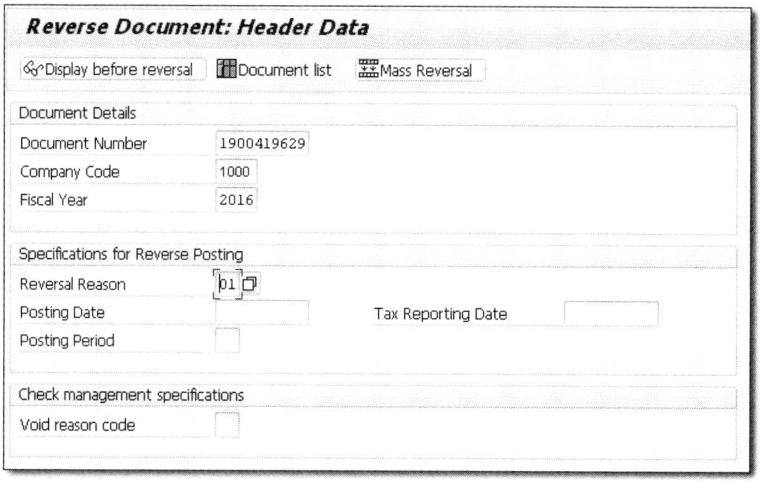

Figure 6.65 Reverse Document: Header Data

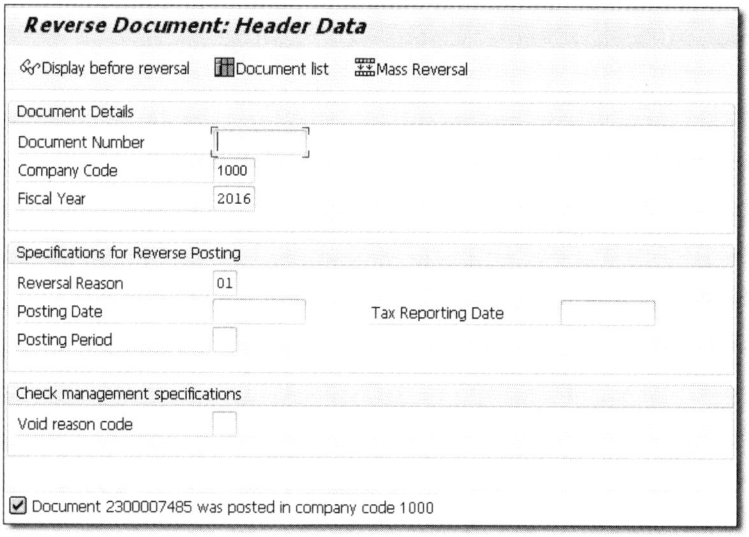

Figure 6.66 Reversal Document Created Message in A/P

Mass document reversal is the name of the functionality that allows you to reverse more than one nonclearing document in a single transaction. To do so, use Transaction F.80 or application menu path Accounting • Financial Accounting • Accounts Payable • Document • Reverse • F.80 — Mass Reversal, as shown in Figure 6.67.

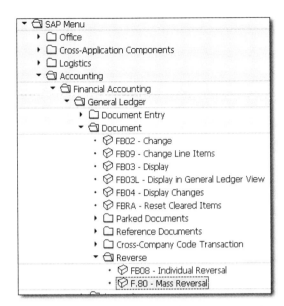

Figure 6.67 Transaction F.80 Application Menu Path in A/P

Double-click F.80—MASS REVERSAL from the menu path, or enter "F.80" in the COMMAND field (as shown in Figure 6.68) and press ⌐Enter⌐.

Figure 6.68 F.80 in Command Field

The MASS REVERSAL OF DOCUMENTS: INITIAL SCREEN screen will open (Figure 6.69). As in Transaction FB08, the COMPANY CODE, DOCUMENT NUMBER, FISCAL YEAR, and REVERSAL REASON fields are required. Note that in Transaction F.80 you can enter a range of values for these fields, whereas in Transaction FB08 you can only enter a single value for each. In Transaction F.80, you also have a LEDGER field, which in most cases will reflect your leading ledger.

Transaction F.80 has some additional features: Under GENERAL SELECTIONS there are several useful input fields, and in the REVERSE POSTING DETAILS section there is a TEST RUN button. For mass reversals, it is always a good idea to run the program in test mode first.

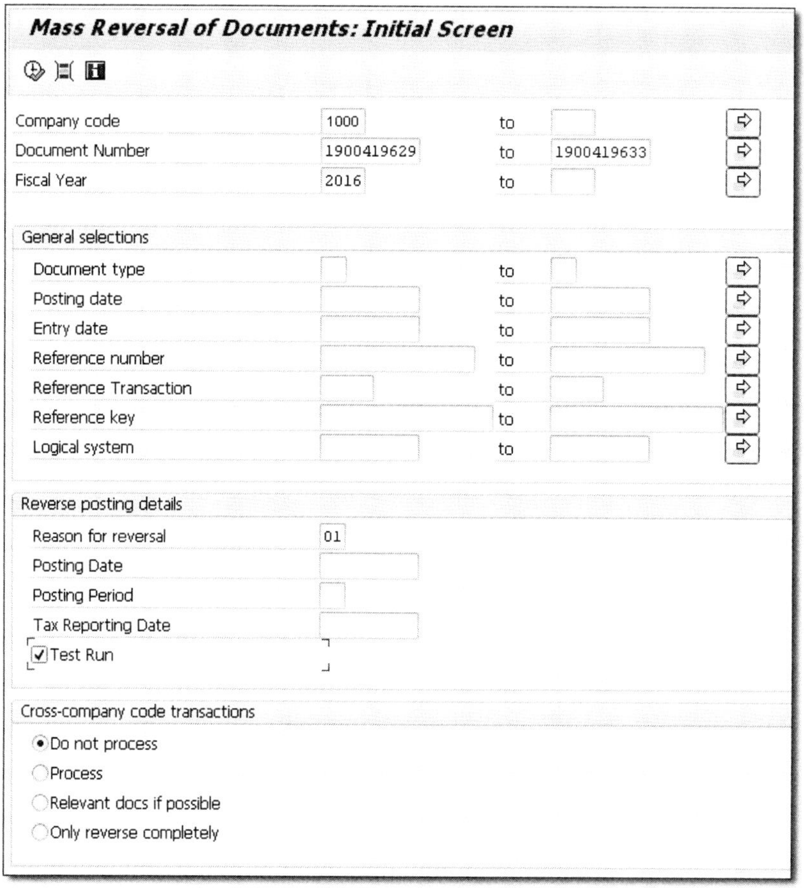

Mass Reversal of Documents: Initial Screen

Company code	1000	to	
Document Number	1900419629	to	1900419633
Fiscal Year	2016	to	

General selections

Document type		to	
Posting date		to	
Entry date		to	
Reference number		to	
Reference Transaction		to	
Reference key		to	
Logical system		to	

Reverse posting details

Reason for reversal	01
Posting Date	
Posting Period	
Tax Reporting Date	
☑ Test Run	

Cross-company code transactions

⦿ Do not process
◯ Process
◯ Relevant docs if possible
◯ Only reverse completely

Figure 6.69 Transaction F.80 Mass Reversal Screen in AP

When all the required fields are entered, click the EXECUTE icon ⊕, or press F8 to post the A/P reversal documents. Detailed results are provided in the MASS REVERSAL OF DOCUMENTS output screen (Figure 6.70).

That concludes our discussion of the individual and mass reversals of nonclearing A/P documents. Next, we will look at the reversal of clearing documents.

To reverse an A/P clearing document, use Transaction FBRA or application menu path ACCOUNTING • FINANCIAL ACCOUNTING • ACCOUNTS PAYABLE • DOCUMENT • FBRA—RESET CLEARED ITEMS, as shown in Figure 6.71.

Mass Reversal of Documents

Reverse documents

```
Test_Refresh_09182015              Mass Reversal of Documents              Time 15:41:38    Date  02/12/2016
                                                                           SAPF080 /C_DBURNS Page           1
                                   Docs which can be reversed

Document Number Company Code    Fiscal Year    Document Type   Posting Date   Document Date   Reference

1900419630      1000            2016           KR              09/16/2015     09/08/2015      117940
1900419631      1000            2016           KR              09/16/2015     09/08/2015      117942
1900419632      1000            2016           KR              09/16/2015     09/08/2015      117943
1900419633      1000            2016           KR              09/16/2015     09/08/2015      117946



Test_Refresh_09182015              Mass Reversal of Documents              Time 15:41:38    Date  02/12/2016
                                                                           SAPF080 /C_DBURNS Page           2
                                   Docs which cannnot be reversed

Document Number Company Code    Fiscal Year    Document Type   Posting Date   Document Date   Reference
                Message

1900419629      1000            2016           KR              09/16/2015     09/08/2015      117939
                F5 361: Document was already reversed
```

Figure 6.70 Transaction F.80 Mass Reversal of Documents Output Screen in A/P

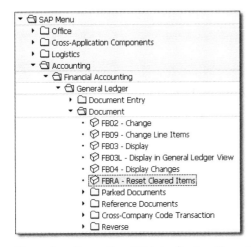

Figure 6.71 Transaction FBRA Application Menu Path in A/P

Double-click FBRA—RESET CLEARED ITEMS from the menu path shown in Figure 6.71, or enter "FBRA" in the COMMAND field (as shown in Figure 6.72) and press Enter.

Figure 6.72 FBRA in Command Field

The RESET CLEARED ITEMS screen will open (Figure 6.73). The CLEARING DOCU-
MENT, COMPANY CODE, and FISCAL YEAR fields are all required.

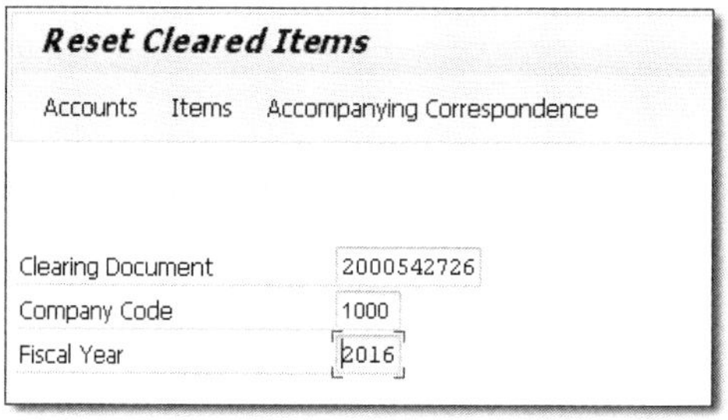

Reset Cleared Items

Accounts   Items   Accompanying Correspondence

Clearing Document	2000542726
Company Code	1000
Fiscal Year	2016

Figure 6.73 Reset Cleared Items

After entering the required screen elements, click the RESET CLEARED ITEMS icon
or press [Ctrl]+[S]. This will bring up the REVERSAL OF CLEARING DOCUMENT
dialog box (Figure 6.74), in which you must choose one of three options: ONLY
RESETTING, RESETTING AND REVERS, or CANCEL.

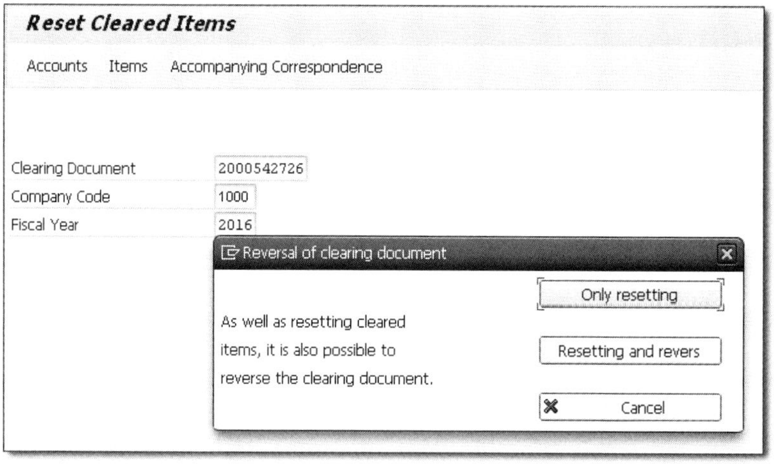

Reset Cleared Items

Accounts   Items   Accompanying Correspondence

Clearing Document	2000542726
Company Code	1000
Fiscal Year	2016

Reversal of clearing document

As well as resetting cleared
items, it is also possible to
reverse the clearing document.

Only resetting

Resetting and revers

Cancel

Figure 6.74 Reversal of Clearing Document Dialog Box

The ONLY RESETTING option does not reverse the clearing document. Instead, it breaks the reference between a clearing document and the A/P item it cleared and changes the status of the cleared A/P item back to open. Only use this option when the A/P item selected for clearing was the wrong line item. The clearing document will become an open item and to be reassigned and clear the correct A/P open item.

The RESETTING AND REVERS option (Figure 6.74) not only resets the cleared item back to open status, but also reverses the clearing document. For this example, select this option to pop up the REVERSAL DATA dialogue box (Figure 6.75).

Figure 6.75 Reversal Data Dialogue Box

The REVERSAL REASON field provides the reason a document is reversed. As previously stated, the reversal reason also determines if an alternative posting date is allowed and if the reversal can be created from a negative posting. In this example, the REVERSAL REASON field is populated with a value of 01, signifying that the reversal will take place in the current period.

Click the CONTINUE icon ☑ or press Enter. Two subsequent information dialogue boxes will appear. The first message, shown in Figure 6.76, states that the clearing document was reset. The second message, shown in Figure 6.77, provides the number of a new document that was posted, which is the document that reversed the clearing document.

Figure 6.76 Clearing Document Reset Message

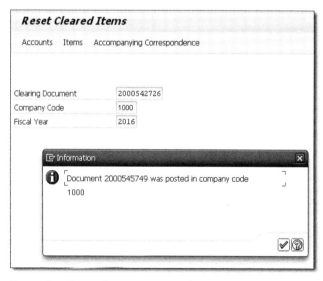

Figure 6.77 Reversal Document Posted Message

This concludes our discussion of A/P document reversals. In this section, you learned the differences between clearing and nonclearing documents and saw examples for each. Now let's discuss the topic of changing and displaying A/P documents.

6.5 Changing and Displaying Documents

This section covers the change and display capabilities for A/P accounting documents. The scope of this section is limited to Transaction FB60, but the same principles apply for other A/P documents.

Rules for changing field values in FI documents are defined in configuration, and separate rules are defined for header and line item fields. In other words, you have some configuration options available, which determine fields in a posted document that can be changed.

It's important to note that there are some limits to this. SAP will never allow you to change fields considered central to the principle of orderly accounting. These are fields that material to A/P and G/L account balances, posting dates, and integration. Such fields include not only the POSTING DATE, DEBIT/CREDIT INDICATOR, and AMOUNT fields, but also update objects (i.e., cost center). If an A/P accounting document contains an incorrect value of this sort, the document should be reversed using Transaction FB08 or Transaction FBRA (see Section 6.4).

To change an A/P document, use Transaction FB02 or application menu path ACCOUNTING • FINANCIAL ACCOUNTING • ACCOUNTS PAYABLE • DOCUMENT • FB02— CHANGE, as shown in Figure 6.78.

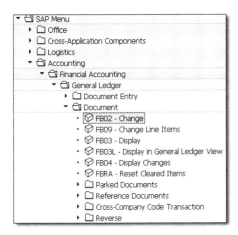

Figure 6.78 Transaction FB02 Application Menu Path in A/P

Double-click FB02—CHANGE from the menu path shown in Figure 6.78, or enter "FB02" in the COMMAND field (as shown in Figure 6.79) and press ⌨Enter.

Figure 6.79 FB02 in Command Field

The CHANGE DOCUMENT: INITIAL SCREEN screen will open (Figure 6.80). The DOC-UMENT NUMBER, COMPANY CODE, and FISCAL YEAR fields are required.

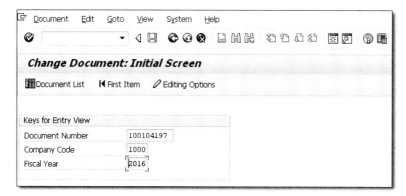

Figure 6.80 Change Document: Initial Screen

After entering all field values, press [Enter]. The CHANGE DOCUMENT: DATA ENTRY VIEW screen will open (Figure 6.81).

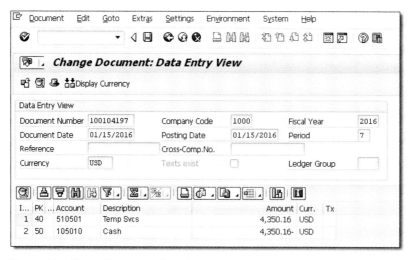

Figure 6.81 Change Document: Data Entry

To change a header field, click the HEADER icon 🐾 to open the document header dialogue box (Figure 6.82). Fields that cannot be changed are greyed out. Fields that can be changed appear white and are ready for field values to be entered or changed.

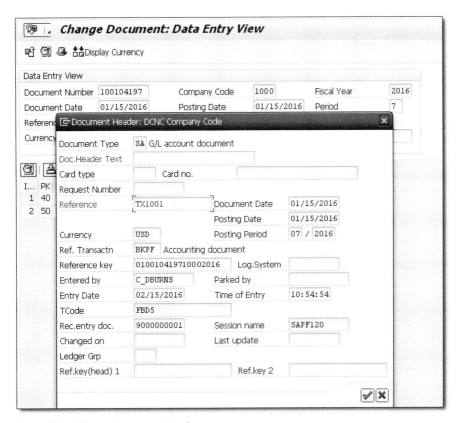

Figure 6.82 Change Document Header

From the CHANGE DOCUMENT: DATA ENTRY VIEW screen (Figure 6.81), you can change line item fields by double-clicking a line. After doing so, the CHANGE DOCUMENT: LINE ITEM screen will open (Figure 6.83).

Fields that cannot be changed are greyed out. Those that can appear white and are ready for field values to be entered or changed. For this example, change the TEXT field (Figure 6.84).

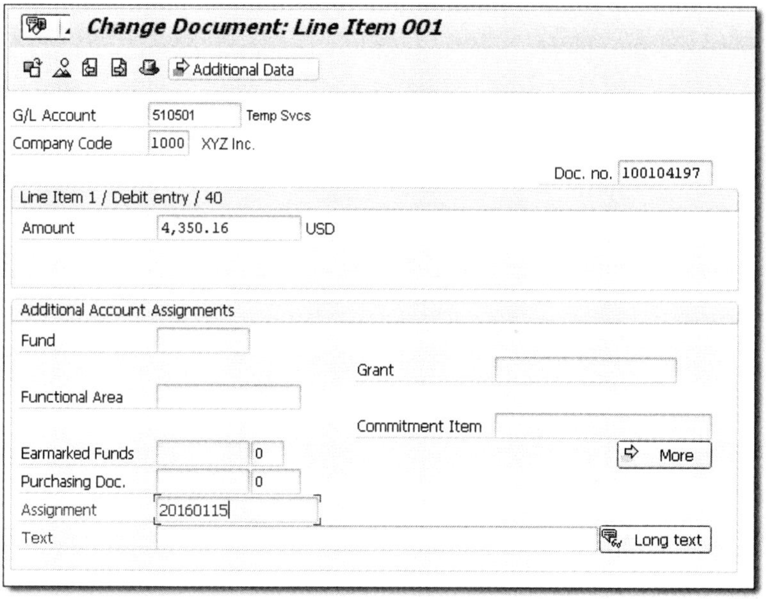

Figure 6.83 Change Document: Line Item

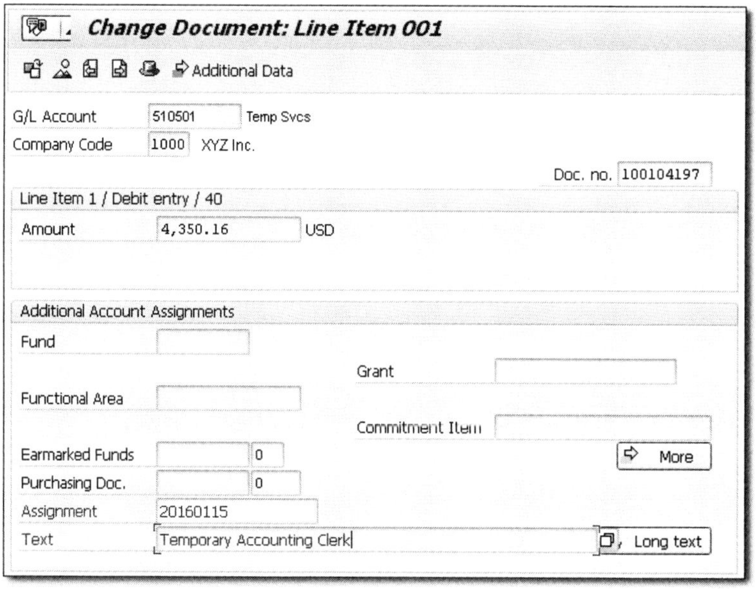

Figure 6.84 Change Line Item with Text Field Change

After changing field values, click the SAVE icon ⊞ or press ⌈Ctrl⌉+⌈S⌉. A message indicates that the document changes have been saved (Figure 6.85).

Figure 6.85 Changes Have Been Saved

To display an A/P accounting document, use Transaction FB03 or application menu path ACCOUNTING • FINANCIAL ACCOUNTING • ACCOUNTS PAYABLE • DOCU-MENT • FB03—DISPLAY, as shown in Figure 6.86.

Figure 6.86 Transaction FB03 Application Menu Path

Double-click FB03—DISPLAY from the menu path, or enter "FB03" in the COM-MAND field (as shown in Figure 6.87) and press ⌈Enter⌉.

Figure 6.87 FB03 in Command Field

The Display Document: Initial Screen screen opens (Figure 6.88). The Document Number, Company Code, and Fiscal Year fields are required.

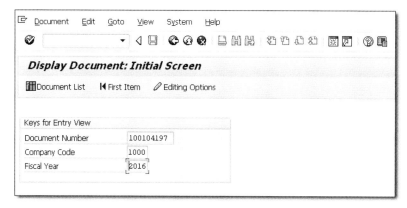

Figure 6.88 Display Document: Initial Screen

After entering field values, press Enter. The Display Document: Data Entry View screen will open (Figure 6.89).

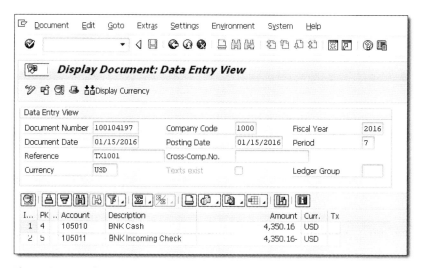

Figure 6.89 Display Document: Data Entry View

From this screen, you can double-click a line to view line item details, or click the Header icon 🖳 to view header details.

This concludes our discussion about changing and displaying A/P documents. In the next session we will discuss the topic of issuing outgoing payments.

6.6   Issuing Outgoing Payments

The basics of A/P are that you create vendor invoices and issue payments. The vendor invoice contains the specific details (e.g., amount and due date) of the outstanding payable owed to a vendor. Issuing payment is the physical transfer of funds to the vendor.

In the A/P module, issuing outgoing payments can be accomplished in mass using the payment program (Transaction F110) or individually using Transaction F-53 (i.e., post payment) or Transaction F-58 (i.e., post and print forms).

Most accounting departments set up a regular schedule to issue payments in mass using Transaction F110. This transaction is covered in detail in Chapter 7. For one-off payments, use Transaction F-53 or Transaction F-58.

Let's begin with an example of posting a manual outgoing payment, using Transaction F-53. It can be executed in the A/P module from application menu path ACCOUNTING • FINANCIAL ACCOUNTING • ACCOUNTS PAYABLE • DOCUMENT ENTRY • OUTGOING PAYMENT • F-53—POST, as shown in Figure 6.90.

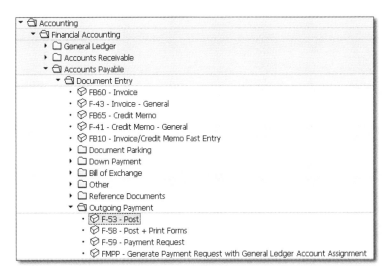

Figure 6.90 Transaction F-53 Application Menu Path

Double-click F-53—Post from the menu path shown in Figure 6.90, or enter "F-53" in the COMMAND field (as shown in Figure 6.91) and press Enter.

Figure 6.91 F-53 in Command Field

The POST OUTGOING PAYMENTS: HEADER DATA screen will open (Figure 6.92). In the top portion of the screen, most field values should contain default values, depending on your configuration and editing options. Make sure to input all required fields that do not contain default values.

In this example, default values populated into the POSTING DATE, TYPE (i.e., document type), PERIOD, COMPANY CODE, and CURRENCY fields. We manually entered a value in the DOCUMENT DATE field.

Post Outgoing Payments: Header Data

Process open items

Document Date	02/12/2016	Type	KZ	Company Code	1000
Posting Date	02/12/2016	Period	8	Currency/Rate	USD
Document Number				Translatn Date	
Reference				Cross-CC no.	
Doc.Header Text				Trading Part.BA	
Clearing text					

Bank data

Account	619100		Business Area	
Amount	500		Amount in LC	
Bank charges			LC bank charges	
Value Date	02/12/2016		Profit Center	
Text			Assignment	

Open item selection			Additional selections	
Account	619100		○ None	
Account Type	K	☐ Other accounts	◉ Amount	
Special G/L ind		☑ Standard OIs	○ Document Number	
Pmnt advice no.			○ Posting Date	
☐ Distribute by age			○ Dunning Area	
☐ Automatic search			○ Others	

Figure 6.92 Post Outgoing Payments: Header Data

In the BANK DATA section, enter values for ACCOUNT, AMOUNT, and any other fields that are required. In the OPEN ITEM SELECTION section, enter the vendor number in ACCOUNT. Finally, in the ADDITIONAL SELECTIONS section, select a button that indicates how the program should select an open invoice. For this example, we selected AMOUNT.

With all relevant fields entered, click the PROCESS OPEN ITEMS button at the top-left portion of the screen (Figure 6.92). The POST OUTGOING PAYMENTS ENTER SELECTION CRITERIA screen will open (Figure 6.93). In this example, we entered the amount of the invoice to be paid ($500) in the FROM and TO fields.

Figure 6.93 Enter Selection Criteria Screen

Once your selection criteria are entered, click the PROCESS OPEN ITEMS button (Figure 6.93) in the top-center portion of the screen. The POST OUTGOING PAYMENTS PROCESS OPEN ITEMS screen will open (Figure 6.94).

Click the SAVE icon 💾 or press Ctrl+S. The program will post the payment document and issue the message shown in Figure 6.95.

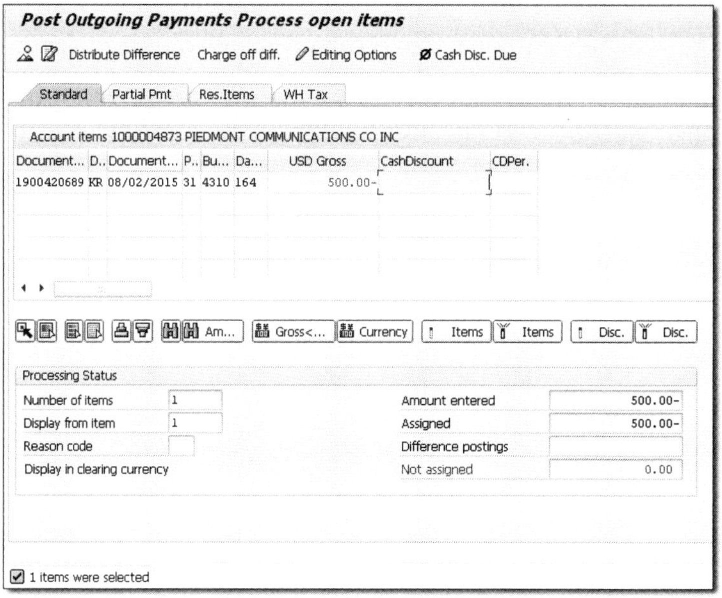

Figure 6.94 Post Outgoing Payments Process Open Items

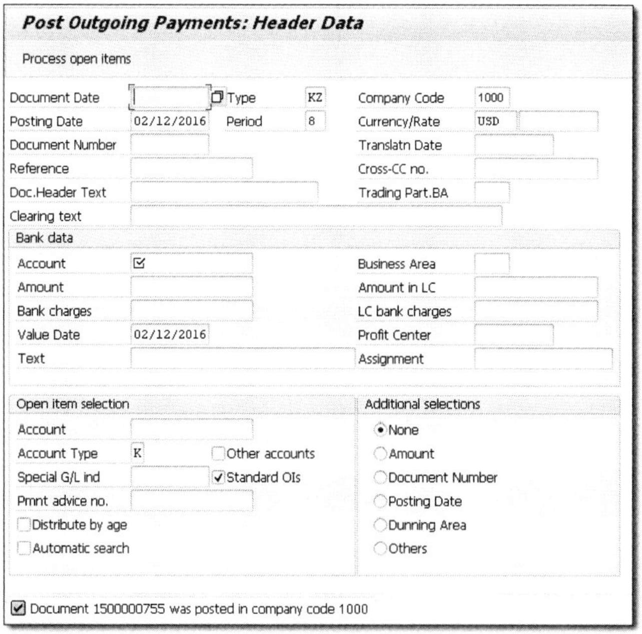

Figure 6.95 Document Posted Message

This concludes our example of issuing a vendor payment using Transaction F-53.

Transaction F-58 is another single-payment transaction. Like Transaction F-53, Transaction F-58 creates a payment entry that credits a bank account balance and clears an open A/P invoice. In addition, Transaction F-58 allows you to print a check.

We will not cover Transaction F-58 in detail in this section because it is so similar to Transaction F-53. However, if you want to try it for yourself, the transaction can be accessed in the A/P module from application menu path ACCOUNTING • FINANCIAL ACCOUNTING • ACCOUNTS PAYABLE • DOCUMENT ENTRY • OUTGOING PAYMENT • F-58 — POST + PRINT FORMS, as shown in Figure 6.96.

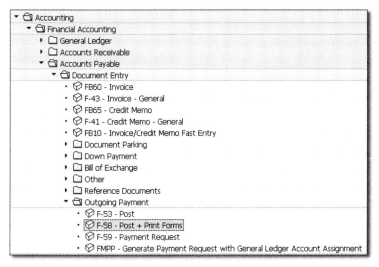

Figure 6.96 Transaction F-58 Application Menu Path

6.7 Summary

In this chapter, we covered A/P account transactions originating in the A/P module. In Chapter 5, during our discussion of the procure-to-pay process, you learned about procurement transactions originating in MM-Purchasing. In this chapter, however, the discussion was limited strictly to A/P transactions, not the procurement cycle as a whole.

The most common A/P transaction is the entry of a vendor invoice using Transaction FB60. Vendor invoices are the documents, which create open vendor liabilities and ultimately get paid. We also walked through examples of other A/P transactions, including the creation of a credit memo, down payment request, manual outgoing payment, and document reversals.

This chapter covered not only the creation of different A/P document types, but also document display, change, reverse, park, saved as completed, and hold. These are all important concepts in the day in the life of an A/P clerk or accounting supervisor.

In this chapter, the examples provided enabled you to learn of the differences between document posting, parking, save as completed, and hold. A posted document is an A/P document that is complete, produces an A/P accounting document number, and updates the A/P subledger and G/L account balances. Parking an A/P document allows you to save an A/P document without impacting the A/P subledger or G/L account balances. Sometimes parking is needed if further edits are required or if document approval is necessary. The save as completed function is similar to document parking, but the document undergoes document check logic, as though it was being posted. A document hold is a function to temporarily save your data. It is most useful when you are interrupted during document creation. The hold function produces no permanent document number until the document is parked or posted. Once again, these concepts are not unique to A/P. They are also applicable to G/L, A/R, and other accounting transactions.

Some other functions were discussed, as they relate to Transaction FB60 and other A/P transactions. These include topics such as the tree display, screen variants, account assignment templates, editing options, and post with reference. All are useful tools and are universal concepts in FI.

This concludes our discussion of A/P transactions. The next chapter is a detailed discussion of the A/P automatic payment program (Transaction F110).

In this chapter, the automatic payment program is discussed in detail. The automatic payment process is one of the more complex transactions in FI.

7   The Automated Payment Program Process

At first glance, the A/P automated payment program (Transaction F110) seems overwhelming—but don't worry. In this chapter, we will walk you through each step in the process and cover the knowledge you need to issue outgoing payments in mass. Repetition is your friend: As you work through the complete payment program a few times, you will begin to recognize the key points needed to complete a successful payment run. The more you practice, the easier it becomes.

To complete a successful payment run requires a mix of various configurations, master data, document settings, and detailed settings in Transaction F110. When errors occur, the key to handling them is to identify their source quickly and accurately. This chapter focuses specifically on the settings within the payment program, not on configuration, master data, or A/P documents. Becoming familiar with the payment program settings will help you learn how to identify the root cause of an error quickly.

This chapter steps you through all the major components of the automated payment program. These components include maintaining payment parameters, creating a payment proposal, and executing a payment run. Other important topics covered include a review of additional payment run logs and payment output.

Let's start by discussing how to access the automatic payment program and enter the payment parameters needed to run it.

7.1 The Automated Payment Program Process

The process steps for executing the automated payment program include maintaining payment program parameters, creating a payment proposal, and executing a payment run, in that order.

Begin by using Transaction F110 or application menu path ACCOUNTING • FINANCIAL ACCOUNTING • ACCOUNTS PAYABLE • PERIODIC PROCESSING • F110—PAYMENTS, as shown in Figure 7.1.

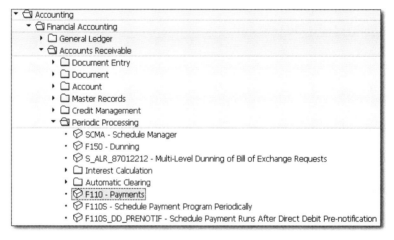

Figure 7.1 F110 Application Menu Path

Double-click F110—PAYMENTS from the menu path shown in Figure 7.1, or enter "F110" in the COMMAND field (Figure 7.2) and press ⌈Enter⌋.

Figure 7.2 F110 in Command Field

The AUTOMATIC PAYMENT TRANSACTIONS: STATUS screen will open (Figure 7.3). On this screen, you must enter values for the RUN DATE and IDENTIFICATION fields. The IDENTIFICATION field is limited to five characters, so building logic into the field value is important for reference. The logic you use will depend on the frequency and makeup of payment runs. You might also build in logic based on geography or your company's organizational structure. For example, you could use US001 to represent a payment run for the United States. Other examples might provide logic based on function. For example, you could use HR001 for issuing payroll or AP001 for vendor payments.

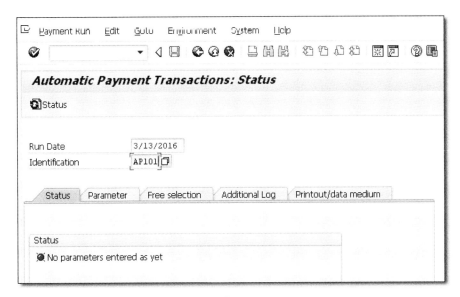

Figure 7.3 Automatic Payment Transaction: Status

7.1.1 Maintain Parameters.

After entering values for RUN DATE and IDENTIFICATION (Figure 7.3), click on the PARAMETER tab. The AUTOMATIC PAYMENT TRANSACTIONS: PARAMETERS screen will open (Figure 7.4). On this screen, the POSTING DATE field defaults to the RUN DATE. In this example, field values were manually entered for DOCS ENTERED UP TO, COMPANY CODES, PMT METHS (i.e., payment methods), NEXT P/DATE (i.e., next payment date), and VENDOR. For simplicity, this example only includes one company code, payment method, and vendor, but an automatic payment run can be executed with multiple values for each of these fields.

Of particular importance is the NEXT P/DATE field. The date you enter is the next date you expect to run the automatic payment program. This date is of particular importance for the program to determine what invoices will come due between the run date and the next payment date so that they can be included in this payment run.

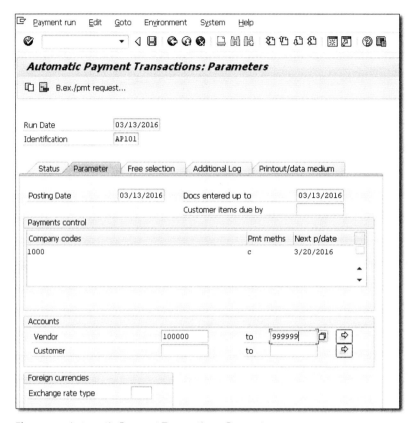

Figure 7.4 Automatic Payment Transactions: Parameters

Once all parameters have been entered, click the Save icon 🖫 to the right of the Command field, or press ⎡Ctrl⎤+⎡S⎤. A message will indicate that the details have been saved (Figure 7.5).

Once the parameter details have been saved, click on the Status tab. The Automatic Payment Transactions: Status screen will reopen (Figure 7.6), but this time with a green status indicator that says Parameters have been entered. In the header, you will see buttons for Proposal and Payment Run.

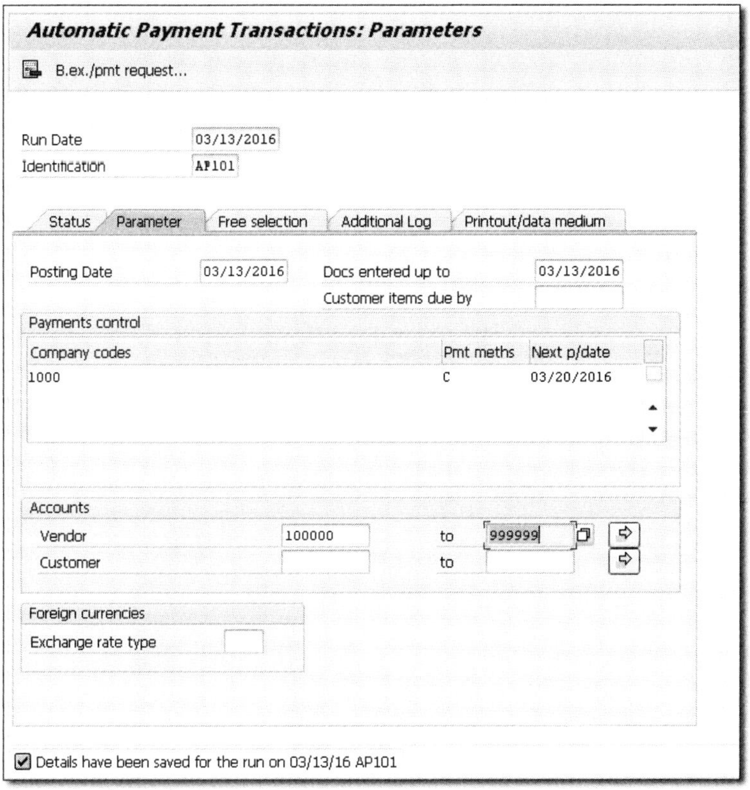

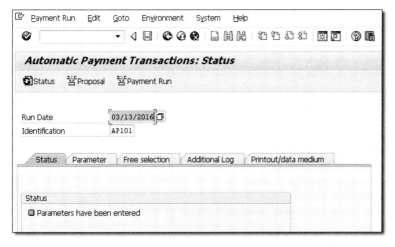

Figure 7.5 Parameter Details Have Been Saved Message

Figure 7.6 F110 Automatic Payment Transactions: Status Screen with Parameters

7.1.2 Create Payment Proposal

Once all payment program parameters have been saved (see Section 7.1.1), the next step is to create a payment proposal. As you likely guessed, this is the step in which the automatic payment program determines what invoices will be paid based on the parameters entered and generates a list of these items for your review. This list is referred to as the *payment proposal*.

To create the payment proposal, click on the PROPOSAL button shown at the top left of Figure 7.6; the SCHEDULE PROPOSAL dialog box will pop up (Figure 7.7). Check the START IMMEDIATELY box to generate the proposal immediately and the CREATE PAYMENT MEDIUM box to automatically schedule the creation of the payment medium (e.g., a check, an ACH file, etc.). Then, click the EXECUTE icon ✅ or press ⌐Enter⌐.

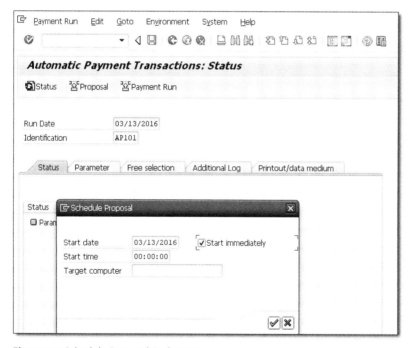

Figure 7.7 Schedule Proposal Dialog Box

When proposal creation is complete, the payment proposal completion message will appear (Figure 7.8), and in the STATUS screen you will see a green status indicator that reads, PAYMENT PROPOSAL HAS BEEN CREATED.

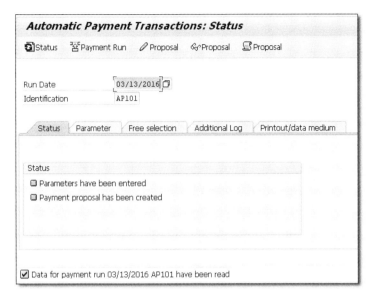

Figure 7.8 Payment Proposal Completion Messsage

To view the items contained in the proposal, click the DISPLAY PROPOSAL icon shown in Figure 7.8, and the DISPLAY PAYMENT PROPOSAL: PAYMENTS screen will open (Figure 7.9). The line with a green indicator in the TYPE field (the top line in Figure 7.9) indicates an item selected for payment, whereas the line with a red indicator (the bottom line in Figure 7.9) indicates an item not selected.

Figure 7.9 Display Payment Proposal: Payments

In this example, double-click the line with the green TYPE indicator to see the detail making up the payment amount. The DISPLAY PAYMENT PROPOSAL: OPEN ITEMS screen will open (Figure 7.10), showing individual documents, which can consist of open invoices, credit memos, and down payments.

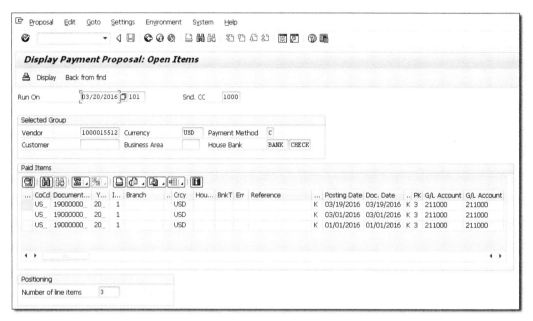

Figure 7.10 Display Payment Proposal: Open Items

Click on the BACK icon ↩ to return to the AUTOMATIC PAYMENT TRANSACTIONS: STATUS screen (Figure 7.8).

7.1.3 Execute Payment Run

Once the payment proposal is been created (see Section 7.1.2), the next step is to execute the payment run. This action creates payment entries in the G/L, creates payment documents, changes the status of open items to cleared status, and creates the payment medium to transfer funds.

To execute the payment run, click on the PAYMENT RUN button shown in the top left of Figure 7.8, and the SCHEDULE PAYMENT dialog box will pop up (Figure 7.11). Check the START IMMEDIATELY box to generate the payment run immediately and the CREATE PAYMENT MEDIUM box to automatically schedule the creation of the payment medium. Then, click the EXECUTE icon ✅ or press [Enter].

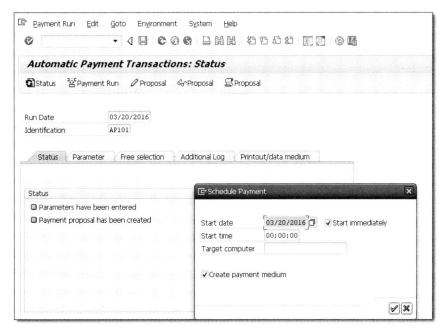

Figure 7.11 Schedule Payment Dialog Box

When the payment run is finished, a green status indicator will appear in the STA-TUS screen saying PAYMENT RUN HAS BEEN CARRIED OUT (Figure 7.12); it will include a list of the number of payment orders generated and completed.

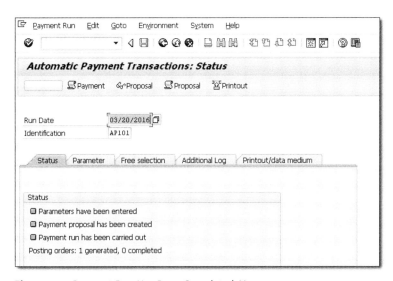

Figure 7.12 Payment Run Has Been Completed Message

In this example, the payment method is a check, which requires physically printing a check. Earlier (see Figure 7.11), we checked the CREATE PAYMENT MEDIUM box, which automatically created a spool request to print the checks. View the spool request using the dropdown menu path SYSTEM • OWN SPOOL REQUESTS.

The LIST OF SPOOL REQUESTS screen will open (Figure 7.13).

Figure 7.13 Output Controller: List of Spool Requests

To preview the output (i.e., checks) in the spool request, check the box in the spool number (SPOOL NO.) column and click the DISPLAY CONTENTS icon 🐾 , or press F6 . In this example, we select the checkbox for spool number 77857, and a print preview of the payment output appears (Figure 7.14).

Figure 7.14 Print Preview Payment Output

7.2   Additional Settings

In Section 7.1, we covered the basic settings to execute Transaction F110, the automated payment program. In this section, we will explore additional settings you can make to customize your payment run. These settings include free selection for field names and values, the additional log, and variants for printout/data medium.

7.2.1   Free Selection

In Section 7.1.1, we covered the topic of maintaining payment parameters for a payment run. When entering payment parameters, as shown in Figure 7.5, the selection criteria can be narrowed further by clicking the FREE SELECTION tab, which makes the AUTOMATIC PAYMENT TRANSACTIONS: FREE SELECTION screen appear (Figure 7.15).

Figure 7.15 Payment Program Free Selection

From this screen, you can select additional single or multiple field values to include or exclude in the payment run. First, select a field name; click on the FIELD NAME selection icon  to view available field selections. By default, only two FIELD LABEL choices appear: SP. G/L TRANS.TYPE (i.e., special G/L transaction types) and OTHERS.

For this example, double-click the OTHERS field label, and a dialogue box pops up with three options: DOCUMENT, VENDOR MASTER RECORD, and CUST. MASTER RECORD (Figure 7.16). This dialogue box allows you to choose the source of additional field selections, which include financial documents, vendor master data, or customer master data. This field selection capability gives you many more fields to choose from than are typically practical to use, but it is better to have too many choices than not enough.

Figure 7.16 Free Selection Dialogue Box for Other Fields

For this example, select DOCUMENT from the dialogue box shown in Figure 7.16 and press ⟨Enter⟩; a list of all specific field selection options will appear on the next screen (Figure 7.17).

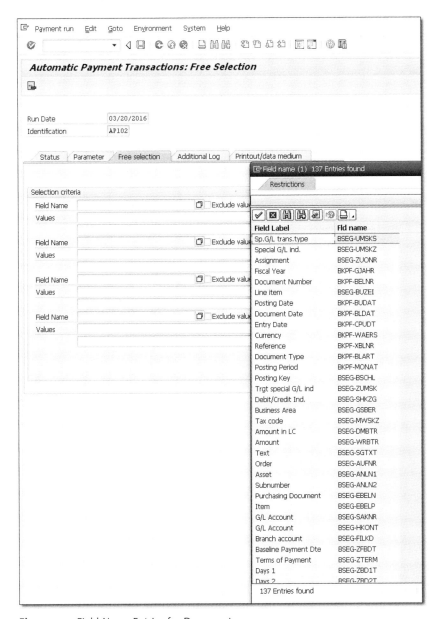

Figure 7.17 Field Name Entries for Documents

From the field entry selection, double-click the field you want to use. For this example, double-click on the Document Number field to return to the Automatic Payment Transactions: Free Selection screen, where the Field Name value is now populated (Figure 7.18).

Figure 7.18 Free Selection Screen with Field Name Value

Once you select a Field Name, specific field Values must be entered. The first notable point is that these values cannot be selected via drop down. In other words, you need to have the specific values for entry and manually enter them. The second notable point is about how you enter the field value. You can enter a single value, a range of values, or a combination thereof. For example, say that you want to enter four document numbers: 1900000001, 1900000004, 1900000005, and 1900000006. You can enter each of these document numbers individually, separated by commas, as shown in Figure 7.19.

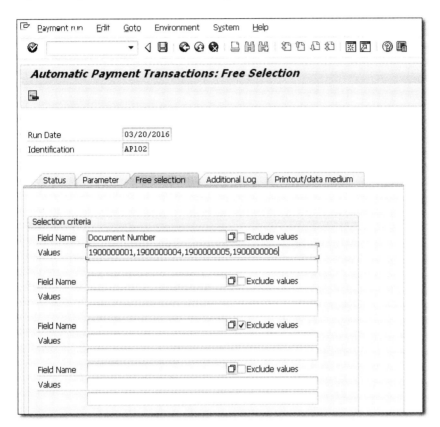

Figure 7.19 Free Selection Single Field Value Entry

Or you can enter the consecutive range of document numbers within brackets, with the start and end range separated by a comma, as shown in Figure 7.20.

Once all free selections are entered, click the SAVE icon 🖫 to the right of the COMMAND field or press Ctrl + S . Notice that multiple SELECTION CRITERIA can be entered, so you can repeat the process shown for additional field selections to further narrow your selection of items for payment.

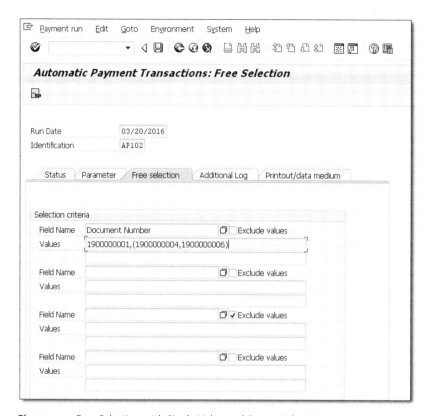

Figure 7.20 Free Selection with Single Value and Range Value Entry

7.2.2 Additional Logs

In Section 7.1.1, we covered the topic of maintaining payment parameters for a payment run. When entering payment parameters, as shown in Figure 7.5, additional trace elements can be selected for the logs created during the payment process by clicking the ADDITIONAL LOG tab. When you do so, the AUTOMATIC PAYMENT TRANSACTIONS: ADDITIONAL LOG screen opens (Figure 7.21). The checkboxes in the REQUIRED LOGGING TYPE portion of the screen allow you to choose additional elements to appear in the automatic payment program logs.

For example, if you select DUE DATE CHECK (Figure 7.22), the due date for open items is captured in the payment program log. This trace is most useful if there is any question about the accuracy of the due date calculation and why an open item is not be selected for payment. The due date check is an example of an additional log option that is frequently used by SAP customers.

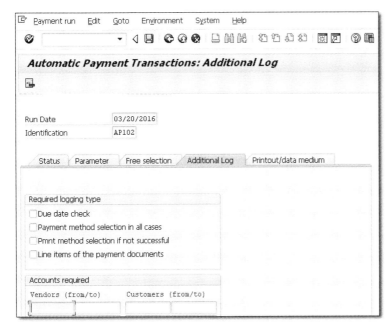

Figure 7.21 Payment Program Additional Log Screen

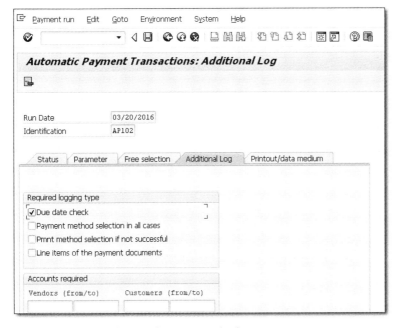

Figure 7.22 Additional Log with Due Date Check

There are three other checkboxes in the REQUIRED LOGGING TYPE section (Figure 7.22):

▶ PAYMENT METHOD SELECTION IN ALL CASES records the payment method and bank in the log for items selected for payment.

▶ PMNT METHOD SELECTION IF NOT SUCCESSFUL records the payment method and bank that are not permitted in the payment run. This option is particularly useful for troubleshooting errors in the payment run. It can point you to corrections that need to be made in either the vendor master record or the payment program configuration. This indicator can also help you determine why a particular open item may not be selected for payment under the payment program parameters you entered.

▶ LINE ITEMS OF THE PAYMENT DOCUMENTS provides a trace in the log of payment documents and line items. This information can be useful for tracking down a clearing document for an open item that was paid in error.

In Figure 7.22, the ACCOUNTS REQUIRED section at the bottom of the screen allows you to narrow your trace selection by vendors and customers. Note that you can enter individual vendor/customer numbers or a range of values.

7.2.3 Variants for Data Medium

In the configuration of payment methods, the format of the outgoing payments is set by assigning a payment medium program. You can also create your own payment formats using the Payment Medium Workbench. The payment program configuration and the Payment Medium Workbench are beyond the scope of this book, but you need to know that when you run the automatic payment program, the payment methods assigned in the payment parameters each have a data medium exchange (DME) program assigned that controls the output format of the payments.

In Section 7.1.1, we covered the topic of maintaining payment parameters for a payment run. When entering payment parameters, as shown in Figure 7.5, variants are assigned to the FORM PRINTING/DATA MEDIUM EXCHANGE programs assigned to the payment methods specified. Click the PRINTOUT/DATA MEDIUM tab to open the Aᴜᴛᴏᴍᴀᴛɪᴄ Pᴀʏᴍᴇɴᴛ Tʀᴀɴsᴀᴄᴛɪᴏɴs: Pʀɪɴᴛᴏᴜᴛ ᴀɴᴅ DME screen (Figure 7.23).

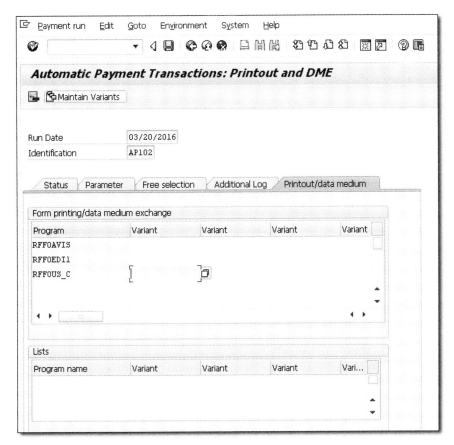

Figure 7.23 Payment Program Printout and DME Screen

Here, we will review a variant of the RFFOUS_C program. RFFOUS_C is a standard SAP DME program for checks. To select a variant from the Aᴜᴛᴏᴍᴀᴛɪᴄ Pᴀʏᴍᴇɴᴛ Tʀᴀɴsᴀᴄᴛɪᴏɴs: Pʀɪɴᴛᴏᴜᴛ ᴀɴᴅ DME screen, click the variant selection dropdown icon 🗗 shown in Figure 7.23 and choose your variant. In this example, we selected variant PRINT_US (Figure 7.24).

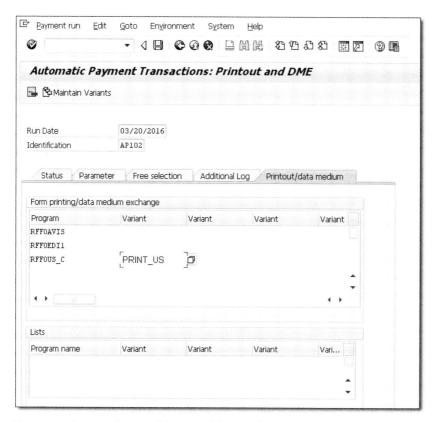

Figure 7.24 Payment Program Printout and DME with Variant Assigned Screen

To review and maintain a variant, have your cursor positioned on the variant you wish to view and click the MAINTAIN VARIANTS button. The EDIT VARIANT screen will open (Figure 7.25). This screen has many different field selections to maintain, and in the remainder of this section, we will discuss the essential fields for the RFFOUS_C program and highlight some of the other, more commonly used fields. Note, however, that the EDIT VARIANT screen will differ based upon the DME program used.

In this variant for program RFFOUS_C, the essential fields to maintain are PAYING COMPANY CODE, PAYMENT METHOD, HOUSE BANK, ACCOUNT ID, CHECK LOT NUMBER, and PRINT CHECKS with a printer specified. All these fields are essential for the program to know how to post in the G/L, the relevant bank account to credit, what check numbers to assign, and where to print checks.

Variant Edit Goto System Help

Maintain Variant: Report RFFOUS_C, Variant PRINT_US

Variant Attributes

Program run date

Identification feature

☐ Proposal run only

Company code selection

Paying company code	1000		
Sending company code		to	➩

Further selections

Payment method	C	to	➩
Pmt meth. supplement		to	➩
Business Area		to	➩
House Bank	BofA		
Account ID	B0001		
Check lot number	1		
Restart from Check Number			
Currency		to	➩
Payment document no.		to	➩

Print control

☑ Print checks	Printer	locl	☑ Print Immediately
☐ Print payment advice notes	Printer		☐ Print Immediately
☐ Print Payment Summary	Printer		☐ Print Immediately
☐ Payment Summary as ALV	Layout		☐ Screen Output

Output control

Alternative check form	
Filler for digits in words	
Number of sample printouts	
No.of items in payment summary	9999

☐ Payment Document Validation

☐ Texts in recipient's lang.

☐ Currency in ISO code

☐ No Form Summary Section

☐ Do not Void any Checks

Reprint checks

☐ Void and reprint checks from payment run already printed

Check number		to	
Void reason code			

Figure 7.25 Payment Program Edit Variant Screen

This variant has some other features that you should be aware of and fields that are not necessarily required but that, depending on your configuration and business processes, may be applicable. The header fields in this variant (Figure 7.26) consist of the PROGRAM RUN DATE and IDENTIFICATION FEATURE fields and a checkbox for PROPOSAL RUN ONLY.

Figure 7.26 Payment Program Variant Header Fields

The PROGRAM RUN DATE field lists the date on which you plan for the program payment run to take place, although you can run the program at an earlier or later date than the one specified. This field may be useful for a one-time payment run that requires unique settings in the variant. For recurring payment runs, you may choose to leave this field blank.

IDENTIFICATION FEATURE is a freely defined six-character field. It is not a required field, but it can be useful as a unique identifier if you use multiple DME variants for the same payment method.

The PROPOSAL RUN ONLY checkbox specifies to use the variant data during execution of the proposal run instead of the during the payment run. This poses some risks, and we do not suggest using this option without a valid need and not without thorough testing. As a general rule of thumb, only use fields on a variant if you need them.

The fields in the FURTHER SELECTIONS section of a variant (Figure 7.27) that may be of use to you include PMT METH. SUPPLEMENT and BUSINESS AREA. The usefulness of these fields depends upon your business requirements and how you use these fields in financial transactions. The main takeaway is that if you do use these fields, additional options exist for their use in the payment variant.

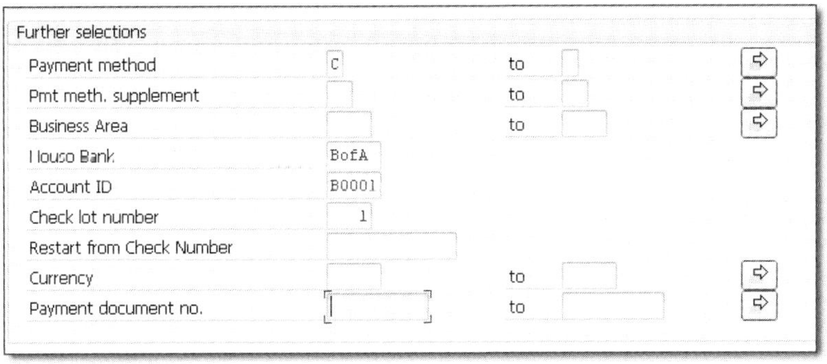

Figure 7.27 Payment Program Variant Further Selections

This concludes our discussion of additional settings in the automatic payment program. In the next section, we will discuss how to find details about and run inquiries on automatic payment runs that have been executed.

7.3 Automatic Payment Run Inquiries

During an automatic payment run or after one has been executed, an AP clerk or supervisor may need to provide summary-level detail about payment run output. CFOs, controllers, and treasury managers all need to know about impact to cash flow, and specific vendor inquiries may be requested for high-visibility vendors. The payment process plays a part in other vital business decisions as well.

For all these reasons and more, you should know how to report the details of a specific automatic payment run. In this section, we will discuss various automatic payment lists and overviews that you can use to provide this useful information.

7.3.1 Proposal Lists

It is common to receive a request from an A/P supervisor for the list of invoices in a payment proposal. The best practice is to thoroughly review the payment proposal and have it approved before an automatic payment run is completed. Upon review of a payment proposal, a supervisor may decide to exclude certain payments by blocking documents or vendors. By reviewing a proposal list, you may also find errors with the payment terms assigned in an A/P invoice or vendor master record. Whatever the issue, the payment proposal allows you to adjust transactions prior to finalizing your automatic payment run.

To generate a payment proposal list from Transaction F110, use the dropdown menu path EDIT • PROPOSAL • PROPOSAL LIST, as shown in Figure 7.28.

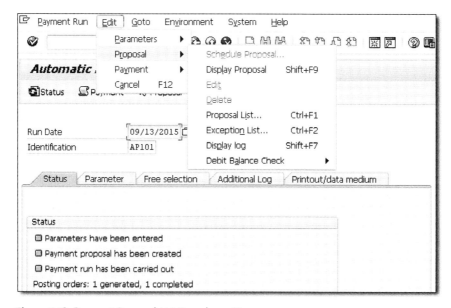

Figure 7.28 Payment Proposal List Dropdown Menu

The PAYMENT LIST screen will open (Figure 7.29) with a list of payment proposal items for the automatic payment run. More details are contained in the report then are shown in Figure 7.29, including a list of blocked items and totals broken out by each of the following categories: business area, company code, country, currency, payment method, and bank account. From this screen, you can also change the layout, download the list to a local file, or email the output.

To view a list of exceptions in the automated payment run, use the same report; the list of exceptions is provided, as shown in Figure 7.30.

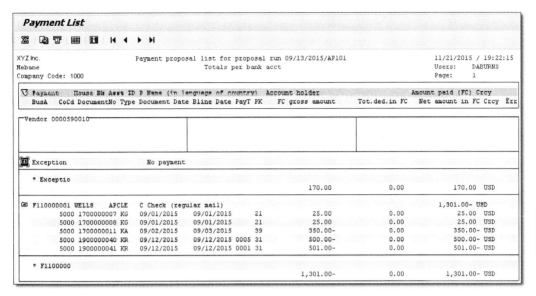

Figure 7.29 Payment Proposal List

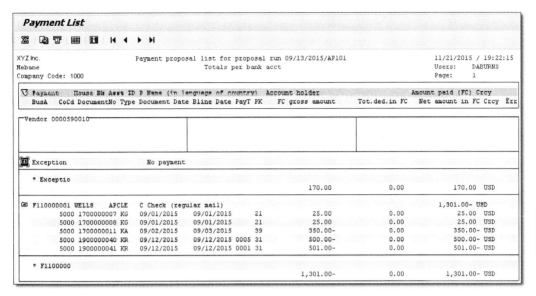

Figure 7.30 Payment Proposal Exceptions List

7.3.2 Payment Lists

It is also a common practice for an A/P supervisor to request the list of invoices paid after the payment run is completed. This should be part of your standard business process. To produce the payment list from Transaction F110 (Figure 7.31), use the dropdown menu path EDIT • PAYMENT • PAYMENT LIST.

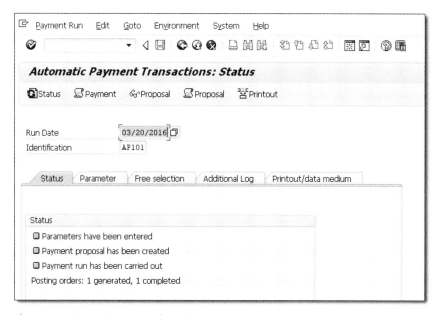

Figure 7.31 Payment List Dropdown Menu

The PAYMENT LIST screen will open (Figure 7.32) with payment items settled in your payment run. More details are contained in the report shown in Figure 7.32, including totals broken out by each of the following categories: business area, company code, country, currency, payment method, and bank account. From this screen, you can also change the layout, download the list to a local file, or email the output.

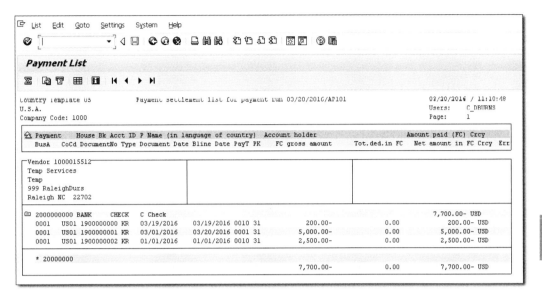

Figure 7.32 Payment Settlement List

7.4 Summary

The automated payment program (Transaction F110) is one of the most complicated transactions in FI. Several aspects of the system come together to make it run successfully, including configuration, master data, and Transaction F110 settings.

In this chapter, we covered the main steps in executing the automatic payment program. The first of these is the entry of payment parameters, which involves specifying exactly what is going to be paid and how payment program parameters establish the selection criteria for documents to be paid.

Next, we covered the creation of a payment proposal. The payment proposal is a list of vendor open items selected for payment, based upon the payment parameters entered. Frequently, SAP customers build in a review of the payment proposal as a process step prior to completing the automatic payment run. This is a safeguard to ensure the accuracy of payments prior to any physical money transfers taking place.

The last step is the execution of the payment run. In this step, payment documents are created, the G/L is updated, and a data medium is ready to be produced for the physical transfer of funds.

This chapter also went into greater detail on certain settings that may be useful to end users, including free selection, additional logs, and variants for DME, all of which play an important role in the automatic payment process.

We also discussed how to produce payment lists and proposal lists. These lists can be generated directly from Transaction F110. Within each list, you can change the report layout, download to a local file, or send the list via email. A thorough review of these lists are important to the validation and verification of outgoing payments.

In most companies, Transaction F110 is set up as a regularly scheduled job. However, it falls on the A/P team to ensure the payment program settings are accurate. When functional errors occur in an automatic payment run, it is the A/P clerks and supervisors who are responsible for identifying the root cause and fixing problems. Knowing the setup of Transaction F110, parameter maintenance, and vendor master data are essential. You also need to know how to execute Transaction F110 manually. Even if you have it setup as a schedule job, there will be times when you need to execute it manually.

Now that we've completed our discussion of the automated payment program, let's move on to discuss A/P inquiries in the next chapter.

In this chapter, well explore transactions and reports you can use on a daily basis for A/P account maintenance. Often, these tools simply validate vendor account details and payments, but they can also reveal errors and discrepancies in vendor account balances and line item details.

8   Accounts Payable Account Inquiries

This chapter provides you with A/P account inquiry and maintenance functions to help you research individual transactions, display account balances, view account transaction details, and run reports and queries.

A/P account inquiry and validation are essential job functions of an A/P clerk or supervisor. Often, you can use these functions to uncover data entry and other posting errors. Knowing how to perform the transactions in this chapter provides you with essential skills needed in the day-to-day operations of an A/P department.

These functions can be useful in the following ways:

▶ To reconcile A/P reconciliation balances against vendor subledger balances

▶ For month-end and year-end account analysis

▶ To assist with cash management needs and forecasting

▶ For vendor account inquiries

One of the ongoing challenges faced by an A/P department is the barrage of inquiries from vendors regarding their account balances and expected payment dates. This chapter provides you with the basic tools you need to address these types of inquiries and more.

In the next section, we will discuss the different types of vendor account balance displays in detail.

8.1   Vendor Account Displays

The A/P vendor account display allows you to view individual or collective vendor account balances and transaction details (i.e., individual A/P documents and line items). The primary transactions used to view vendor account details are Transaction FK10N and Transaction FBL1N.

One powerful feature of SAP is its drilldown capability. Specifically, within certain views of summary data, you have the ability to drilldown directly from that view to the line item details making up an account balance. Transactions FK10N and FBL1N provide good examples of this drilldown functionality. Starting directly in Transaction FK10N, you can double-click any account balance and automatically transfer to Transaction FBL1N to see a detailed view of the transaction details that make up the balance.

Now that we have discussed the basic capabilities of vendor account balances, let's look at specific examples in the following sections.

8.1.1   Vendor Account Balance

Transaction FK10N is the vendor account balance display transaction. It allows you to view the account balance of one or more vendors by accounting period. The display screen breaks down the vendor account balance into debit balance, credit balance, period balance, cumulative balance, and sales/purchases amounts, and you can double-click any of these numbers to drill down to the detailed transactions making up the balance.

To display vendor balances, use Transaction FK10N or application menu path ACCOUNTING • FINANCIAL ACCOUNTING • ACCOUNTS PAYABLE • ACCOUNT • FK10N — DISPLAY BALANCES, as shown in Figure 8.1.

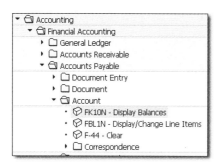

Figure 8.1 FK10N Application Menu Path

Double-click FK10N—DISPLAY BALANCES from the menu path shown in Figure 8.1, or enter "FK10N" in the COMMAND field (as shown in Figure 8.2) and press Enter .

Figure 8.2 FK10N in Command Field

The VENDOR BALANCE DISPLAY selection screen appears (Figure 8.3). Enter values for the VENDOR, COMPANY CODE, and FISCAL YEAR fields, then click the EXECUTE icon ⊕.

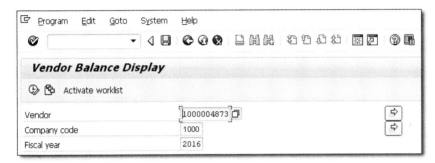

Figure 8.3 FK10N Vendor Balance Display Screen

The VENDOR BALANCE DISPLAY output screen appears (Figure 8.4). From this screen, you can double-click any account display to view balance details, or you can click the SPECIAL G/L tab to view balances for specific Special G/L transactions, such as down payments.

Transaction FK10N is frequently used to reconcile A/P with G/L liabilities. At a high level, it also provides the period breakdowns needed for reconciling month-end activities.

Although there are several standard reports from which you can obtain vendor account balances, Transaction FK10N is by far the most powerful and flexible tool available.

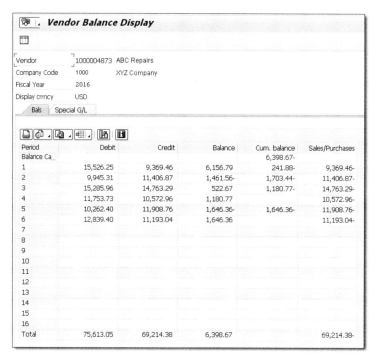

Figure 8.4 Vendor Balance Display Output

This concludes our discussion of vendor account balances. In the next section, let's discuss vendor account line items.

8.1.2 Vendor Account Line Items

Transaction FBL1N is the vendor line item display. It provides all the individual documents and accounting line items posted to a vendor account. When using this transaction code, selection screens give you the flexibility to filter data by vendor account, company code, posting date, type of transaction, and more. These selection options can be saved as variants, making them reusable. In addition, you can filter, search, sort, subtotal, and more from the output screen. The output can be downloaded into various file formats (e.g., Excel) making further analysis outside SAP possible when needed.

Before going any further, it's important for you to understand the concept of open item management. This SAP concept is how the system tracks, matches, and manages vendor line items that are supposed to be offset (i.e., cleared) by other accounting entries and net to zero. For example, when a vendor invoice is received, an accounting document will post a line item credit to the vendor account. This credit is considered an open item because it has created an open payable (i.e., liability) due to the vendor. Once payment is issued to the vendor, the open liability is matched with an offsetting debit to the vendor account and its status is changed from open to cleared.

Issuing an outgoing vendor payment creates a payment document, which also acts as a system clearing document. This clearing document creates a debit entry to the vendor account and a credit to cash. Therefore, the vendor liability is matched with the outgoing payment and nets to zero, indicating that the open liability no longer exists.

With the concept of open item management in mind, Transaction FBL1N is particularly useful for showing the status of an invoice (i.e., open or cleared) and the due date for each invoice. It is an essential tool for handling vendor inquiries regarding the status of invoices and payments. Often, when a vendor claims that a payment is overdue, an A/P clerk's first response will be to use Transaction FBL1N to verify that the invoice does indeed have an open status.

Transaction FBL1N is often a frequently used tool during month-end and year-end close. For details on financial close processes, see Chapter 16 and Chapter 17.

To display vendor line items using Transaction FBL1N, follow application menu path ACCOUNTING • FINANCIAL ACCOUNTING • ACCOUNTS PAYABLE • ACCOUNT • FBL1N—DISPLAY/CHANGE LINE ITEMS, as seen in Figure 8.5.

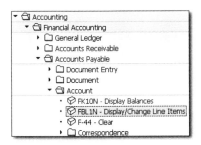

Figure 8.5 FBL1N Application Menu Path

Double-click FBL1N—DISPLAY/CHANGE LINE ITEMS from the menu path shown in Figure 8.5, or enter "FBL1N" in the COMMAND field (as shown in Figure 8.6) and press Enter.

Figure 8.6 FBL1N in Command Field

The VENDOR LINE ITEM DISPLAY selection screen will open (Figure 8.7). Enter values in the VENDOR ACCOUNT and COMPANY CODE fields. The most notable components of this selection screen are the STATUS and TYPE sections under LINE ITEM SELECTION. The STATUS buttons allow you to choose to see OPEN ITEMS, CLEARED ITEMS, or both (i.e., ALL ITEMS). You can also narrow your data selection by entering relevant date parameters.

The checkboxes in the TYPE section allow you to choose the types of documents to display on the output screen.

Figure 8.7 FBL1N Vendor Line Item Display Selection

Once you have entered all your selection parameters, click the EXECUTE icon ⊕. The VENDOR LINE ITEM DISPLAY output screen will open (Figure 8.8).

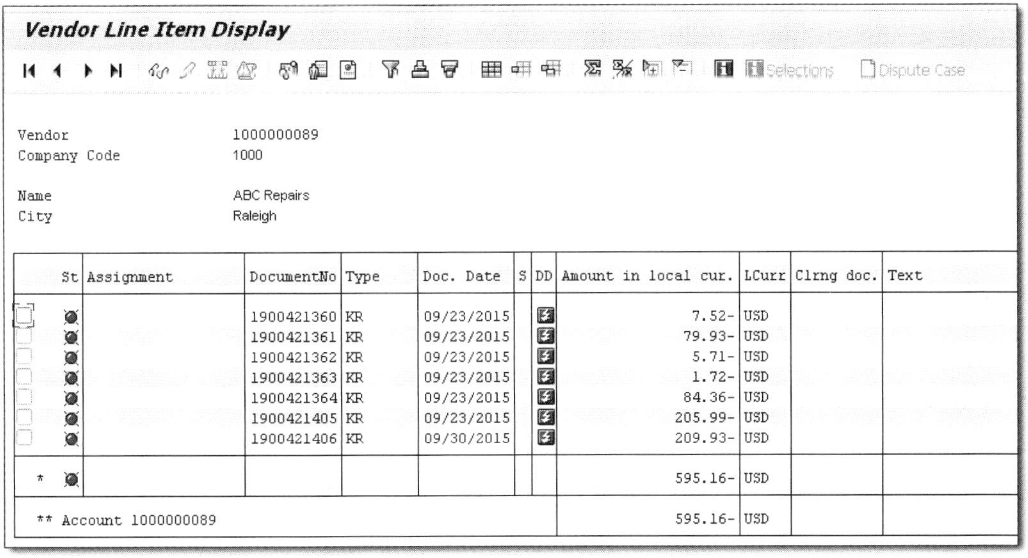

Vendor Line Item Display

	St	Assignment	DocumentNo	Type	Doc. Date	S	DD	Amount in local cur.	LCurr	Clrng doc.	Text
			1900421360	KR	09/23/2015			7.52-	USD		
			1900421361	KR	09/23/2015			79.93-	USD		
			1900421362	KR	09/23/2015			5.71-	USD		
			1900421363	KR	09/23/2015			1.72-	USD		
			1900421364	KR	09/23/2015			84.36-	USD		
			1900421405	KR	09/23/2015			205.99-	USD		
			1900421406	KR	09/30/2015			209.93-	USD		
*								595.16-	USD		
**	Account 1000000089							595.16-	USD		

Vendor 1000000089
Company Code 1000

Name ABC Repairs
City Raleigh

Figure 8.8 FBL1N Vendor Line Item Display Output

Now, you can change the layout, sort, filter, total, subtotal, and so on by using icons on the toolbar. Transaction FBL1N also allows you to double-click an individual line item to drill down directly into an A/P invoice or other A/P document, such as a credit memo or down payment. Once in an A/P document, you can then drill down into individual line items in the document.

Table 8.1 below is a list some useful icons frequently used in Transaction FBL1N.

Icon	Description
𝒢	Click once on the document you want to display and then click on this display document icon.
𝒫	Click once on the document you want to change and then click on this change document icon.
🖫	If a vendor invoice was paid by check, click once on the document and then click on this display check information icon.

Table 8.1 Frequently Used Icons in Transaction FBL1N

Icon	Description
▼	To filter data in the view, click on this icon. Then define your field criteria (i.e. select fields to filter and values).
▲	To sort data in ascending order, click once on a column header and then this sort in ascending order icon.
▼	To sort data in descending order, click once on a column header and then this sort in descending order icon.
▦	To change the screen layout, click on the change layout icon. Then select fields and order of display.
▦	To select a different predefined screen layout, click on the select layout icon. In the popup window, double-click on the screen layout you wish to use.
▦	Use the save layout icon to save changes you've made to the screen layout.
Σ	To total data, click once on a column header and then this display sum icon.
‰	To subtotal data, click once on a column header and then this subtotal icon

Table 8.1 Frequently Used Icons in Transaction FBL1N (Cont.)

In addition to the icons in Table 8.1, several additional actions are available from the drop-down menu. For example, the drop-down menu path LIST • EXPORT • SPREADSHEET allows you to export vendor line item detail from the screen to a spreadsheet.

The vendor line item display is the most powerful tool at your disposal for checking the status of an invoice or payment. A/P clerks and supervisors use it frequently, and it is often the first stop when fielding an inquiry about a vendor account balance, the status of an invoice, or the status of a payment.

8.2   Due Date Analysis

One of the most common inquiries sent to an A/P department is the question of when a particular invoice is due for payment. The quickest and easiest way to find the answer is using Transaction FBL1N, which is covered in detail in Section 8.1.2.

Within vendor line item display, two fields are most relevant to due date determination: NET DUE DATE and NET DUE DATE SYMBOL. The NET DUE DATE SYMBOL graphically represents whether an item is not due, due, or overdue. All three symbols are represented in Figure 8.9 in the column DD.

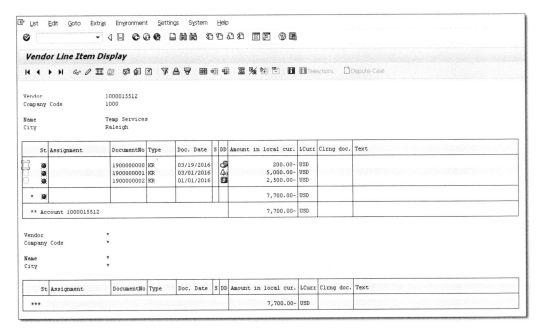

Figure 8.9 FBL1N Output with Due Date Symbols

The OVERDUE symbol ![icon] will appear anytime an invoice is unpaid and the current date is past the payment due date.

The DUE symbol ![icon] will appear anytime an invoice is unpaid and the current date equals the payment due date.

The NOT DUE symbol ![icon] will appear anytime an invoice is unpaid and the current date is less than the payment due date.

See Figure 8.21 for further discussion of due date analysis.

8.3 Payment History

After a vendor invoice has been paid, it will show up as a cleared item in Transaction FBL1N. A paid invoice will appear in the vendor line item display with a clearing document, payment date, and payment method.

To view a cleared vendor line item using Transaction FBL1N, follow application menu path ACCOUNTING • FINANCIAL ACCOUNTING • ACCOUNTS PAYABLE • ACCOUNT • FBL1N—DISPLAY/CHANGE LINE ITEMS, as shown in Figure 8.10.

Figure 8.10 FBL1N Application Menu Path

The VENDOR LINE ITEM DISPLAY selection screen will open (Figure 8.11). Enter values in the VENDOR ACCOUNT and COMPANY CODE fields. For this example, to see a payment issued, we selected the CLEARED ITEMS status option and entered a value in the CLEARING DATE field.

Vendor Line Item Display

⊕ 🗗 ⨮ 🔢 Data Sources

Vendor selection

Vendor account	1000000089	to		➡
Company code	1000	to		➡

Selection using search help

Search help ID	
Search string	
➡ Search help	

Line item selection

Status

○ Open items
Open at key date

◉ Cleared items

Clearing date		to	➡
Open at key date			

○ All items

Posting date		to	➡

Type

☑ Normal items
☐ Special G/L transactions
☐ Noted items
☐ Parked items
☐ Customer items

Figure 8.11 FBL1N Vendor Line Item Display with Cleared Items Selected

With all field values entered, click the EXECUTE icon ⊕. The VENDOR LINE ITEM DISPLAY screen will open, showing the date the vendor invoice was paid, the payment method, and the clearing document number (Figure 8.12).

Vendor Line Item Display

Vendor   1000000089
Company Code   1000

Name   ABC Repairs
City   Raleigh

Account	Reference	BusA	DocumentNo	Doc. Date	Check number	Amount in local cur.	EncashDate	Pstng Date
1000000089	2100514954	5100	1900001640	09/19/2005	0000000100987	84.11-	11/03/2005	10/20/2005
1000000089		5100	2000001260	10/20/2005	0000000100987	84.11	11/03/2005	10/20/2005
1000000089	2100514954A	5100	1900001641	09/19/2005	0000000101040	7.13-	11/04/2005	10/20/2005
1000000089	2100514970	5100	1900001868	09/19/2005	0000000101040	9.17-	11/04/2005	10/24/2005
1000000089	2100517381	5100	1900001871	09/26/2005	0000000101040	82.18-	11/04/2005	10/24/2005
1000000089	2100517381A	5100	1900001873	09/26/2005	0000000101040	7.13-	11/04/2005	10/24/2005
1000000089	2100517398	5100	1900001878	09/26/2005	0000000101040	9.17-	11/04/2005	10/24/2005
1000000089		5100	2000001314	10/26/2005	0000000101040	114.78	11/04/2005	10/26/2005
1000000089	2100524122	6110	1900001556	10/12/2005	0000000101409	21.41-	11/07/2005	10/19/2005
1000000089	2100519914	5100	1900002126	10/03/2005	0000000101409	82.27-	11/07/2005	10/25/2005
1000000089	2100519914	5100	1900002127	10/03/2005	0000000101409	36.61-	11/07/2005	10/25/2005
1000000089	2100519931	5100	1900002136	10/03/2005	0000000101409	9.35-	11/07/2005	10/25/2005
1000000089		6110	2000001679	10/27/2005	0000000101409	21.41	11/07/2005	10/27/2005
1000000089		5100	2000001679	10/27/2005	0000000101409	128.23	11/07/2005	10/27/2005
1000000089	2100521535	4190	1900003208	10/05/2005	0000000101723	15.51-	11/10/2005	11/01/2005
1000000089	2100526713	4190	1900003210	10/19/2005	0000000101723	319.31-	11/10/2005	11/02/2005
1000000089	2100526715	4190	1900003211	10/19/2005	0000000101723	15.51-	11/10/2005	11/02/2005
1000000089	2100524121	4190	1900003212	10/12/2005	0000000101723	15.51-	11/10/2005	11/02/2005
1000000089	2100524119	4190	1900003213	10/05/2005	0000000101723	261.63-	11/10/2005	11/02/2005
1000000089	2100521533	4190	1900003214	10/05/2005	0000000101723	287.10-	11/10/2005	11/02/2005
1000000089		4190	2000002017	11/02/2005	0000000101723	914.57	11/10/2005	11/02/2005
1000000089	2100519916	5100	1900002128	10/03/2005	0000000102405	36.61-	11/21/2005	10/25/2005
1000000089	2100524120	5100	1900003704	10/12/2005	0000000102405	14.17-	11/21/2005	11/08/2005
1000000089	2100522536	5100	1900003706	10/10/2005	0000000102405	81.99-	11/21/2005	11/08/2005
1000000089	2100522536	5100	1900003707	10/10/2005	0000000102405	7.13-	11/21/2005	11/08/2005
1000000089	2100522537	5100	1900003708	10/10/2005	0000000102405	34.94-	11/21/2005	11/08/2005
1000000089	2100522538	5100	1900003709	10/10/2005	0000000102405	36.55-	11/21/2005	11/08/2005
1000000089		5100	2000002698	11/09/2005	0000000102405	211.39	11/21/2005	11/09/2005
1000000089	2100519915	5100	1900002135	10/03/2005	0000000103886	35.45-	11/30/2005	10/25/2005
1000000089	2100529305	4190	1900006468	10/26/2005	0000000103886	278.61-	11/30/2005	11/22/2005
1000000089	2100531968	4190	1900006470	11/02/2005	0000000103886	15.51-	11/30/2005	11/22/2005

Figure 8.12 FBL1N Vendor Line Item Display with Paid Invoice

Transaction FBL1N is frequently used to find out when a vendor invoice was paid. The program's flexibility makes it a valuable tool in making this kinds of inquiries. You can search for cleared items for one or more vendors, on specific date, or by referencing a specific invoice or clearing document number.

8.4 Check Register

Check management is an important function in A/P. You can issue checks using the automatic payment program or manually. Check management also includes voiding checks, replacing lost or stolen checks, renumbering, reassignment, canceling payment, and deleting checks.

The complete list of check information functions is provided in Figure 8.13. To get to these folders, follow application menu path ACCOUNTING • FINANCIAL ACCOUNTING • ACCOUNTS PAYABLE • ENVIRONMENT • CHECK INFORMATION.

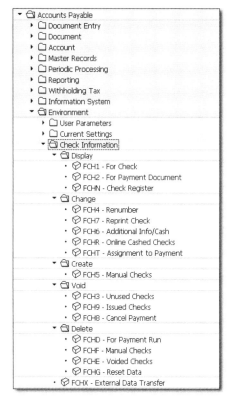

Figure 8.13 Application Menu Path for Check Information

You need to be aware of these functions and transactions. There are many circumstances where you will need to reprint a check using Transaction FCH7, or cancel a check using Transaction FCH8.

The remainder of this section focuses on the central check management tool: the *check register*. This program generates a list of all check registers belonging to a company code, based on the selection criteria you choose. It also allows you to create checklists, which may consist of outstanding checks, voided checks, payroll checks, or other options.

The check register is a one-stop shop for information about checks on an individual or collective basis. It allows you to see all the information associated with a check, including payment date, amount, vendor, encashment/void date, and much more.

To view the check register, follow application menu path ACCOUNTING • FINANCIAL ACCOUNTING • ACCOUNTS PAYABLE • ENVIRONMENT • CHECK INFORMATION • DISPLAY • FCHN — CHECK REGISTER, as shown in Figure 8.14.

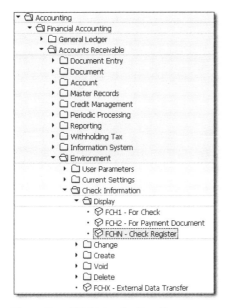

Figure 8.14 FCHN Application Menu

Double-click FCHN — CHECK REGISTER from the menu path, or enter "FCHN" in the COMMAND field (as shown in Figure 8.15) and press [Enter].

Figure 8.15 FCHN in Command Field

The CHECK REGISTER selection screen will open (Figure 8.16). In the header, enter field values for the PAYING COMPANY CODE, HOUSE BANK, and ACCOUNT ID fields; you also have the option to include payroll checks.

In the main body of the selection screen, you will see two selection tabs: Under GENERAL SELECTIONS, you can narrow your search by bank, bank account, specific check number, currency, or amount, and you will see selection options that influence output control and layouts. If you want to narrow your selection even more, move to the FURTHER SELECTIONS tab for additional field selection options.

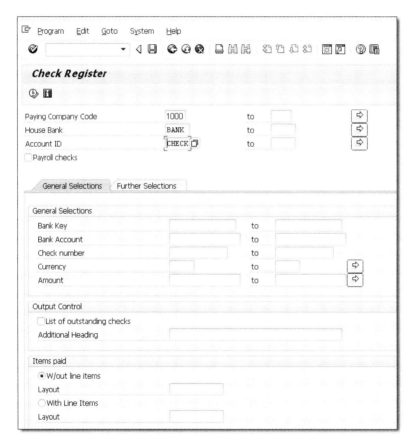

Figure 8.16 FCHN Check Register Selection Screen

Once you have entered all your selection parameters, click the EXECUTE icon ⊕. The CHECK REGISTER output screen will open (Figure 8.17).

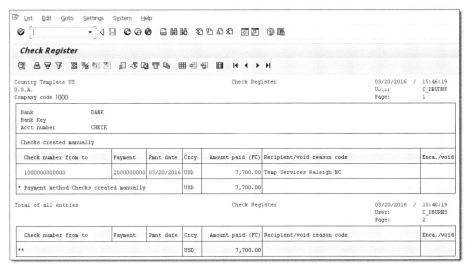

Figure 8.17 FCHN Check Register Output Screen

From this screen, you can see virtually any data associated with a check. You can also drill down, sort, filter, total, subtotal, export, and change the line layout.

Double-click on a line item within the check registry and the DISPLAY CHECK INFORMATION screen appears (Figure 8.18).

Display Check Information

Check recipient | Check issuer... | Accompanying docs | Payment document

Paying company code: 1000   Payment document no.: 2000001260

Bank details

House Bank	BAMER	Bank Key	061101223
Account ID	0001	Bank Account	123456789
Bank name	Bank of America		
City			

Check information

Check number	0000000100001	Currency	USD
Payment date	10/20/2005	Amount paid	84.11
Check encashment	11/03/2005	Cash discount amount	0.00

Check recipient

Name	Unilever
City	Raleigh
Payee's country	US
Regional code	NC

Figure 8.18 Display Check Information Screen

Click on the CHECK RECIPIENT button to display the name and address where the check was sent (Figure 8.19).

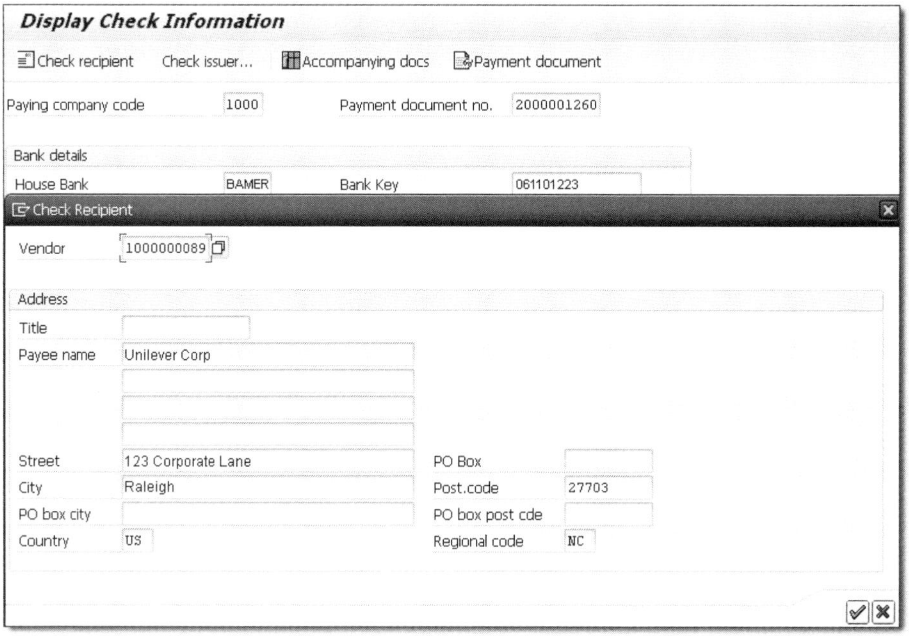

Figure 8.19 Display Check Recipient

From Figure 8.18, click on the CHECK ISSUER... icon to display the payment run from which the check was generated. This information is displayed in Figure 8.20. As you can see, the screen displays associated information, such as the payment run date, identification, user, date and time.

As you can see, the check register is an indispensable tool and frequently used by any A/P department. As an alternative to Transaction FCHN, you can also view the check register via standard report S_P99_41000101 – Check Register. You can access this report using follow application menu path ACCOUNTING • FINANCIAL ACCOUNTING • ACCOUNTS PAYABLE • INFORMATION SYSTEM • REPORTS FOR ACCOUNTS PAYABLE ACCOUNTING • PAYMENT TRANSACTIONS • S_P99_41000101 — CHECK REGISTER, as shown in Figure 8.21.

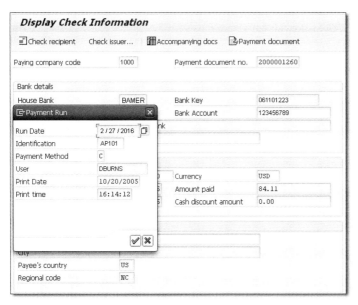

Figure 8.20 Display Check Issuer

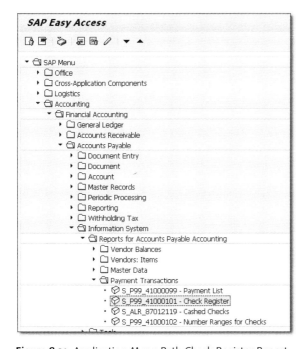

Figure 8.21 Application Menu Path Check Register Report

This concludes our discussion of the check register. In the next section, we'll discuss other standard reports available in A/P.

8.5   Reports and Queries

In Section 8.1, we discussed vendor account displays in detail, including Transactions FK10N and FBL1N. For validating vendor account balances and transaction details, these transactions are the most beneficial, particularly because of their ability to drill down into accounting documents. However, other tools do exist to view vendor account balances and transaction details. In this section, we will show you where to find these alternatives in A/P reports and queries.

Standard reports are SAP delivered and are universally found in the INFORMATION SYSTEM folder of the application menu. The most useful general-purpose A/P account balance reports can be accessed from application menu path ACCOUNTING • FINANCIAL ACCOUNTING • ACCOUNTS PAYABLE • INFORMATION SYSTEM • REPORTS FOR ACCOUNTS PAYABLE ACCOUNTING, as shown in Figure 8.22.

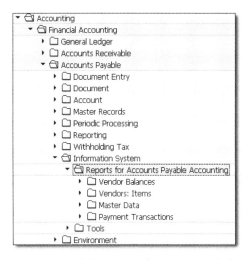

Figure 8.22 A/P Reports Application Menu Path

Many standard reports exist for viewing vendor balances, line items, payment transactions, and master data. Let's look at one report in more detail as an example.

Vendor due date analysis is the process of determining how much is due to be paid in a given period of time. The most comprehensive tool is Report S_ALR_87012078 – Due Date Analysis for Open Items.

To perform due date analysis, use Transaction S_ALR_87012078 or application menu path ACCOUNTING • FINANCIAL ACCOUNTING • ACCOUNTS PAYABLE • INFORMATION SYSTEM • REPORTS FOR ACCOUNTS PAYABLE ACCOUNTING • VENDOR ITEMS • S_ALR_87012078 – DUE DATE ANALYSIS FOR OPEN ITEMS, as shown in Figure 8.23.

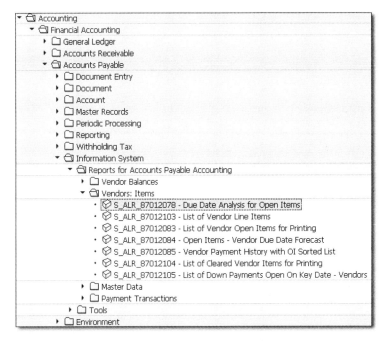

Figure 8.23 S_ALR_87012078 Application Menu Path

Double-click S_ALR_87012078 – DUE DATE ANALYSIS from the menu path shown in Figure 8.23, and the S_ALR_87012078 report selection screen will open (Figure 8.24). For this example, we entered one value each for VENDOR ACCOUNT and COMPANY CODE, although multiple values are permitted. The field value for OPEN ITEMS AT KEY DATE defaults to the current date, but it can be overwritten. In the OUTPUT TYPE section, multiple choices exist, and you should try them all. For this example, we selected the first option: GRAPHICAL REPORT OUTPUT.

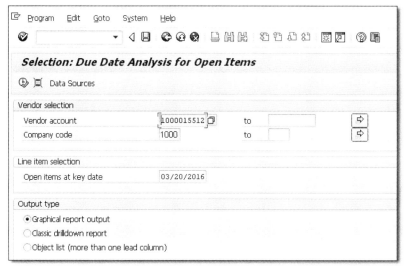

Figure 8.24 Report S_ALR_87012078 Selection Screen

When all screen field values are entered, click the EXECUTE icon ⊕. The output screen for the due date analysis report will open (Figure 8.25), showing amounts currently due for the vendor selected.

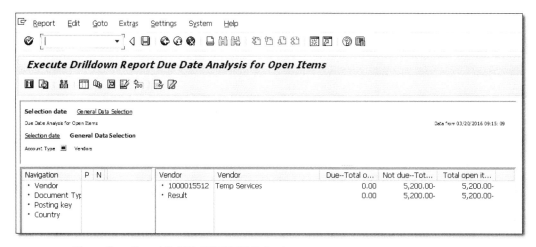

Figure 8.25 Report S_ALR_87012078 Output

From the output screen, you can drill down, navigate using other objects, or export the data.

Another useful standard A/P report is Report S_ALR_87012082—Vendor Balances in Local Currency. Access Report S_ALR_87012082 using application menu path ACCOUNTING • FINANCIAL ACCOUNTING • ACCOUNTS PAYABLE • INFORMATION SYSTEM • REPORTS FOR ACCOUNTS PAYABLE ACCOUNTING • VENDOR BALANCES • S_ALR_87012082—VENDOR BALANCES IN LOCAL CURRENCY, as shown in Figure 8.26.

Figure 8.26 S_ALR_87012082 Application Menu Path

Double-click S_ALR_87012082—VENDOR BALANCES IN LOCAL CURRENCY from the menu path shown in Figure 8.26, and the VENDOR BALANCES IN LOCAL CURRENCY selection screen will open (Figure 8.27). For this example, we entered values for the VENDOR ACCOUNT and COMPANY CODE fields. Values will default into the FISCAL YEAR and REPORTING PERIODS fields.

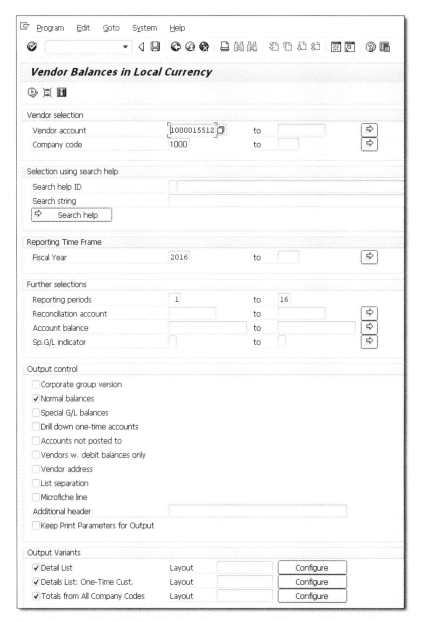

Figure 8.27 S_ALR_87012082 Vendor Balances in Local Currency Selection Screen

When all screen field values are entered, click the Execute icon ⊕. The output screen for the report will open (Figure 8.28), showing vendor balances.

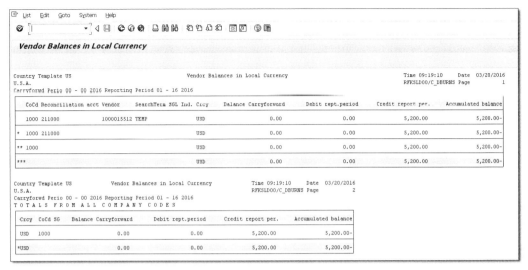

Figure 8.28 S_ALR_87012082 Vendor Balances in Local Currency Output Screen

Drilldown capability does not exist in Report S_ALR_87012082, but for a nice view of vendor balances, this report serves the purpose well.

8.6 Summary

In Chapter 6, we covered transactions in A/P that you will use on a daily basis, and in Chapter 7, we covered the automatic payment program. Then, in this chapter, we demonstrated transactions and reports you can use in your day-to-day work in vendor account maintenance. The topics covered in this chapter also assist you in making inquiries and troubleshooting problems, based on vendor transaction detail in the A/P module. Often, you will use these tools simply to validate vendor account details and payments, but these are essential tools utilized daily in an accounting department.

Transaction codes FK10N and FBL1N are used to view account balances and line item details. These are among the most common A/P transactions executed in the system. Frequent use of these transactions and reports is essential to understanding the activity in A/P. Their drilldown capability makes them powerful and flexible tools. Drilldown capability exists within them to drill all the way from an A/P vendor account balance down to an individual document.

In A/P, account maintenance is the name of the game. The tools provided in this chapter provide you with the ability to answer inquiries, adjust vendor account balances, and perform account maintenance. A/P is not a static event, and you need programs at your disposal.

In an A/P department, it is essential to quickly track down the status of an invoice, a payment, and other vendor account transactions. Vendor account displays and standard reports give you the ability to do this. Check management is another important function, and the transaction register (i.e., Transaction FCHN) is a one-stop shop for check information. Transaction FCHN is used to display the check register. As an alternative, standard report S_P99_41000101 also displays the check register.

This concludes our discussions of A/P. In the next chapter, we look at the Accounts Receivable module and accounts receivable processes.

In this chapter, we discuss A/R business processes and integration with the Sales and Distribution module through the order-to-cash business process.

9   Accounts Receivable Processes

The purpose of the Accounts Receivable (A/R) module is to manage customer accounts and internal payments. From a finance and accounting perspective, this is a critical part of doing business—some would argue the most important part, because without customers and revenue, there is no business.

In many ways, this argument holds true. The sustainability of a company depends upon a solid business model and revenue growth. This does not mean that you should ignore other aspects of business operations. However, revenue is necessary to build and sustain a business and a fundamental factor in the profitability of a company.

There are several different A/R business processes. These include such processes as credit management, disputes management, and bad debt. These business functions are all important. The objective of this chapter, however, is to focus on the order-to-cash business process. This business process consists of the following steps:

1. Create sales order
2. Create outbound delivery
3. Customer billing
4. Receivables management
5. Payment receipt

As we explore the order-to-cash process in detail, we cover two distinct business functions. The first is sales. Sales involves customer-facing activities that ultimately result in a commitment from customers to buy goods or services from your company. Sales always involves product delivery, customer satisfaction, and other associated functions.

The second business function we will discuss is A/R management, which is the operational management of customer accounts and outstanding receivables. This accounting function involves monitoring and maintaining customer accounts, collecting money, reporting, and more. Together, sales and A/R management influence revenue forecasts, profitability, cash management, human resources, and more.

Now that you understand the basics, let's begin to discuss the order-to-cash process in detail. SAP business processes often consist of steps that are cross-modular, and the order-to-cash process is an example of this. Order to cash is a core business process within SAP and serves as an excellent example of SAP ERP integration. We will focus on this process in this chapter in order demonstrate the integration between the Sales and Distribution (SD) module and A/R.

Transactions in SD are many and can be complex, and we will not attempt to discuss them all in detail here. The intent of this chapter is to provide you with enough knowledge to understand the basic integration of A/R with SD. In addition, it's important for accountants and financial managers to understand the dependencies in A/R. This knowledge will serve you well in better performing certain functions, such as financial close.

Beyond providing you with an understanding of SD and FI integration, the primary objective of this chapter is to distinguish a billing document and an A/R invoice created as a subsequent document to a billing document. We also differentiate direct invoices from those invoices created automatically in the order-to-cash process. Finally, we will discuss A/R process exceptions in order to give you an understanding of when and how transactions can be used for credit memos, document reversals, or to change to a posted document.

9.1 Logistics

The order-to-cash process begins in the Sales and Distribution module (SD), which is a component of logistics. Logistics functionality in SAP covers a broad spectrum of capabilities and SAP modules. Some of the modules in logistics include SD, Material Management, Production, Plant Maintenance and Quality Management (see Figure 9.1).

Figure 9.1 Application Menu for Logistics

Within the SD module, there are also numerous capabilities. As you can see in Figure 9.2, the capabilities that exist in SD include sales support, sales, shipping and transportation, billing, etc.

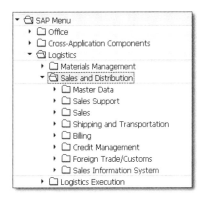

Figure 9.2 Application Menu Path for Sales and Distribution

In this chapter, our discussions are limited to those portions of SD relevant to the sale, delivery, and billing of goods or services—specifically, transactions in SD-Sales and SD-Billing.

As finance and accounting professionals, we like to think that revenue just shows up at our doorstep, and all we have to do is tend to the accounting and maintenance associated with it. The reality is that much goes on at the front end of the order to cash process. The customer may have been shipped the wrong product or quantity, goods may have been damaged and returned, or the customer may be unhappy for any number of reasons. The point is that A/R management is a dynamic function, and understanding the moving parts is key to knowing how to manage A/R. Furthermore, to effectively managing the accounting, you need a complete understanding of the order-to-cash process and the integration between SD and AR.

Let's start at the beginning. A customer sale is the starting point of the order to cash business process and takes the form of a sales order (SO). SOs are handled in the portion of logistics referred to as SD-Sales, which is where transactions exist for sales inquiries, quotations, scheduling agreements, contracts, and more. SD-Sales is also where outbound deliveries are created. The application menu path for SD-Sales is shown in Figure 9.3.

Figure 9.3 Application Menu Path for SD Sales

> **Note**
>
> The setup and configuration of SD is more complex than A/R. It requires special expertise in areas such as pricing. Therefore, your company should ensure it has specialized SD expertise in house.

In the next section, we will discuss the first step in the order-to-cash process: the creation of a sales order.

9.1.1   Sales Orders

According to SAP, an *SO* is a request from a customer to a company to deliver a defined quantity of products or provide a service at a certain time. The SO is typically considered a contractual agreement between a buyer and seller to deliver goods or services of a particular price and quantity by a set date.

There is a lot of complexity behind the creation of a SO, which is beyond the scope of this book. Keep in mind that companies have entire customer service departments whose job it is to create SOs all day. This process involves taking customer orders over the phone or electronically, entering SOs, and handling customer inquiries. The point is that creating SOs is a specialized function that requires knowledge of customers, products, pricing, and the sales organization. The job of finance and accounting is to have a basic understanding of the sales process and to know when and how it affects accounting. Furthermore, it's important to communicate with sales and customer service on questions of revenue recognition, status of orders, and billing.

The intent of this book is not to teach you how to create SOs or other logistics transactions. To obtain an understanding of the integration between SD and AR in the order-to-cash process, displaying logistics documents will suffice. For purposes of our discussion, however, you should know that SOs contain pricing information, materials and quantities, shipping methods, and much more.

The transaction codes used for SOs are as follows:

▶ Transaction VA01 — Create Sales Order

▶ Transaction VA02 — Change Sales Order

▶ Transaction VA03 — Display Sales Order

Figure 9.4 shows an example SO displayed using Transaction VA03. An SO contains a header and several tabs, and the bottom section shows all SO line items and line item tabs. To an accountant, the complexity of a SO can seem overwhelming. It is important to understand the key pieces of information that impact accounting when the time comes. Note that the SO itself does not update accounting until subsequent steps are performed; the primary impact to accounting occurs when an SD billing document is created. This billing function also produces an open receivable to the customer's account in A/R.

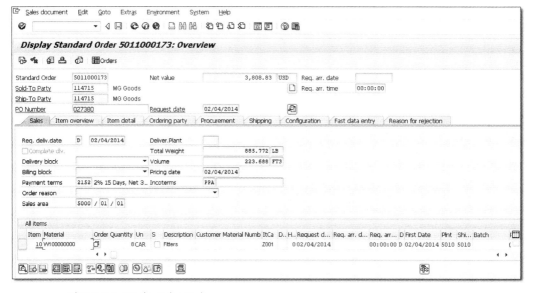

Figure 9.4 Display Sales Order

9.1.2 Outbound Deliveries

Once an SO has been created, the next step is to deliver the goods or services. This is referred to as a *goods issue* and results in an inventory posting in accounting.

A user creates an outbound delivery using Transaction VL01N, referencing the SO. When an outbound delivery is created, the SO will display an outbound delivery document number in DOCUMENT FLOW (Figure 9.5).

Document Flow

Status overview   Display document   Service documents

Business partner 0000114715 MG Goods
Material

Document	Quantity	Unit	Ref. value	Currency	On	Status
▼ ⇒ Standard Order 5011000173 / 10	32	TIN	802.89	EUR	02/04/2014	Completed
▼ Outbound Delivery 5061000312 / 10	32	TIN			02/04/2014	Completed
· Shipment 5070000285 / 1					02/04/2014	Complet.status set
· WMS transfer order 0000011781 / 1	32	TIN			02/07/2014	Completed
· GD goods issue:delvy 4902251394 / 1	32	TIN	467.79	USD	02/07/2014	complete
▼ Invoice 5091000208 / 10	32	TIN	802.89	EUR	02/10/2014	Completed
· Accounting document 5091000208	32	TIN			02/10/2014	Cleared

Figure 9.5 Outbound Delivery in Document Flow

Click on the outbound delivery document number and then the DISPLAY DOCU-
MENT button to enter the outbound delivery document (Figure 9.6). Note that
the outbound delivery document number highlighted in Figure 9.5 is the same
as the outbound delivery document number shown in the header of Figure 9.6.

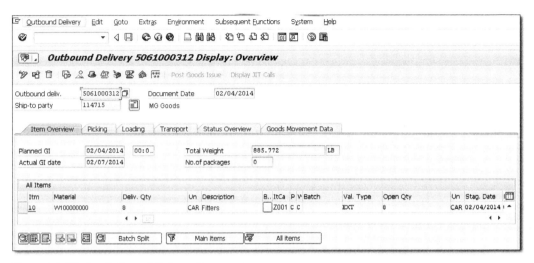

Figure 9.6 Display Outbound Delivery Document

Notice in Figure 9.6 that tabs exist for several logistical functions relevant to the
selection of goods, shipping, and transport. These tabs are aptly named PICKING,
LOADING, and TRANSPORT. One other tab of particular importance to FI is the
GOODS MOVEMENT DATA tab. Movement of goods reduces inventory and produces a financial document. This is one of the key integration points between SD
and FI.

9.1.3   Billing Documents

Following outbound delivery, the next step is the creation of a customer billing
document. In accounting, the term *bill* is synonymous with *invoice*. An SD billing
document is created in either SD-Sales or SD-Billing using Transaction VF01.
When a customer bill is created in SD, it always references an SO. See the example billing document in Figure 9.7.

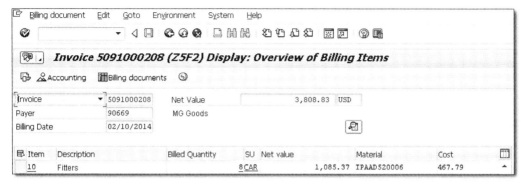

Figure 9.7 Display Billing Document Screen

An SD billing document has a unique feature: Once created, it does not automatically transfer information to accounting. To transfer information, use Transaction VF02 and follow the dropdown menu path BILLING DOCUMENT • RELEASETOACCOUNTING. Once released, RELEASETOACCOUNTING will be greyed out, indicating this step has already been completed.

Once outbound delivery items have been released to accounting, click the ACCOUNTING button in Transaction VF02 or Transaction VF03 to view the A/R invoice.

9.1.4 Automatic Creation of Accounting Invoice

When a billing document has been posted, as shown in Section 9.1.3, a corresponding A/R invoice is created once the bill has been released to accounting. At the end of the bill creation process, the billing document created using Transaction VF01 creates two documents: an SD invoice (i.e., a bill) and an A/R invoice. Here, things become a little tricky. Both documents can have the same document number, and typically do for most SAP customers. Let's take a look, using the example shown in Figure 9.7.

Within DOCUMENT FLOW in Transaction VF03, you can see both the SD invoice number (i.e., billing document) and the accounting document invoice number (Figure 9.8).

Figure 9.8 VF03 Display Document Flow

View the invoice document in A/R by clicking the accounting document number and then the DISPLAY DOCUMENT button. You will see the open receivable created in A/R and awaiting payment receipt (Figure 9.9).

Figure 9.9 Display Acccounts Receivable Invoice Document

Now that you have learned about the front end of the order-to-cash business process, in the next section we will discuss the creation of a direct invoice in the A/R module. It is important to understand that accounting integration from SD to A/R is a one-way street, meaning that updates to accounting documents can flow from SD to A/R, but not from A/R to SD.

9.2 Direct Invoices

Direct invoices is a term often used to refer to A/R invoices created using Transaction FB70. These are A/R invoices created directly in the A/R module, independent of SD-Sales and the creation of billing documents.

There are a few distinguishing features of direct invoices. First, they have no corresponding SD billing document. SD billing documents are only created using Transaction VF01, either in SD-Sales or SD-Billing. Another difference is that the standard document type for direct A/R invoices is DR, whereas those from SD are document type RV. Using Transaction FBL5N, you can therefore distinguish direct invoices from those transferred from SD. The document number ranges are also different, since number ranges are assigned to document types.

When do you use direct invoices? There are several different scenarios that are applicable, which we will discuss in the following subsections.

9.2.1 Outside Sales Ordering System

It would be nice to think that every company takes advantage of the full integration that SAP has to offer, but this is not always the case. Sometimes, a company will use a sales ordering system outside of SAP. It could be that this system was already in place when SAP was implemented and the decision was made to keep it. In a situation like this, management may have decided to keep the sales ordering system because the sales force and customer service representatives were already trained on it. The cost of transitioning to SAP SD may have been another deciding factor.

Whatever the reason, if a non-SAP system is used for sales order management, then accounting data for receivables may simply be interfaced to SAP A/R. In this situation, some direct invoicing in SAP may be required.

9.2.2 No Sales Order Exists

It is a best practice to create an SO for any sale. However, sometimes one size does not fit all. For various reasons, a company may decide not to create SOs for all sales. There are several factors that come into play, including lines of business, size of the company, and industry. Moreover, for small or one-time purchases, a company may decide that creating an SO is neither necessary nor worth the effort. In such situations, a company may decide to create direct invoices instead.

9.2.3 Miscellaneous Receivables

Let's face facts: Business models have become very creative over the years. Although the majority of businesses generate revenue by providing goods, there are a lot of service-based business models that do not require shipping and inventory movement. A collection agency is a good example. Other examples include the collection of a service fee, fines, tax, or subscription fees. For some business models, it makes more sense to create direct invoices and fully manage receivables in the A/R module.

For more information on direct A/R invoices, see Chapter 10, Section 10.1.1.

Now that you have learned about A/R invoices, let's discuss customer account maintenance and payment receipt.

9.3 Customer Account Maintenance and Incoming Payments

Accounting offices typically have a department responsible for A/R account maintenance. One metric the A/R department is responsible for is the days sales outstanding (DSO). DSO is a measure of the average number of days it takes a company to collect revenue after a sale has been made. DSO is a key performance indicator (KPI) that is monitored at the highest echelons of a company.

Keeping DSO at acceptable levels involves several moving parts, such as monitoring customer accounts through account statements, dunning, credit management, and more. Processes need to be in place for collecting on overdue accounts, establishing customer credit ratings, and setting payment terms.

Now, let's discuss terms of payment. First, it is important to establish favorable payment terms with customers. Usually there are standards such as *net 30*. Yet, important customers often demand payment terms more favorable to them and their cash flow. Balancing this aspect of the business can be tricky. Many companies offer payment terms with discounts that reward early payment. This all plays into cash management and liquidity forecasting. The quicker you receive payment from your customers, the better the health of the business.

In addition, the form of payment and your ability to process payments quickly makes a big difference. Most companies have Lockboxes to centrally process incoming check payments quickly. In addition, receiving payment electronically (e.g., direct deposit) reduces processing costs and makes the funds available quicker.

There are a couple ways to post incoming payments electronically in SAP. First is lockbox. A *lockbox* is a post office (PO) box that is accessible by your bank. Your customers send their payments to the PO Box, and then the bank collects and processes these payments directly and deposits them to your bank account. You can obtain an electronic file from your bank to process lockbox transactions in SAP. A more detailed look at the lockbox is beyond the scope of this book, but it is an important concept to understand.

Your company can also receive an electronic bank statement (EBS) from your bank and automatically clear customer invoices in SAP. For further details on EBS, see Chapter 15.

Finally, you can create incoming payments manually in A/R. Whether an A/R invoice is created as a follow-on document from SD or created as a direct invoice using Transaction FB70, the next step in the order-to-cash process is to receive payment from the customer.

Incoming payments are created in A/R using Transaction F-28. This transaction is covered in detail in Chapter 10, Section 10.6. When an incoming payment is posted, a clearing document is created, and the status of the A/R invoice changes from open to cleared.

9.4 Process Exceptions

Throughout the order to cash business process, exceptions happen. Goods sent to your customers may arrive damaged and need to be returned. Invoices may contain an incorrect amount or quantity. Documents may be posted with incorrect information. In this section, we will not attempt to identify all the possible exceptions that can occur; instead, we will discuss three transactions in the A/R module that users frequently use to correct errors or to make adjustments: credit memos, document reversals, and changing documents.

9.4.1 Credit Memos

A *credit memo* is exactly what it appears to be: a credit back to a customer's account. A credit memo may be created because of a defective good, overcharge, or other adjustment needed to a customer's account. Credit memos net against open receivable amounts at the time of payment receipt to properly net the balance in the customer account.

There are two ways to create credit memos. The first is in the A/R module, using Transaction FB75. This is covered in detail in Chapter 10, Section 10.2. Transaction FB75 should be used for general customer account credit adjustments not specific to sales transactions originating in SD. When you need to issue a credit memo for a transaction originating in SD, the best approach is to create it using Transaction VF01.

Figure 9.10 shows the Transaction VF01 BILLING TYPE dropdown box, with the CREDIT MEMO option highlighted.

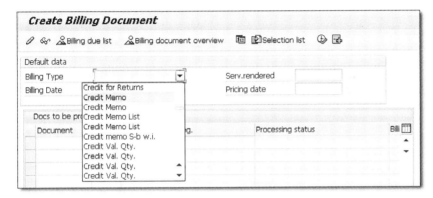

Figure 9.10 VF01 Billing Type Dropdown List

Once you create a credit memo, the SO referenced in the credit memo displays the credit memo document number in DOCUMENT FLOW. A credit memo originating in SD also transfers to FI so that the customer account reflects the credit. These credit memos can be seen in A/R using Transaction FBL5N.

As noted earlier, credit memos can be created both in A/R and SD. Remember, SD and A/R integration is a one-way street: Financial information flows from SD to A/R, but not vice versa. Therefore, if the credit memo needs to tie back to an SO, create the credit memo in SD, not in A/R.

Next, let's discuss document reversals.

9.4.2   Document Reversals

An SAP best practice is to reverse documents in the module in which they originate. This concept is important for keeping modules in sync.

In Chapter 10, Section 10.4, we discussed resetting and reversing A/R documents in detail. However, for documents originating in SD, document reversals should be made in that module rather than reversing follow-on documents in A/R.

In this chapter, we discuss several SD transactions: The first, Transaction VA01, creates a SO. To cancel an SO, use Transaction VA02. To delete an SO, from Transaction VA02, choose the DELETE option from the dropdown menu (Figure 9.11). You can only do so if no subsequent documents have been created, however.

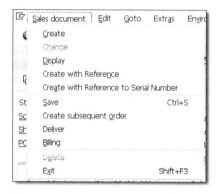

Figure 9.11 VA02 Drop-Down Selection Menu

Keep in mind that SOs can be large documents with numerous line items. Just because there is an error or issue in one line of the SO does not mean that you must cancel the entire SO. SO line items can be changed, deleted, and inserted, so before cancelling an entire SO due to a line item issue, make sure you attempt to fix the document first. If a customer truly cancels an order, then the delete option is applicable.

The next SD transaction discussed is an outbound delivery, created using Transaction VL01N in SD-Sales. Changes to the outbound delivery document cancel or modify all subsequent documents, ensuring that the outbound delivery document shows the current status of the whole outbound delivery. To reverse or cancel the goods movement portion of an outbound delivery, use Transaction VL09.

The third SD transaction discussed in this chapter is the billing document. To cancel the billing document, use Transaction VF11. In this way, the A/R invoice is also reversed, and the current status is correctly updated for the SO. Remember, reversing a document in the module of origin also triggers a reversal in FI. You can validate this in an A/R customer accounting using Transaction FBL5N.

9.4.3 Change Posted Documents

As noted previously, SAP best practice is to change posted documents in the module in which they originated. However, there is an exception to this rule with the A/R invoice, as we will discuss towards the end of this section. See Chapter 10, Section 10.5 for more on changing A/R documents.

Transaction VA01 is used for the creation of an SO. SOs can be cancelled, and SO line items can be deleted or added. The transaction to change a SO is Transaction VA02. Any change to a SO should be made by the office responsible for entering and managing sales orders in the system. An accountant or accounting supervisor may request that a change to a SO be made but should not make the change directly unless it is part of his or her job responsibilities and he or she has been trained. Before making any change, it is important to understand the dependency on subsequent documents and the impact any change will have to the statuses of an SO.

Another important SD transaction is outbound deliveries. To make a subsequent adjustment to an outbound delivery, you can use Transaction VL02N. Keep in mind that outbound deliveries involve several other steps related to transportation and shipping. Other steps or transactions made be needed to perform the changes you require.

The last transaction discussed is the billing document, created using Transaction VF01. To change the billing document, use Transaction VF02. In this transaction, you release billing information to accounting. Certain accounting information cannot be changed in SD after this release has taken place. In the case of an A/R invoice, you need to make any change directly in the A/R invoice in FI, which was created as a follow-on document when the release to FI took place. The FI transaction to change the A/R invoice is Transaction FB02.

One of the more commonly changed fields in an A/R invoice is the BASELINE DATE. You may also need to change the payment terms or the payment method assigned in the document. These are simple changes that cause no reconciliation problems between A/R and SD.

Throughout this chapter, we have mentioned numerous times that SD to A/R is a one-way street as far as integration and the exchange of financial information. It's important to keep the integrated documents in sync as much as possible. Moreover, keeping all documents centrally tied to the SO makes life a lot easier. Yet, here we must stress the different business functions between SD and A/R, because these differences are relevant to changing customer invoices directly in A/R.

In the order-to-cash business process, the frontend steps are executed in SD. When a customer bill is created and is transferred to accounting, a customer invoice is created. From this point on, customer account maintenance and collections are the responsibility of accounting.

As a result, there are times when it is absolutely essential that accounts receivable change an invoice in A/R that is a follow-on document from SD. Remember that an accounts receivable department is responsible for the following tasks:

▸ Keeping DSO at acceptable levels

▸ Monitoring customer accounts

▸ Dunning

▸ Credit management

▸ Collecting on overdue accounts

▸ Establishing customer credit ratings

▸ Setting payment terms

▸ Processing incoming payments

▸ Blocking customer accounts

If the accounts receivable department needs to make a change to a posted document to fulfill these responsibilities and the change cannot be made in SD, then the accounts receivable department will make the changes necessary in A/R.

9.5   Summary

In this chapter, we focused on A/R business processes and integration with the SD module. The steps that make up the sale of goods and services are not isolated to the A/R module, but rather reach back into transactions in the SD module. Sales functions originate in SD-Sales. The complete business process includes creating sales orders, outbound deliveries, billing, and payment receipts. Together, these make up the order to cash business process.

The significance of the order to cash process is that it begins with the receipt of a customer order, ends with payment receipt from the customer, and demonstrates integration between SD and FI. Integration between SD and FI is essential.

A complete order-to-cash process is not complete without it, and the sales process makes up an important part of any business.

SD supports the business in taking customer orders, revenue recognition, goods movements, shipping and transportation, pricing, and much more. It's important for any accountant, particularly A/R clerks and supervisors, to have a base knowledge of SD and FI integration.

The first step in the sales process is a customer sales order. After an order has been placed, the goods must be picked, packed, and shipped. These functions involve the creation of an outbound delivery document in SD, with several subsequent documents associated with it and displayed in document flow.

An outbound delivery document references an SO. It is in this step that the power of SAP ERP first demonstrates itself in the order-to-cash process. Once posted, the outbound delivery document is displayed in SO document flow and statuses are updated. Linking documents to an SO makes the management of the order-to-cash process streamlined and efficient.

Following outbound delivery, the next step is the creation of a customer bill via Transaction VF01 in either SD-Sales or SD-Billing. The result is the creation of an SD billing document. Once a billing document is released to accounting, a partner invoice is created in A/R. This invoice in A/R is referred to as a subsequent document and is shown in document flow.

It is an SAP best practice to change or reverse a document in the module in which it was created. Both SOs and outbound deliveries can be changed in SD, with limitations based upon the subsequent steps already performed.

Bills can be reversed in SD-Billing, but your ability to change the documents has limits. To change a field such as PAYMENT TERMS, change the A/R invoice directly in FI. For more complex changes, such as to a cost object, the billing document should be cancelled in SD-Billing and reposted.

Transactions in both SD and FI make the order-to-cash process complete. In this chapter, you learned about each step in the process, integration points, and when and how to reverse or change documents.

This concludes the discussion of A/R processes and integration with SD. In the next chapter, we will discuss A/R transactions in detail.

In this chapter, we cover A/R transactions in detail. These transactions consist of line items that include a customer subledger entry. A customer invoice can be created directly in the A/R module or as a part of a document chain created in the SD module through the order-to-cash business process.

10   Accounts Receivable Transactions

This chapter covers A/R transactions originating in the A/R module. The most common of these is the entry of a customer invoice document using Transaction FB70. This chapter covers not only the creation of an A/R customer invoice document but also associated A/R functions, such as document display, change, reverse, park, and more.

In essence, A/R serves to collect money from customers. First, you create a customer invoice. Then, you receive payment and apply the amount received against an open invoice. However, this seemingly straightforward process can take many twists and turns. Posting credit memos and down payments received, clearing accounts, making document corrections, and reconciling balances are just some of the functions that have to be performed by accountants in the A/R department.

This chapter begins by covering the basics of creating a customer invoice in the A/R module. We then take a deep dive into each associated function in the A/R module.

Some of the transactions covered in this chapter, such as the creation of a customer invoice, are tasks you are likely to perform on a daily basis. Other transactions, such as document reversal, are executed less frequently. This chapter can be revisited as a reference point for less frequently used transactions and can provide you with an overall refresher on the A/R module. Let's begin our discussion by looking into A/R customer invoices.

10.1   Customer Invoices

This section covers the A/R customer invoice creation process, which includes document entry, park, post, save as complete, and hold. It also covers the Transaction FB70 tree display, screen variants, account assignment templates, editing options, and post with reference, all of which provide valuable insights to help you be more productive and organized within the A/R module.

To create a customer invoice in SAP using Transaction FB70, you must enter document header details (e.g., posting date) and at least one noncustomer line item that nets the document balance to zero. You may find that you cannot complete a document while you are in the middle of processing it or that a field you need to enter is not present on the screen; this section gives you the tools you need to deal with these and other challenges and provides you with the knowledge to enter A/R transactions more efficiently.

10.1.1   Document Entry

To create an A/R customer invoice document, use Transaction FB70 or application menu path Accounting • Financial Accounting • Accounts Receivable • Document Entry • FB70—Invoice, as shown in Figure 10.1.

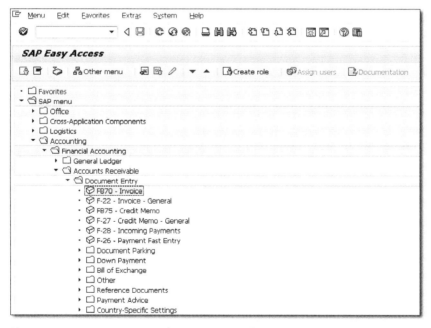

Figure 10.1 Transaction FB70 Application Menu Path

Double-click on FB70—Invoice from the menu path, or enter "FB70" in the Command field (as shown in Figure 10.2) and press Enter.

Figure 10.2 FB70 in Command Field

The ENTER CUSTOMER INVOICE entry screen will open (Figure 10.3). The fields that appear on the header with prepopulated values may vary, depending upon your system configuration and editing options. In this example, field values defaulted into the POSTING DATE, DOCUMENT TYPE, CURRENCY, and COMPANY CODE fields, whereas field values were entered into the CUSTOMER, INVOICE DATE, REFERENCE, and AMOUNT fields.

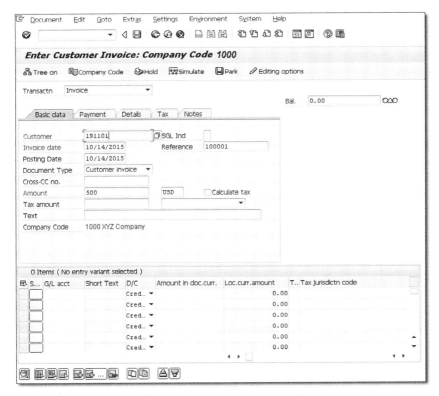

Figure 10.3 Transaction FB70 Enter Customer Invoice Entry Screen

The customer invoice REFERENCE field can contain the document number of the customer or a different value. This field is used as a search criterion when displaying or changing documents. In addition, take special note of the INVOICE DATE field. The invoice date is the start date of the due date calculation. In other words, if the payment terms are net 30, the clock starts ticking based on the date in the INVOICE DATE field, not the POSTING DATE field. After entering header details, the next step is to enter at least one line item, as shown in Figure 10.4.

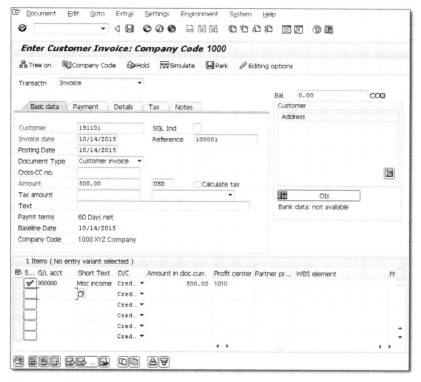

Figure 10.4 Transaction FB70 Enter Customer Invoice Screen with Line Item Entry

In Figure 10.4, the line item entered is a credit to a revenue account. For a revenue line item, you are required to enter values for the G/L ACCOUNT, DEBIT/CREDIT INDICATOR, andAMOUNT fields at a minimum. In addition, PROFIT CENTER may be required, and we entered a profit center in this example. Your SAP system may have additional field entry requirements based upon your configuration and field status settings.

After entering document line items, click the SIMULATE button in the top center of the entry screen. This initiates simulation of the customer invoice posting logic to determine if the document can be properly posted. If the simulation is unsuccessful, an error message will appear. If successful, the document overview screen appears, as shown in Figure 10.5.

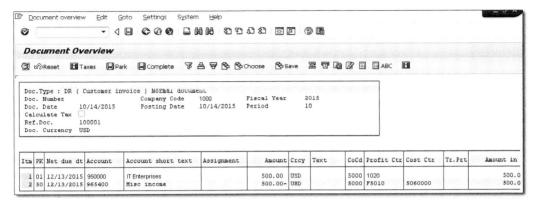

Figure 10.5 Transaction FB70 Document Overview Screen

Once simulation is complete, click the Post icon 🔲 to the right of the Command field in the upper-left-hand corner of the screen. This will post the customer invoice, and a message will appear with the new document number, as shown in Figure 10.6.

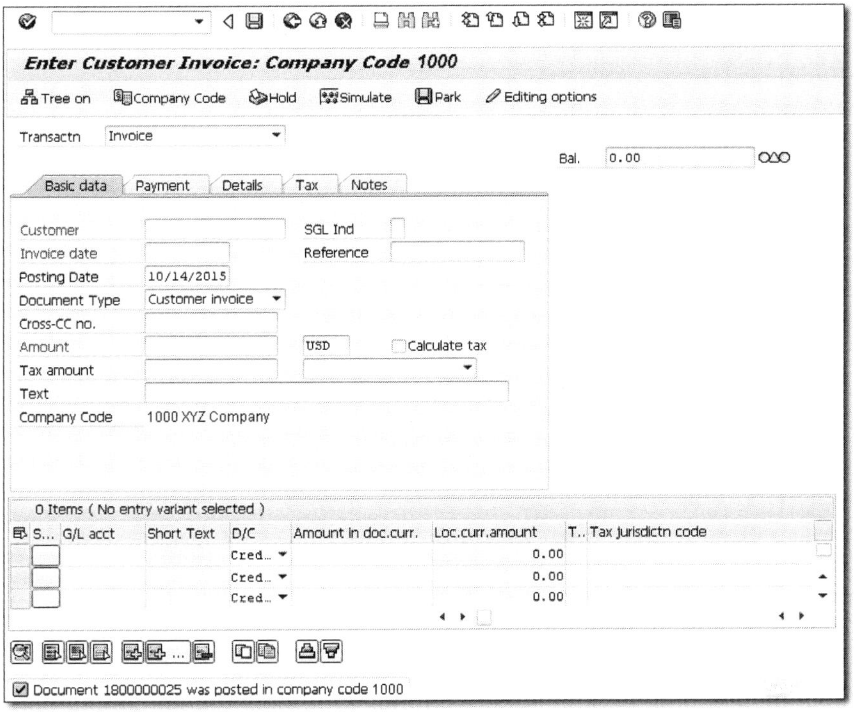

Figure 10.6 Transaction FB70 Document Posted Message

10.1.2 Post, Park, Save as Complete, and Hold

This section describes the different ways to create customer invoice documents: post, park, save as complete, and hold. All are universal concepts within FI and therefore are not unique to customer invoices and Transaction FB70, but their discussion in this section is confined to their use for customer invoices. These functions work the same in G/L and A/P, so if you read Chapter 3 and Chapter 6, you will see that the content in this section is very similar.

Post

Posting a customer invoice was covered in its entirety in Section 10.1.1. A posted document is a customer invoice that is considered complete, produces an accounting document number, and updates the customer account and G/L account balances.

Once a customer document is posted, the only way to reverse its impact on the customer account and G/L account balances is to reverse the document. Reversing G/L documents is covered in Section 6.4.

Park

Document parking allows you to save a customer invoice document without impacting customer account and G/L account balances. This may be necessary if the document is incomplete or if further edits, data validation, or document approval is required prior to posting.

Because parked documents are considered incomplete, they can be changed or deleted. When parked, these customer documents do not update transaction figures and account balances. Moreover, a parked document does not go through the extensive entry checks performed when documents are posted.

To park a customer invoice document, use Transaction FV70 or follow application menu path ACCOUNTING • FINANCIAL ACCOUNTING • ACCOUNTS RECEIVABLE •

DOCUMENT ENTRY • DOCUMENT PARKING • FV70 — PARK/EDIT INVOICE, as shown in Figure 10.7.

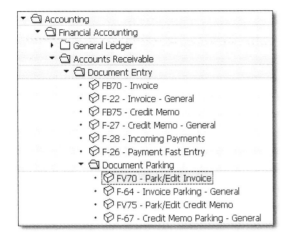

Figure 10.7 Transaction FV70 Application Menu Path

Double-click FV70 — PARK/EDIT INVOICE from the menu path, or enter "FV70" in the COMMAND field (as shown in Figure 10.8) and press ⌜Enter⌟.

Figure 10.8 FV70 in Command Field

The PARK CUSTOMER INVOICE entry screen will open (Figure 10.9). The fields that default values into the document header will vary depending upon your system configuration and editing options. In this example, the CUSTOMER, INVOICE DATE, REFERENCE, and AMOUNT fields were manually entered, whereas field values defaulted for the POSTING DATE, DOCUMENT TYPE, CURRENCY, and COMPANY CODE fields.

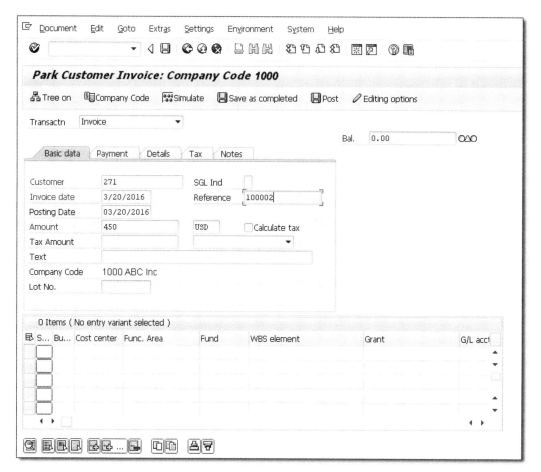

Figure 10.9 Park Invoice Initial Screen

After inputting field values on the header screen, enter at least one line item, as shown in Figure 10.10.

Figure 10.10 Entry Screen with Line Items

Once the line items are entered, click the PARK icon 🖫 to the right of the COM-MAND field in the upper-left-hand portion of the screen. This will park the customer invoice, and a message will appear with the new parked document number, as shown in Figure 10.11.

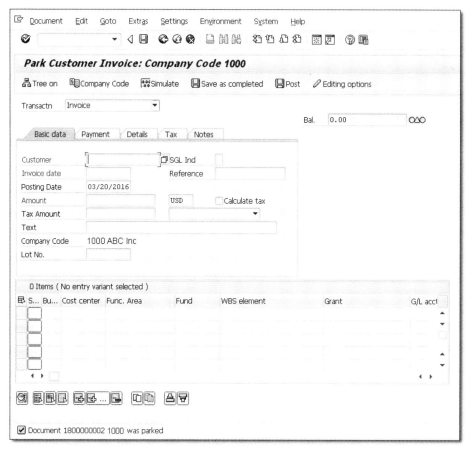

Figure 10.11 Document Parked Message

Save as Completed

The *save as completed* function is similar to document parking, but with some key distinctions. When you save a document as completed, the program goes through more extensive document check logic, just as if the document were being posted. Like parked documents, however, documents that are saved as completed can be edited and changed prior to posting.

Although the park and save as completed functions are similar, the latter should generally only be used when you are sure the document is accurate and complete and only needs final approval before being posted.

To save a customer invoice as completed, use Transaction FV70 or follow application menu path ACCOUNTING • FINANCIAL ACCOUNTING • ACCOUNTS RECEIVABLE • DOCUMENT ENTRY • DOCUMENT PARKING • FV70—PARK/EDIT INVOICE, as seen in Figure 10.12.

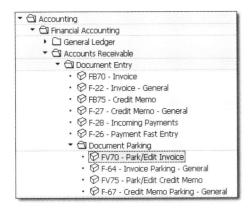

Figure 10.12 Application Menu Path for Save as Complete Function

Double-click FV70—PARK/EDIT INVOICE from the menu path shown in Figure 10.12, or enter "FV70" in the COMMAND field (Figure 10.13) and press Enter.

Figure 10.13 FV70 in Command Field

The PARK CUSTOMER INVOICE entry screen will open (Figure 10.14). The fields that appear on the header with prepopulated values may vary depending upon your system configuration and editing options. In this example, the CUSTOMER, INVOICE DATE, REFERENCE, and AMOUNT fields were manually entered, whereas field values defaulted for the POSTING DATE, DOCUMENT TYPE, CURRENCY, and COMPANY CODE fields.

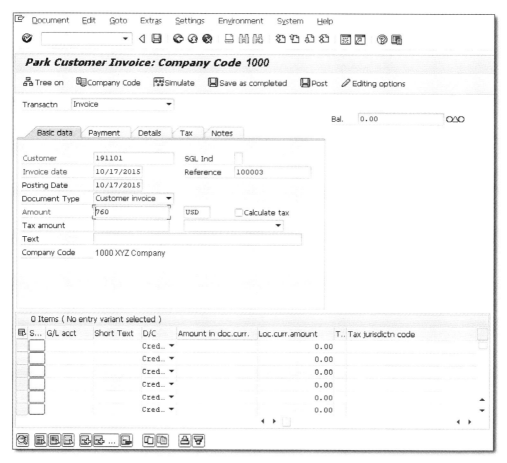

Figure 10.14 Entry Screen for Save as Complete Function

After the PARK CUSTOMER INVOICE header screen is complete, enter at least one line item, as shown in Figure 10.15.

After entering line items, click the SAVE AS COMPLETED icon at the top-center portion of the screen. This will save the customer invoice as completed, and a message will appear with the new document number, as shown in Figure 10.16.

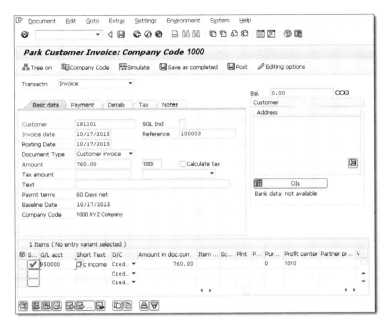

Figure 10.15 Line Item Entry for Save as Complete Function

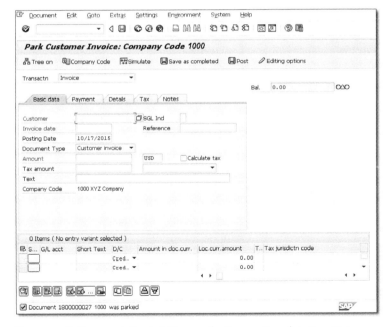

Figure 10.16 Document Created Message for Save as Complete Function

Hold

Document hold allows you to temporarily save your data. It is most useful when you are interrupted during document entry. Because held documents are temporary, they do not update A/R and G/L transactions and balances. Furthermore, in subsequent processing they can be edited, deleted, parked, or posted. Unlike post, park, and save as completed, the hold function produces no permanent document number until the document is parked or posted.

To hold an A/R accounting document, use Transaction FB70 or application menu path Accounting • Financial Accounting • Accounts Receivable • Document Entry • FB70—Invoice, as shown in Figure 10.17.

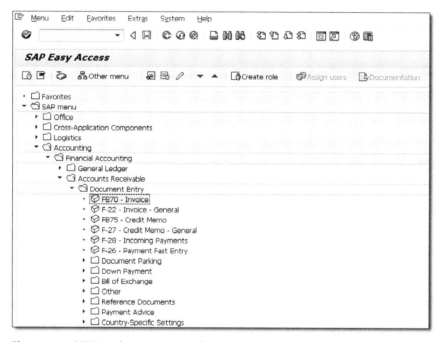

Figure 10.17 FB70 Application Menu Path

Double-click FB70—Invoice from the menu path shown in Figure 10.17, or enter "FB70" in the Command field (Figure 10.18) and press Enter.

Figure 10.18 FB70 in Command Field

At any point in Transaction FB70, you can use the hold function. You can do so regardless of how much or little information has been entered, because no system checks take place when you hold an A/R document.

In the example shown in Figure 10.19, the CUSTOMER, INVOICE DATE, REFERENCE, and AMOUNT fields have been entered, along with one partially complete line item. In the screen header, field values were prepopulated for the CURRENCY, POSTING DATE, DOCUMENT TYPE, andCOMPANY CODE fields.

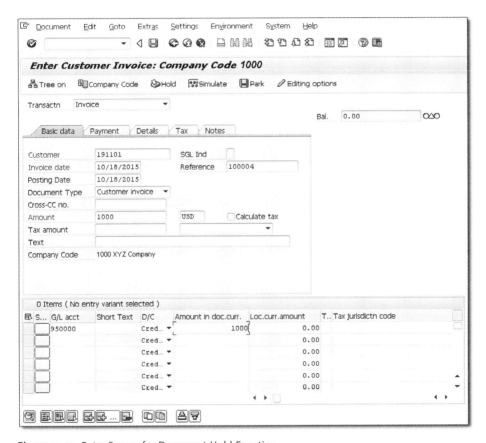

Figure 10.19 Entry Screen for Document Hold Function

At any point, the document can be held by pressing [F5] or selecting DOCUMENT • HOLD from the dropdown menu, as shown in Figure 10.20.

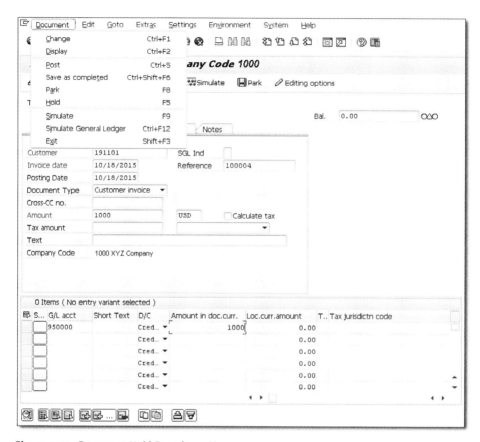

Figure 10.20 Document Hold Dropdown Menu

When you select DOCUMENT • HOLD, a dialogue box will open (Figure 10.21) and prompt you to enter a temporary document number. This ten-character preliminary document number can contain numbers, letters, and special characters. This is a temporary document number, meaning that it is no longer valid when a permanent number is assigned, such as when the document is posted, parked, or saved as completed.

After entering a temporary document number, press Enter or click on the HOLD DOCUMENT button. A temporary accounting document will be created, and a message will appear with the held document number, as shown in Figure 10.22.

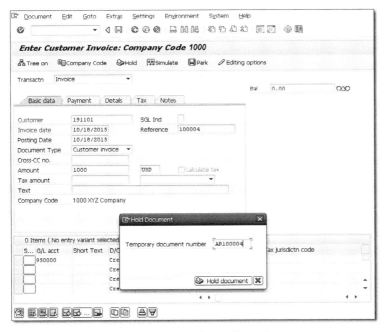

Figure 10.21 Temporary Document Number Dialogue Box

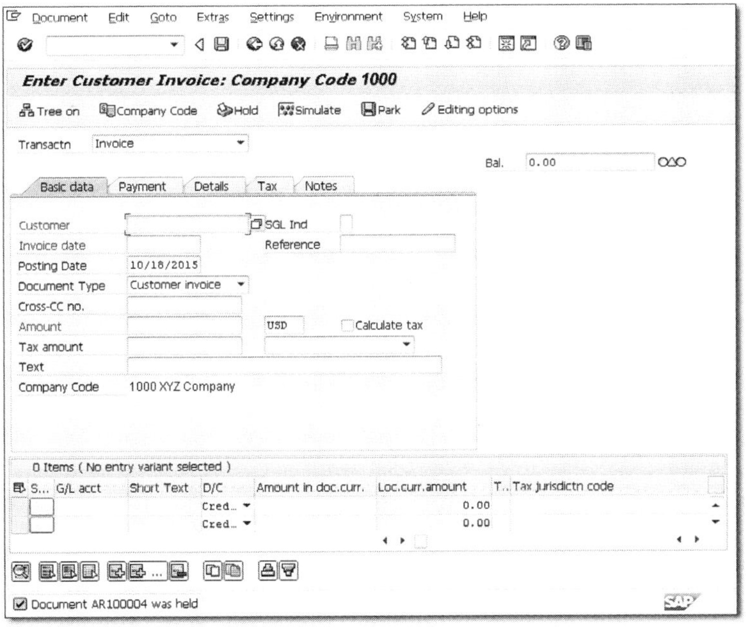

Figure 10.22 Document Held Message

10.1.3 Tree Display

The *tree display* provides an easy-to-use visual display for several functions that can also be accessed from the dropdown menu in Transaction FB70. The tree display is a universal concept, or shortcut, for accessing accounting documents and document entry tools in FI. In this section, we will confine the discussion of the tree display to Transactions FB70 and FV70, but this capability can be used in any FI transaction for which the tree display is available.

The tree display is a toggle function, meaning that it can be turned on (i.e., made visible) or off (i.e., made invisible) with the click of a button or via a keyboard combination.

Figure 10.23 shows Transaction FB70 with the tree display on, visible as a panel on the left-hand side of the transaction screen.

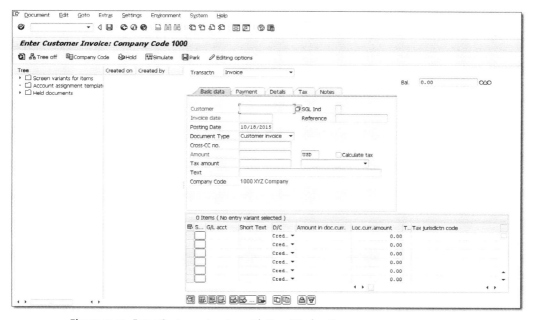

Figure 10.23 Enter Customer Invoice with Tree Display On

With the tree display on, you will see a panel containing folders on the left. The folders that appear in the display vary by transaction code. In Transaction FB70, you will see the following folders:

▸ Screen Variants for Items

▸ Account Assignment Templates for Items

▸ Held Documents

Screen variants and account assignment templates are covered in detail in Section 10.1.4.

In Section 10.1.2, we demonstrated how to hold a customer invoice document. View held documents in the tree display by clicking on the triangle to the left of the HELD DOCUMENTS folder. This action opens the folder and displays all the held documents created by the user.

By double-clicking on a held document in the tree display, the details appear in the ENTER CUSTOMER INVOICE entry screen, as shown in Figure 10.24. Once displayed, held document details can be edited, parked, or posted.

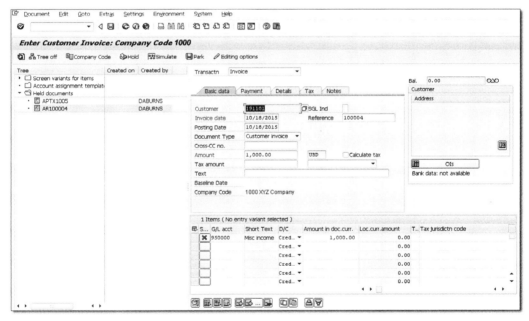

Figure 10.24 Held Documents with Tree Display On

The tree display function in Transaction FV70 is the same as in Transaction FB70 and has the same toggle capability. Transaction FV70 with tree display on is shown in Figure 10.25.

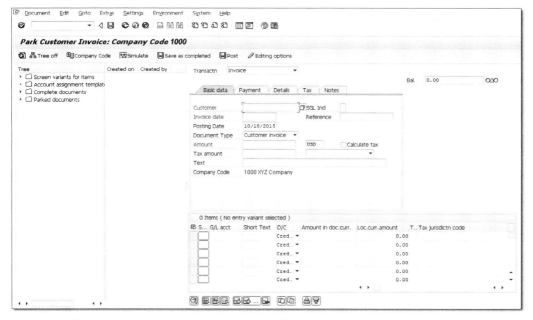

Figure 10.25 Transaction FV70 with Tree Display On

In Transaction FV70, you will see the following folders:

- SCREEN VARIANTS FOR ITEMS
- ACCOUNT ASSIGNMENT TEMPLATES FOR ITEMS
- COMPLETE DOCUMENTS
- PARKED DOCUMENTS

In the Transaction FV70 tree display, folders for screen variants and account assignment templates appear at the top, as they did in Transaction FB70. However, folders for complete and parked documents appear in FV70, but did not in the Transaction FB70 tree display. Finally, the folder for held documents, which appeared in Transaction FB70's tree display, does not appear in Transaction FV70. As you can see, the tree display default folders vary by transaction.

10.1.4 Using Screen Variants and Account Assignment Templates

Screen variants and *account assignment templates* are tools available in FI to simplify entry of customer documents. They are not unique to A/R or Transaction

FB70, but in this section we will confine our discussion of them to this transaction. Note that both screen variants and account assignment templates can be accessed and maintained from both the tree display in Transaction FB70 and the dropdown menu. In this section, we focus on using the tree display, the most user-friendly and frequently used method.

Use of Screen Variants

A screen variant sets the columns for line item entry in Transaction FB70 (Figure 10.26). In other words, it controls the fields displayed on the screen and the order in which they appear.

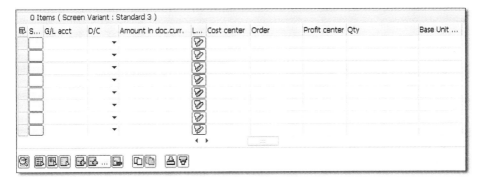

Figure 10.26 Transaction FB70 Screen Variant

A well-developed screen variant reduces data entry time and the number of data entry errors. Your goal is to have appear on the screen only the fields you need to enter or display. For example, if you use profit center accounting (PCA), your A/R screen variants should make the profit center field available and prominently placed. In addition, if you use the Segment dimension, you should make it prominently place in the screen layout, even if it is derived from the profit center.

Transaction FB70 has a default screen variant assigned, which is displayed each time you execute the transaction. However, the default may not be your preferred line item entry screen, or you may prefer different screen variants depending on the type of customer document you are creating. In Transaction FB70, you have the ability to select different screen variants at any point in time via the tree display or the dropdown menu. In A/R, you may want different screen variants created based on the major types of customer invoices created. If you work for a global company, you may need multiple A/R screen variants setup for intercompany and international transactions.

Let's look at screen variant selection in action. Go to Transaction FB70, and make sure the tree display is on (see Section 10.1.3). Click on the triangle next to the SCREEN VARIANTS FOR ITEMS folder to see a list of available variants to choose from (Figure 10.27).

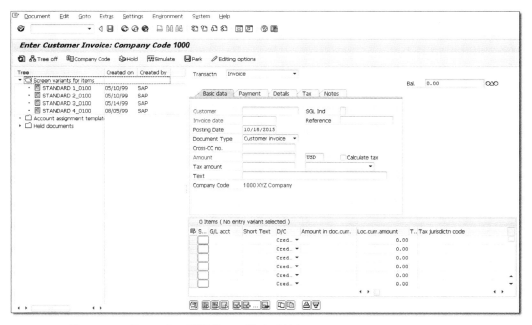

Figure 10.27 Transaction FB70 Screen Variant List

Double-click the screen variant you want to use (Figure 10.28), and the line layout in the bottom right of the screen will change.

The creation and maintenance of screen variants is beyond the scope of this book. They are cross-client dependent, meaning that if a screen variant change is made in one SAP client, the change is reflected in every other client within that SAP instance. For this reason, screen variant creation and maintenance is a function usually restricted to an SAP support team or system administrator.

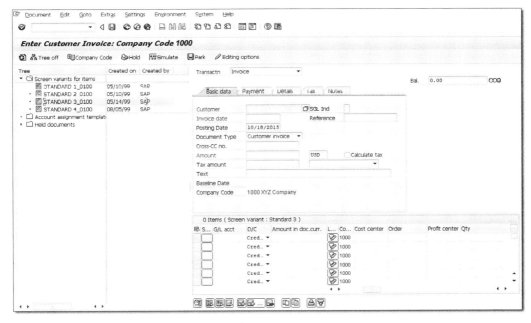

Figure 10.28 Transaction FB70 Screen Variant Selection

Use of Account Assignment Templates

Account assignment templates are prepopulated field values in document line items. This is a useful concept in A/R that helps reduce data entry requirements for customer invoices, which are frequent and consistent in their makeup. These templates allow you to quickly enter customer invoices without the hassle of reentering all the necessary field values each time you create a new document.

In A/R, account assignment templates are used heavily for repetitive transactions that post to the same G/L accounts and profit centers. They may also be used for intercompany transactions. Account assignment templates in A/R not only make data entry easier, but also ensure consistency in your A/P accounting entries.

The next time you find yourself entering a customer invoice from scratch that you have created multiple times in the past, consider creating an account assignment template.

Let's take a closer look at account assignment templates. Go to Transaction FB70, and make sure the tree display is on (see Section 10.1.3). Click on the triangle next to the ACCOUNT ASSIGNMENT TEMPLATE FOR ITEMS folder to see a list of avail-able templates to choose from (Figure 10.29).

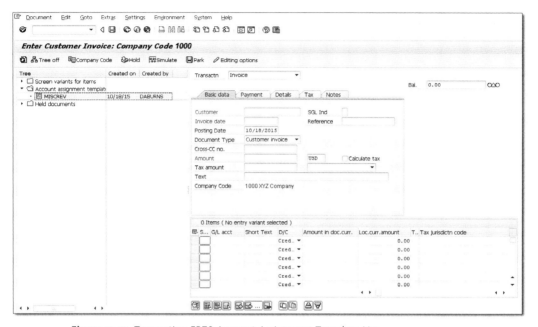

Figure 10.29 Transaction FB70 Account Assignment Template List

Double-click the template you want to use (Figure 10.30), and the line layout in the line item entry screen will change to reflect the prepopulated values con-tained in the account assignment template. Afterwards, you can add or edit these prepopulated field values.

In this example, account assignment template MISCREV contains prepopulated values for the G/L ACCOUNT, DEBIT/CREDIT INDICATOR, andTAX CODE fields. With these fields prepopulated, let's manually enter additional fields to walk through completing an A/R customer invoice from an account assignment template.

In the header, the VENDOR, REFERENCE, and INVOICE DATE fields were manually entered. In the line item, PROFIT CENTER was manually entered. With all the other required fields populated, you simply need to enter a value in the AMOUNT field to complete the document entry requirements (Figure 10.31).

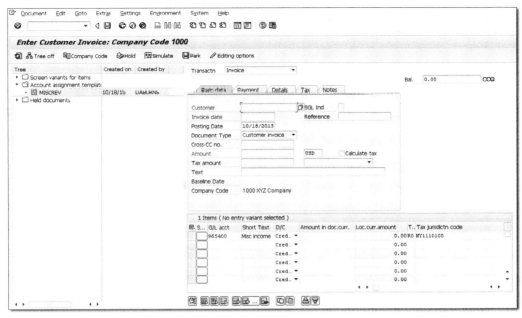

Figure 10.30 Transaction FB70 Account Assignment Template Selection

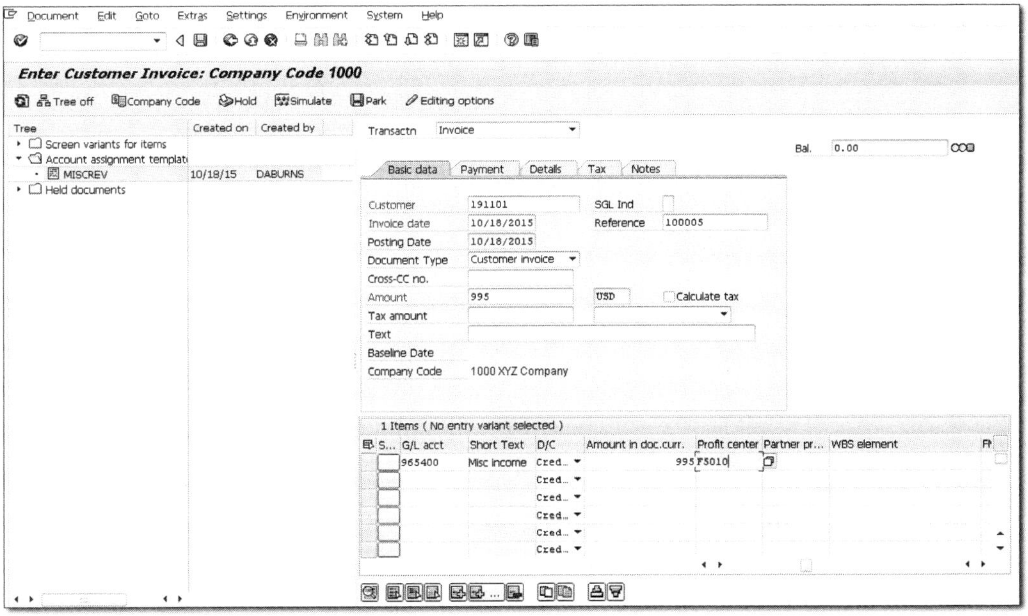

Figure 10.31 Account Assignment Template Entry Complete

With document entry complete, you can post, park, or hold this vendor invoice. In this example, we posted the document (Figure 10.32).

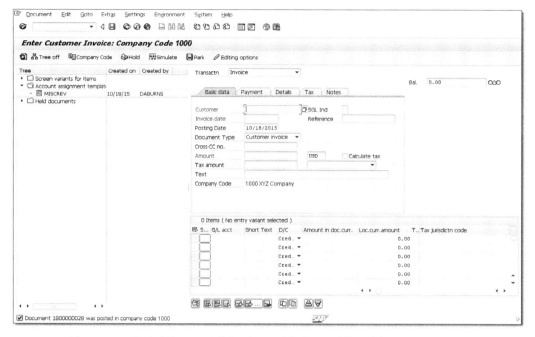

Figure 10.32 Posted Document Using Account Assignment Template

10.1.5 Controlling Document Entry with Editing Options

Controlling document entry with editing options allows you to make user-specific settings for transactions in accounting. Editing options are useful tools that give you some level of field control over the entry screen, what is displayed, and values that are defaulted, and they determine the interpretation of certain field entry values.

Editing options are a universal concept in FI, but our discussion in this section is limited to their use in Transaction FB70. The settings you make are not transaction-specific, meaning that once you have made an editing option in Transaction in FB70, it will also apply to other accounting transactions, such as Transactions FB50 and FB60.

In this section, we will demonstrate some of the most commonly used settings and provide a complete list of all editing options and their descriptions (Table 10.1).

To access editing options from Transaction FB70 (Figure 10.33), click on the EDITING OPTIONS button at the top of the ENTER CUSTOMER INVOICE screen, or press Shift + F4 .

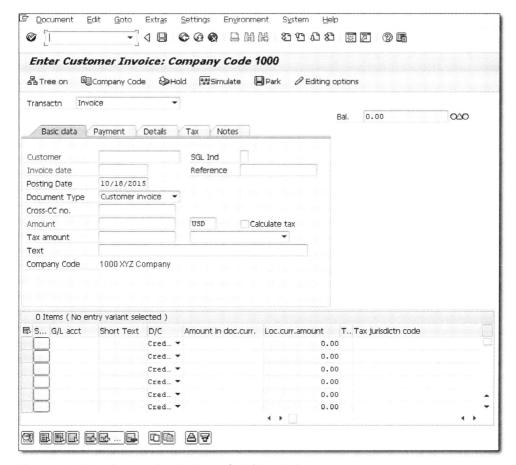

Figure 10.33 Enter Customer Invoice Screen for Editing Options

The ACCOUNTING EDITING OPTIONS screen will open (Figure 10.34). Editing options fall into four general categories, each with its own section of the screen:

▶ General Entry Options

▶ Special Options for Single Screen Transactions

▶ Default Document Currency

▶ Default Company Code

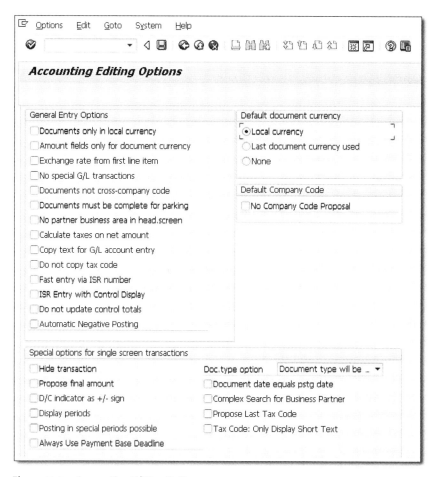

Figure 10.34 Accounting Editing Options

In the upper-right-hand corner of Figure 10.34 the Local Currency radio button is selected in the Default Document Currency section. With this setting, the local currency of the company code will default into Transaction FB70.

For this example, change the DEFAULT DOCUMENT CURRENCY to NONE (Figure 10.35). Once this selection is made, click the SAVE icon ⊟ or press ⌈Ctrl⌉+⌈S⌉.

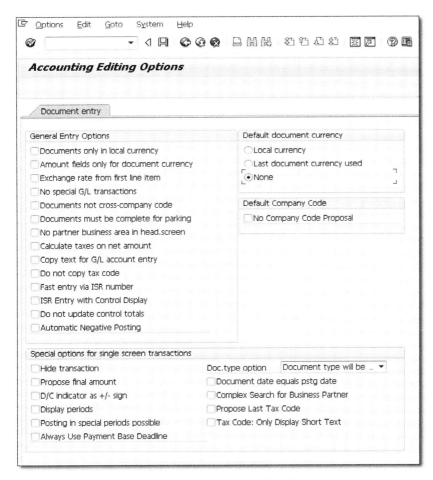

Figure 10.35 Accounting Editing Options with No Default Currency

Once the editing options are saved, return to Transaction FB70 to find that the CURRENCY field in the header is now blank (Figure 10.36), meaning that no value defaulted into this field. This currency setting is relevant to A/R when posting receivable transactions for multiple regions. It forces you to think about the correct currency to use, instead of using the local currency when you shouldn't.

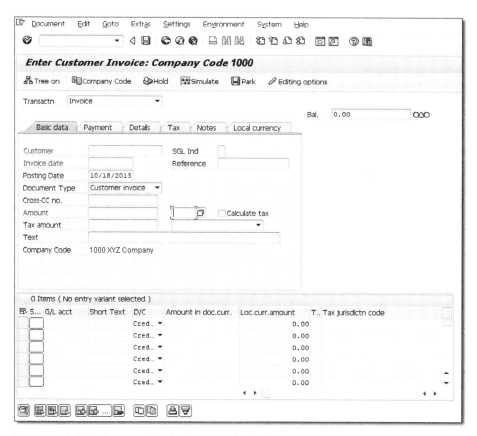

Figure 10.36 Enter Customer Invoice Screen with Blank Currency

Similarly, you can use editing options to change the transaction entry screen so that no company code is proposed. For this example, do so by selecting the checkbox next to No COMPANY CODE PROPOSAL checkbox in the ACCOUNTING EDITING OPTIONS screen (Figure 10.37). Once this selection is made, click the SAVE icon 🖫 or press ⌈Ctrl⌉+⌈S⌉.

Once the editing options are saved, return to Transaction FB70; you are immediately prompted to enter a COMPANY CODE (Figure 10.38). Again, this option may be useful in A/R when you are responsible for creating receivable entries in multiple regions.

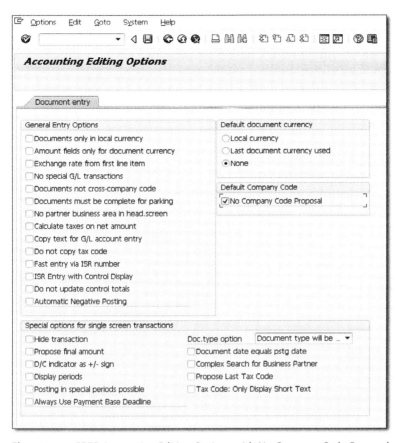

Figure 10.37 FB70 Accounting Editing Options with No Company Code Proposal

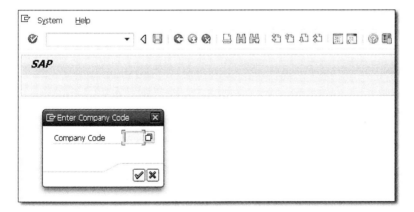

Figure 10.38 Enter Company Code Dialogue Box

Another common use of editing options is to change the document type setting. For this example, change the DOC.TYPE OPTION field to DOCUMENT TYPE HIDDEN (Figure 10.39). Once this selection is made, click the SAVE icon 🖫 or press [Ctrl]+[S].

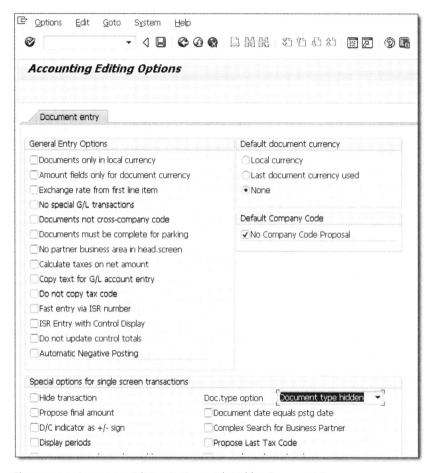

Figure 10.39 Accounting Editing Options with Hidden Document Type

Once the editing options are saved, return to Transaction FB70 and see that the DOCUMENT TYPE field is now hidden from view (Figure 10.40).

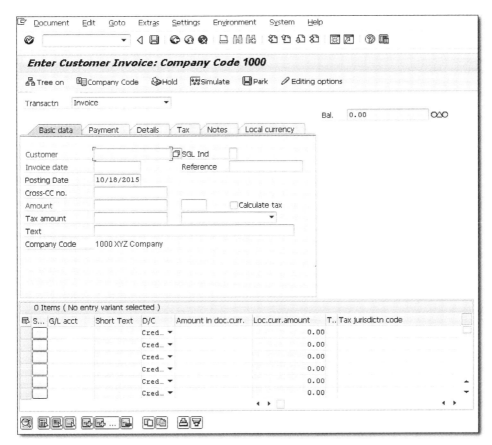

Figure 10.40 Document Entry Screen with Document Type Hidden

That concludes our discussion of editing options. Table 10.1 provides a complete list of editing options and their descriptions. This table is also provided in Chapter 3 and Chapter 6, since these editing options are also relevant to G/L and A/P. For your convenience, the table is also provided here.

Editing Option	Description
DOCUMENTS ONLY IN LOCAL CURRENCY	Only allows entry of documents in local currency.
AMOUNT FIELDS ONLY FOR DOCUMENT CURRENCY	Only allows entry amounts in foreign currency when entering documents in foreign currency.

Table 10.1 Editing Options and Descriptions

Editing Option	Description
EXCHANGE RATE FROM FIRST LINE ITEM	When posting foreign currency documents, the exchange rate in the document header is corrected automatically using the amounts in the first line item.
NO SPECIAL G/L TRANSACTIONS	Prevent entry of special G/L transactions.
DOCUMENTS NOT CROSS-COMPANY CODE	Cross-company code entries are prevented.
DOCUMENTS MUST BE COMPLETE FOR PARKING	Prevents incomplete documents from being parked.
NO PARTNER BUSINESS AREA IN HEAD.SCREEN	Default partner business area cannot be entered in document header.
CALCULATE TAXES ON NET AMOUNT	Indicates the G/L account amounts entered are net of taxes.
COPY TEXT FOR G/L ACCOUNT ENTRY	Automatically copies text from last G/L line item to subsequent line items.
DO NOT COPY TAX CODE	Deactivates the setting that the last tax code entered is automatically copied to G/L account line items.
FAST ENTRY VIA ISR NUMBER	Enables the fast entry of incoming invoices using the ISR subscriber number.
ISR ENTRY WITH CONTROL DISPLAY	Provides the ability to enter an alternative vendor number in cases where several vendors may have the same ISR number.
DO NOT UPDATE CONTROL TOTALS	Control totals are not updated.
AUTOMATIC NEGATIVE POSTING	When the negative postings indicator is set for at least one manually entered line, also makes any automatically generated lines negative postings.
DEFAULT DOCUMENT CURRENCY	1. Default local currency used in header currency field. 2. Default last currency used in header currency field. 3. Default no currency in the header currency field.
DEFAULT COMPANY CODE	When the NO COMPANY CODE PROPOSAL indicator is checked, you must manually select the company code to be used.
HIDE TRANSACTION	Hides the TRANSACTION field on the entry screen.
PROPOSE FINAL AMOUNT	The system proposes the final invoice amount in the customer or vendor line, after a G/L line has been entered.

Table 10.1 Editing Options and Descriptions (Cont.)

Editing Option	Description
D/C INDICATOR AS +/- SIGN	Allows the entry of +/- sign with amounts; the debit/credit indicator is thus derived.
DISPLAY PERIODS	Enables the display of period on the entry screen under basic data.
POSTING IN SPECIAL PERIODS POSSIBLE	Enables the period field for data input.
ALWAYS USE PAYMENT BASE DEADLINE	Only permits payment deadline calculation based on the baseline date.
DOCUMENT TYPE OPTION	1. Displays document type in header.
	2. Document type is ready for input.
	3. Displays document type using short name.
	4. Document type is ready for input using short name.
	5. Document type is hidden.
DOCUMENT DATE EQUALS POSTING DATE	Defaults the document date from the posting date.
COMPLEX SEARCH FOR BUSINESS PARTNER	Specifies when entering a vendor invoice if a complex search is possible for the number of the trading partner.
PROPOSE LAST TAX CODE	Proposes the last tax code used the next time the transaction is called.
TAX CODE: ONLY DISPLAY SHORT TEXT	Changes the tax code dropdown list in the transaction to only display the short text of the tax code.

Table 10.1 Editing Options and Descriptions (Cont.)

This concludes our discussion of editing options. In the next section we'll present material on the post with reference functionality.

10.1.6 Post with Reference

Post with reference is a quick and easy way to create a new customer invoice by replicating all or most of the accounting data from a document that has already been posted. It is much like a document copy function, except for flow control indicators provided by SAP that allow you to select specific actions to control in the process. For example, there is a DO NOT PROPOSE AMOUNTS flow control indicator. When this indicator is selected, you must enter document line item amounts.

Post with reference is a universal concept in FI, but the scope of our discussion in this section is limited to its use in Transaction FB70. We will demonstrate its use with a simple example and provide a complete list of flow control options and their descriptions (Table 10.2 later in this section). Bear in mind that post with reference offers no unique functionality to A/R. If in Chapter 3 and Chapter 6 you found the post with reference useful for G/L and A/P transactions, you are likely to find it useful for A/R transactions as well.

Post with reference can be used when you enter a customer invoice document via Transaction FB70 or application menu path ACCOUNTING • FINANCIAL ACCOUNTING • ACCOUNTS RECEIVABLE • DOCUMENT ENTRY • FB70—INVOICE, as shown in Figure 10.41.

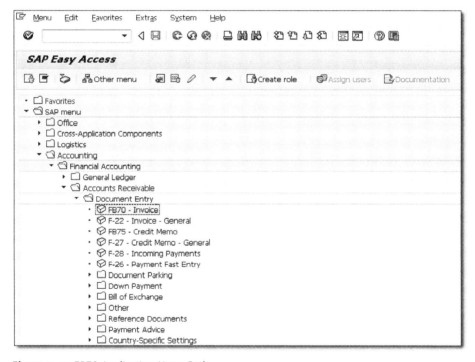

Figure 10.41 FB70 Application Menu Path

Double-click FB70—INVOICE from the menu path shown in Figure 10.41, or enter "FB70" in the COMMAND field (Figure 10.42) and press Enter.

Figure 10.42 FB70 in Command Field

From the ENTER CUSTOMER INVOICE entry screen (Figure 10.43), initiate the post with reference function from the dropdown menu GOTO • POST WITH REFERENCE (Figure 10.43), or press [Shift]+[F9].

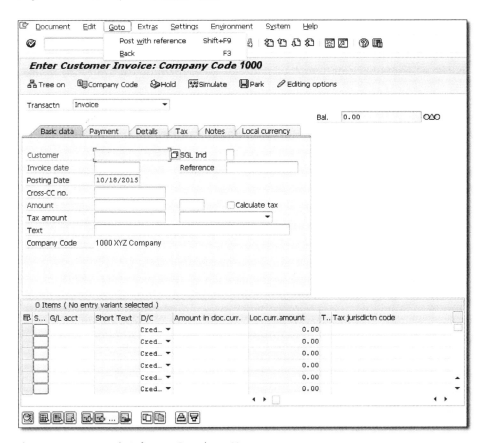

Figure 10.43 Post with Reference Dropdown Menu

The post with reference POST DOCUMENT: HEADER DATA selection screen will open (Figure 10.44). Here, enter the DOCUMENT NUMBER, COMPANY CODE, and FISCAL YEAR fields in the REFERENCE section. For this example, select the DO NOT PROPOSE AMOUNTS indicator in the FLOW CONTROL section.

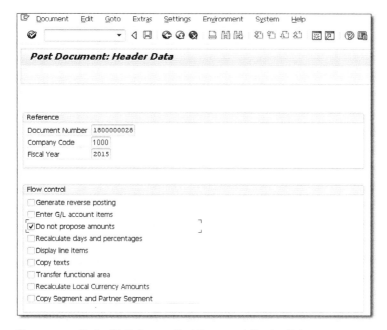

Figure 10.44 Post with Reference Post Document Header Data

Once the relevant fields are populated in the Post Document: Header Data screen, press [Enter] to access the first screen of the new customer invoice document (Figure 10.45). Header data in this new document contains the field values copied from the reference document. Note that you can edit many field values at this point.

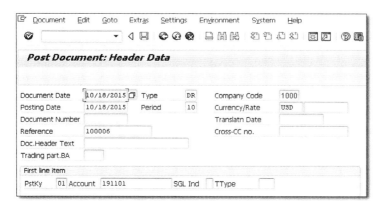

Figure 10.45 Post with Reference Header Data

In this example, we changed the DOCUMENT DATE, POSTING DATE, and REFERENCE fields (Figure 10.46).

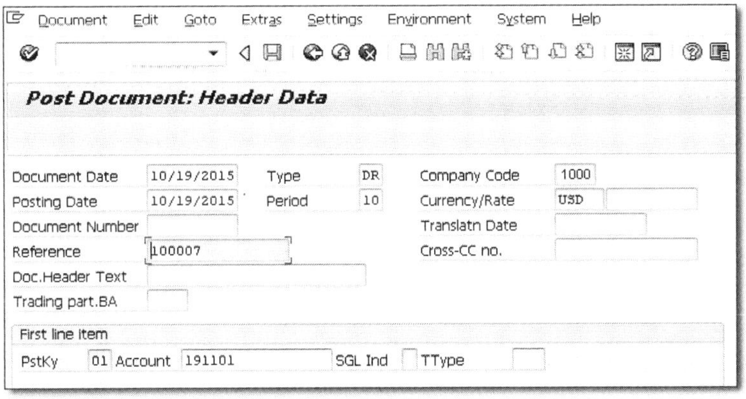

Figure 10.46 Post with Reference Header Data with Changes

Once you have changed the header fields as needed, press Enter, and the POST DOCUMENT ADD CUSTOMER ITEM screen will open (Figure 10.47).

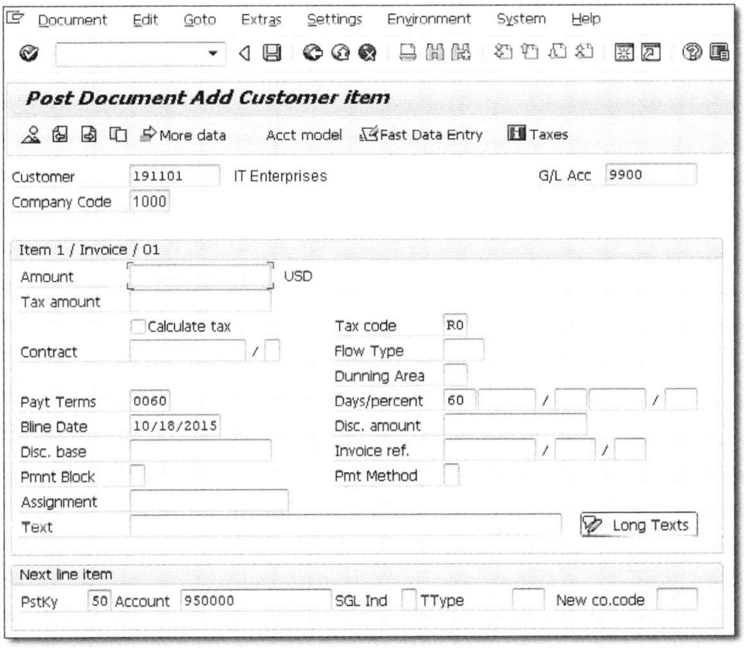

Figure 10.47 Post with Reference Add Customer Item

Note that the AMOUNT field is blank. This is because you selected the DO NOT PROPOSE AMOUNTS indicator in the FLOW CONTROL section (Figure 10.44) when you initiated the post with reference transaction.

For this example, entered "2000" in the AMOUNT field (Figure 10.48).

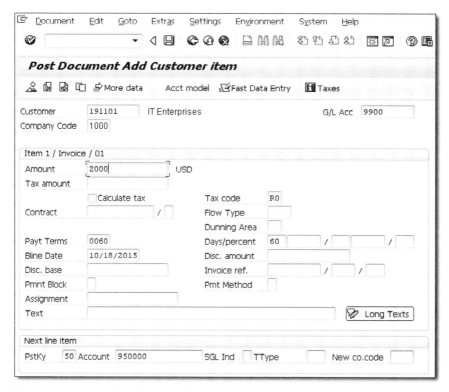

Figure 10.48 Post with Reference Add Customer Item with Amount Change

Once the AMOUNT field is entered, press ⌊Enter⌋, and a second POST DOCUMENT ADD G/L ACCOUNT ITEM screen will open (Figure 10.49). Again, the AMOUNT field is blank.

For this example, again enter "2000" in the AMOUNT field (Figure 10.50).

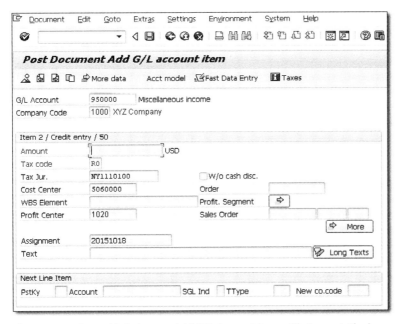

Figure 10.49 Post with Reference Add G/L Account Item with Amount Blank

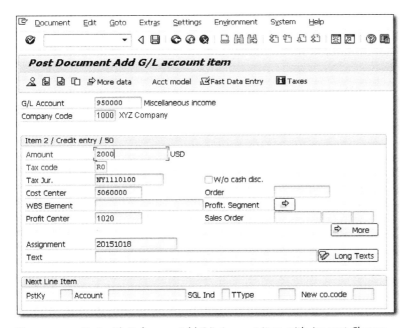

Figure 10.50 Post with Reference Add G/L Account Item with Amount Change

After entering all G/L account line items, click the Post icon 🖫 or press ⌃Ctrl⌃+ ⌃S⌃ to post the customer invoice document (Figure 10.51). A message appears with the new customer invoice document number.

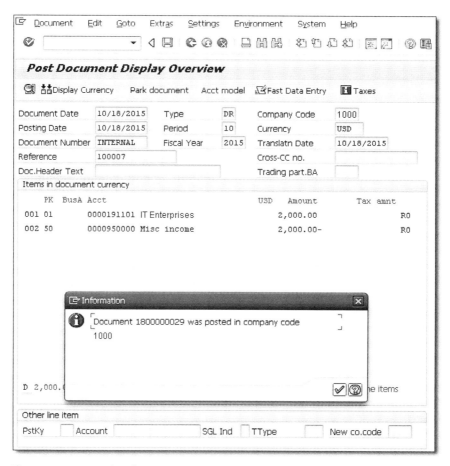

Figure 10.51 Post with Reference Document Created Message

This completes our post with reference example in A/R. Table 10.2 provides a complete list of flow control options and their descriptions (as seen in Figure 10.44). Flow control indicators are the same for all post with reference transactions, so you will not see any unique indicators for A/R.

Flow Control Indicator	Description
GENERATE REVERSE POSTING	Automatically generates reverse debit/credit indicators to offset the reference document.
ENTER G/L ACCOUNT ITEMS	Line items are transferred to the fast entry screen for G/L accounts so that several line items can be displayed and processed from one screen.
DO NOT PROPOSE AMOUNTS	Line item amounts must be manually entered in the new document.
RECALCULATE DAYS AND PERCENTAGES	Days and percentages from payment terms will be recalculated.
DISPLAY LINE ITEMS	Displays each individual line item separately so that default field values can be changed if necessary.
COPY TEXTS	Copies long texts from reference document to the new document.
TRANSFER FUNCTIONAL AREA	Functional area is normally derived; therefore, this option transfers the reference functional area instead of rederiving it.
RECALCULATE LOCAL CURRENCY AMOUNTS	Recalculates local currency amounts to account for changes in exchange rates.
COPY SEGMENT AND PARTNER SEGMENT	These fields are normally derived; therefore, this option transfers them instead of rederiving their values.

Table 10.2 Flow Control Indicators and Descriptions

10.2 Credit Memos

Customer invoices are amounts owed to you by customers for goods or services purchased. *Credit memos*, on the other hand, are credits issued back to the customer's account. A credit may be due for any number of reasons, such as overpayment, damaged goods, additional discounts, and erroneous bill amounts.

Credit memos allow you to correct erroneous customer balances and to offset incoming payment balances. In other words, the amount paid to you is the invoice amount less any credit memos posted to the customer's account.

In the A/R module, you can post a credit memo via Transaction FB75 or application menu path ACCOUNTING • FINANCIAL ACCOUNTING • ACCOUNTS RECEIVABLE • DOCUMENT ENTRY • FB75 — CREDIT MEMO, as seen in Figure 10.52.

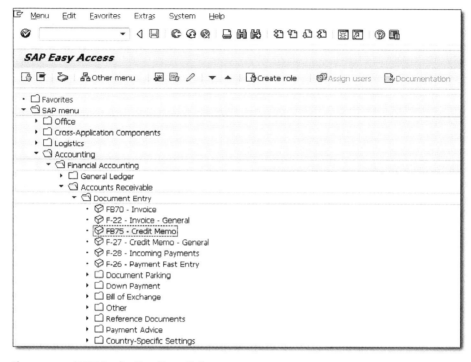

Figure 10.52 FB75 Application Menu Path

Double-click FB75 — CREDIT MEMO from the menu path shown in Figure 10.52, or enter "FB75" in the COMMAND field (Figure 10.53) and press [Enter].

Figure 10.53 FB75 in Command Field

The ENTER CUSTOMER CREDIT MEMO screen will open (Figure 10.54). In the document header, enter values for the CUSTOMER, DOCUMENT DATE, and AMOUNT fields and any other fields that are required, but do not default a value. In this example, field values defaulted for Posting Date, Company Code, and Currency.

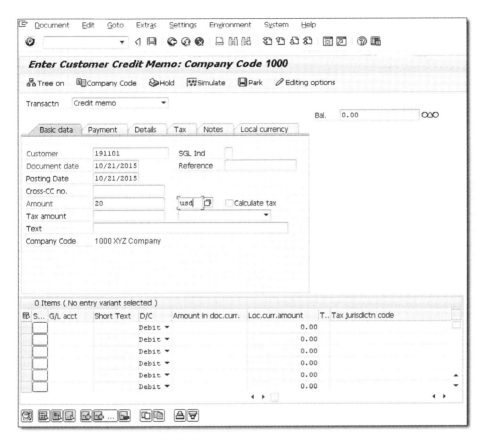

Figure 10.54 Enter Customer Credit Memo

With header entry complete, enter at least one G/L line item (Figure 10.55). In this example, the line item is an offset (i.e., debit) to a revenue account. Values were manually entered here in the G/L Acct, D/C (i.e., debit/credit indicator), Amount, Tax Code, and Profit Center line item fields.

After entering document line items, click the Simulate button in the top center of the Enter Customer Credit Memo screen to initiate simulation of the customer credit memo posting logic, which will determine if the document can be properly posted. If the simulation is unsuccessful, an error message will appear. If successful, the document overview screen opens, as shown in Figure 10.56.

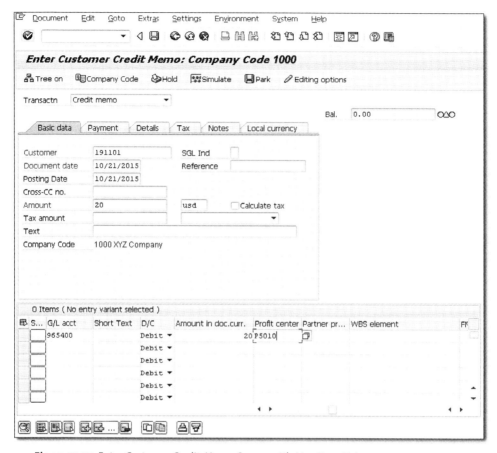

Figure 10.55 Enter Customer Credit Memo Screen with Line Item Entry

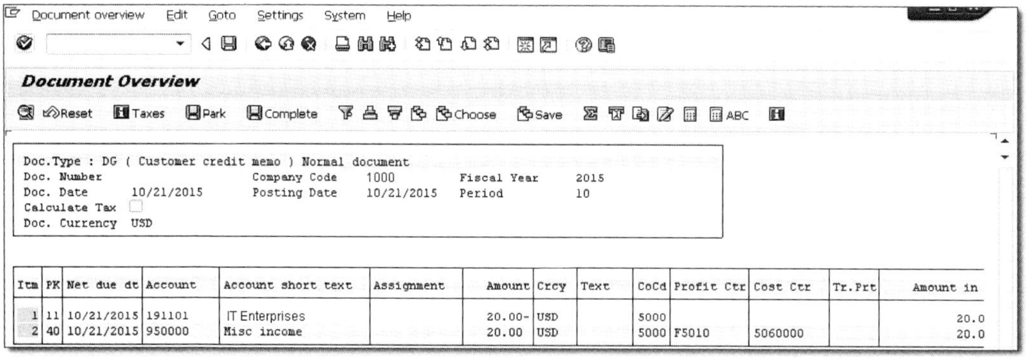

Figure 10.56 Enter Customer Credit Memo Document Overview

Once simulation is complete, click the POST icon 🖫 to the right of the COMMAND field in the upper-left-hand corner of the screen. This will post the customer credit memo, and a message will appear with the new document number, as shown in Figure 10.57.

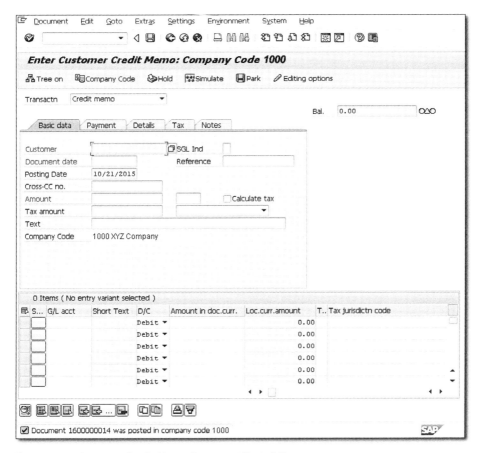

Figure 10.57 Customer Credit Memo Document Posted Message

10.3 Down Payments Received

Down payments received are prepayments from a customer in advance of receiving goods or services. A down payment may be requested as a sign of good faith or required in order to reserve a product.

An optional step in the down payment process in A/R is the *down payment request*. You enter a customer down payment request and then clear it against an incoming down payment. Down payment requests are *noted items* in FI, meaning that they do not update G/L account balances. In other words, down payment requests are not reflected in either the transaction figures or the balance displays. They can only be viewed in line item displays by specifying that you want to see noted items.

To enter a customer down payment request in the A/R module, use Transaction F-37 or application menu path ACCOUNTING • FINANCIAL ACCOUNTING • ACCOUNTS RECEIVABLE • DOCUMENT ENTRY • DOWN PAYMENT • F-37—REQUEST, as shown in Figure 10.58.

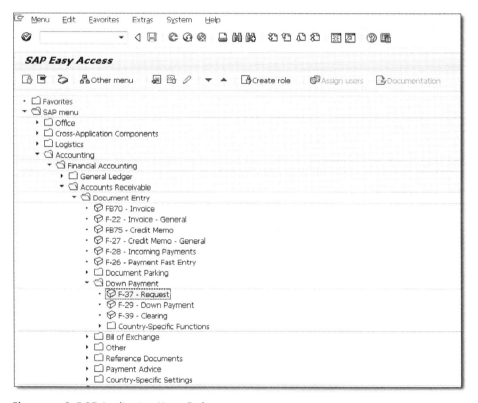

Figure 10.58 F-37 Application Menu Path

Double-click F-37—Request from the menu path shown in Figure 10.58, or enter "F-37" in the Command field (Figure 10.59) and press ⌷Enter⌷.

Figure 10.59 F-37 in Command Field

The Customer Down Payment Request: Header Data screen will open (Figure 10.60). In the document header, enter a value for Document Date and any other fields that are required, but do not prepopulate a field value. In this example, field values defaulted for Posting Date, Type (i.e., document type), Period, Company Code, and Currency.

In the Customer section at the bottom of the screen, you must also enter an Account and special G/L indicator (in the Trg.sp.G/L ind. field).

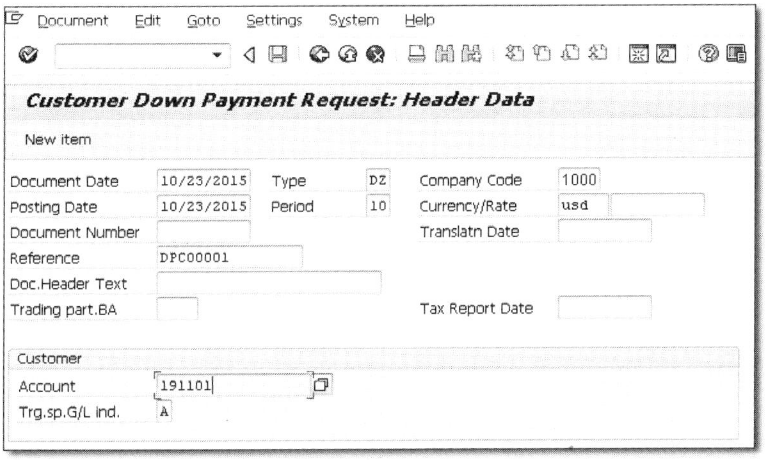

Figure 10.60 Customer Down Payment Request Header Data

With header data complete, click on the New Item button. The Customer Down Payment Request Correct Customer Item screen will open (Figure 10.61). Here, enter values for the Amount, Due on, and any other required fields.

369

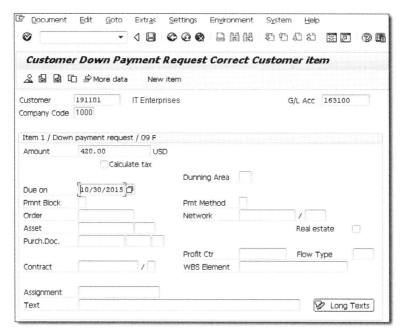

Figure 10.61 Add Customer Item to Customer Down Payment Request

After entering the customer line item, click the SAVE icon 🖫 in the top of the entry screen to the right of the COMMAND field. This will post the customer down payment request, and a message will appear with the new document number, as shown in Figure 10.62.

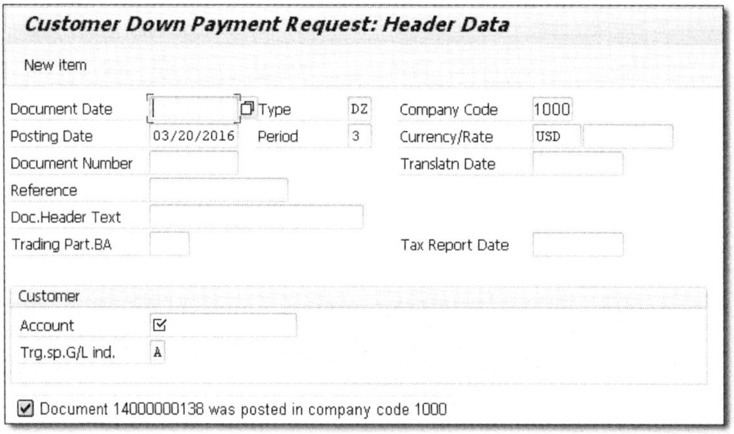

Customer Down Payment Request: Header Data

New item

Document Date		Type	DZ	Company Code	1000
Posting Date	03/20/2016	Period	3	Currency/Rate	USD
Document Number				Translatn Date	
Reference					
Doc.Header Text					
Trading Part.BA				Tax Report Date	

Customer

Account ☑
Trg.sp.G/L ind. A

☑ Document 14000000138 was posted in company code 1000

Figure 10.62 Customer Down Payment Request Document Posted Message

When a down payment is received, enter the customer down payment in the A/R module using Transaction F-29 or application menu path ACCOUNTING • FINANCIAL ACCOUNTING • ACCOUNTS RECEIVABLE • DOCUMENT ENTRY • DOWN PAYMENT • F-29 DOWN PAYMENT, as shown in Figure 10.63.

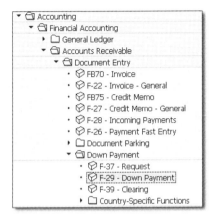

Figure 10.63 F-29 Application Menu Path

Double-click F-29—DOWN PAYMENT from the menu path shown in Figure 10.63. The POST CUSTOMER DOWN PAYMENT REQUEST: HEADER DATA screen will open. In the document header, enter a value for DOCUMENT DATE and any other fields that are required but that do not contain a default value. In our example, field values defaulted for POSTING DATE, TYPE (i.e., document type), PERIOD, COMPANY CODE, and CURRENCY.

In the CUSTOMER section, at the bottom of the screen, you must also enter an ACCOUNT and special G/L indicator (in the TRG.SP.G/L IND. field). In the BANK section, you must enter an ACCOUNT and AMOUNT. In this example, we also entered a value for PROFIT CENTER.

When all field values are entered, click the REQUESTS button at the top of the screen. The POST CUSTOMER DOWN PAYMENT CHOOSE REQUESTS screen will open. Select your request. After selecting your down payment request, click the CREATE DOWN PAYMENTS button in the top-left portion of the screen. The POST CUSTOMER DOWN PAYMENT DISPLAY OVERVIEW screen will open.

Click the SAVE icon 🖫 to post the customer down payment.

Now that you understand customer down payments, let's move on to the next topic: resetting and reversing A/R documents.

10.4 Resetting and Reversing Documents

The most important thing to know before attempting to reverse an A/R document is what type of document you are working with. It may be a customer invoice or credit memo, and for reversal purposes these documents can be classified as either clearing or nonclearing documents.

Clearing documents are those produced through a post with clearing transaction, such as Transaction F-04 (see Chapter 3, Section 3.2), or those documents produced as an incoming payment using Transaction F-28. These documents have two technical components: First, a clearing document contains complete header data and at least two completed line items with debit/credit amounts netting to zero. The second component of a clearing document is account clearing. Through the clearing process, a customer open item is selected and its status changed from open to cleared when the clearing document posts.

A *nonclearing accounting document* has the same attributes as a clearing document, except that it does not clear a customer open item. Therefore, a nonclearing document does not change the status of a customer line item from open to cleared. Nonclearing documents are the simplest to reverse.

To reverse a single A/R document, use Transaction FB08 or application menu path Accounting • Financial Accounting • Accounts Receivable • Document • Reverse • FB08 — Individual Reversal, as shown in Figure 10.64.

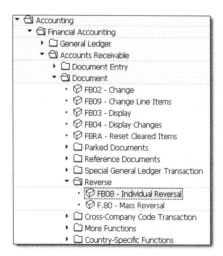

Figure 10.64 FB08 Application Menu Path in A/R

Double-click on FB08 from the menu path shown in Figure 10.64, or enter "FB08" in the COMMAND field (Figure 10.65) and press ⌑Enter⌑.

Figure 10.65 FB08 in Command Field

The REVERSE DOCUMENT: HEADER DATA screen opens (Figure 10.66). At a minimum, the DOCUMENT NUMBER, COMPANY CODE, FISCAL YEAR, and REVERSAL REASON fields are required.

The REVERSAL REASON field is noted in the reversed document. It also determines if an alternative posting date is allowed or if the reversal can be created from a negative posting. In this example, the REVERSAL REASON field is populated with a value of 01, indicating that the reversal will take place in the current period.

```
 Document   Edit   Goto   System   Help

 Reverse Document: Header Data

 Display before reversal    Document list    Mass Reversal

 Document Details
 Document Number      1800000003
 Company Code         1000
 Fiscal Year          2016

 Specifications for Reverse Posting
 Reversal Reason      01
 Posting Date                          Tax Reporting Date
 Posting Period

 Check management specifications
 Void reason code
```

Figure 10.66 FB08 Reverse Document Header Data Screen in A/R

When all the required fields are entered, click the POST icon 🖫 or press ⌑Ctrl⌑+⌑S⌑ to post the A/R reversal document. A message appears with the new G/L document number (Figure 10.67).

373

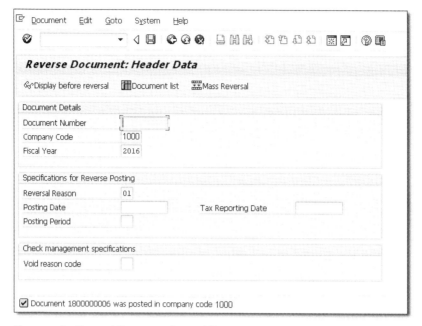

Figure 10.67 Reversal Document Created Message in A/R

If you have more than one nonclearing document to reverse, use Transaction F.80 or application menu path ACCOUNTING • FINANCIAL ACCOUNTING • ACCOUNTS RECEIVABLE • DOCUMENT • REVERSE • F.80—MASS REVERSAL, as shown in Figure 10.68.

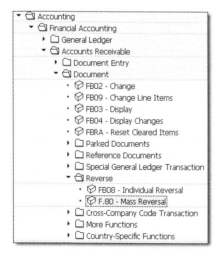

Figure 10.68 F.80 Application Menu Path in A/R

Double-click F.80—MASS REVERSAL from the menu path shown in Figure 10.68, or enter "F.80" in the COMMAND field (Figure 10.69) and press Enter.

Figure 10.69 F.80 in Command Field

The MASS REVERSAL OF DOCUMENTS: INITIAL SCREEN opens (Figure 10.70). As in Transaction FB08, the COMPANY CODE, DOCUMENT NUMBER, FISCAL YEAR, and REVERSAL REASON fields are required. Note that you can enter a range of values for these fields in Transaction F.80, whereas in Transaction FB08 you can only enter a single value for each. In Transaction F.80, you also have a LEDGER field, which in most cases will reflect your primary ledger.

| Program | Edit | Goto | System | Help |

Mass Reversal of Documents: Initial Screen

Company code	1000	to	
Document Number	1800000004	to	1800000005
Fiscal Year	2016	to	
Ledger	0L		

General selections

Document type		to	
Posting date		to	
Entry date		to	
Reference number		to	
Reference Transaction		to	
Reference key		to	
Logical system		to	

Reverse posting details

Reason for reversal	01
Posting Date	
Posting Period	
Tax Reporting Date	
✓ Test Run	

Cross-company code transactions

- ⦿ Do not process
- ◯ Process
- ◯ Relevant docs if possible
- ◯ Only reverse completely

Figure 10.70 Mass Document Reversal Screen in A/R

Transaction F.80 has other notable features. Under GENERAL SELECTIONS, you will see have several input fields that may be useful. In addition, in the REVERSE POSTING DETAILS section you will see a TEST RUN button. For mass reversals, it is always a good idea to run the program in test mode first.

When all the required fields are entered, click the EXECUTE icon ⊕ or press [F8] to post the A/R reversal documents. Detailed results are provided on the MASS REVERSAL OF DOCUMENTS output screen (Figure 10.71).

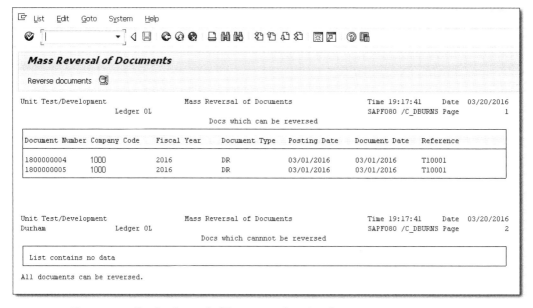

Figure 10.71 Massive Reversal of Documents Overview Screen

That concludes our discussion of the individual and mass reversals of nonclearing A/R documents. Now, let's discuss how to reverse clearing documents.

To reverse an A/R clearing document, use Transaction FBRA or application menu path ACCOUNTING • FINANCIAL ACCOUNTING • ACCOUNTS RECEIVABLE • DOCUMENT • FBRA—RESET CLEARED ITEMS, as shown in Figure 10.72.

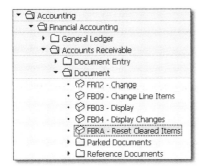

Figure 10.72 FBRA Application Menu Path in A/R

Double-click FBRA—Reset Cleared Items from the menu path shown in Figure 10.72, or enter "FBRA" in the Command field (Figure 10.73) and press Enter.

Figure 10.73 FBRA in Command Field

The Reset Cleared Items screen opens (Figure 10.74). The Clearing Document, Company Code, and Fiscal Year fields are all required.

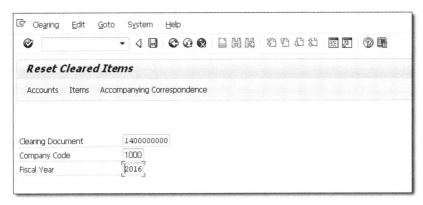

Figure 10.74 Reset Cleared Items

After entering the required fields, click the Reset Cleared Items icon ⊕, or press Ctrl+S. This will prompt the Reversal of Clearing Document dialog box

(Figure 10.75) to pop up. In this box, you must choose one of three options: ONLY RESETTING, RESETTING AND REVERS, or CANCEL.

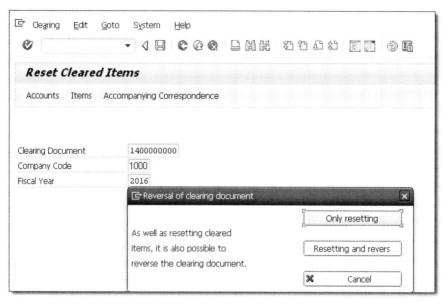

Figure 10.75 Reversal of Clearing Document Dialogue Box

The ONLY RESETTING option does not reverse the clearing document. Instead, it breaks the reference between a clearing document and the A/R item it cleared and changes the status of the cleared A/R item back to open. Only use this option when the A/R item selected for clearing was the wrong line item. The clearing document thus becomes an open item and can be reassigned to clear the correct A/R open item.

The RESETTING AND REVERS option not only resets the cleared item back to open status but also reverses the clearing document. For this example, select this option; the REVERSAL DATA dialogue box will pop up (Figure 10.76).

The REVERSAL REASON field is required, and the value selected is noted in the reversed document. This value also determines if an alternative posting date is allowed or if the reversal can be created from a negative posting. In this example, the REVERSAL REASON field is populated with a value of 01, signifying that the reversal will take place in the current period.

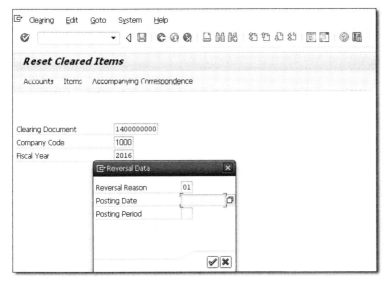

Figure 10.76 Reversal Data Dialogue Box

Click the CONTINUE icon ☑, or press ⌈Enter⌋. Two subsequent information dialogue boxes will appear. The first, shown in Figure 10.77, states that the clearing document was reset. The second, shown in Figure 10.78, provides the number for a new document that has been posted, which is the document that reversed the clearing document.

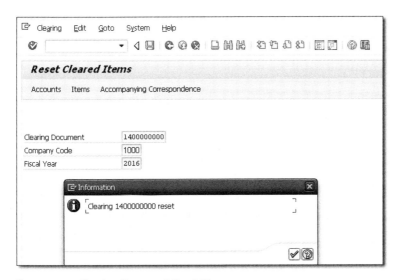

Figure 10.77 Clearing Document Reset Message

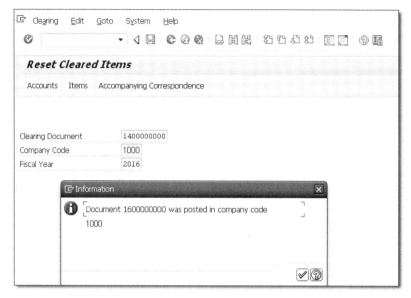

Figure 10.78 Reversal Document Posted Message

You should now have a good understanding of clearing versus nonclearing documents, how to reverse individual A/R documents, and reversing multiple documents. In the next section the topic of changing and displaying documents is discussed.

10.5   Changing and Displaying Documents

This section covers the change and display capabilities for A/R accounting documents. The scope of this section is limited to Transaction FB70, but the same principles apply for other A/R documents.

Rules for changing field values in SAP accounting documents are defined in configuration, and separate rules are defined for header and line item fields. Note, however, that SAP will never allow you to change fields considered central to the principle of orderly accounting. In other words, fields that are material to A/R and G/L account balances, posting dates, and integration cannot be changed after an A/R accounting document has been posted. These include not only the POST-ING DATE, DEBIT/CREDIT INDICATOR, and AMOUNT fields, but also update objects (i.e., cost center). If an A/R accounting document contains an incorrect value of this sort, the document should be reversed using Transaction FB08 or Transaction FBRA (see Section 10.4).

Note that the principle of orderly accounting is applicable to more than just A/R documents. It holds true for G/L, A/P, asset accounting, banking, and any accounting entry. To change an A/R document, use Transaction FB02 or application menu path ACCOUNTING • FINANCIAL ACCOUNTING • ACCOUNTS RECEIVABLE • DOCUMENT • FB02—CHANGE, as shown in Figure 10.79.

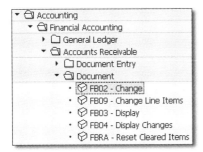

Figure 10.79 FB02 Application Menu Path in A/R

Double-click FB02—CHANGE from the menu path shown in Figure 10.79. The CHANGE DOCUMENT: INITIAL SCREEN opens (Figure 10.80). The DOCUMENT NUMBER, COMPANY CODE, and FISCAL YEAR fields are required.

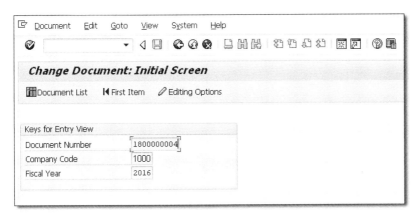

Figure 10.80 Change Document: Initial Screen

After entering all field values, press [Enter]. The CHANGE DOCUMENT: DATA ENTRY VIEW screen opens (Figure 10.81).

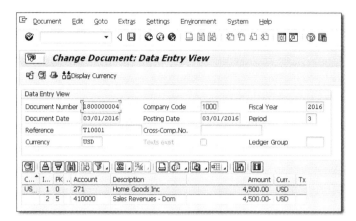

Figure 10.81 Change Document: Data Entry View

To change a header field, click on the HEADER icon 🖳 , and the document header dialogue box will pop up (Figure 10.82). Fields that cannot be changed are greyed out. Fields that can be changed appear white and are ready for field values to be entered or changed.

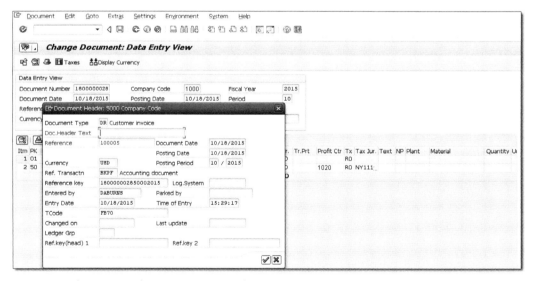

Figure 10.82 Change Document Header Screen

From the CHANGE DOCUMENT: DATA ENTRY VIEW screen (Figure 10.81), you can change line item fields by double-clicking a line. After doing so, the CHANGE DOCUMENT: LINE ITEM screen opens (Figure 10.83).

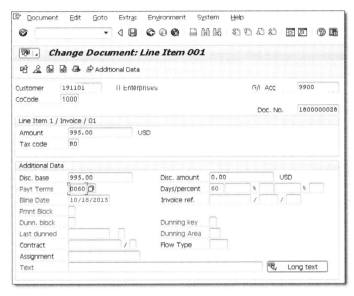

Figure 10.83 Change Document: Line Item

Fields that cannot be changed are greyed out. Those that can be changed appear white and are ready for field values to be entered or changed. In this example, we changed the TEXT field (Figure 10.84).

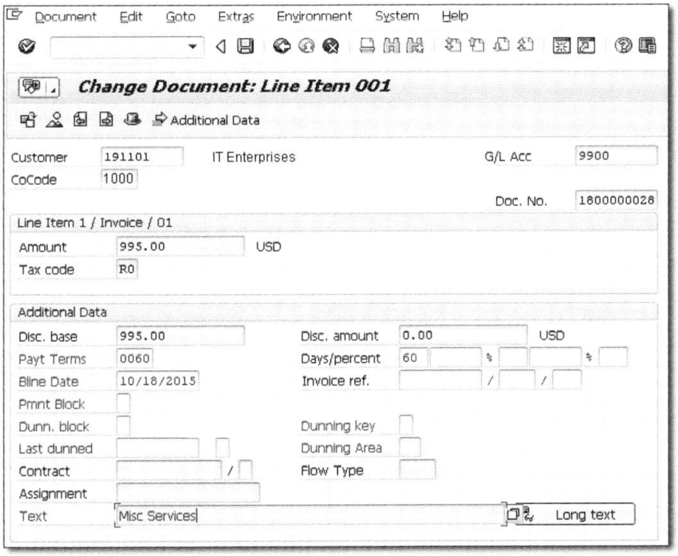

Figure 10.84 Change Document with Line Item Text Change

After changing field values, click the SAVE icon 🖫 , or press ⌈Ctrl⌉+⌈S⌉. A message indicates that the document changes have been saved (Figure 10.85).

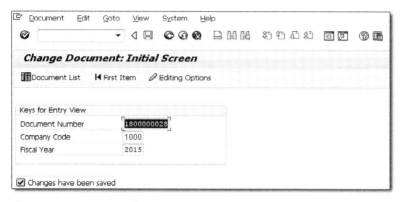

Figure 10.85 Document Changes Have Been Saved Message

To display an A/R accounting document, use Transaction FB03 or application menu path ACCOUNTING • FINANCIAL ACCOUNTING • ACCOUNTS RECEIVABLE • DOCUMENT • FB03—DISPLAY, as shown in Figure 10.86.

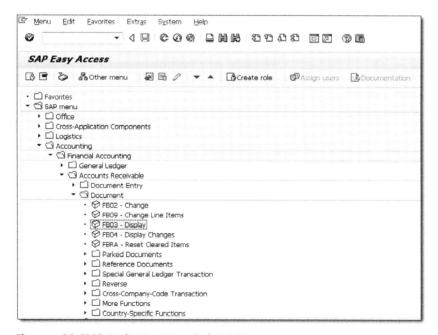

Figure 10.86 FB03 Application Menu Path in A/R

Double-click FB03—Display from the menu path shown in Figure 10.86, or enter "FB03" in the Command field (Figure 10.87) and press ⌈Enter⌉.

Figure 10.87 FB03 in Command Field

The Document Display: Initial Screen screen opens (Figure 10.88). The Document Number, Company Code, and Fiscal Year fields are required.

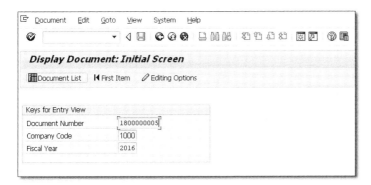

Figure 10.88 Document Display: Initial Screen

After entering the required field values, press ⌈Enter⌉. The Display Document: Data Entry View screen opens (Figure 10.89).

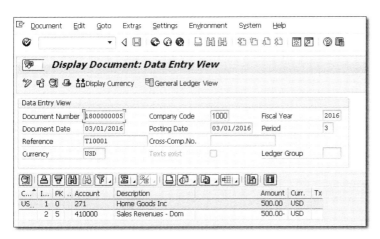

Figure 10.89 Display Documen:Data Entry View

385

From this screen, you can double-click a line to view line item details, or click the
HEADER icon ⏺ to view header details.

10.6 Process Incoming Payments

Among other things, A/R includes steps for creating a customer invoice and processing payment receipt. The customer invoice includes specific details (e.g.,
amount, due date) about the receivables owed by a customer. Processing an
incoming payment involves the physical transfer of funds from a customer.

A customer payment can be received several different ways, including check,
wire transfer, and direct deposit. Electronic payments can automatically clear
open customer invoices through the electronic bank reconciliation process in
SAP, which is beyond the scope of this chapter. This section covers the manual
creation of an incoming payment using Transaction F-28.

To post a manual incoming payment using Transaction F-28, follow the application menu path ACCOUNTING • FINANCIAL ACCOUNTING • ACCOUNTS RECEIVABLE •
DOCUMENT ENTRY • F-28—INCOMING PAYMENTS, as shown in Figure 10.90.

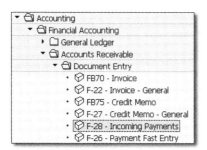

Figure 10.90 F-28 Application Menu Path

Double-click F-28—INCOMING PAYMENTS from the menu path, or enter "F-28" in
the COMMAND field (Figure 10.91) and press ⌨Enter.

Figure 10.91 F-28 in Command Field

The POST INCOMING PAYMENTS: HEADER DATA screen will open (Figure 10.92). In the top portion of the screen, most field values should contain default values, depending on your configuration and editing options. Make sure to input all required fields that do not list default values. In this example, default values populated into the POSTING DATE, TYPE (i.e., document type), PERIOD, COMPANY CODE, and CURRENCY fields. We manually input a value into the DOCUMENT DATE field.

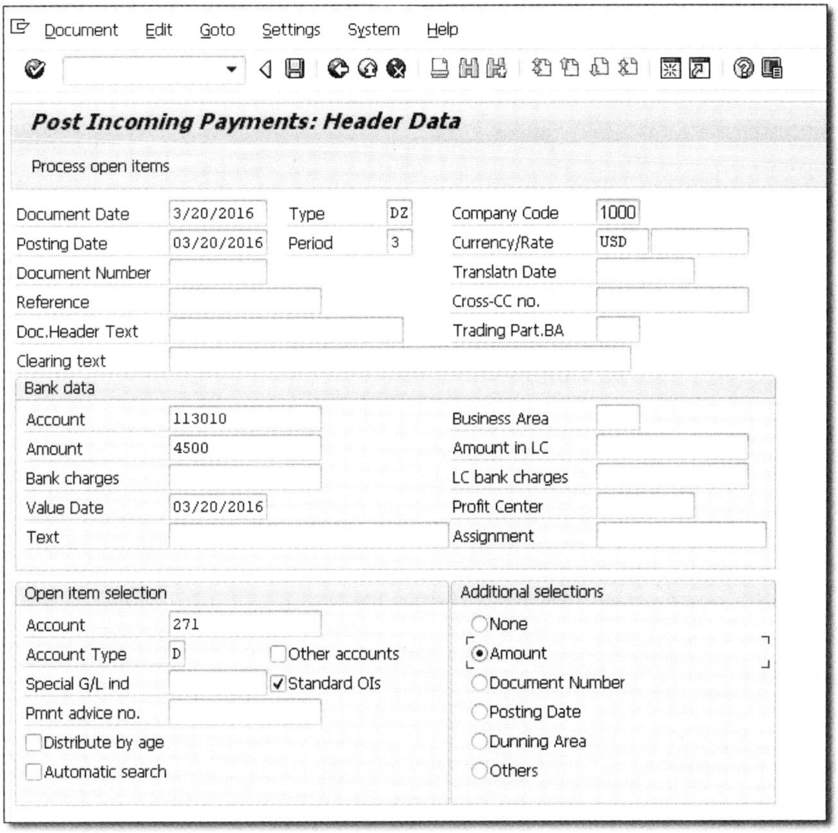

Figure 10.92 Post Incoming Payments: Header Data

In the BANK DATA section, enter values for ACCOUNT, AMOUNT, and any other fields that are required. In this example, we also entered a value in the PROFIT

CENTER field. In the OPEN ITEM SELECTION section, enter the customer number in ACCOUNT.

Finally, in the ADDITIONAL SELECTIONS section, choose a button that indicates how the program should search for and select open invoices. For this example, select the AMOUNT button.

With all relevant fields entered, click the PROCESS OPEN ITEMS button in the top-left portion of the screen (Figure 10.92). The POST INCOMING PAYMENTS ENTER SELECTION CRITERIA screen will open (Figure 10.93). In this example, we entered the amount of our invoice to be paid ($2000) in the FROM and TO fields.

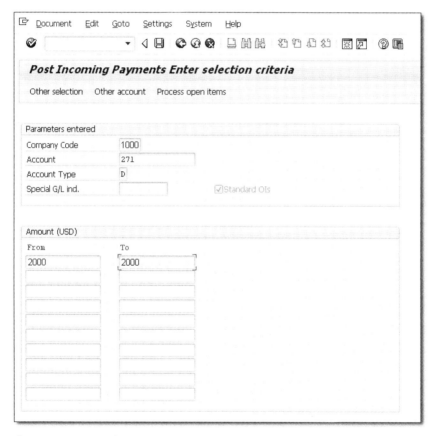

Figure 10.93 Enter Selection Criteria

Once your selection criteria are entered, click the PROCESS OPEN ITEMS button (Figure 10.93) in the top-center portion of the screen. The POST INCOMING PAYMENTS PROCESS OPEN ITEMS screen will open (Figure 10.94).

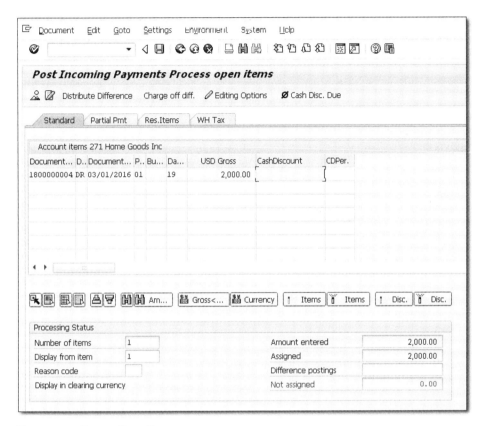

Figure 10.94 Process Open Items

If the correct open items have been selected, click the SAVE icon ▣ , or press Ctrl+S . The program will post the payment document and issue a "document posted" message (Figure 10.95).

This ends our discussion of incoming payments. The next topic, dunning, is important when customers aren't paying their invoices on time. Let's move on to discuss the details in the next section.

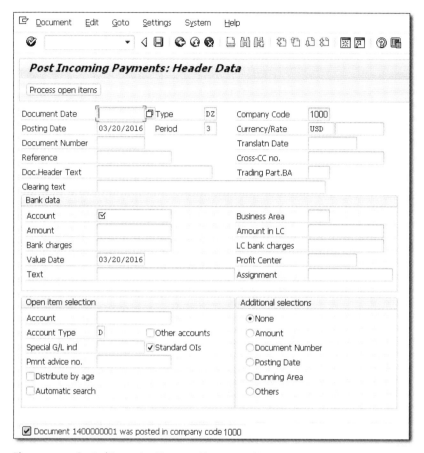

Figure 10.95 Posted Incoming Payment Document Message

10.7 Dunning

Dunning is the process of sending periodic notices to customers regarding overdue payments. Setting up dunning requires configuration and settings within customer master data that are beyond the scope of this book. However, it is essential for an A/R clerk to know how to execute the dunning program, a process we cover in the remainder of this section.

To execute a dunning run, follow application menu path ACCOUNTING • FINANCIAL ACCOUNTING • ACCOUNTS RECEIVABLE • PERIODIC PROCESSING • F150—DUNNING, as shown in Figure 10.96.

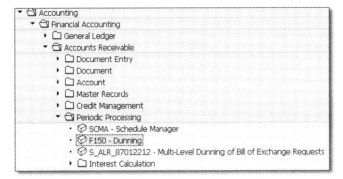

Figure 10.96 F150 Application Menu Path

Double-click F150—DUNNING from the menu path shown in Figure 10.96. The DUNNING program initial screen will open (Figure 10.97). In this screen, enter values for the RUN ON and IDENTIFICATION fields.

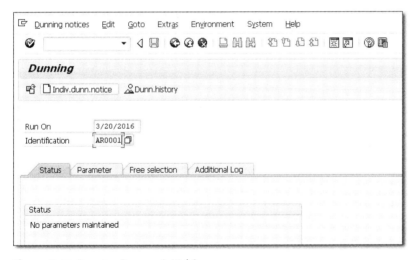

Figure 10.97 Dunning Program Initial Screen

Click on the PARAMETER tab. The DUNNING: PARAMETERS screen opens (Figure 10.98). Enter values for the DUNNING DATE, DOCMNTS POSTED UP TO, COMPANY CODE, and CUSTOMER (or VENDOR, in some circumstances) fields.

Once all the parameters are entered, click the SAVE icon ⊞ or press ⌈Ctrl⌉+⌈S⌉ and return to the STATUS tab (Figure 10.99). A message now appears: PARAMETERS WERE MAINTAINED.

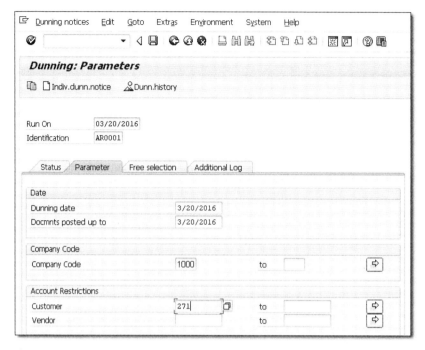

Figure 10.98 F150 Dunning Parameters Screen

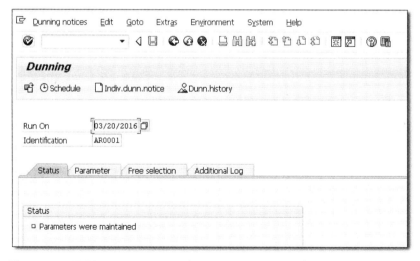

Figure 10.99 F150 Dunning Status with Parameters Maintained

Now, click on the SCHEDULE button in the top-left portion of the screen. The SCHEDULE SELECTION AND PRINT dialogue box will pop up (Figure 10.100) and immediately prompted you to enter a value for OUTPUTDEVICE. To schedule the dunning run and print the dunning notices immediately, enter a value for START DATE and select the checkboxes for START IMMEDIATELY and DUNN.PRINT WITH SCHEDULING?. Then, click the SCHEDULE button in the dialogue box.

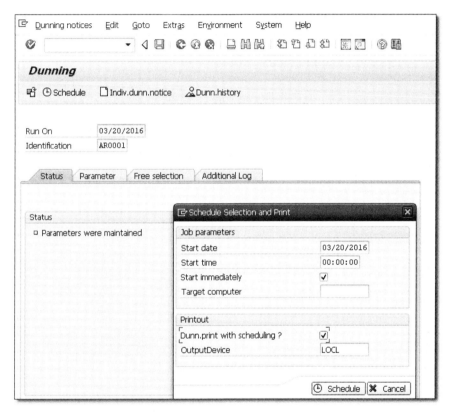

Figure 10.100 Dunning Schedule Selection and Print Dialogue Box

A message will indicate that dunning has been scheduled successfully. Once the printing is complete, you can email your dunning notices or set them up to be automatically emailed to your customers. In addition, the dunning date and dunning level are updated in the customer's SAP master record.

10.8   Credit Management

Credit management is an essential part of working in A/R. There are several parts to the credit management setup, one of which is the definition of groups (e.g., accounting clerk groups) and categories (e.g., risk categories). Customers are allocated to these groups for purposes of reporting and monitoring.

The credit management setup is highly personalized from company to company. Many factors can influence how it is configured. Much depends on your risk tolerance and exposure, credit limits, and customer history.

To see the standard tools and reports available in A/R Credit Management, follow application menu path ACCOUNTING • FINANCIAL ACCOUNTING • ACCOUNTS RECEIVABLE • CREDIT MANAGEMENT, as shown in Figure 10.101.

Figure 10.101 Credit Management Application Menu Path

10.9   Summary

In this chapter, we covered A/R account transactions originating in the A/R module. In Chapter 9, during our discussion of the order-to-cash process, you learned about sales transactions originating in SD-Sales. The discussion in this chapter is limited to A/R transactions, not the sales cycle as a whole.

The most common A/R transaction is the entry of a customer invoice using Transaction FB70. Customer invoices are the documents, which create open customer receivables and result in revenue recognition. We also walked through examples of other A/R transactions, including the creation of a credit memo, down payment request, incoming payment, and document reversals.

Like the other FI modules, A/R requires a host of tools to correct errors and to keep accurate track of receivables and revenue. Resetting and reversing, changing, and displaying documents are just some of the essential tasks of an A/R clerk and A/R supervisor. In addition, dunning and credit management are utilized for monitoring, management, and risk mitigation. Although they do not produce transactions per se, dunning and credit management are important A/R business processes.

In addition to transactions and tools specific to A/R, there are several pieces of standard functionality available in A/R that exist in other modules as well. These include the ability to park, hold, and save documents as completed, along with the tree display, account assignment templates, screen variants, and more. By learning these functions in A/R, you have also acquired knowledge that transcends other areas of FI.

This concludes our discussion of A/R transactions. In the next chapter, we will discuss A/R account inquiries.

In this chapter, we explore transactions and reports you can use to make inquiries about customer accounts and balances in A/R. The transactions and reports in this chapter are used for customer account maintenance and can reveal user entry errors, document interface errors, and account code block mishaps.

11 Accounts Receivable Account Inquiries

In Chapter 9 and Chapter 10 you learned about the order-to-cash business process and many A/R transactions. This chapter provides you with information about A/R account inquiry and maintenance functions that help you research individual transactions, display account balances, view account transaction details, and run reports and queries. Many of the tools discussed in this chapter have practical application not only in month-end and year-end closing, but also in the day-to-day functions performed by A/R clerks and supervisors.

A/R account inquiry and validation are essential job functions of A/R personnel. Often, you can use these functions to uncover data entry and other posting errors. They also play a vital role in the validation and verification of customer account activity. Knowing how to perform the transactions in this chapter provides you with essential skills required in the day-to-day operations of an A/R department. We will discuss the basic tools of the trade and provide guidance about the best transactions to use in different scenarios.

One of the ongoing challenges faced by an A/R department is the large number of inquiries from customers regarding their account balances, expected due dates, and payment receipts. This chapter provides you with the basic tools needed to satisfy these types of inquiries and more.

These functions can be useful in the following ways:

▸ To reconcile A/R reconciliation balances with customer subledger balances

▸ For month-end and year-end account analysis

▸ To assist with cash management needs and forecasting

▸ To perform customer account inquiries

Next, we will discuss the different types of customer account display in detail, including customer balances and line item displays.

11.1   Customer Account Displays

The A/R customer account display allows you to view individual or collective customer account balances and transaction details (i.e., individual A/R documents and line items). The primary transactions used to view customer account balances and account details are Transaction FD10N and Transaction FBL5N.

Drilldown capability is particularly powerful within these two transactions. From Transaction FD10N, you can double-click a balance and immediately drill down into a customer line item display in Transaction FBL5N. Then, within Transaction FBL5N, you can double-click an individual customer line item and immediately be taken into the individual accounting document that contains that customer line item.

Let's take a look at the customer account balance transaction.

11.1.1   Customer Account Balance

Transaction FD10N is the customer account balance display. It allows you to view the account balance by accounting period of one or more customers. The display screen breaks the customer account balance down into a debit balance, credit balance, period balance, cumulative balance, and sales/purchases amounts. By double-clicking any of these numbers, you can drill down to see the detailed transactions making up the balance.

Transaction FD10N is frequently used in A/R to reconcile with G/L receivables account balances. At a high level, this transaction provides the period breakdowns needed for reconciling month-end activities, and it is also useful if you need to drill down into a specific account balance to see the documents that make up that balance.

To display customer balances, use Transaction FD10N or application menu path ACCOUNTING • FINANCIAL ACCOUNTING • ACCOUNTS RECEIVABLE • ACCOUNT • FD10N—DISPLAY BALANCES, as shown in Figure 11.1.

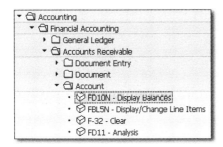

Figure 11.1 FD10N Application Menu Path

Double-click FD10N—DISPLAY BALANCES from the menu path, or enter "FD10N" in the COMMAND field (Figure 11.2) and press ⌷Enter⌷.

Figure 11.2 FD10N in Command Field

The CUSTOMER BALANCE DISPLAY selection screen will open (Figure 11.3). Enter values for the CUSTOMER, COMPANY CODE, and FISCAL YEAR fields and click the EXE-CUTE icon ⊕.

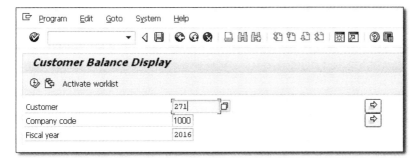

Figure 11.3 FD10N Customer Balance Display Screen

The CUSTOMER BALANCE DISPLAY output screen will open (Figure 11.4). From this screen, you can double-click any number to display balance details, or you can click on the SPECIAL G/L tab to view balances for specific Special G/L transactions, such as down payments.

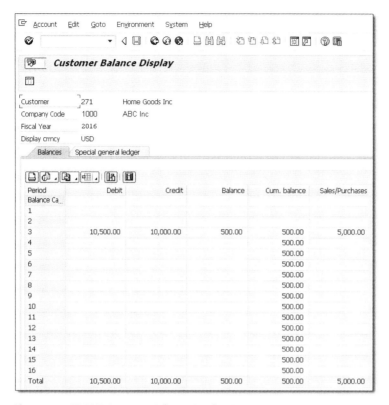

Figure 11.4 FD10N Customer Balance Display Output

Now that we have discussed customer account balance displays, let's look at customer line item displays in the next section.

11.1.2 Customer Account Line Items

Transaction FBL5N is the customer line item display. It provides all the individual documents and account line items posted to a customer account. When using this transaction, the selection screens give you the flexibility to filter data by customer account, company code, posting date, type of transaction, and more. These selection options can be saved as variants", making them reusable. In addition, from the output screen you can filter, search, sort, subtotal, and more. The output can be downloaded into various file formats (such as Excel) making further analysis outside SAP possible when needed. This functionality works the same in A/R as it does in G/L and A/P using Transaction FBL3N and Transaction FBL1N.

Believe it or not, spreadsheets are more in use than ever before in accounting and finance. It is very common to use Transaction FBL5N to query, filter, and sort data, only to export the results into a spreadsheet for further analysis.

The SAP concept of open item management is inherent in A/R, just as it is in A/P and fixed assets. Open item management is a way of tracking, matching, and managing customer accounting line items that are supposed to be offset (i.e., cleared) by other items and net to zero. For example, when a customer invoice is received, an accounting document will post a debit to the customer account. The debit entry to the customer account is considered an open item because, in essence, it has created an open receivable due from the customer. Once payment is received, the open receivable is matched with an offsetting credit to the customer account and its status is changed from open to cleared.

With the concept of open item management in mind, Transaction FBL5N is particularly useful in showing the status of an invoice (i.e., open or cleared) and the due date for each invoice. It is an essential tool for handling customer inquiries regarding the status of invoices and payments. Moreover, Transaction FBL5N can be very telling in finding common errors in a customer account, such as duplicate invoice posting.

To display customer line items using Transaction FBL5N, follow application menu path ACCOUNTING • FINANCIAL ACCOUNTING • ACCOUNTS RECEIVABLE • ACCOUNT • FBL5N—DISPLAY/CHANGE LINE ITEMS, as shown in Figure 11.5.

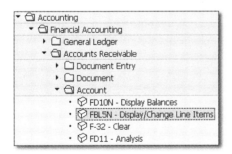

Figure 11.5 FBL5N Application Menu Path

Double-click FBL5N—DISPLAY/CHANGE LINE ITEMS from the menu path, or enter "FBL5N" in the COMMAND field (as shown in Figure 11.6) and press Enter .

Figure 11.6 FBL5N in Command Field

The CUSTOMER LINE ITEM DISPLAY selection screen will open (Figure 11.7). Enter values in the CUSTOMER ACCOUNT and COMPANY CODE fields. The most notable components of this selection screen are the STATUS and TYPE sections under LINE ITEM SELECTION. The STATUS buttons allow you to choose whether to output OPEN ITEMS, CLEARED ITEMS, or both (i.e., ALL ITEMS). You can also narrow your selection of data by entering relevant date parameters.

The checkboxes in the TYPE section allow you to choose the types of documents to display on the output screen.

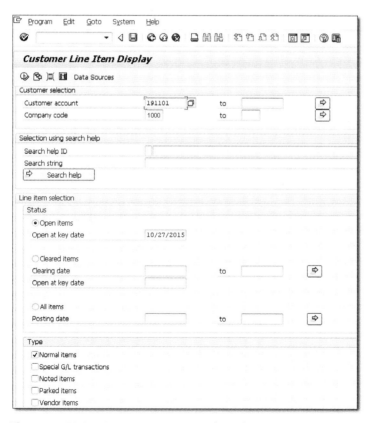

Figure 11.7 FBL5N Customer Line Item Display Selection Screen

Once you have entered all your selection parameters, click the EXECUTE icon ⊕. The CUSTOMER LINE ITEM DISPLAY output screen will open (Figure 11.8).

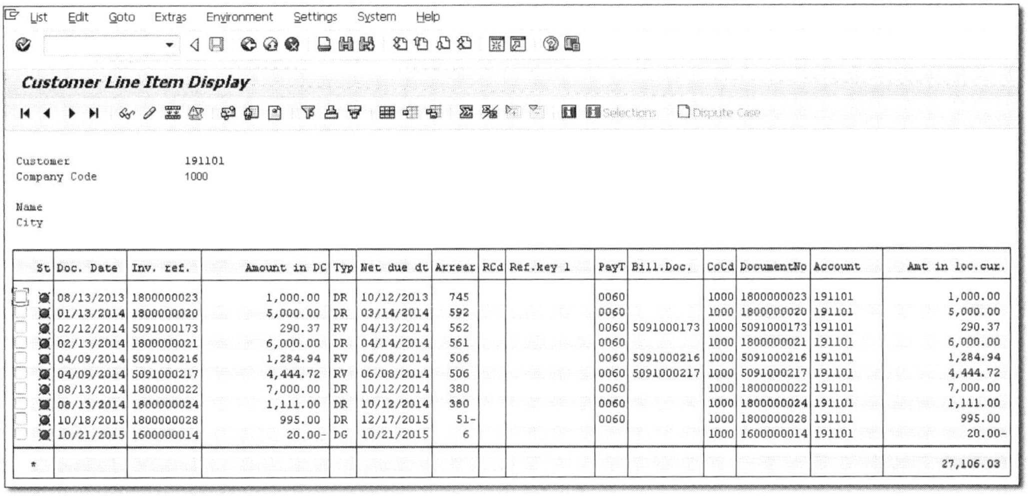

Figure 11.8 FBL5N Customer Line Item Display Output

Once the output is displayed, you can change the layout, sort, filter, total, subtotal, and so on, and your layouts can be saved and reused. In Transaction FBL5N, you can also double-click an individual line item to drill down directly into an A/R invoice or other A/R document. Once in an A/R document, you can then drill down into individual line items in the document. This demonstrates the power of system integration and drilldown capability.

In Chapter 8 a table of frequently used icons in line item display is provided. For your convenience, this table is also provided here (Table 11.1). Nothing new or unique to A/R is provided in this table. In fact, you will discover that most of the icons you need to use repetitively in A/P are the same ones you use regularly in A/R.

Icon	Description
✋	Click once on the document you want to display and then click on this display document icon.
✎	Click once on the document you want to change and then click on this change document icon.

Table 11.1 Frequently Used Icons in Transaction FBL1N

Icon	Description
▼	To filter data in the view, click on this icon. Then define your field criteria (i.e. select fields to filter and values).
⇧	To sort data in ascending order, click once on a column header and then this sort in ascending order icon.
⇩	To sort data in descending order, click once on a column header and then this sort in descending order icon.
⊞	To change the screen layout, click on the change layout icon. Then select fields and order of display.
⊞	To select a different predefined screen layout, click on the select layout icon. In the popup window, double-click on the screen layout you wish to use.
⊞	Use the save layout icon to save changes you've made to the screen layout.
Σ	To total data, click once on a column header and then this display sum icon.
⅀	To subtotal data, click once on a column header and then this subtotal icon

Table 11.1 Frequently Used Icons in Transaction FBL1N (Cont.)

The customer line item display is the most powerful tool at your disposal for checking the status of an invoice or payment. A/R clerks and supervisors use it frequently and it is often the first stop when fielding an inquiry about a customer account balance, the status of an invoice, or the status of a payment. Several standard reports can provide the same or similar output, but without the same drill-down capability.

11.2 Customer Analysis

When it comes to analyzing details of a customer account, there are several transactions available in A/R that are useful. In this section, we will cover three common scenarios in the day-to-day work of an A/R clerk or supervisor and discuss the best tool to use in each.

The first scenario is finding the due date and status for an open A/R invoice. One of the most frequent tasks requested of an A/R department is to find out when a particular invoice is due for payment. One way to find the answer is via Transaction FBL5N, which was covered in detail in Section 11.1.2.

Within the customer line item display (Transaction FBL5N), there are two fields most relevant to due date determination: NET DUE DATE and NET DUE DATE SYMBOL. The NET DUE DATE SYMBOL graphically represents whether an item is not due, due, or overdue. All three symbols are shown in Figure 11.9, each with an individual open customer invoice.

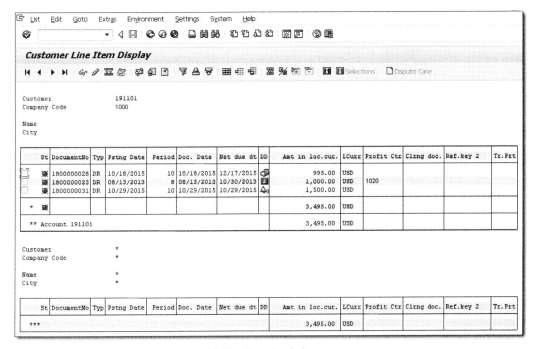

Figure 11.9 Transaction FBL5N Output with Due Date Symbols

The OVERDUE symbol ⚡ will appear anytime an invoice is unpaid and the current date is past the payment due date. This is the symbol you want to watch out for because it means a customer account is past due.

The DUE symbol 🔔 will appear anytime an invoice is unpaid and the current date equals the payment due date. This is also one you want to keep an eye on, particularly if the customer has a history of making late payments.

The NOT DUE symbol 🗓 will appear anytime an invoice is unpaid and the current date is less than the payment due date.

A second common A/R task is to find the payment date of a customer invoice for which payment has been received and applied against a customer account. After a customer payment has been received and applied against an open invoice, that invoice will show up as a cleared item in Transaction FBL5N. A paid invoice will appear in the customer line item display with a clearing document number and payment date.

To view a cleared customer line item using Transaction FBL5N, follow application menu path Accounting • Financial Accounting • Accounts Receivable • Account • FBL5N—Display/Change Line Items, as shown in Figure 11.10.

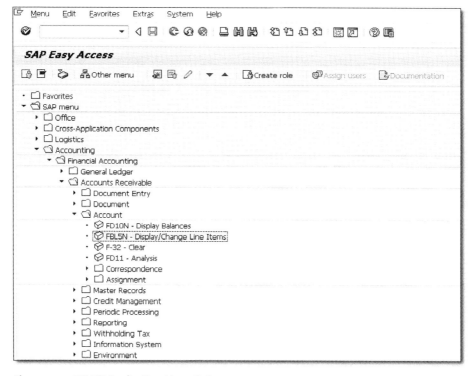

Figure 11.10 FBL5N Application Menu Path

The Customer Line Item Display selection screen will open (Figure 11.11). Enter values in the Customer account and Company code fields. For this example, to see a payment received, we selected the Cleared items status option and entered a date range in the CLEARING DATE field. Note that this is not the only way to see if a customer payment has been received, but it is the most frequent method used in accounting departments because it is the most flexible and powerful tool available.

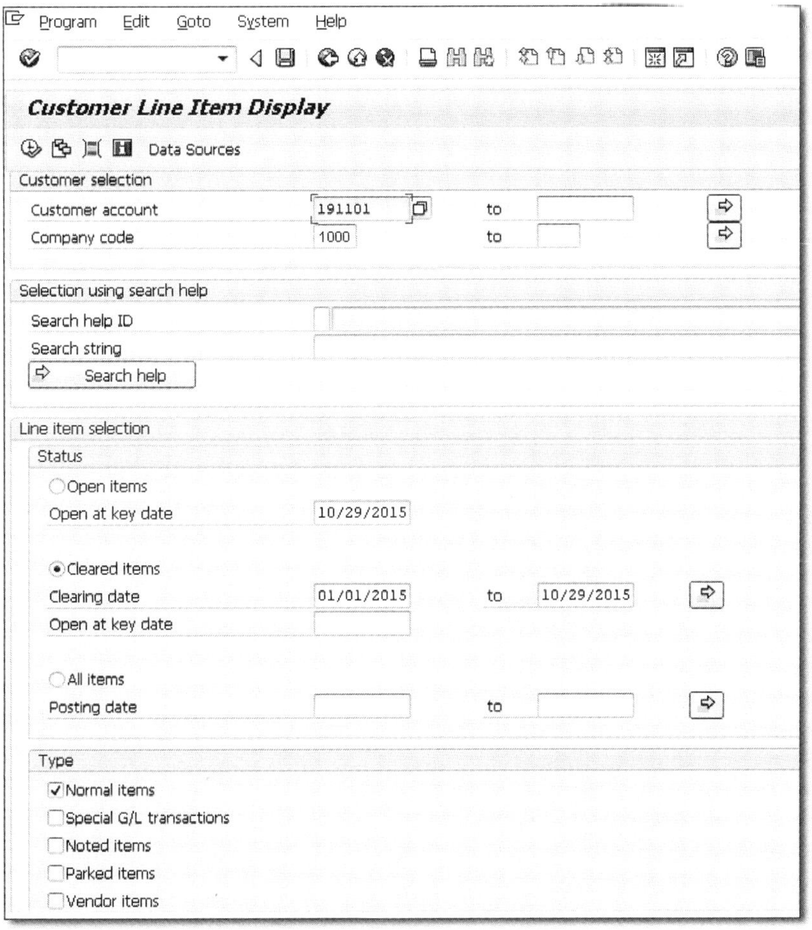

Figure 11.11 Selection Screen with Cleared Item Selections

With all field values entered, click the EXECUTE icon ⊕. The CUSTOMER LINE ITEM DISPLAY screen appears, showing the payment date the customer payment was received and the clearing document number (Figure 11.12).

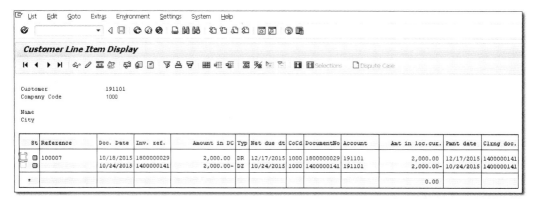

Figure 11.12 Output with Paid Invoice

Searching for cleared customer items in Transaction FBL5N is frequently used to answer the question of if and when a customer payment was received. You can search for cleared items for one or more customers, on specific date, or by referencing a specific invoice or clearing document number. These are just some of the ways to search for cleared customer items.

Using Transaction FBL5N to search for cleared invoices and payments received is also valuable when looking for a misapplied payment—that is, one that was applied to the wrong invoice or to the wrong customer account altogether. The best way to identify misapplied payments is to validate the customer number and reference number of the cleared invoice.

The third common task covered in this section is performing general customer analysis using Transaction FD11. This transaction is not necessarily used for only one specific purpose. Instead, provides a breadth of information on a customer account. It is a one-stop shop to view balances, look at Special G/L transactions, view payment history, and much more. Transaction FD11 is designed to show the most common types of customer analysis required.

To review a customer accounting using Transaction FD11, follow application menu path ACCOUNTING • FINANCIAL ACCOUNTING • ACCOUNTS RECEIVABLE • ACCOUNT • FD11—ANALYSIS, as shown in Figure 11.13.

Double-click FD11—ANALYSIS from the menu path shown in Figure 11.13, or enter "FD11" in the COMMAND field (Figure 11.14) and press [Enter].

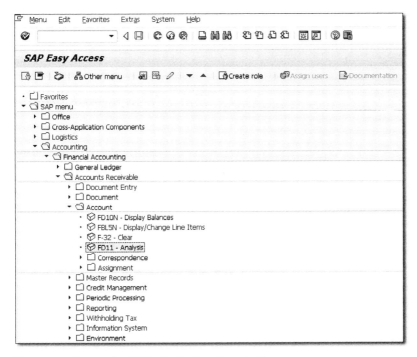

Figure 11.13 Transaction FD11 Application Menu Path

Figure 11.14 FD11 in Command Field

The CUSTOMER: INITIAL SCREEN ACCOUNT ANALYSIS selection screen will open (Figure 11.15). Enter values in the CUSTOMER ACCOUNT, COMPANY CODE, and FISCAL YEAR fields.

With all field values entered, press ⎡Enter⎤, and the ACCOUNT BALANCE ACCOUNT ANALYSIS screen will open (Figure 11.16). Seven different tabs exist to take you directly to the type of data that you want to see. These tabs filter certain types of data (e.g., sales, down payments, discounts) that are commonly needed for customer account analysis. Transaction FD11 also has drilldown capability to see line item detail. To see this detail, double-click any number in a screen, or click once on a number to place your cursor on it and click the LINE ITEMS button in the top-left portion of the screen.

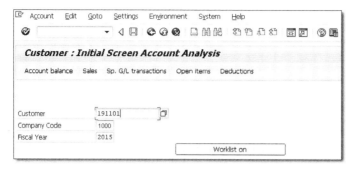

Figure 11.15 Customer: Initial Screen Account Analysis

Period	Deb.	Cred.	DC bal.	0.00
JAN	0.00	0.00	0.00	"
FEB	0.00	0.00	0.00	"
MAR	0.00	0.00	0.00	"
APR	0.00	0.00	0.00	"
MAY	0.00	0.00	0.00	"
JUN	0.00	0.00	0.00	"
JUL	0.00	0.00	0.00	"
AUG	0.00	0.00	0.00	"
SEP	0.00	0.00	0.00	"
OCT	5,990.00	3,515.00	2,475.00	2,475.00
NOV	0.00	0.00	0.00	"
DEC	0.00	0.00	0.00	"
SP1	0.00	0.00	0.00	"
SP2	0.00	0.00	0.00	"
SP3	0.00	0.00	0.00	"
SP4	0.00	0.00	0.00	"
	5,990.00	3,515.00	2,475.00	2,475.00

Figure 11.16 Account Balance Account Analysis

Now that we've completed our discussion on customer account displays and customer account analysis, let's move on to discuss some standard reporting capabilities in A/R.

11.3 Reports and Queries

In Section 11.1, we discussed customer account displays in detail, including a discussion of Transaction FD10N and Transaction FBL5N. For validating customer account balances and transaction details, these transactions are the most beneficial, particularly because of their ability to drill down all the way to accounting documents. However, other tools do exist to view customer account balances and transaction details. In this section, you will see where to find these alternatives in A/R reports and queries.

Standard reports are SAP delivered and are universally found in the INFORMATION SYSTEM folder of the application menu. The most useful general-purpose A/R reports can be accessed from application menu path ACCOUNTING • FINANCIAL ACCOUNTING • ACCOUNTS RECEIVABLE • INFORMATION SYSTEM • REPORTS FOR ACCOUNTS RECEIVABLE ACCOUNTING, as shown in Figure 11.17.

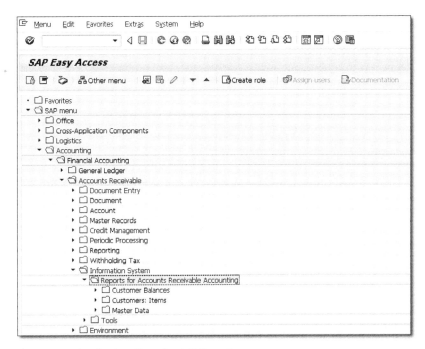

Figure 11.17 Application Menu for A/R Reports

Many standard reports exist for viewing customer balances, line items, and master data; let's take a closer look at one example.

Customer due date analysis is the process of determining how much is due to be paid by a customer in a given period of time. The most comprehensive tool for this task is Report S_ALR_87012168—Due Date Analysis for Open Items.

To perform A/R due date analysis, use Transaction S_ALR_87012168 or application menu path Accounting • Financial Accounting • Accounts Receivable • Information System • Reports for Accounts Receivable Accounting • Customer: Items • S_ALR_87012168—Due Date Analysis for Open Items, as shown in Figure 11.18.

Figure 11.18 Report S_ALR_87012168 Application Menu Path

Double-click S_ALR_87012168—Due Date Analysis for Open Items from the menu path shown in Figure 11.18, and the Report S_ALR_87012168 selection screen will open (Figure 11.19). For this example, we entered one Customer Account and Company Code, although multiple values are permitted. The field value for Open Items at Key Date defaults to the current date, but can be over-written. In the Output Type section, multiple choices exist; you should try them all. For this example, we selected the first option: Graphical report output.

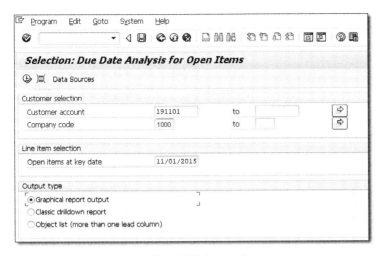

Figure 11.19 Report S_ALR_87012168 Selection Screen

With all screen field values entered, click the Execute icon ⊕; the output screen for the due date analysis report will open (Figure 11.20), showing amounts currently due for the customer selected.

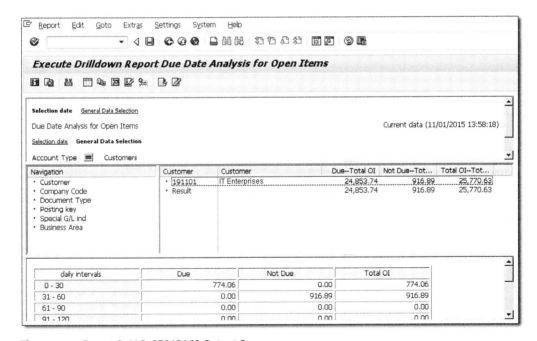

Figure 11.20 Report S_ALR_87012168 Output Screen

From the output screen, you can drill down, navigate using other objects, export the data, and more. Report S_ALR_87012168 can be a valuable tool in forecasting cash balances .

Another useful standard A/R report is Report S_ALR_87012175—Open Items—Customer Due Date Forecast. Access Report S_ALR_87012175 using application menu path ACCOUNTING • FINANCIAL ACCOUNTING • ACCOUNTS RECEIVABLE • INFORMATION SYSTEM • REPORTS FOR ACCOUNTS RECEIVABLE ACCOUNTING • CUSTOMER ITEMS • S_ALR_87012175—OPEN ITEMS—CUSTOMER DUE DATE FORECAST, as shown in Figure 11.21.

Figure 11.21 Report S_ALR_87012175 Application Menu Path

Double-click S_ALR_87012175—OPEN ITEMS—CUSTOMER DUE DATE FORECAST from the menu path shown in Figure 11.21, and the OPEN ITEMS—CUSTOMER DUE DATE FORECAST selection screen will open (Figure 11.22). For this example, we entered values for the CUSTOMER ACCOUNT and COMPANY CODE fields. A value defaulted into the OPEN ITEMS AT KEY DATE field. Additional output selections can be made in the FURTHER SELECTIONS and OUTPUT CONTROL sections.

Figure 11.22 Report S_ALR_87012175 Selection Screen

With all screen field values entered, click the EXECUTE icon ⊕. The output screen for the report appears (Figure 11.23), showing customer due date forecasts.

Drilldown capability does not exist in Report S_ALR_87012175, but for a nice summary view of customer balances, this report serves the purpose well.

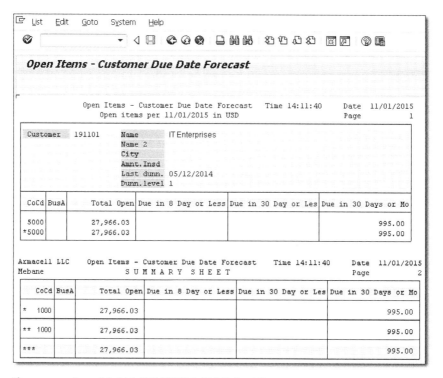

Figure 11.23 Report S_ALR_87012175 Initial Output Screen

Now that we have discussed several specific methods for handling customer account inquiries using customer analysis and standard reports, let's discuss more reasons that these methods are useful.

11.4   Uses for Customer Inquiries

A/R departments have a lot of responsibility. Although their job functions are operational in nature, A/R clerks and supervisors play an important part in the overall success of a company.

As was discussed in Chapter 10, A/R departments are responsible for the days sales outstanding (DSO) metric. DSO is a measure of the average number of days it takes a company to collect revenue after a sale has been made. DSO is a key performance indicator (KPI) that is monitored at the highest levels of a company, because it is a measure of the company's health.

Keeping DSO at acceptable levels involves monitoring customer accounts through account statements, dunning, credit management and more. Processes need to be in place for collecting on overdue accounts, establishing customer credit ratings, and setting payment terms.

Part of DSO tracking and performance is monitoring overdue payments. In addition, the form of payment and your ability to process payments quickly makes a big difference.

Let's summarize some of the ways the tools in this chapter can be of most use to the A/R department in meeting its responsibilities, as described in this section — for example:

▸ Transaction FD10N: Reconcile customer account balances to G/L reconciliation account balances

▸ Transaction FBL5N: Track open receivables, find the status of a payment or invoice, answer customer inquiries, and find misapplied payments

▸ Transaction FD11: Perform comprehensive customer account analysis on sales, down payments, discounts, open items, and more

▸ Standard reports, such as Report S_ALR_87012168: Perform due date analysis for open items

▸ Reports such as Report S_ALR_87012175: Forecast customer due payment dates

▸ Include the reports and transactions presented in month-end and year-end close procedures

▸ Transactions to monitor processes for outstanding receivables, overdue payments, and customers in collection or those with poor credit ratings

As you can see from the preceding list, the transactions and reports covered in this chapter have many uses within the A/R department. The key is to identify those tools most useful to your company and department, build them into your day-to-day processes, and train your employees to use them efficiently.

11.5   Summary

In this chapter, we covered some of the most essential tools for A/R account inquiries. These tools include the A/R account balances transaction (i.e., Transaction FD10N), the A/R account line item display transaction (i.e., Transaction

FBL5N), and standard A/R reports. Frequent use of these transactions and reports is essential to understanding the activity in A/R.

In A/R, account maintenance is a frequent and ongoing event. The tools provided in this chapter provide you with the ability to answer inquiries, adjust customer account balances, and perform account maintenance. A/R is not a static event; you need programs at your disposal to remain on top of changes.

In performing customer account analysis, Transactions FD10K and FBL5N play a useful role because of their drilldown capability. Moreover, Transaction FD11 provides predefined subsets of data, such as payment history, that can allow you to quickly and easily perform the customer account analysis needed.

In an A/R department, it is essential to quickly and accurately track down the status of an invoice, a payment, and other customer account transactions. Customer account displays and standard reports give you the ability to do so. Many standard A/R reports are delivered by SAP; before writing custom reports or queries, make sure you thoroughly review the standard reports and know that you are not recreating capabilities that already exist within the standard reports.

This concludes our A/R discussions. In the next chapter, we move on to the topic of fixed asset accounting and processes.

In this chapter, we discuss fixed asset business processes with an emphasis on integration in the asset lifecycle.

12   Fixed Asset Processes

Business processes in FI often consist of steps that are cross-modular. In other words, all steps in the business process aren't isolated to one SAP module. We saw this in Chapter 5 with the procure-to-pay process, where purchase requisitions, purchase orders, and other logistics transactions are executed in MM-Purchasing, while vendor account maintenance and outgoing payments take place in A/P. We also saw this in Chapter 9 with the order-to-cash business process, where sales orders, deliveries, and billing takes place in SD-Sales, while customer account maintenance and incoming payments are managed in A/R.

Another great example of a business process that crosses SAP modules is acquire-to-retire in FI Asset Accounting (FI-AA), often referred to as the asset lifecycle. Throughout this chapter, you will see the term Acquire-to-Retire used synonymously with asset lifecycle.

Acquire-to-retire is a core business process within SAP and it's important for you to understand how it is comprised of multiple transactions, some of which reside in FI-AA and others which are outside of FI-AA. Using this business process as the basis of our discussion, we cover the overall asset lifecycle and some of it's key points of integration with other modules.

We will discuss several key business process steps in the acquire-to-retire process, but will focus most heavily on the acquisition step. This is a process step with a great amount of potential integration, with several acquisition methods available. In an effort to keep this chapter centered on FI-AA integration, we will begin with a discussion of the asset lifecycle and then delve into the specifics of asset acquisition. For details on FI-AA transactions, see Chapter 13.

> **Note**
>
> SAP provides functionality for leased assets but they are beyond the scope of this book.

12.1 The Fixed Asset Lifecycle

FI-AA is used for acquiring, managing, valuing, and supervising fixed assets within SAP. FI-AA is a subledger ledger to the G/L. The subledger is an important concept to understand, so we'll discuss it a little more before getting into the specifics of the fixed asset lifecycle. This is not the first time in this book that subledgers are described. The concept is also relevant to A/P and A/R and is discussed in those chapters as well.

A subledger stores individual transaction detail in separate tables and is managed via individual master records, such as vendors, customers, and fixed assets. FI-AA is it's own subledger, with all asset accounting entries stored in separate tables. Transaction detail is managed and viewed via asset master records and the FI-AA subledger.

Like A/R and A/P, the FI-AA subledger links back to the G/L by means of G/L reconciliation accounts. Each subledger account must link back to a G/L reconciliation account. When an accounting entry is posted to the FI-AA subledger, the system automatically updates the balance in the corresponding G/L reconciliation account. Therefore, the transaction detail is stored in the subledger, but balances are updated in the G/L.

Now that you understand the concept of a FI-AA subledger, let's discuss the stages within the asset lifecycle.

12.1.1 Stages of the Asset Lifecycle

An asset's lifecycle isn't always a straight line from acquisition to retirement. We will not attempt to discuss all the variations that can occur, but rather will highlight a few scenarios to provide a good understanding of the acquire-to-retire business process and the relationship of FI-AA to other modules.

To provide a basis for the remainder of this chapter, let's take a look at the major parts of the asset lifecycle:

1. **Acquisition**

   This is the first step in the Acquire-to-Retire business process. It is important that the acquisition value accurately reflect the true cost of the asset. This step in the lifecycle requires entering into a contractual agreement with a business partner to acquire goods. In FI-AA, it requires the creation of an asset master record and the capitalization of an asset.

2. **Maintenance**

   Many types of assets need periodic maintenance. Over the life of an asset, it may need repairs, improvements, and replacement parts. Routine maintenance and repair costs to sustain performance are considered expenses, unless major upgrades or overhauls improve the value of an asset.

3. **Depreciation**

   Depreciation is the consumption of the asset over a period of time. Depreciation methods in SAP determine the rate at which an asset is depreciated. An assets net book value is the original cost less depreciation, amortization, and impairment costs.

4. **Retirement**

   Retirement is the final stage in the asset lifecycle. It is the removal of an asset or part of an asset from the asset portfolio. In FI-AA, asset retirement is done by either selling or scrapping the asset.

It's important to point out that prior to entering an asset acquisition FI-AA, you need to have a good understanding of your company's fixed asset types and valuation methods. Fixed assets types come in many varieties, including tangible assets, such as furniture and computers, and intangibles, such as software, copyrights, and trademarks.

Fixed asset valuations need to reflect the true and relevant cost of an asset. Asset values should absolute costs, not estimates. These include purchase price and costs associated with bringing the asset into workable condition.

Regardless of how the asset is acquired, there are two steps in the fixed asset acquisition process: the creation of an asset master record and the posting of capitalization value. Once these steps are complete, the life of the fixed asset begins. For more information on fixed asset master data, see Chapter 2.

As the lifecycle of an asset progresses, many events can cause a required adjustment to the asset or its value. For example, asset maintenance or improvements may change the value of the asset, or the asset could be damaged or destroyed. Whatever the circumstance, FI-AA provides the means to adjust an asset's valuation.

The final stages of the fixed asset lifecycle involve selling, transferring, or scrapping the asset. Figure 12.1 shows the application menu paths for FI-AA transfer and retirements.

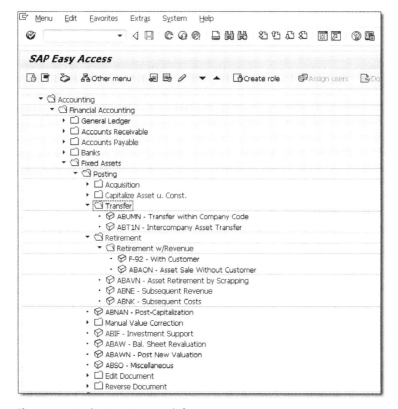

Figure 12.1 Application Menu Path for FI-AA Retirements

For details on asset transfer and retirement transactions, see Chapter 13.

12.1.2 Structure of FI-AA Application Menu

Now, let's take a look at specific FI-AA transactions and show they are organized. Figure 12.2 shows the FI-AA application menu path ACCOUNTING • FINANCIAL

ACCOUNTING • FIXED ASSETS. The POSTING folder contains transactions for acquisitions, capitalization, transfers, retirements, value corrections, and document edits and reversals. These are all the core financial transactions relevant to the lifecycle of an asset (except depreciation).

The ASSET folder contains all the transactions for fixed asset master data. This includes fixed asset creation, change, and display. This folder also contains transactions to lock or delete fixed assets.

The PERIODIC PROCESSING folder contains many transactions, the most important of which is the transaction to execute depreciation (Transaction AFAB).

The INFORMATION SYSTEM folder is where the standard reports for FI-AA reside.

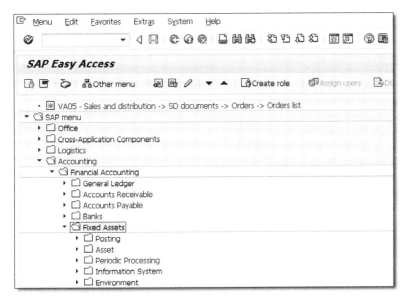

Figure 12.2 FI-AA Application Menu

Let's open the POSTINGS folder and see the folders and transactions it contains. The first application subfolder shown is ACQUISITION (Figure 12.3). This folder contains transactions for the acquisition of a fixed asset. There are several ways a fixed asset can be acquired. The asset can be produced in house, procured directly in FI-AA, transferred from an affiliate company, or procured and capitalized through MM-Purchasing.

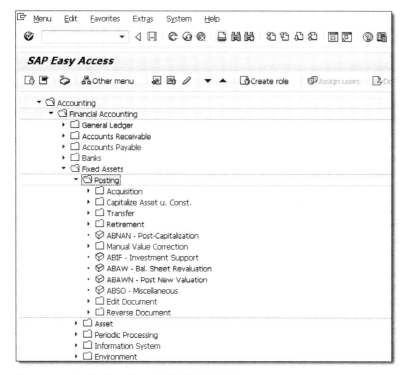

Figure 12.3 Application Menu Path FI-AA Postings

12.1.3 FI-AA Configuration

At this point, it is important to mention that FI-AA involves a good amount of configuration. This book is not a configuration guide, but it is important to know that FI-AA configuration is substantial. It includes asset classes, account determinations, depreciation areas, and much more. In this section, we discuss a few critical points of configuration to help in your overall understanding of FI-AA.

At the top of the list are asset classes. They are an important building block in FI-AA configuration in that they control such things as account determinations and screen layouts. Normally, asset classes correlate to specific asset types and fixed asset G/L accounts. They are configured to correlate with G/L accounts to meet the necessary reporting requirements on the balance sheet. In addition, an asset class determines the depreciation method used in calculating depreciation expense.

Below are some examples of typical asset classes.

- Land
- Buildings
- Machinery and Equipment
- Furniture and Fixtures
- Vehicles
- Computer Hardware
- Computer Software
- Leasehold Improvements
- Low Value Assets
- Capital Leases
- Assets Under Construction (AuC)

The next element of FI-AA configuration we will discuss is account determinations, which establish which G/L accounts to post to for each FI-AA transaction type. Account determinations are not unique to FI-AA; they exist throughout FI. They are of particular importance in FI-AA, however, because they automatically update all relevant transactions in the G/L. Among them are the following:

- Acquisition and Production Costs (APC)
- Down payments
- Gain/Loss/Revenue from sale
- APC revaluation
- Depreciation
- Transfer of reserves
- Depreciation revaluation
- Interest expense

See Chapter 14 for a more in-depth discussion on the topics of asset classes and FI-AA account determinations.

The last notable point on configuration in this section has to do with depreciation expense. In configuration, a depreciation area and depreciation types are defined.

They determine how depreciation will be calculated and posted in the G/L. Depreciation calculations are an important step in month-end and year-end close and in the calculation of an asset's net book value. For these reasons, accountants and accounting supervisors give depreciation a lot of attention. Yet, preceding steps in the asset lifecycle are essential to achieve accurate depreciation postings.

Together, asset classes, account determinations, and depreciation are all critical areas of configuration, and a basic understanding of these areas goes a long way when troubleshooting errors in FI-AA.

12.1.4 Depreciation

Depreciation is covered at a high level in this section because of its special significance in the asset lifecycle. It is also covered in detail in Chapter 13.

As previously mentioned, depreciation is essential to the calculation of an asset's net book value. Net book value is the original cost of an asset less depreciation, amortization, and impairment costs.

Depreciation is calculated over the course of a fixed asset's lifetime. In configuration, you determine the how the asset will depreciate. FI-AA configuration is designed to be flexible in accommodating the needs of any country and industry. In addition, the type of asset and its expected life play important roles in the setup of FI-AA and depreciation.

Let's put depreciation in perspective in terms of the overall accounting for fixed assets. Fixed asset master records are created in FI-AA. When capitalization occurs, the FI-AA subledger and G/L are updated with APC values. At this point, a fixed asset's value is reflected on the balance sheet. In FI-AA, ongoing adjustments are made to master data and asset values. Moreover, as depreciation is posted at regular increments (e.g. monthly), the balance sheet will contain accumulated depreciation amounts, whereas the profit and loss statements will contain postings for depreciation expense amounts. All these postings are controlled through FI-AA account determinations.

Figure 12.4 shows the application menu path for Transaction AFAB, the transaction to execute depreciation. Most companies set up depreciation to run automatically as a scheduled job, and asset accountants are then responsible for reviewing the depreciation postings, validating them, and making any necessary adjustments. When the system posts depreciation, it creates collective documents. It does not create separate documents for each asset.

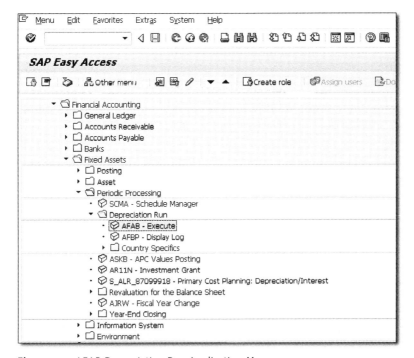

Figure 12.4 AFAB Depreciation Run Application Menu

Now that we have covered the basics of the overall asset lifecycle, let's discuss asset acquisitions in more detail.

12.2 Asset Acquisition

Acquiring an asset is the first step in the acquire-to-retire business process. The focus of this section is on the various methods of acquiring fixed assets. An asset can be produced in house, procured directly in FI-AA, transferred from an affiliate company, or procured and capitalized through MM-Purchasing.

12.2.1 Fixed Asset Acquisition Types

It is important to understand each of these asset acquisition methods. This is important not only to gain an understanding of SAP's capabilities, but also for insights into how your company's internal acquisition processes work.

There are three basic types of fixed asset acquisitions:

▶ **Internal acquisition**
An acquisition of an asset from an affiliate company or an asset that is produced in house.

▶ **Assets under construction (AuC)**
A special form of tangible assets. These are assets being constructed (e.g., a building) and are accounted for separately until the asset is put into service, at which time the cost of the asset is transferred into the appropriate asset class.

▶ **External acquisition**
The acquisition of an asset from a business partner (i.e. vendor).

In this section, we do not attempt to cover these transactions in detail. It is more than can be covered in a single chapter. Instead, we elaborate on external acquisition types to give you an understanding of FI-AA integration. In Section 12.2.2, an example is provided of an external acquisition using a purchase order (PO). In addition, Chapter 13 provides a detailed example of an external procurement using Transaction F-90 and other FI-AA transactions.

Transaction F-90 is designed to debit an asset and credit a vendor account, thereby capitalizing the asset value while at the same time producing an open invoice payable to the vendor. This is a frequently used external acquisition transaction.

Figure 12.5 also shows other external acquisition transaction types. These options often confuse people and warrant some discussion.

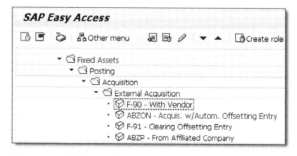

Figure 12.5 F-90 Application Menu

Transaction ABZON is used to capitalize an asset with an offsetting entry to the G/L. Using this transaction, a debit is made to an asset and a credit to an offsetting

G/L account. This transaction is used when there is no need to create an A/P invoice, such as when a vendor has been prepaid for the asset. This may be the case for large-ticket assets for which vendors need to be prepaid to produce the asset. Transaction F-91 will capitalize an asset with an offsetting entry to a G/L clearing account. Using this transaction, a debit is made to an asset and a credit to an offsetting G/L clearing account. For more details on these transactions, see Chapter 13.

12.2.2 External Asset Acquisition with Purchase Order

The final external fixed asset acquisition method we will discuss in this section is the acquisition of a fixed asset directly through a PO created in MM-Purchasing. If your company uses the MM-Purchasing module and creates POs for all asset acquisitions, this is the preferred method for capitalizing assets.

To use this method, when creating the PO you must use account assignment category A in the line item of the PO. In configuration, you can designate a different account assignment category for use in POs, but category A is delivered by SAP.

Prior to creating the PO, the fixed asset master record must be created. Figure 12.6 shows an example PO with line items containing account assignment A. In the PURCHASE ORDER HISTORY tab, you can click the invoice receipt document to view the material invoice number associated with the procurement instance.

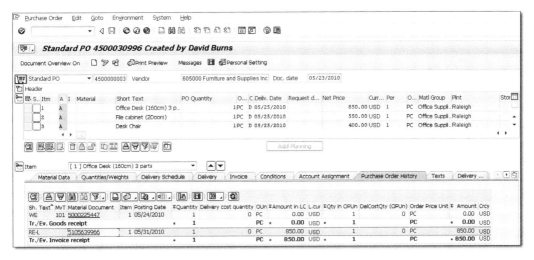

Figure 12.6 Example PO with Account Assignment A

Figure 12.7 shows the material invoice document number. Click the FOLLOW-ON DOCUMENTS... button to review the FI documents automatically created by MM-LIV.

Figure 12.7 Display Material Invoice Document

The LIST OF DOCUMENTS IN ACCOUNTING dialog box will pop up (Figure 12.8). Notice that there is one accounting document and one asset document.

Double-click the accounting document number to display the document (Figure 12.9). This document demonstrates that by using the procurement process in MM-Purchasing, ultimately you can produce an A/P invoice that posts a credit to a vendor account and a debit to fixed assets.

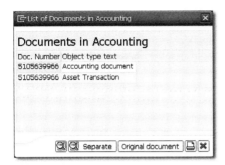

Figure 12.8 List of Documents in Accounting Dialog Box

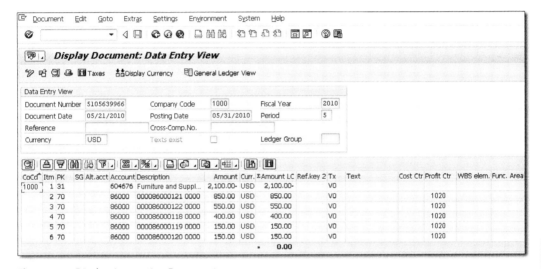

Figure 12.9 Display Accounting Document

This concludes our discussion of external fixed asset acquisitions. Next, we will discuss internal acquisitions.

12.2.3 Internal Acquisition

As discussed in the previous section, there is a clear difference between internal and external asset acquisitions. An internal acquisition of an asset is one from an affiliate company or an asset that is produced in house, as opposed to an external acquisition, which is made from a business partner.

There are two standard transactions that fit under the category of an internal acquisition. The first occurs when a company acquires an asset from an affiliate company and uses Transaction ABZP. The second is for assets produced in house, in which case Transaction ABZE is used.

Both Transactions ABZP and ABZE use standard transaction types. You only need to create custom transaction types if you need them to only post to certain depreciation areas in your chart of depreciation or if there is no standard transaction type with the necessary limitations.

12.2.4 Assets under Construction and Settlements

As straightforward as the Acquire-to-Retire process may seem, it is not so simple for all fixed assets, particularly during the acquisition phase. For example, assets under construction (AuC) can be cumbersome to manage. The difficulty lies in trying to put together all the pieces of the puzzle to ensure the accounting is correct.

Typically, AuC need to be shown separately on the balance sheet. To begin using AuC, an asset class is required with specific AuC settings in configuration. Figure 12.10 shows an example asset class. The STATUS OF AUC setting determines if the asset class is designated AuC or not. LINE ITEM SETTLEMENT means that final line item settlement to an asset or cost center can be performed. The INVESTMENT MEASURE setting indicates that assets cannot be created or posted to using FI-AA. Instead, the AuC are posted via internal orders or WBS elements.

It is important to note that AuC are not final assets. Costs are accumulated in the AuC until final settlement takes place. Then, the AuC value is transferred to a final asset.

There are several ways to accumulate costs that settle to AuC. For example, you can create an internal order (IO) using Transaction KO01. The IO type INVESTMENT MEASURE should be selected when creating the IO. Subsequently, costs are accumulated using the IO as the cost collector. A settlement rule is created that designates the asset as the receiver, and the IO is settled to the asset using Transaction KO88.

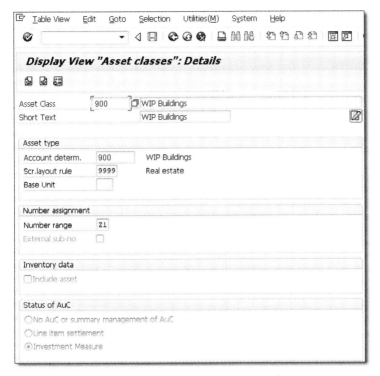

Figure 12.10 Example Assets under Construction Asset Class

There are multiple ways to accumulate and settle costs to AuC, including use of WBS elements. It is important that you understand the AuC cost collectors being used in your company, the timing of their settlement to AuC, and the process steps used during the settlement process.

12.3 Summary

Fixed assets are a major component of the balance sheet. Asset values and accumulated depreciation are broken down into their component parts—that is, asset classes correlating to G/L accounts. In addition, depreciation expense is posted at regular increments and reported on profit and loss statements.

There is no question that understanding asset accounting is an essential part of the job in any accounting department. To understand asset accounting in SAP, it is important to understand the integration between FI-AA and other modules. Such an understanding helps provide complete knowledge of the Acquire-to-Retire process.

It is important to note that many accounting departments have a specific position called asset accountant. From a strictly accounting perspective, this makes sense. Accounting rules, reporting requirements, and asset valuation methods justify the need for specialized accounting expertise in fixed assets.

From an SAP perspective, it also makes sense to have a specialized role for an asset accountant. This is the go-to person for questions on asset classes, account determinations (i.e., how FI-AA transactions post), and depreciation. At month end and year end, the asset accountant is responsible not only for running and validating depreciation but also for reconciling G/L to fixed asset balances. Keeping FI-AA reconciled and accurate is a lot easier than going back in time to clean up discrepancies.

In this chapter, we focused heavily on the FI-AA acquisition process, a step that has much variability. We introduced several fixed asset acquisition transactions, including Transactions F-90, F-91, ABZON, ABZP, and ABZE. The most important example we discussed was the procurement of a fixed asset through MM-Purchasing. Using Transaction ME21N and account assignment category A, we showed how an asset was capitalized and an A/P invoice created automatically using the MM-Purchasing module.

AuC is another important concept in FI-AA. AuCs are accounted for separately on the balance sheet, until a certain point in time when the asset is put into service. AuCs are an example of FI-AA flexibility in their integration with other modules. They need a separate asset class in which specific AuC settings are made, and cost collectors are needed (e.g., WBS, IO) that settle to an AuC.

When cost collectors for AuC are created, they will not work without specific settings. We introduced you to the settings specific to an IO for AuC. There are multiple ways to accumulate and settle costs to AuC, including use of WBS elements. It is important that you understand the AuC cost collectors being used in your company, the timing of their settlement, and the process steps used during the settlement process.

This concludes our discussion of fixed asset processes. The next chapter discusses fixed asset transactions in detail.

In this chapter, we discuss fixed asset transactions covering the complete acquire-to-retire business process.

13   Fixed Asset Transactions

This chapter covers fixed asset transactions originating in the FI-AA module. It is important to understand the concept of a fixed asset's lifecycle, often referred to as the *acquire-to-retire* business process. The first step in this process is the creation of the asset master record.

After an asset master record is created, it can be capitalized, giving life to the asset. Throughout its lifetime, the asset depreciates until it is eventually sold, transferred, or retired. Along the way, an asset's lifecycle can take many twists and turns. It may be improved, damaged, revaluated, and maintained. End users must know the FI-AA transactions to make the necessary adjustments to asset values.

We discussed the asset lifecycle in Chapter 12. In this chapter, we will take a more in-depth look at it the lifecycle of an asset using FI-AA transactions.

Let's begin by discussing how to create a fixed asset master record.

13.1   Creating an Asset

The first step is to create an asset master record. To create an asset, use Transaction AS01 or application menu path ACCOUNTING • FINANCIAL ACCOUNTING • FIXED ASSETS • ASSET • CREATE • AS01—ASSET, as shown in Figure 13.1.

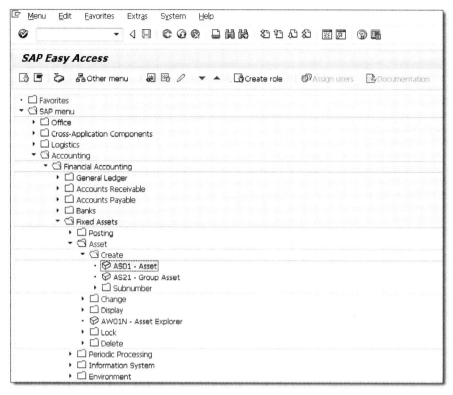

Figure 13.1 AS01 Application Menu Path

Double-click AS01—Asset from the menu path, or enter "AS01" in the Command field (as shown in Figure 13.2) and press Enter.

Figure 13.2 AS01 in Command Field

The Create Asset: Initial Screen screen will open (Figure 13.3). Here, enter an Asset Class. Note that once an asset master record is created, the asset class cannot be changed. If the wrong asset class is selected, the asset must be transferred to a new asset with the correct asset class. See Section 13.4 for more details on asset transfers.

In this example, the COMPANY CODE field defaults from the company code assigned to your user ID. The NUMBER OF SIMILAR ASSETS field enables you to create multiple similar assets in one master transaction. These assets differ from each other only by their main and/or sub number. For this example, we entered "1".

The REFERENCE section allows you to create a new asset referencing an existing one. In this way, many fields default into the new asset master record from the reference asset, thereby expediting the creation of a new asset master record.

Finally, selecting the POST-CAPITALIZATION checkbox makes the capitalization date in the asset master record a required field, and the system automatically sets the acquisition date based on the capitalization date. When you check this field, you must also manually set the historical capitalization date and the acquisition date for the asset in the asset master record. For this example, leave it unselected, which gives you the most flexibility. Check this flag if you want an asset accountant or manager to manually set the acquisition and capitalization dates.

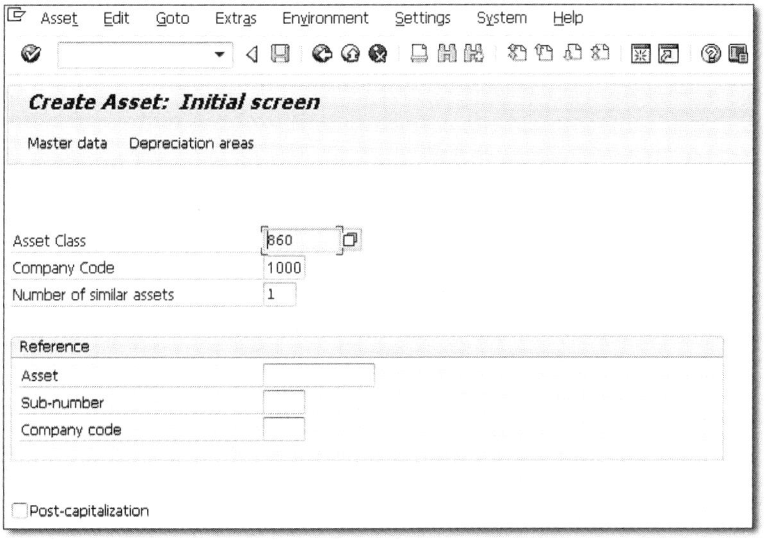

Figure 13.3 Create Asset Initial Screen

When all field values in Figure 13.3 have been added, press ⌑Enter⌑. The CREATE ASSET: MASTER DATA screen appears (Figure 13.4). Here, we entered values for DESCRIPTION, QUANTITY, and UNIT OF MEASURE.

We also selected the MANAGE HISTORICALLY checkbox, which enables functionality that displays the asset in an asset chart. It also prevents reorganization of the asset and its transactions until the asset is deactivated.

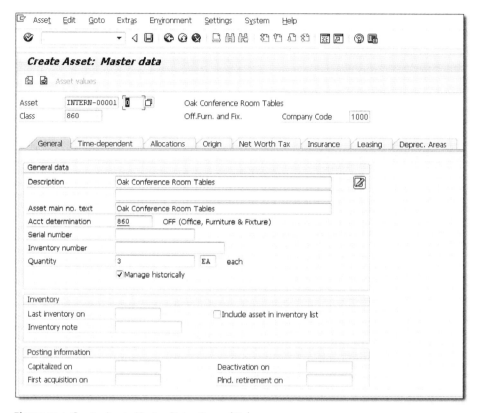

Figure 13.4 Create Asset: Master Data, General Tab

When all the information is entered in the GENERAL tab, click the TIME-DEPENDENT tab (Figure 13.5). On this tab, the asset is assigned master data, organizational objects, and other specifications as required. In this example, the only assignment made is to a COST CENTER.

Several other tabs exist on the asset master record, which we will not cover in detail here, but you should have a basic understanding of them. The ALLOCATIONS tab is where evaluation groups and investment information is entered. The ORIGIN tab contains information that further identifies specific attributes of the asset's origin and acquisition. The NET WORTH TAX tab holds information on net worth valuation and fields relevant for real estate holdings. Insurance and Leasing have their own respective tabs.

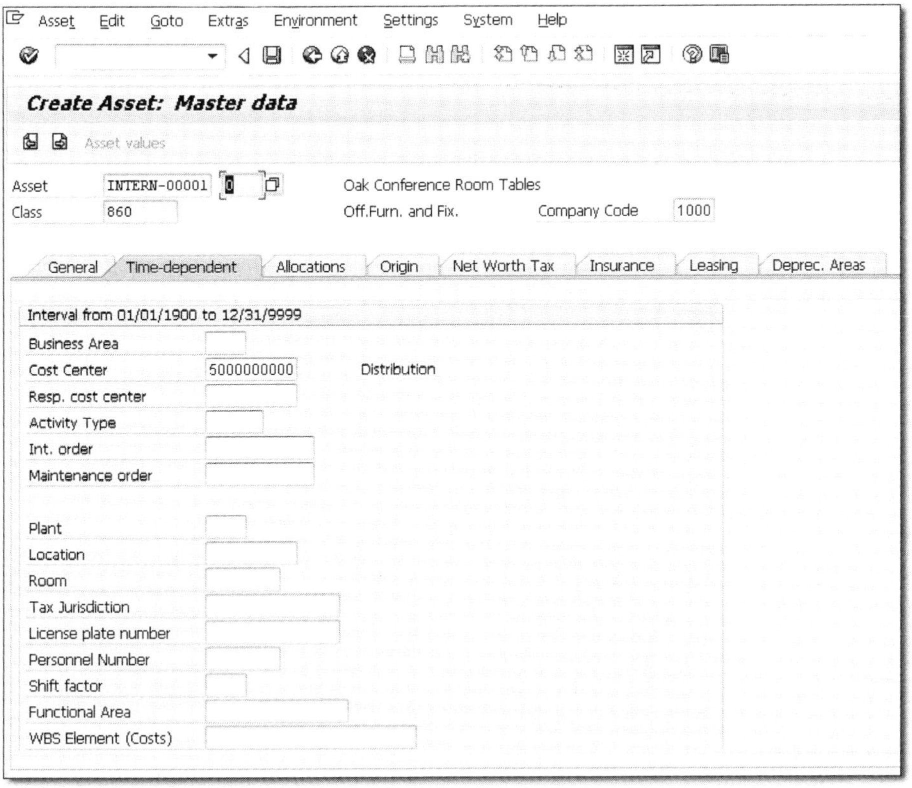

Figure 13.5 Create Asset: Master Data, Time-Dependent Tab

The last tab on the asset master screen is the Deprec. Areas tab (Figure 13.6). Depreciation areas are assigned to asset classes in configuration and default into the asset master record when created, based on the asset class selected in Figure 13.3. However, flexibility exists within the asset master record to change depreciation areas and valuation attributes.

With all data entered in the asset master record, click the Post icon to the right of the Command field in the upper-left-hand corner of the screen. This will create the asset master record, and a message will appear with the new asset number, as shown in Figure 13.7.

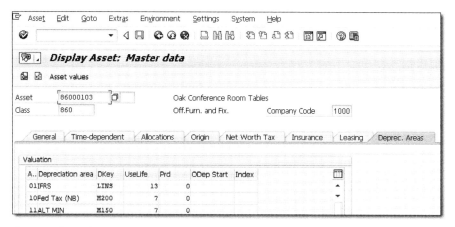

Figure 13.6 Display Asset: Master Data, Depreciation Areas Tab

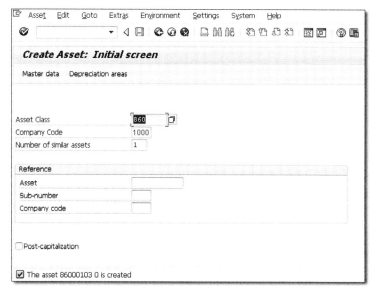

Figure 13.7 Asset Master Created Message

Once an asset master record has been created, it can be capitalized. There are several ways to capitalize an asset, depending on how it is procured. The asset can be produced in house, procured directly in FI-AA, transferred from an affiliate company, or ordered through MM-Purchasing. In the remainder of this section, we focus on external acquisitions posted directly in FI-AA.

The external purchase of a fixed asset is a daily event for most companies. As we discussed in Chapter 12, there are multiple transactions in FI-AA to accomplish this. Transaction F-90 was designed to debit an asset and credit a vendor account, thereby capitalizing the asset value while at the same time producing an open A/P invoice. Next is Transaction ABZON, which is used to capitalize an asset with an offsetting entry to the G/L. Using this transaction, a debit is made to an asset and a credit to an offsetting G/L account. Finally, Transaction F-91 is used to capitalize an asset with an offsetting entry to a G/L clearing account. This transaction makes a debit entry to an asset and a credit to an offsetting G/L clearing account.

In the remainder of this section, we will use Transaction F-90 to demonstrate asset capitalization. Transaction F-90 is used to post an external fixed asset acquisition with an external vendor. To see an example of fixed asset capitalization through a PO, see Chapter 12.

To post an external asset acquisition, use Transaction F-90 or follow application menu path ACCOUNTING • FINANCIAL ACCOUNTING • FIXED ASSETS • POSTING • ACQUISITION • EXTERNAL ACQUISITION • F-90—WITH VENDOR, as shown in Figure 13.8.

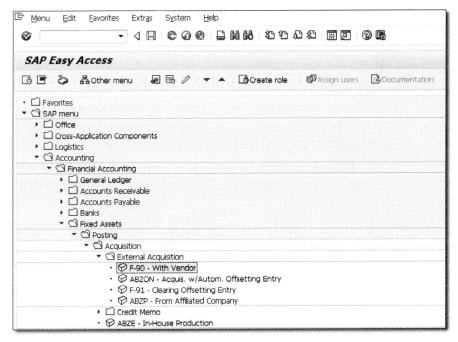

Figure 13.8 F-90 Application Menu Path

Double-click F-90—WITH VENDOR from the menu path shown in Figure 13.8 and the ACQUISITION FROM PURCHASE W. VENDOR: HEADER DATA screen will open (Figure 13.9). The fields on the header with prepopulated values may vary depending upon your system configuration and editing options. In this example, the DOCUMENT DATE and REFERENCE fields were manually entered, whereas field values defaulted for the POSTING DATE, TYPE, PERIOD, CURRENCY, and COMPANY CODE fields.

At the bottom of the screen, the first part of the first accounting line item is entered. In the FIRST LINE ITEM section, enter a posting key (PSTKY) and vendor number were entered in the ACCOUNT field. Posting key 31 indicates a credit to a vendor account.

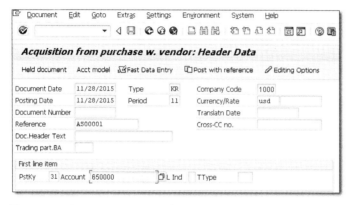

Figure 13.9 Asset Acquisition Header Data

When the header and first line item fields are complete, press [Enter]. The ENTER VENDOR INVOICE: ADD VENDOR ITEM screen will open (Figure 13.10). We manually entered a value into the AMOUNT field, whereas other field values defaulted from the vendor master record, including payment terms (PAYT TERMS) and baseline date (BLINE DATE).

At the bottom of the screen, the first part of the second accounting line item is entered. In the NEXT LINE ITEM section, enter a posting key (PSTKY), asset number in the ACCOUNT field, and transaction type (TTYPE). Posting key 70 indicates a debit to an asset account, and a value of 100 for the transaction type specifies that the line item is an external asset transaction.

With all field values added as in Figure 13.10, press [Enter]. The ENTER VENDOR INVOICE: ADD ASSET ITEM screen will open (Figure 13.11). In this example, we entered values in the AMOUNT and TAX CODE fields.

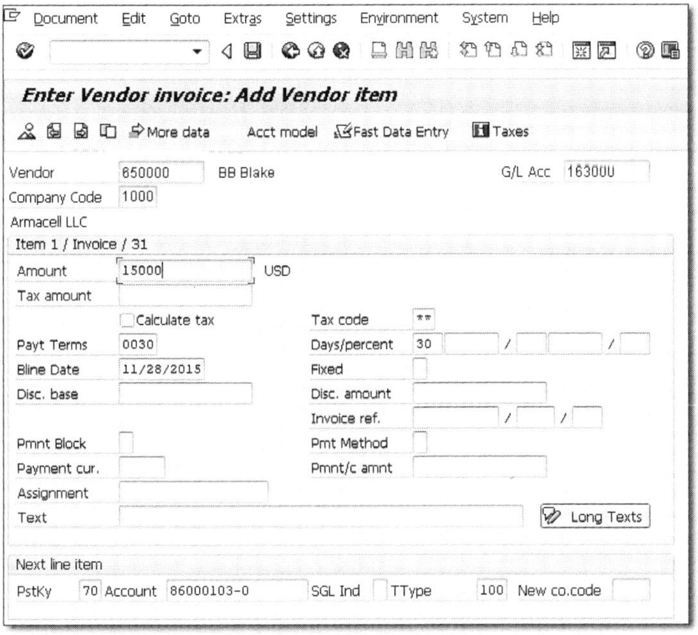

Figure 13.10 Add Vendor Item

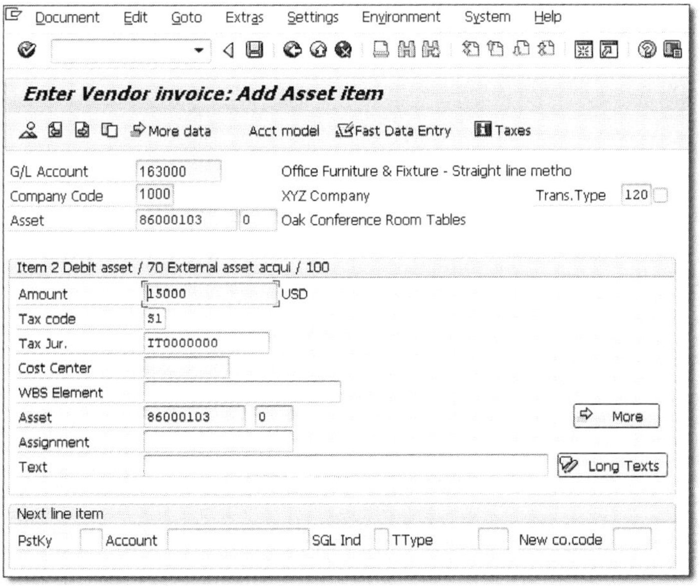

Figure 13.11 Add Asset Item

With all data entry complete, click the Post icon ⊟ to the right of the Command field in the upper-left-hand corner of the screen. This will create the asset acquisition document, and a message will appear with the new document number, as shown in Figure 13.12.

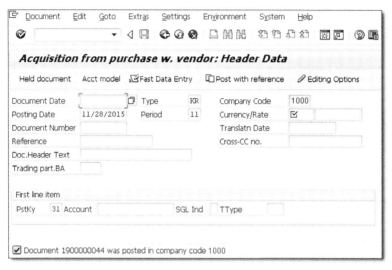

Figure 13.12 Document Created Message

Notice that the document type KR defaulted into Transaction F-90, which is a standard document type for A/P invoices. This is because Transaction F-90 creates an open A/P invoice. In addition, note that because document type KR was used, the document number created used the same number range as other A/P invoices.

Now that you have learned how to create an asset master record and post an external fixed asset acquisition, let's discuss how to change, display, and lock asset master records.

13.2   Changing, Displaying, and Locking

Regardless of the FI modules you use, master data maintenance is an important function that includes master data creation, change/edit, display, lock/block, and delete. FI-AA is no exception.

In Section 13.1 we demonstrated the creation of an asset master record. Some of the other day-to-day master data functions in FI-AA include changing, displaying, and locking asset master records. FI-AA also provides the capability to delete an asset master record, but only when no transactions have been created (i.e., the asset has not been capitalized).

To change to an asset master record, use Transaction AS02 or application menu path ACCOUNTING • FINANCIAL ACCOUNTING • FIXED ASSETS • ASSET • CHANGE • AS02—ASSET, as shown in Figure 13.13.

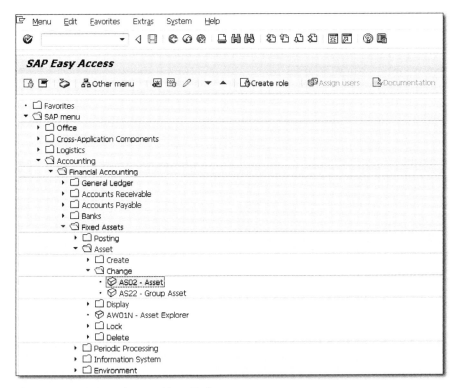

Figure 13.13 AS02 Application Menu Path

Double-click AS02—ASSET from the menu path shown in Figure 13.13 and the CHANGE ASSET: INITIAL SCREEN screen will appear (Figure 13.14). Enter an ASSET number and press ⌐Enter⌐. Note that you also need to enter a SUBNUMBER if applicable; otherwise, the field will default to 0.

Figure 13.14 Change Asset: Initial Screen

After you press Enter, the CHANGE ASSET: MASTER DATA screen will open (Figure 13.15). Editable fields have white backgrounds.

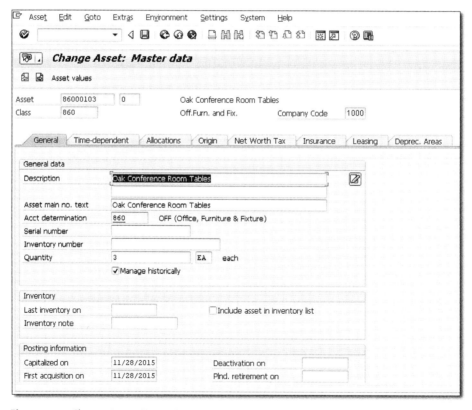

Figure 13.15 Change Asset: Master Data

For this example, click the ORIGIN tab and check the ASSET PURCH. NEW box (Figure 13.16).

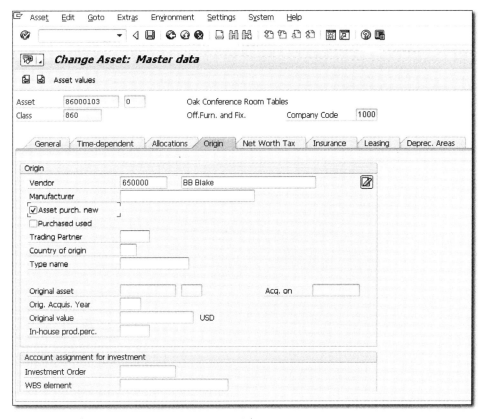

Figure 13.16 Change Asset: Master Data, Origin Tab

Once asset master record changes have been made, click the SAVE icon 🖫 to the right of the COMMAND field in the upper-left-hand corner of the screen. This will save changes to the asset master record, and a confirmation of change message will appear, as shown in Figure 13.17.

To display an asset master record, use Transaction AS03 or application menu path ACCOUNTING • FINANCIAL ACCOUNTING • FIXED ASSETS • ASSET • DISPLAY • AS03 — ASSET, as shown in Figure 13.18.

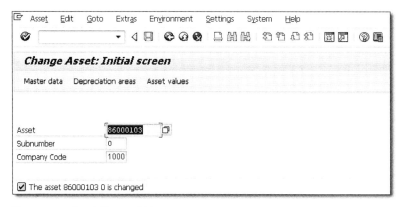

Figure 13.17 Asset Changed Message

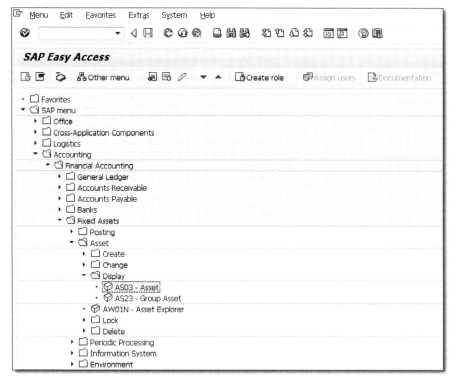

Figure 13.18 Transaction AS03 Application Menu Path

Double-click AS03 from the menu path shown in Figure 13.19 and the DISPLAY ASSET: INITIAL SCREEN screen will open. Enter an ASSET number and press Enter.

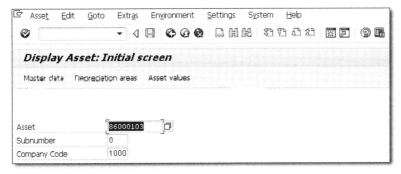

Figure 13.19 Display Asset: Initial Screen

The DISPLAY ASSET: MASTER DATA screen will open (Figure 13.20). Click any of the available tabs to view relevant information.

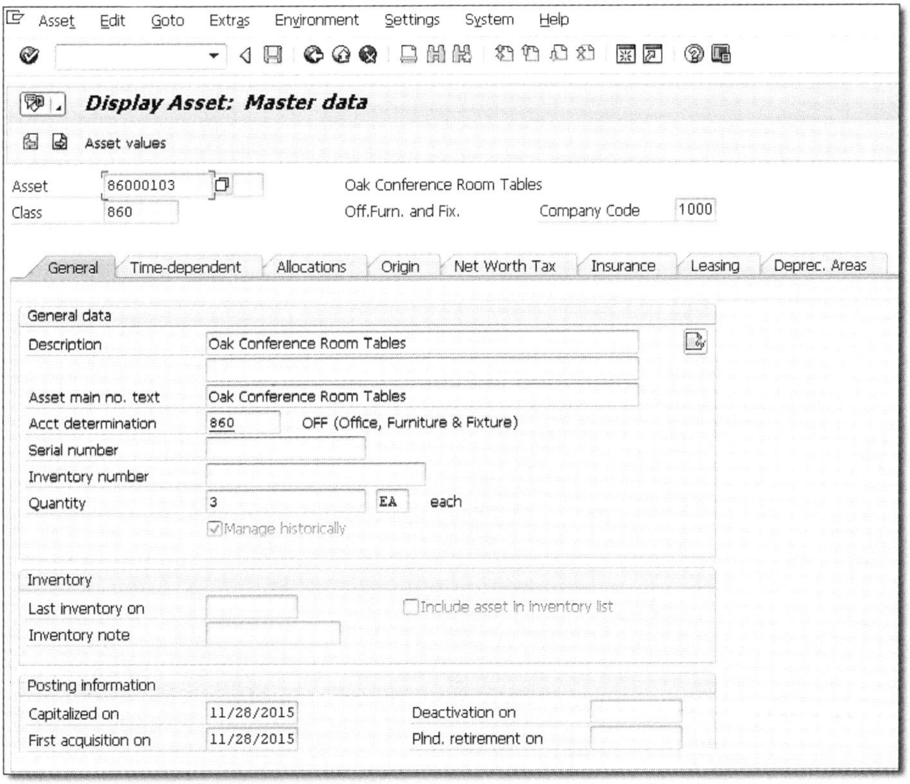

Figure 13.20 Display Asset: Master Data

The last topic we will discuss in this section is locking an asset. In FI-AA, the terms *lock* and *block* are used synonymously. The lock transaction prevents further acquisition postings to an asset master record.

To lock an asset master record, use Transaction AS05 or application menu path Accounting • Financial Accounting • Fixed Assets • Asset • Lock • AS05—Asset, as shown in Figure 13.21.

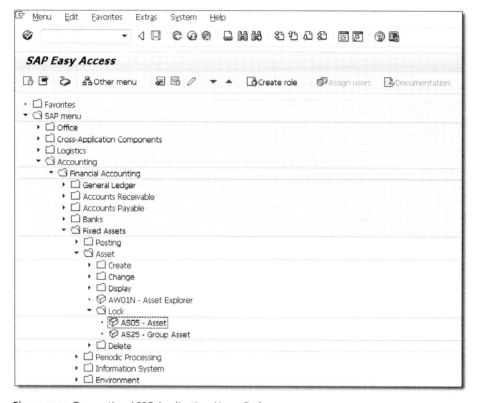

Figure 13.21 Transaction AS05 Application Menu Path

Double-click AS05—Asset from the menu path shown in Figure 13.21 and the Block Asset: Initial Screen screen will open (Figure 13.22). Enter an Asset number, and click the Block icon or press Enter.

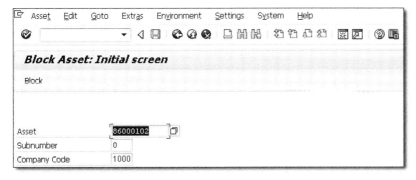

Figure 13.22 Block Asset: Initial Screen

The BLOCK ASSET: PROCESSING SCREEN screen will open (Figure 13.23).

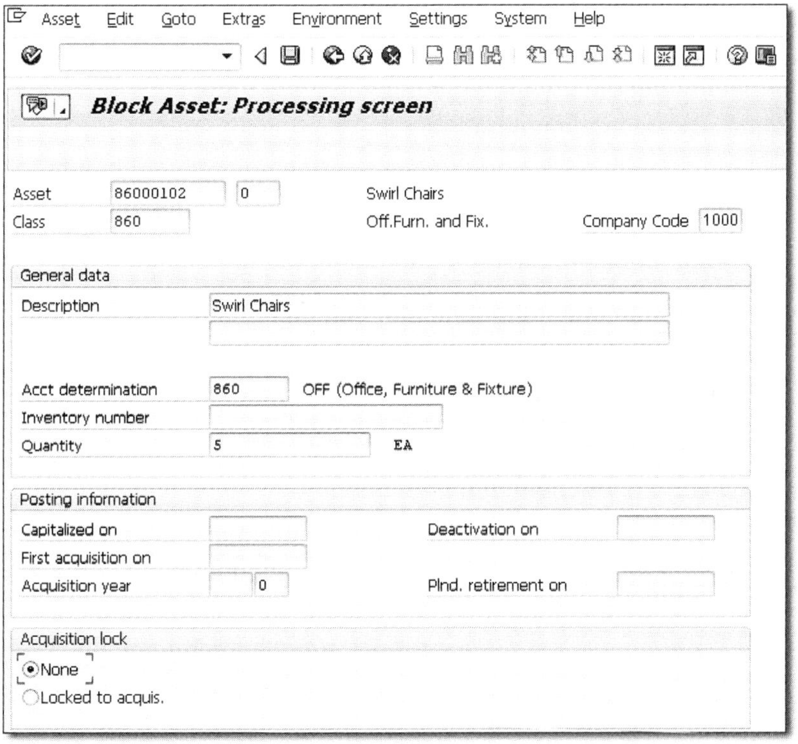

Figure 13.23 Block Asset: Processing Screen

As shown in Figure 13.24, change the ACQUISITION LOCK selection to LOCKED TO ACQUIS. This setting prevents any further acquisition transactions from posting to the asset master record.

Figure 13.24 Acquisition Lock Selection

Click the SAVE icon 🖫 to the right of the COMMAND field in the upper-left-hand corner of the screen. This will save the asset master record block, and a message confirming the block will appear, as shown in Figure 13.25.

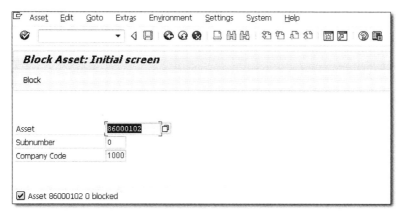

Figure 13.25 Asset Blocked Message

There are several reasons that you might block an asset. For example, when the asset master record is initially created, there may be information that is still missing, such as a serial number. In a situation like this, the asset master record is blocked for safety reasons.

Another reason for locking/blocking an asset is if there a discrepancy has been found, in which case further postings are prevented until the errors have been corrected.

This concludes our discussion of changing, displaying, and locking asset master records. In the next section, you will learn how to best navigate assets using the Asset Explorer.

13.3   Navigating the Asset Explorer

Managing fixed assets is not an easy job. The number of assets within a company can number in the thousands or tens of thousands and spread across numerous asset classes. Asset managers and accountants need user-friendly tools and comprehensive views of fixed assets and their financial information. SAP's primary solution is the Asset Explorer.

The Asset Explorer (Transaction AW01N) is an essential tool for any asset manager. Within this transaction, the system allows you to view all transactions tied to an asset. In essence, it is a one-stop shop. In addition, it allows you to see planned and actual depreciation, net book values over time, and depreciation parameters.

Now, let's take a closer look at the Asset Explorer in action.

To use the Asset Explorer, use Transaction AW01N or application menu path Accounting • Financial Accounting • Fixed Assets • Asset • AW01N – Asset Explorer, as shown in Figure 13.26.

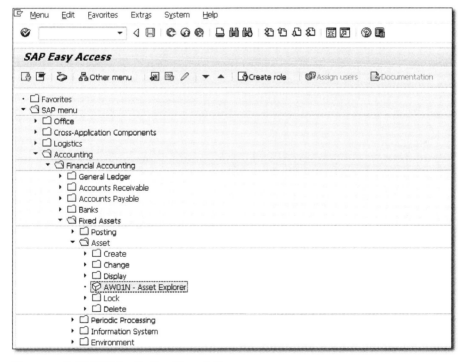

Figure 13.26 AW01N Application Menu Path

Double-click AW01N—ASSET EXPLORER from the menu path shown in Figure 13.26 and the ASSET EXPLORER screen will open (Figure 13.27). This initial screen defaults to the PLANNED VALUES tab, where acquisition values and planned depreciation can be viewed by depreciation area. To change depreciation areas, use the navigation pane to the left of the screen.

In the TRANSACTIONS section at the bottom of the screen, you will see all transactions posted to this asset. The Asset Explorer has drilldown capability; double-click a transaction document number to view an individual document associated with the asset.

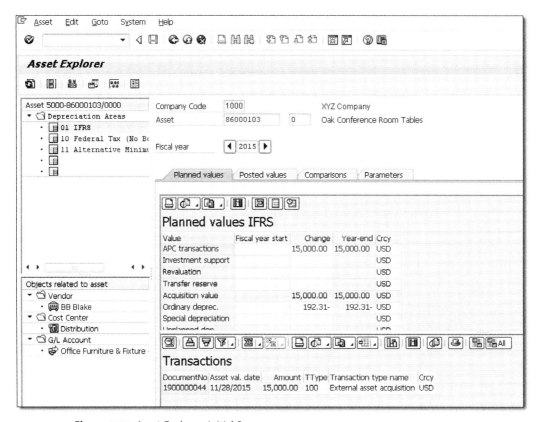

Figure 13.27 Asset Explorer, Initial Screen

Click on the POSTED VALUES tab (Figure 13.28) to see all posted and planned depreciation for an asset by period. This powerful capability is used frequently by accountants, asset managers, and accounting supervisors.

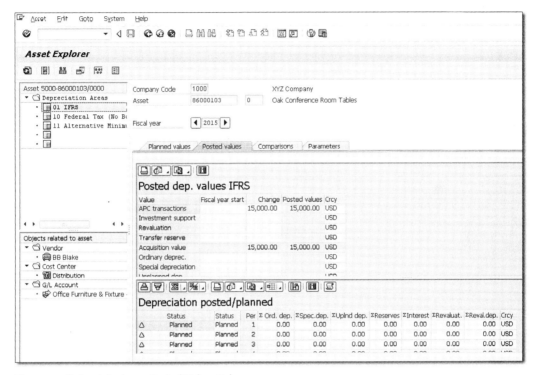

Figure 13.28 Asset Explorer, Posted Values Tab

Click on the COMPARISONS tab (Figure 13.29) to see annual breakouts for depreciation and net book value.

Click on the PARAMETERS tab (Figure 13.30) to see specific settings relevant to the depreciation of the asset. The depreciation key is fundamental, as it determines the assets method of depreciation. Useful life and other relevant settings also can be viewed on this screen. Most of these settings are made in configuration and are associated with the asset class. However, if you ever question the validity of an asset's depreciation calculation, the PARAMETERS tab is where you can go to validate an asset's depreciation settings.

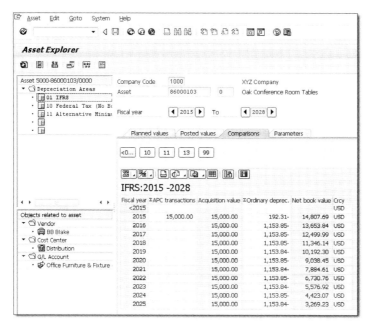

Figure 13.29 AS05 Asset Explorer, Comparisons Tab

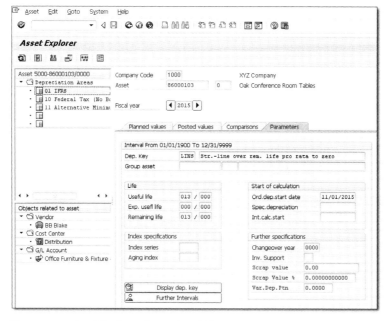

Figure 13.30 Asset Explorer, Parameters Tab

Now that you know how to navigate fixed assets with Asset Explorer, let's discuss fixed asset transfers in the next section.

13.4   Transfers

There are two types of asset transfers in FI-AA: intracompany transfers and inter-company transfers.

The transactions codes used include the following:

1. **ABUMN—Transfer within Company Code**
   Use this transaction when you need to transfer an asset to another business unit or location (e.g., plant) within the same company code.
2. **ABT1N—Intercompany Asset Transfer**
   Use this transaction to transfer an asset to another company code within your organization.

In addition to transferring an asset to another business unit, Transaction ABUMN can be used to correct an asset that was created with the wrong asset class. In both situations, Transaction ABUMN is an asset transfer within the same company code.

Transaction ABUMN can also be used to perform a partial asset transfer. In this situation, you need to split up an asset or move part of it to another asset. This is common for assets with component or interchangeable parts.

Finally, you can use Transaction ABUMN to transfer an asset under construction (AuC) to a finished asset.

To access Transaction ABUMN, follow application menu path ACCOUNTING • FINANCIAL ACCOUNTING • FIXED ASSETS • POSTING • TRANSFER • ABUMN – TRANSFER WITHIN COMPANY CODE, as shown in Figure 13.31.

Double-click on Transaction ABUMN and the ENTER ASSET TRANSACTION: TRANSFER WITHIN COMPANY CODE selection screen appears (Figure 13.32). This is where you enter the details to transfer an asset.

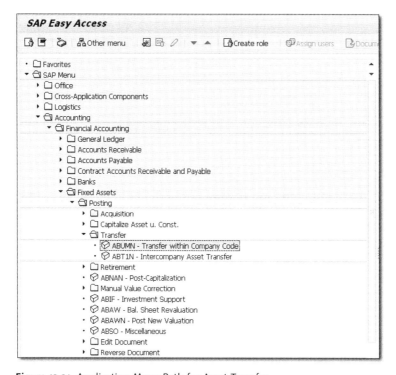

Figure 13.31 Application Menu Path for Asset Transfer

Figure 13.32 Transaction ABUMN Selection Screen

Transaction ABT1N is used if the asset transfer takes place between company codes. This is required when another company code is taking ownership of the asset.

To access Transaction ABT1N, follow application menu path ACCOUNTING • FINANCIAL ACCOUNTING • FIXED ASSETS • POSTING • TRANSFER • ABT1N, as shown in Figure 13.33.

Figure 13.33 Application Menu Path Intercompany Asset Transfer

Double-click on Transaction ABT1N and the ENTER ASSET TRANSACTION: INTERCOMPANY ASSET TRANSFER selection screen appears (Figure 13.34).

Enter Asset Transaction: Intercompany Asset Transfer

     Line items   Change company code   Multiple assets

Company Code	1000	ABC Inc	
Asset		0	Printer Standds

Transaction Data   Additional Details   Partial Transfer   Note

Document Date	
Posting Date	03/05/2016
Asset Value Date	
Text	

Specifications for revenue

- ● No revenue
- ○ Manual Revenue
- ○ Rev. from NBV

Interco. transfer to

Company Code	☑
● Existing asset	
○ New asset	
	Business Area

Figure 13.34 Enter Intercompany Asset Transfer

There are similarities between Transaction ABT1N and Transaction ABUMN, but there are some key differences. The most obvious difference is that Transaction ABT1N has different company codes for the sender and receiver assets. In other words, an asset is being transferred from the balance sheet of one company code to another.

In addition, intercompany asset transfers require that you make revenue specifications.You must specify if a revenue exchange will take place. Revenue may be associated with an intercompany transfer if it is sold to another part of the company with a separate company code.

Transaction ABT1N offers the following three options for revenue specification:

1. No revenue

2. Manual revenue

3. Revenue from Net Book Value (NBV)

This concludes our discussion of fixed asset transfers. In the next section, we will discuss asset retirements.

13.5   Retirement

Most people think *asset retirement* means that the asset has no more value or future use. In actuality, asset retirement is simply the removal of an asset or part of an asset from the asset portfolio.

There are several FI-AA business transactions that are relevant to asset retirement. If an asset is sold to a customer and it generates revenue, Transaction F-92 is used. This transaction creates a debit to A/R through the creation of an A/R invoice and a credit to the asset.

Instead of posting a retirement to a customer, you can instead post against a G/L clearing account using Transaction ABAON. Both Transaction F-92 and Transaction ABAON are considered asset sales. Transaction ABAON creates a debit to a G/L clearing account and a credit to the asset. Revenue is either manually specified or based upon NBV.

Another common scenario is to scrap an asset. In this case, the asset is scrapped and no revenue is associated with the retirement of the asset. Transaction ABAVN is used in this scenario.

In the next section, value adjustments to fixed assets are discussed.

13.6   Value Adjustments

There are many reasons that adjustments may need to be made to an asset's valuation. We do not intend to identify and discuss them all here, but we will highlight some key points.

A change to an asset value is referred to as a *write-up*. There are several reasons that a write-up may be necessary, such as when an asset was not capitalized in a fiscal year that is now closed, or when an incorrect depreciation key was used in the past, causing excess depreciation to be posted.

Several transactions exist in FI-AA to make value adjustments. These transactions, along with transaction types, provide you with the tools needed to make asset value adjustments for just about any circumstance.

Transaction ABZU is the primary transaction. It is used to post write-ups to ordinary depreciation, special depreciation, unplanned depreciation, reserves by specifying the appropriate transaction type.

Other write-up transactions include Transaction ABMA for write-up of manual depreciation, Transaction ABAA for write-up of unplanned depreciation, and Transaction ABMR for write-up of transfer of reserves.

Another type of write-up is called *write-up to APC*. These are corrections to the acquisition and production costs of an asset. Transaction ABNAN is used to correct APC valuations.

Although each of these transactions has an intended purpose, the main differences among them are the transaction type defaults and selection options. We will not cover transaction types in detail here, but for value adjustments you should become familiar with them and understand when and how to use them.

This concludes our discussion of value adjustments. In the next section, the topic of depreciation is discussed.

13.7 Depreciation

Depreciation of an asset is typically referred to as *asset consumption*. In accounting terms, depreciation refers to the following:

- A decrease in the value of the asset
- The allocation of costs of an asset to periods in which the asset is used

Long-term assets are depreciated for both tax and accounting purposes. The former affects the balance sheet of a company, and the latter affects net income. Cost is allocated as depreciation expense in the periods in which the asset is expected to be used.

Depreciation expense is recognized by companies for financial reporting and tax purposes. Methods of computing depreciation, and the periods over which assets are depreciated, may vary between asset types, countries, and industries. Specific laws or accounting standards, which may vary by country, may dictate standards for depreciation.

There are several standard methods of computing depreciation expense, including fixed percentage, straight line, and declining balance methods. Depreciation expense begins when the asset is placed in service.

Now, let's see how depreciation expense is executed in FI-AA.

The calculation of depreciation is an important step in month-end and year-end closing. To execute an asset depreciation run, use Transaction AFAB or application menu path Accounting • Financial Accounting • Fixed Assets • Periodic Processing • AFAB—Execute, as shown in Figure 13.35.

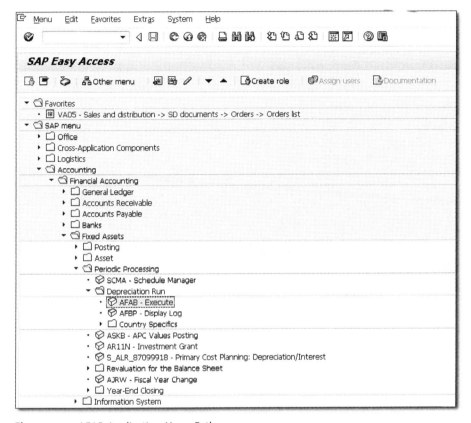

Figure 13.35 AFAB Application Menu Path

Double-click AFAB—Execute from the menu path shown in Figure 13.35 and the Depreciation Posting Run initial screen will open (Figure 13.36). Here, enter the parameters for your depreciation posting run. The Company Code, Fiscal year, and Posting Period fields are required.

The default selection in Reason for Posting Run is Planned Posting Run. However, occasionally there will be a need to repeat or restart a run, or to run unplanned depreciation.

The FURTHER OPTIONS section of the screen provides additional options for output. One common selection is LIST ASSETS, which specifies that all assets will be listed for which depreciation is posted on the depreciation log.

It is always a good idea to run depreciation in test mode first. The PARAMETERS FOR TEST RUN section at the bottom of the screen provides settings for you to do so.

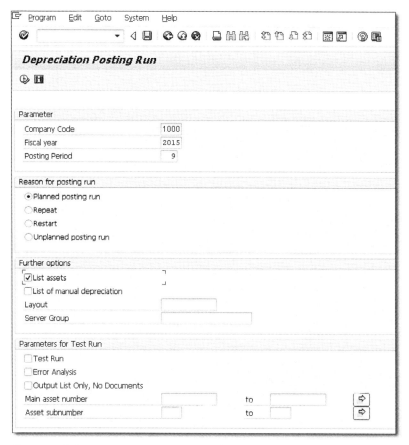

Figure 13.36 Depreciation Posting Run Initial Screen

With all the field values entered as in Figure 13.36, click the EXECUTE icon ⊕. The depreciation run will execute in a background job.

To view the results of a depreciation run, use Transaction AFBP or application menu path ACCOUNTING • FINANCIAL ACCOUNTING • FIXED ASSETS • PERIODIC PROCESSING • DEPRECIATION RUN • AFBP—DISPLAY LOG, as shown in Figure 13.37.

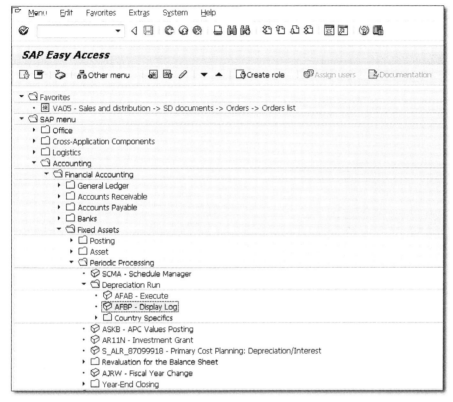

Figure 13.37 Transaction AFBP Application Menu Path

Double-click AFBP—DISPLAY LOG from the menu path shown in Figure 13.37 and the LOG OF POSTING RUN screen will open (Figure 13.38). The COMPANY CODE, FISCAL YEAR, and POSTING PERIOD fields are required. Further options also are available, including the LIST ASSETS selection box, which indicates that all posted assets with depreciation will be listed on the output log.

With all field values entered, click the EXECUTE icon ⊕. The LOG FOR POSTING RUN screen will open (Figure 13.39). All the details from the depreciation run are provided. Within the log, you can change the layout, sort, filter, subtotal, download to Excel, and so on.

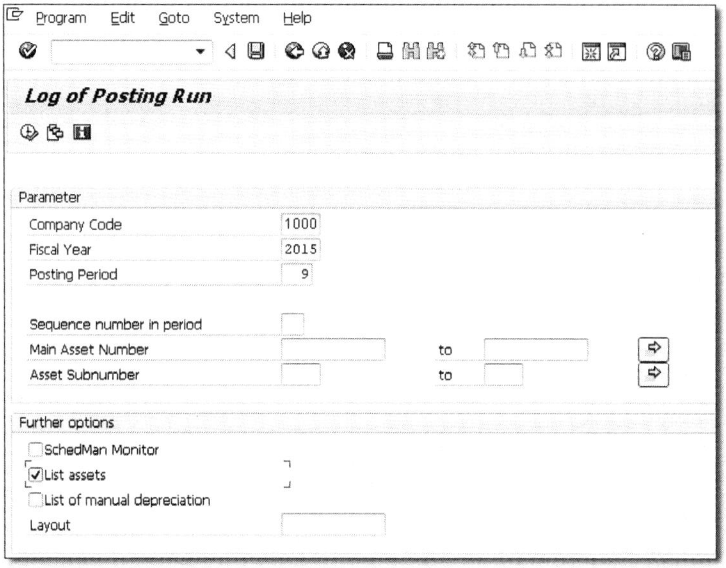

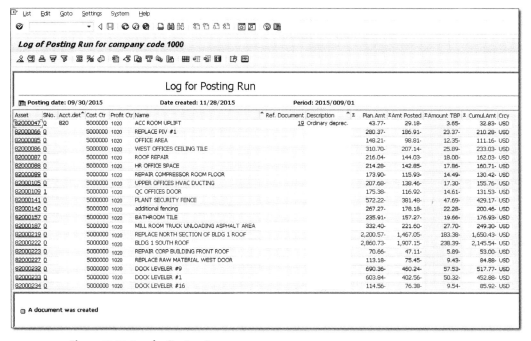

Figure 13.38 Log of Posting Run Initial Screen

Log for Posting Run

Posting date: 09/30/2015 **Date created: 11/28/2015** **Period: 2015/009/01**

Asset	SNo.	Acct.det	Cost Ctr	Profit Ctr	Name	Ref. Document	Description	Plan.Amt	Amt Posted	Amount TBP	Cumul.Amt	Crcy
82000047	0	820	5000000	1020	ACC ROOM UPLIFT	19	Ordinary deprec.	43.77-	29.18-	3.65-	32.83-	USD
82000066	0		5000000	1020	REPLACE PIV #1			280.37-	186.91-	23.37-	210.28-	USD
82000085	0		5000000	1020	OFFICE AREA			148.21-	98.81-	12.35-	111.16-	USD
82000086	0		5000000	1020	WEST OFFICES CEILING TILE			310.70-	207.14-	25.89-	233.03-	USD
82000087	0		5000000	1020	ROOF REPAIR			216.04-	144.03-	18.00-	162.03-	USD
82000088	0		5000000	1020	HR OFFICE SPACE			214.28-	142.85-	17.86-	160.71-	USD
82000089	0		5000000	1020	REPAIR COMPRESSOR ROOM FLOOR			173.90-	115.93-	14.49-	130.42-	USD
82000105	0		5000000	1020	UPPER OFFICES HVAC DUCTING			207.68-	138.46-	17.30-	155.76-	USD
82000109	1		5000000	1020	QC OFFICES DOOR			175.38-	116.92-	14.61-	131.53-	USD
82000141	0		5000000	1020	PLANT SECURITY FENCE			572.22-	381.48-	47.69-	429.17-	USD
82000142	0		5000000	1020	additional fencing			267.27-	178.18-	22.28-	200.46-	USD
82000157	0		5000000	1020	BATHROOM TILE			235.91-	157.27-	19.66-	176.93-	USD
82000187	0		5000000	1020	MILL ROOM TRUCK UNLOADING ASPHALT AREA			332.40-	221.60-	27.70-	249.30-	USD
82000219	0		5000000	1020	REPLACE NORTH SECTION OF BLDG 1 ROOF			2,200.57-	1,467.05-	183.38-	1,650.43-	USD
82000222	0		5000000	1020	BLDG 1 SOUTH ROOF			2,860.73-	1,907.15-	238.39-	2,145.54-	USD
82000223	0		5000000	1020	REPAIR CORP BUILDING FRONT ROOF			70.66-	47.11-	5.89-	53.00-	USD
82000227	0		5000000	1020	REPLACE RAW MATERIAL WEST DOOR			113.18-	75.45-	9.43-	84.88-	USD
82000232	0		5000000	1020	DOCK LEVELER #9			690.36-	460.24-	57.53-	517.77-	USD
82000233	0		5000000	1020	DOCK LEVELER #1			603.84-	402.56-	50.32-	452.88-	USD
82000234	0		5000000	1020	DOCK LEVELER #16			114.56-	76.38-	9.54-	85.92-	USD

A document was created

Figure 13.39 Log for Posting Run

This concludes our discussion of fixed asset depreciation. You should now have a good understanding of what depreciation is, how to execute a depreciation run in FI-AA, and how to view the log of a depreciation run.

13.8   Summary

The concept of the fixed asset lifecycle is important to understand. The fixed asset lifecycle is often referred to as the *acquire-to-retire* process. In this chapter, the different parts of the lifecycle were covered in detail.

The first step in the acquire-to-retire process is the creation of the asset master record using Transaction AS01. Once an asset master record is created, it is capitalized, giving life to the asset. There are several ways to capitalize an asset, depending upon its origin and how it is procured. The asset can be produced in house, procured directly in FI-AA, transferred from an affiliate company, or procured through MM-Purchasing. In this chapter, capitalization of an asset was demonstrated using Transaction F-90 to debit an asset and credit a vendor account, thereby capitalizing the asset value, while at the same time producing an open A/P invoice for a vendor.

Throughout the lifecycle of an asset, the Asset Explorer (Transaction AW01N) is an indispensable tool for managing assets. In essence, it serves as a one-stop shop for asset information. It allows you to see planned and actual depreciation, net book values over time, and depreciation parameters. The Asset Explorer is used frequently by accountants, asset managers, and accounting supervisors.

The calculation of depreciation is an important step in month-end and year-end closing. In this chapter, we demonstrated how to execute a depreciation run (Transaction AFAB) and how to view a depreciation run log (Transaction AFBP). In most companies, depreciation runs are scheduled jobs that run automatically at month end, but it is important to know the details of how such a run works. Frequently, questions arise about depreciation calculations, and troubleshooting asset depreciation tends to be a common occurrence.

Other steps in the asset lifecycle discussed in this chapter include asset transfers, retirements, and value adjustments. Each of these transaction types have multiple FI-AA transactions. It is important to understand them all and their associated transaction types to know when and how to use them.

FI-AA provides the capability for full asset lifecycle management, but business processes tend to be cross-modular, and fixed asset processes are no exception. Understanding the basics of FI-AA is an important first step for gaining a broader perspective on integrated asset processes.

This concludes our discussion of fixed asset transactions. In the next chapter, we will discuss fixed asset posting logic and the validation of FI-AA postings.

In this chapter, we cover useful topics in FI-AA for understanding the validation of asset postings. Several factors make the validation of asset postings a challenge, including a large number of account determinations, transaction types, and G/L accounts.

14   Fixed Asset Posting Logic

Trying to validate asset postings can, at times, feel like wandering in the dark. This is because, by the very nature of FI-AA, a lot happens in the background when you execute a transaction. When FI-AA is configured, there is a wide range of system settings and integration to sort out, requiring close collaboration with the chart of accounts, procurement, production, and more.

In this chapter, our intent is to give you a better understanding of the FI-AA design and posting logic, thereby empowering asset managers and accountants to execute their day-to-day job functions.

Specific topics addressed in this chapter include fixed asset G/L accounts, asset classes, and account determinations, and covering these topics requires delving into configuration at times. However, the intent is not to teach configuration but to provide you with a base level of understanding for how certain configurations influence the G/L account postings in FI-AA.

Asset accountants frequently encounter two types of issues: The first occurs when an asset transaction does not post to the expected G/L account—for example, when an asset acquisition posts to the wrong asset class and G/L reconciliation account.

The second common issue occurs when an asset manager finds that depreciation postings are incorrect. This is seen commonly during month-end or year-end close, when depreciation is run and postings are validated.

In this chapter, you will gain insights to help you deal with these types of postings errors and more.

14.1   General Ledger Accounts

Asset accounting is a specialty. Numerous G/L accounts are needed to support FI-AA. It is a best practice to set up G/L reconciliation accounts in a one-to-one relationship with asset classes, which makes FI-AA more organized and easier to manage and streamlines FI-AA configuration with financial reporting.

Now, let's discuss some other aspects of G/L accounts in FI-AA. The specific G/L accounts you choose to use in FI-AA depend primarily on your business processes. Not all FI-AA steps are executed by every customer. Therefore, you need to carefully define your FI-AA business processes and implement the G/L accounts and configuration necessary to support those processes.

This chapter does not attempt to identify each possible G/L account you may need. Instead, we address the core G/L accounts to support acquisition and production cost (APC) and depreciation transactions. These include fixed asset balance sheet accounts (i.e., reconciliation and accumulated depreciation accounts) and profit and loss (P&L) accounts (i.e., depreciation expense).

Now, let's delve into balance sheet accounts in the next section.

14.1.1   Balance Sheet Accounts

In configuration, G/L account groups are defined prior to creating G/L accounts. These account groups determine the allowable number range for G/L accounts and control the layout of the G/L account master record and whether fields are required, optional, or suppressed. When creating a G/L account, an account group must be specified.

This is critical to know when your company is setting up its chart of accounts in SAP. Each type of G/L account (e.g., bank accounts, liabilities, assets) should have a distinct number range and account group. If your asset accounts are not aligned, but scattered, then it they will be more difficult to manage.

G/L account groups are especially important to FI-AA because a company should have at least one account group for fixed assets. This account group should designate an allowable number range consistent with your numbering scheme for asset classes. Asset classes are discussed in detail in Section 14.2. *Consistency* is the name of the game when setting up FI-AA in a way that is easy to understand and manage. Consistency between fixed asset G/L accounts and asset classes is especially important.

Figure 14.1 is an example of FI-AA balance sheet accounts.

```
Chart of Accounts ABC Inc

G/L acct   G/L Acct Long Text

140210    LAND
140211    EASEMENTS
140212     BUILDINGS
140213    OFFICE FURNITURE AND EQUIPMENT
140214    MACHINERY AND EQUIPMENT
140215     COMPUTER EQUIPMENT
140216     COMPUTER SOFTWARE
140217    VEHICLES
140218     CONSTRUCTION IN PROGRESS
140219    LEASEHOLD IMPROVEMENTS
140220    CAPITAL LEASES
```

Figure 14.1 FI-AA Balance Sheet Accounts

The core balance sheet fixed asset accounts include APC reconciliation accounts (Figure 14.1) and accumulated depreciation and amortization accounts.

Figure 14.2 is an example of accumulated depreciation accounts that correlate to the APC accounts in Figure 14.1.

```
Chart of Accounts ABC Inc

G/L acct   G/L Acct Long Text

140110    LAND
140111    EASEMENTS
140112     BUILDINGS
140113    OFFICE FURNITURE AND EQUIPMENT
140114    MACHINERY AND EQUIPMENT
140115     COMPUTER EQUIPMENT
140116     COMPUTER SOFTWARE
140117    VEHICLES
140118     CONSTRUCTION IN PROGRESS
140119    LEASEHOLD IMPROVEMENTS
140120    CAPITAL LEASES
```

Figure 14.2 FI-AA Accumulated Depreciation Accounts

A streamlined design will have a one-to-one relationship between fixed asset balance sheet accounts and asset classes (Figure 14.3).

There may be regulatory, industry, or country-specific requirements that dictate otherwise for some customers. Moreover, for each fixed asset reconciliation account, there should be a corresponding accumulated depreciation and amortization account.

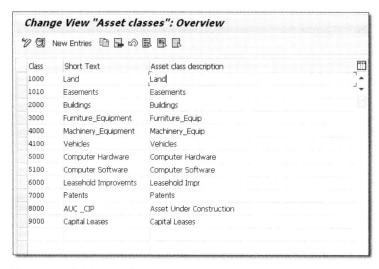

Figure 14.3 FI-AA Asset Classes

Balance sheet accounts are designated in FI-AA account determinations and are discussed in detail in Section 14.3.

Now that you understand FI-AA balance sheet accounts, we'll discuss FI-AA P&L accounts in the next section.

14.1.2 Profit and Loss Accounts

In the P&L, many different G/L accounts may be used for fixed assets. These include G/L accounts for revenue, gain/loss, interest, and more. The focus of this section, however, is on P&L depreciation expense accounts.

When a depreciation run is executed (Transaction AFAB), a debit is posted to a P&L depreciation and amortization expense account and a credit is posted to a balance sheet accumulated depreciation account.

Depreciation expense accounts are designated in FI-AA account determinations and are discussed in detail in Section 14.3.

From an accounting perspective, depreciation expense postings affect the net income of a company.

As you learned in this section, there is a close relationship between asset classes and FI-AA G/L accounts. In the next section, we will discuss asset classes in detail.

14.2 Asset Classes

Asset classes are a fundamental part of the FI-AA design and provide a structure for fixed assets from an accounting point of view. Each asset master record is assigned to only one asset class, and an asset class, in turn, is assigned to an asset when it is created. Asset classes serve other important functions in FI-AA, including assigning default values when creating assets (e.g., depreciation terms) and grouping assets for reporting. The asset class also determines the screen variant and account determinations.

An important system limitation to be aware of is that once an asset is created with an asset class, the asset class cannot be changed. To fix the error, you have to create a new asset with the proper asset class and transfer the asset to a new one. Be especially careful when you create a new asset master record to ensure that the correct asset class is selected.

Although asset classes are configurations and typically accessed via the IMG (Transaction SPRO), they also can be accessed using Transaction OAOA. This transaction opens the DISPLAY VIEW "ASSET CLASSES": OVERVIEW screen (Figure 14.4).

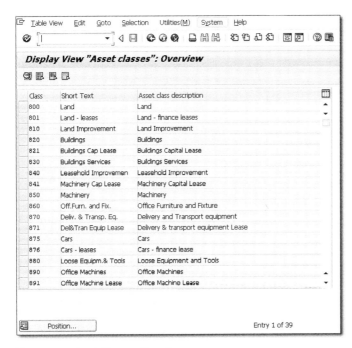

Figure 14.4 Asset Classes: Overview

Double-click an asset class, or highlight it and click the DISPLAY icon 🔍 . The DIS-PLAY VIEW "ASSET CLASSES": DETAILS screen will open (Figure 14.5). Note that several important control parameters exist within the asset class, including screen layout rules for asset master records, number ranges, a setting to allow subasset numbers, and so on.

Figure 14.5 Asset Classes: Details

In Figure 14.5, take note of the ACCOUNT DETERM . field. This field provides a link to specific account determinations for this asset class. Account determination designates the reconciliation accounts in the G/L and their offsetting accounts posted to when certain business transactions are executed. The ACCOUNT DETERM. field is required in the asset class. Several asset classes can use the same account determination, but they must use the same chart of accounts and post in the same way to G/L accounts.

In this section, you have seen that asset classes are a fundamental structure in FI-AA. Moreover, through assignment of account determination, asset classes provide the link to G/L reconciliation accounts and offsetting accounts with certain business transactions. In the next section, we will discuss FI-AA account determinations.

14.3 Account Determinations

Account determinations specify the G/L accounts posted to for specific FI-AA transaction types. They are required for the integration of FI-AA with the G/L.

Initially setting up and testing account determinations is no small task. Just think about all the different transaction types in FI-AA and you'll get the picture. These transactions include acquisitions, retirements, revaluations, investment support, depreciation, and more.

Prior to setting up account determinations, a chart of depreciation must be created and assigned to a company code. This is an essential link between FI-AA and G/L. Figure 14.6 shows an example chart of depreciation assigned to a company code. Although this assignment is made in configuration using Transaction SPRO, you can go directly to this setting using Transaction OAOB (Figure 14.6).

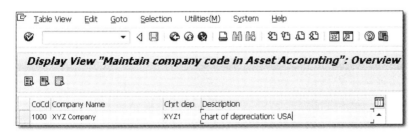

Figure 14.6 Assign Chart of Depreciation to Company Code

The chart of depreciation contains a set of depreciation areas. Figure 14.7 shows an example chart of depreciation that contains multiple depreciation areas. Notice in the G/L column the value 1 in depreciation area 1. This setting specifies that that postings are to be made to the G/L in real time.

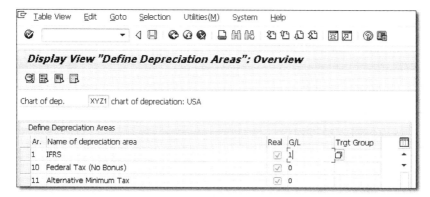

Figure 14.7 Define Chart of Depreciation

With the framework established, FI-AA account assignments can be made. Initially setting up FI-AA account assignments is tedious. Account determinations must be completed for each combination of transaction type and asset class, and these account determinations should be well documented in your company's accounting models, especially because any future changes to G/L asset accounts also need to be made in account determinations.

Several different account assignment transaction codes exist in FI-AA. They are broken out to allow account determinations by business transaction groupings. Table 14.1 provides a list of these transaction codes.

Transaction Code	Transaction Name
AO85	Acquisitions
AO86	Retirements
AO87	Revaluation of APC
AO88	Investment Support
AO89	Settlement AuC to CO Objects
AO93	Ordinary Depreciation
AO94	Special Depreciation
AO95	Unplanned Depreciation

Table 14.1 FI-AA Account Determination Transaction Codes

Transaction Code	Transaction Name
AO96	Transfer of Reserves
AO97	Revaluation of Depreciation
AO98	Interest

Table 14.1 FI-AA Account Determination Transaction Codes (Cont.)

Rather than going through each of the transactions in Table 14.1 individually, we will focus on Transaction AO90, which provides a comprehensive view of FI-AA account determinations. Transaction AO90 includes account determinations for acquisitions, retirements, revaluations, balance sheet accounts, ordinary depreciation, special depreciation, unplanned depreciation, transfer of reserves, interest, and more.

When you execute Transaction AO90, the DISPLAY VIEW "CHART OF ACCOUNTS ": OVERVIEW screen will open (Figure 14.8).

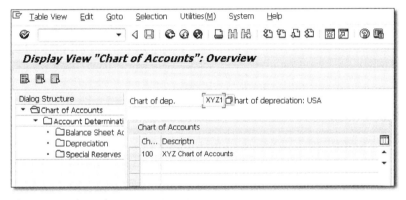

Figure 14.8 Chart of Accounts: Overview

By drilling down into the ACCOUNT DETERMINATION folder, you will open the DISPLAY VIEW "ACCOUNT DETERMINATION": OVERVIEW screen (Figure 14.9). Notice that the ACCOUNT DETERM. values and names directly mirror the asset classes discussed in section Section 14.2. It is not required that they have a one-to-one correlation, but it helps keep your FI-AA setup organized and easy to manage.

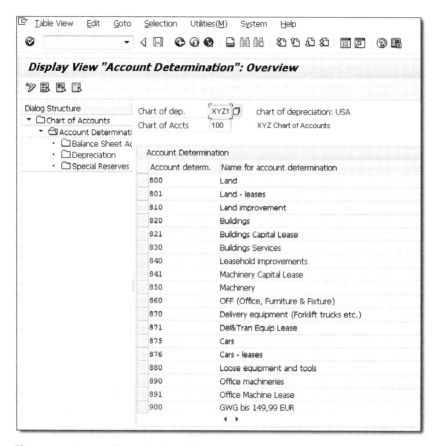

Figure 14.9 Account Determination: Overview

Drilling down in the BALANCE SHEET ACCOUNTS folder lets you view specific account determination settings (Figure 14.10). It's important to note that not all G/L accounts are specified. More possibilities exist than always are needed. A company typically only enters account determinations when it knows for certain they will be used. For example, if down payments are not part of your company's acquisition process, you might choose not to enter a G/L account in the ACQUISITION: DOWN PAYMENTS field.

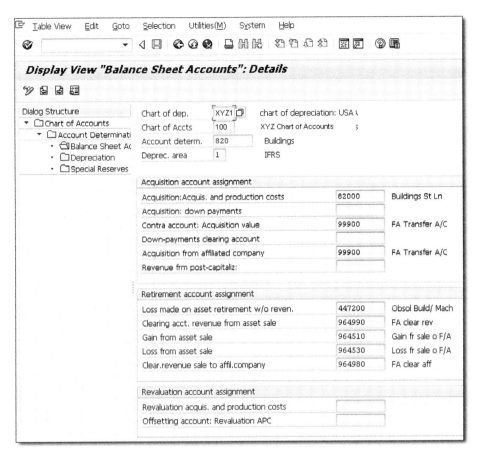

Figure 14.10 Balance Sheet Accounts: Details

Drilling down into the DEPRECIATION folder, you can view specific account determination settings (Figure 14.11). Notice that separate account determinations have to be made for ordinary, special, and unplanned depreciation. For accounting purposes, each type of depreciation may need to be accounted for separately.

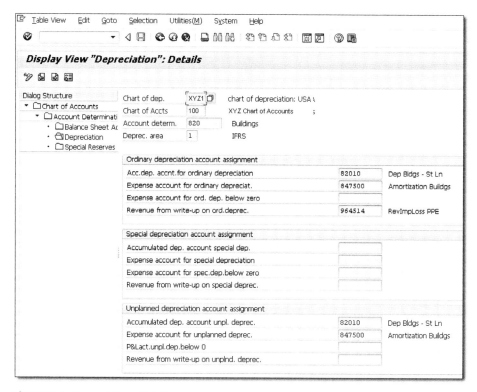

Figure 14.11 Depreciation: Details

A word of caution related to the setup of FI-AA account determinations and testing: Because so many FI-AA account determinations exist, it is important to keep FI-AA posting models with your expected results and to test all relevant account determinations before you go live with SAP. If you are already live on FI-AA and make a change to account determinations, the same applies.

In today's world, people are under a lot of pressure to complete tasks quickly. As a result, testing easily can be compromised or skipped altogether. Whether you are going live with FI-AA for the first time or making a change to account determinations, make sure to test all FI-AA postings before promoting a change to production. It is likely that fixing FI-AA posting errors in production will be a lot more time-consuming than testing.

In this section, you learned about FI-AA account determinations and how to view them, as well as the importance of testing them all and having good posting models with expected results. Understanding account determinations is critical for understanding of asset accounting, and it gives you a greater understanding of the FI-AA posting logic necessary for validating and troubleshooting asset postings.

14.4 Reports and Tools

In the previous sections of this chapter, you learned about asset G/L accounts, asset classes, and account determinations. Knowing the setup of FI-AA is important to recognize a posting problem when you see it. In this section, you are directed to specific reports and tools to aid you in your analysis.

The first and most frequently used is Transaction AW01N. Its application menu path is shown in Figure 14.12. Transaction AW01N is best used to get an overview of an asset, including posting history, planned depreciation, and NBV.

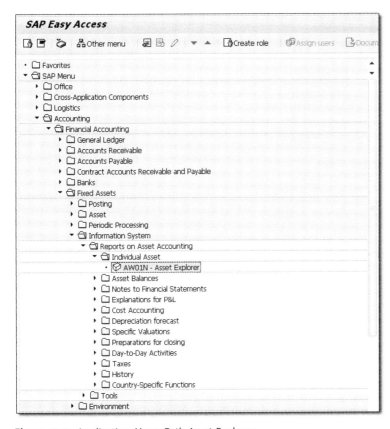

Figure 14.12 Application Menu Path Asset Explorer

A multitude of additional standard reports exists to get details on asset balances. As shown in Figure 14.13, individual folders contain reports categorized as Bal-ance Lists, Inventory Lists, Leased Assets, and Country Specifics.

Figure 14.13 Application Menu Path Asset Balances

Within BALANCE Lists is the ASSET BALANCES folder (Figure 14.14), where report selections exist by individual asset and other dimensions (e.g. BUSINESS AREA, COST CENTER, etc.).

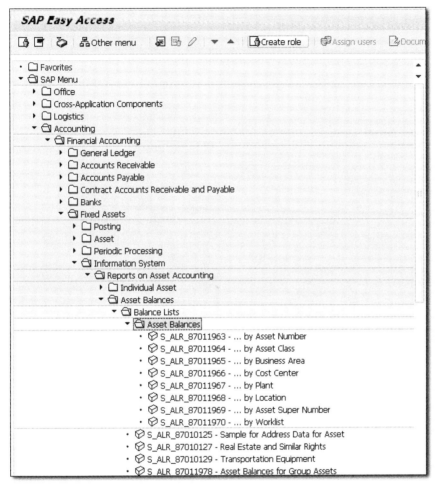

Figure 14.14 Application Menu Path Asset Balances Reports

Also within the BALANCES LIST folder is a compilation of physical inventory list reports (Figure 14.15).

Figure 14.15 Application Menu Path Physical Inventory List

Also available in asset reports are reports on COST ACCOUNTING (Figure 14.16). These reports are particularly useful for inquiries into depreciation and revaluation.

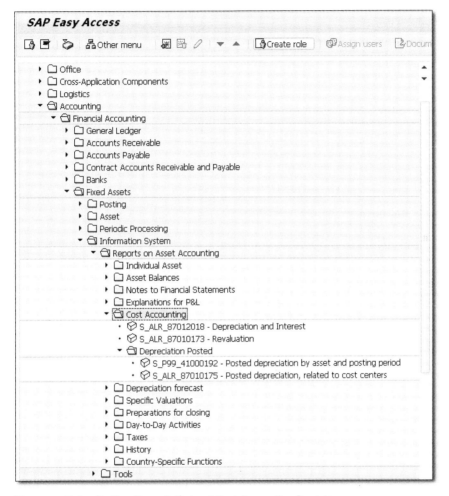

Figure 14.16 Application Menu Path Asset Cost Accounting Reports

If you still haven't found the reports you need, try looking in the PROBLEM ANALY-SIS folder (Figure 14.17). Many useful tools exist here, such as Transaction ABST. Build this transaction into your financial close procedures.

Figure 14.17 Application Menu Path Problem Analysis

Within PROBLEM ANALYSIS is the ASSET SUMMARY folder (Figure 14.18), which contains numerous transactions to view postings, value determination, intercompany transfers, and much more.

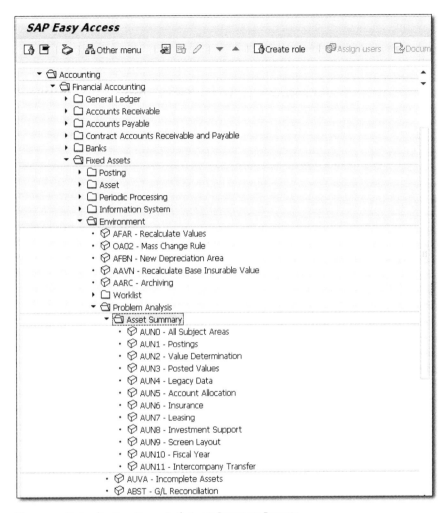

Figure 14.18 Application Menu Path Asset Summary Reports

Now you should have a good understanding of the important elements required to understand and validate FI-AA postings.

14.5 Summary

This chapter discussed three topics in FI-AA essential to understanding asset postings: G/L accounts, asset classes, and account determinations. FI-AA consists of much more than these topics, but these provide essential knowledge you need to identify potential posting problems.

The fixed asset G/L account structure is the backbone of asset accounting. The essential G/L accounts needed are fixed asset reconciliation accounts, accumulated depreciation and amortization accounts, and depreciation expense accounts. Depending upon your business processes, several additional G/L accounts and account determinations may be needed. Some of the possibilities that exist are accounts for revenue, interest, gain/loss, special depreciation, and unplanned depreciation.

FI-AA is a subledger, meaning that transaction detail is maintained in the asset master record. Individual assets will each maintain details for all related transactions, including capitalization, depreciation, revaluation, and so on. Individual assets in the same asset class have their values rolled up to a cumulative balance in the reconciliation account for the asset class.

A streamlined FI-AA design will have a one-to-one relationship between fixed asset balance sheet accounts and asset classes. There may be regulatory, industry, or country-specific requirements that dictate otherwise for some customers. Moreover, for each fixed asset reconciliation account, there should be a corresponding accumulated depreciation and amortization account.

Asset classes are a fundamental part of the FI-AA design. They provide the structure of fixed assets from an accounting point of view. Each asset master record is assigned to only one asset class. An asset class, in turn, is assigned to an asset when an asset master record is created. Asset classes serve other important functions in FI-AA, including assigning default values when creating assets (e.g., depreciation terms) and grouping assets for reporting. The most important points to remember about asset classes are that they should correlate with your balance sheet reconciliation accounts and that all account determinations must be made for each combination of asset class and transaction type.

Account determinations specify the G/L accounts posted to for specific FI-AA transaction types. They are required for the integration of FI-AA with the G/L.

Although several account determination transaction codes exist, the most useful is Transaction OA90, which provides the most comprehensive list of account determinations.

The topics of FI-AA G/L accounts, asset classes, and account determinations are important for gaining a greater understanding of asset posting logic and dependencies. Understanding them is essential for asset managers and accountants when validating and troubleshooting asset-related postings.

This completes the discussion of fixed assets. In the next chapter, we discuss bank master data and processes.

In this chapter, we discuss bank master data and processes. This includes bank master records, house banks, and bank reconciliation.

15 Bank Master Data and Processes

At this point, you are familiar with master data from our discussions in prior chapters on FI master data, G/L, A/P, A/R, and fixed assets. SAP defines *master data* as data that remains unchanged over a long period of time. It contains information that is needed repeatedly in the same way. In FI, master data primarily includes G/L accounts, vendors, customers, banks, and fixed assets. Each of these is important in its own way to specific business processes.

In this chapter, we will cover house banks and vendor and customer bank accounts. The distinction between house banks and bank master records is simply that *house banks* are the banks with which your company has a bank account. That is, they are the banks with which your company does business. House bank accounts are used to hold cash, disburse payments, and receive money.

Customer and vendor bank accounts, on the other hand, are the bank accounts of your business partners. For external bank accounts that you send money to or receive money from, a bank account master record is created and assigned in a business partner's master record.

As you can imagine, several business processes use bank accounts. This includes any business process in which you send or receive money, calculate interest or fees, or manage cash and account balances. We cannot cover all these business processes in one chapter, so the focus here is on the bank reconciliation business process.

Let's begin with a detailed discussion of bank master data.

15.1   Bank Master Data

In this section, we will discuss vendor and customer bank master records and house banks. It is important to understand how to create and maintain bank master records, how assign them to customer and vendor accounts, and the relationship of the House Bank to G/L accounts and bank reconciliation.

15.1.1   Vendor and Customer Bank Data

For each business partner (i.e., vendors and customers) there is an expected exchange of money. You procure goods and services from vendors. In exchange, outgoing payments are made to the vendor to compensate them for the goods or services provided.

On the flip side, goods and services are sold to customers. Goods are issued, services provided, and payments received from a customer in exchange for these goods and services.

There are two steps necessary to set up and use vendor and customer bank data. First is the creation of a bank master record. The second is the assignment of bank master data to a vendor or customer account.

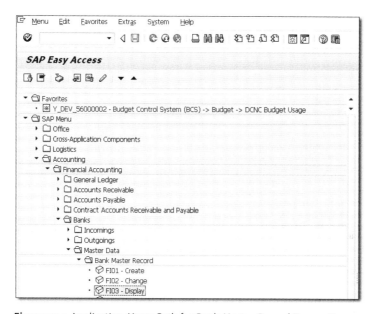

Figure 15.1 Application Menu Path for Bank Master Record Transactions

To access bank master record transactions, follow application menu path ACCOUNT-ING • FINANCIAL ACCOUNTING • BANKS • MASTER DATA • BANK MASTER RECORD, as shown in Figure 15.1.

As you can see, transactions exist to create (Transaction FI01), change (Transaction FI02), and display (Transaction FI03) bank master records. Double-click FI03—DIS-PLAY from the menu path shown in Figure 15.1. The DISPLAY BANK: INITIAL SCREEN will open (Figure 15.2). Enter a BANK COUNTRY and BANK KEY and press Enter.

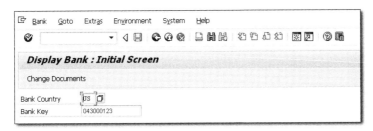

Figure 15.2 Display Bank: Initial Screen

The DISPLAY BANK: DETAIL SCREEN screen will open (Figure 15.3). Once a bank with all its details has been created, as in this example, the bank can be assigned in a vendor or customer master record.

| Bank | Goto | Extras | Environment | System | Help |

Display Bank : Detail Screen

Change Documents

Bank Country   US   USA
Bank Key   021000021

Address
Bank name   NC Regional Bank
State   NC
Street   123 Banker Drive
City   Raleigh
Bank Branch

Control data
SWIFT/BIC
Bank group
☐ Postbank Acct
Bank number   043000123

Figure 15.3 Display Bank: Detail Screen

Let's see an example of a bank assigned to a vendor master record. To view a vendor master record, follow application menu path Accounting • Financial Accounting • Accounts Payable • Master Records • FK03—Display, as shown in Figure 15.4.

Figure 15.4 Transaction FK03 Application Menu Path

Double-click FK03—Display from the menu path shown in Figure 15.4. The Display Vendor : Initial Screen screen will open (Figure 15.5). Select the Payment Transactions checkbox under General Data and press ⌷Enter⌷.

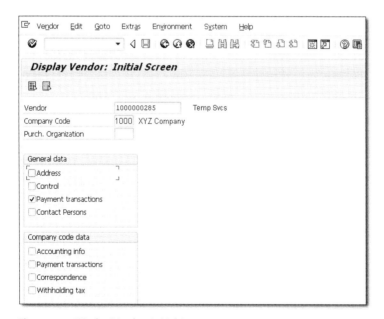

Figure 15.5 Display Vendor: Initial Screen

The DISPLAY VENDOR: PAYMENT TRANSACTIONS screen will open (Figure 15.6). In this example, Figure 15.6 shows that the BANK KEY from the bank master record was entered into the vendor master record, along with a specific BANK ACCOUNT number for the vendor.

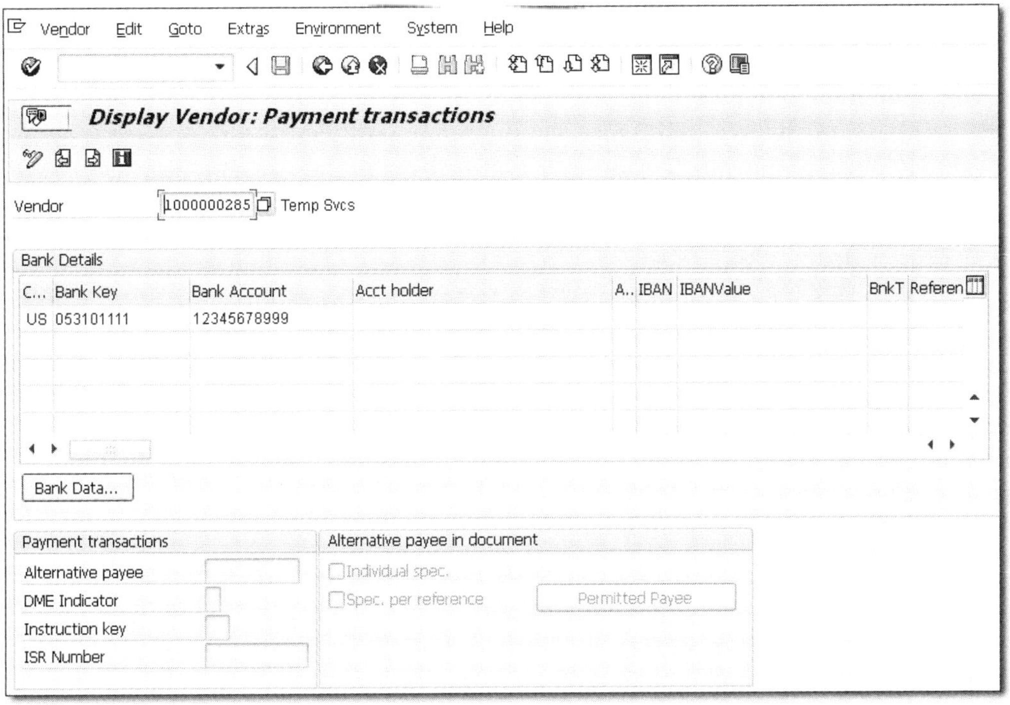

Figure 15.6 Display Vendor: Payment Transactions

These bank account details are needed in the business partner account to transact electronic money transfers.

Entries in the bank directory (table BNKA) can be entered either manually or uploaded from an electronic file using Transaction BAUP. Prior to using Transaction BAUP, the upload file must be registered in Transaction BA01 to convert the external structure to the SAP data structure.

15.1.2 House Banks

In SAP, house banks are the banks with which your company maintains a bank account. They are the banks with which your company does business and are used to hold cash, disburse payments, and receive money. House banks are defined using an account ID, a unique system identifier.

For each house bank account, you create a unique G/L account in the system. In addition, if you use SAP to reconcile bank statements, additional G/L subaccounts are created for each bank account. This bank account to G/L account structure is covered in detail in Section 15.2.

Bank master data is stored centrally. This includes address data and other control data, such as the SWIFT code. By specifying the country and a country-specific key, such as the bank number or the SWIFT code, you establish the connection between house banks and the bank master data.

To edit house banks and bank accounts, follow application menu path ACCOUNTING • FINANCIAL SUPPLY CHAIN MANAGEMENT • TREASURY RISK MANAGEMENT • BASIC FUNCTIONS • MASTER DATA • HOUSE BANKS • FI12—EDIT HOUSE BANKS AND BANK ACCOUNTS, as shown in Figure 15.7.

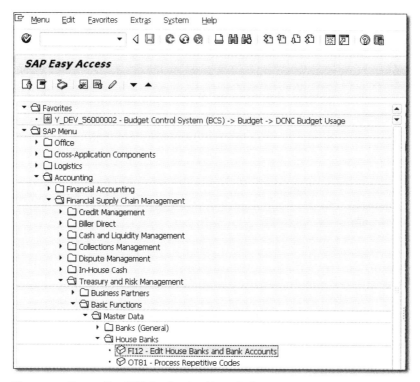

Figure 15.7 Transaction FI12 Application Menu Path

Double-click FI12—EDIT HOUSE BANKS AND BANK ACCOUNTS from the menu path shown in Figure 15.7. The DETERMINE WORK AREA: ENTRY screen will open (Figure 15.8). Here, enter your COMPANY CODE and press ⌈Enter⌉ or click on the CONTINUE button ✓.

Figure 15.8 Determine Work Area: Entry

The CHANGE VIEW "HOUSE BANKS": OVERVIEW screen will open (Figure 15.9). Click a specific house bank in the HOUSE BANKS section in the center of the screen and then double-click the BANK ACCOUNTS folder.

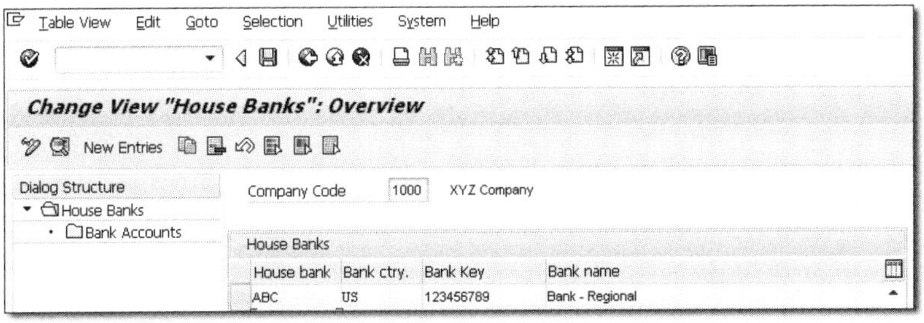

Figure 15.9 Change House Banks: Overview

The specific bank accounts at a house bank will appear in the BANK ACCOUNTS section (Figure 15.10) in the center of the screen. Double-click a bank account, or single-click a bank account and click the DETAILS icon 🖳 .

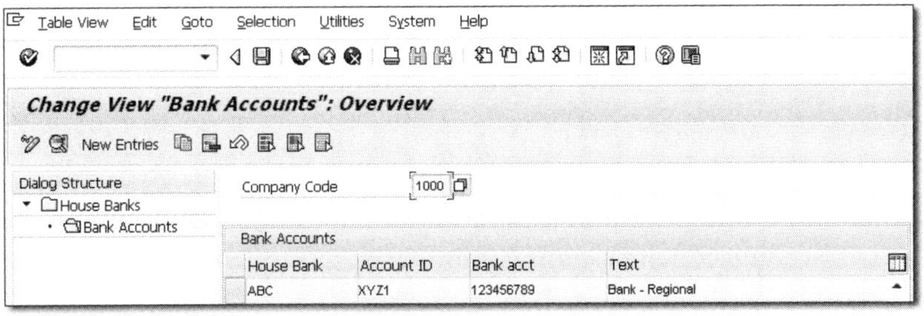

Figure 15.10 Bank Accounts Folder View

The CHANGE VIEW "BANK ACCOUNTS": DETAILS screen will open (Figure 15.11). All the details for the bank account appear, including COMPANY CODE, HOUSE BANK, ACCOUNT ID, DESCRIPTION, BANK ACCOUNT NUMBER, CURRENCY, ADDRESS, and so on.

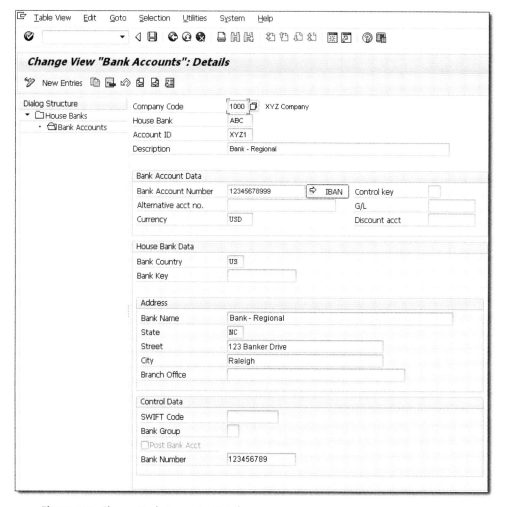

Figure 15.11 Change Bank Accounts: Details

Notice the entry of a G/L account in Figure 15.11. This is an important link; it specifies the G/L account to which transaction figures are to be updated and is a necessary element to use bank reconciliation capabilities.

House bank accounts are specified in various places. For example, in the configuration of the automatic payment program (Transaction F110), a house bank is linked to an individual payment method.

This is accomplished using Transaction FBZP. When you execute Transaction FBZP, the CUSTOMIZING: MAINTAIN PAYMENT PROGRAM screen appears (Figure 15.12).

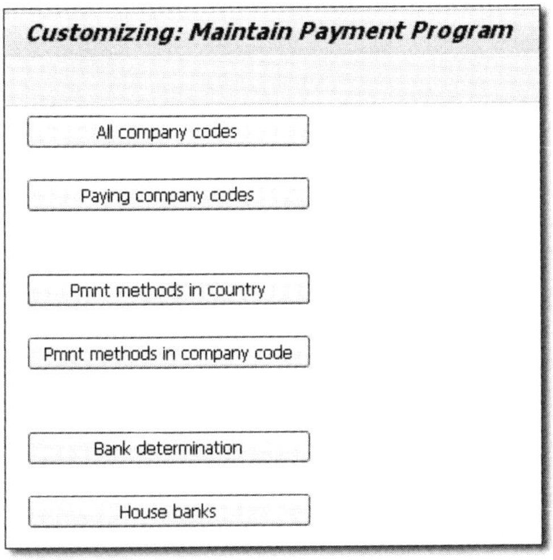

Figure 15.12 Customizing Maintain Payment Program Screen

Click on the BANK DETERMINATION button. The DISPLAY VIEW "BANK SELECTION": OVERVIEW screen appears (Figure 15.13). Highlight your bank selection, then double-click on BANK ACCOUNTS folder in the DIALOG STRUCTURE to the left of the screen.

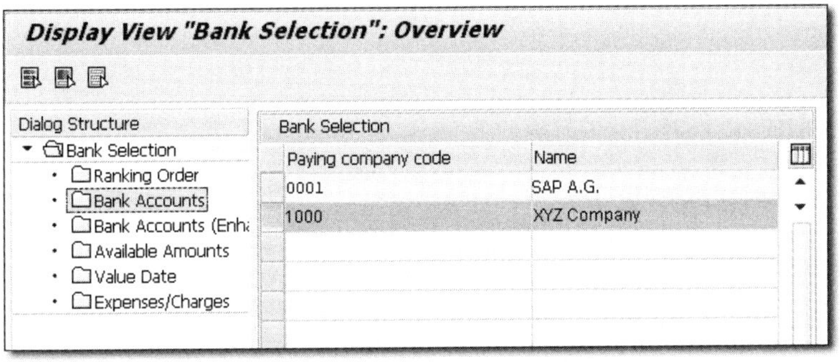

Figure 15.13 Display Bank Overview Screen

The CHANGE VIEW "BANK ACCOUNTS": OVERVIEW screen appears. In this screen you can see the house bank and account specifications (Figure 15.14).

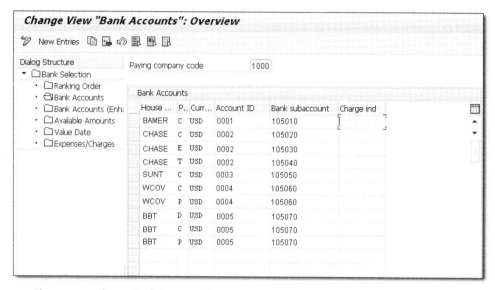

Figure 15.14 Change Bank Accounts Overview Screen

House banks are also specified in bank reconciliation and the Data Medium Exchange (DME) variants in Transaction F110.

Now that you understand house banks and bank master records, let's discuss how bank accounts are structured in the G/L for your company's bank accounts. As we walk through this material, keep in mind the distinction between bank master records in the system for your business partners, which are assigned in vendor and customer master records, and bank accounts owned by your company (i.e. house banks).

15.2   Structuring Bank Accounts in the G/L

In this section, you will learn how to represent your company's bank accounts in the G/L chart of accounts. This is a tricky topic and one that continues to confuse even experienced users and consultants. It is tricky for several reasons: First, it forces you to think beyond how you are accustomed to seeing your bank accounts represented in your chart of accounts. Second, it requires you to organize your

G/L bank account numbers in a methodical manner to plan for bank reconciliation in SAP, even if your company currently has no plans to do so. Lastly, if you do plan to use the electronic bank statement functionality, setting up bank clearing accounts requires that you know all the types of transactions you expect to come through in your electronic bank statements. Bank clearing accounts are discussed in detail in Section 15.2.2.

Before moving on to the specifics of setting up G/L bank accounts, it is important to note that the bank account structure in the chart of accounts and use of electronic bank statements in SAP is the springboard into using SAP's cash and liquidity forecasting functionality. In turn, forecasting cash flow and liquidity are important functions for treasury managers, who need to know on a daily basis how much they can invest, what types of instruments to invest in, and how much cash needs to be kept on hand to cover upcoming expenses.

Cash management, liquidity forecasting, and treasury functions can be automated in SAP using the Financial Supply Chain Management (FIN-FSCM) solution. Although FIN-FSCM is beyond the scope of this book, it is important to understand the relationship it has with FI.

Now that you understand the importance of the G/L bank account structure, let's discuss the G/L bank accounts themselves in more detail.

15.2.1 Bank Balance Sheet Accounts

There are two main types of G/L bank accounts: First are the main bank accounts, which have a one-to-one relationship with a house bank account. Second are bank clearing accounts, which are used for bank reconciliation. Both types are balance sheet accounts. The remainder of this section focuses on the main bank balance sheet accounts. Bank clearing accounts are discussed in detail in Section 15.2.2.

As noted, main G/L bank accounts are set up with a one-to-one relationship with house bank accounts. They are set up with a bidirectional link. In other words, in the house bank account, the G/L account is specified, and in the G/L bank account, the house bank and account ID are specified.

Figure 15.15 shows a house bank account using Transaction FI12. Notice in the G/L field that a G/L bank account number is linked to the bank account. This particular link designates the G/L account to which transaction figures will be updated.

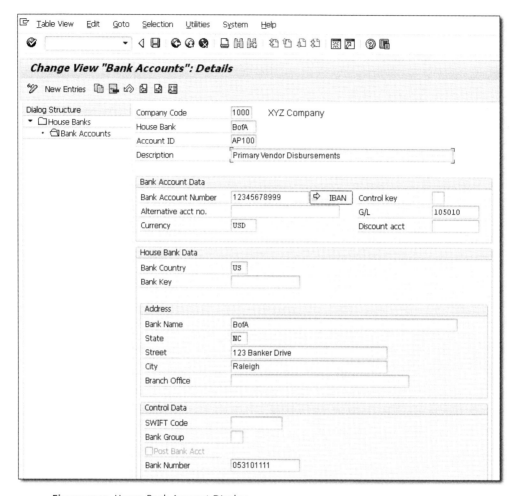

Figure 15.15 House Bank Account Display

Figure 15.16 shows a G/L bank account using Transaction FS03. Notice in the House Bank and Account ID fields that a link is provided back to the bank master record shown in Figure 15.15.

Note that the main G/L bank accounts should end in "0" to allow the last digit of the account (i.e., 1–9) to be used for bank clearing accounts. We will discuss this further in the next section.

Now that you understand the relationship of a house bank account and a main G/L bank account, let's move on to discuss bank clearing accounts.

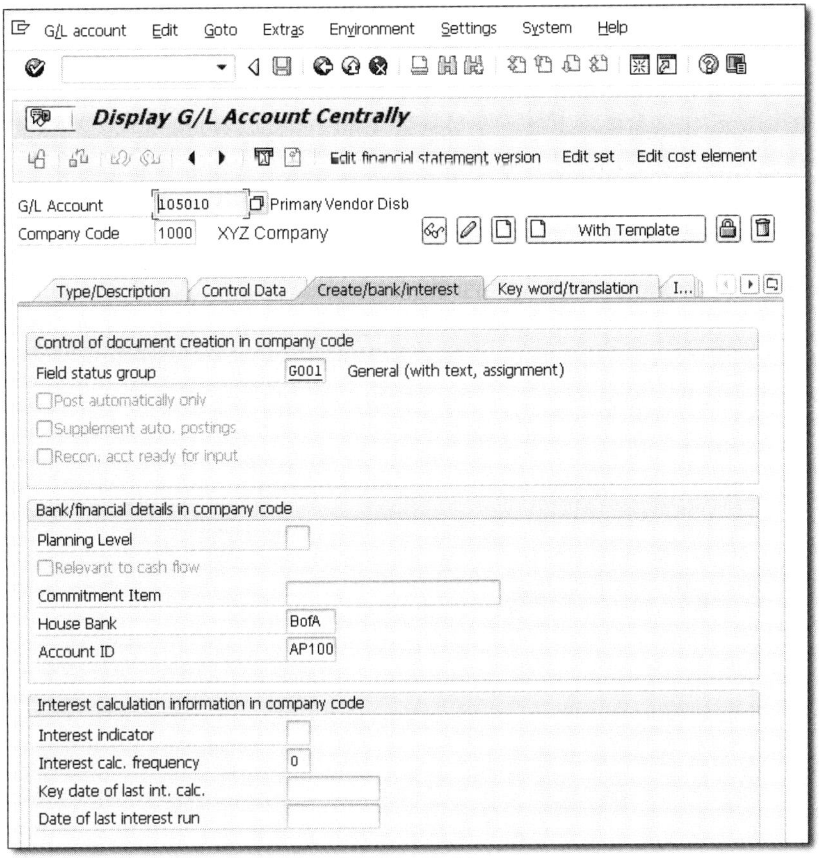

Figure 15.16 G/L Bank Account Display

15.2.2 Bank G/L Clearing Accounts

In SAP, a *G/L clearing account* is an open item managed account in which G/L transactions are posted with a status of open, awaiting another G/L entry to offset and clear them. When this clearing process is complete, the status of an item in the G/L changes from open to cleared.

Open item management is an important concept to understand when using SAP's electronic bank statement functionality for bank reconciliation. G/L clearing accounts are used to account for in-transit transactions and the matching of book-to-bank.

Let's discuss this in a little more detail to ensure you understand the concept. G/L clearing accounts are used to house transactions posted in FI that have not yet been reconciled with a transaction on an incoming bank statement. A transaction in a bank clearing account with an open status is one that has been posted to the G/L, but hasn't cleared at the bank. In contrast, a transaction in a clearing account with cleared status is a transaction that has cleared the bank and been posted to the main G/L bank account.

Creating G/L bank accounts in a structured fashion is critical to keeping your G/L clean and organized. As discussed in Section 15.2.1 there is a one-to-one relationship between a house bank account and a G/L account, and the G/L account should have "0" as the last digit. Moreover, G/L bank clearing accounts should be structured with a consistent naming convention utilizing the last digit of the account (i.e., 1–9). In this way, posting logic for bank reconciliation can be established.

A clearing account should be created for each major type of transaction on a bank account. Table 15.1 is an example G/L bank account structure for a bank account with transaction types that include check, ACH, and wire transfer.

Account Structure	G/L Accounts
130100	Main Bank Account 1
130101	Outgoing Check
130102	Incoming Check
130103	Outgoing ACH
130104	Incoming ACH
130105	Outgoing Wire Transfer
130106	Incoming Wire Transfer
130109	Miscellaneous

Table 15.1 G/L Account Structure for Transaction Types

As you can see in this example, a G/L clearing account is created for each major transaction type. Using a consistent clearing account structure is important for account determinations. It also makes it easier to conduct post-processing for bank items that don't clear automatically when an electronic bank statement is imported. See Section 15.4 for details on post-processing of electronic bank statements.

For each bank account, you only need to create a clearing account for each of the relevant transaction types. However, the numbering convention should be used consistently across all bank accounts. For example, if another bank account is only used for outgoing wire transfers, the G/L accounts would be set up as shown in Table 15.2.

Account Structure	G/L Accounts
130110	Main Bank Account 2
130115	Outgoing Wire Transfer
130119	Miscellaneous

Table 15.2 G/L Account Numbering Convention

On a final note, not all bank transactions exist on the books when bank statements are imported into SAP. Examples include fees and interest. In such cases, it is advantageous to post these transactions to a miscellaneous clearing account to be manually reconciled at a later point in time.

That concludes the discussion of bank G/L accounts. In the next section, we discuss bank reconciliation.

15.3 Bank Reconciliation

The *bank reconciliation* process is all about matching bank statement transactions with those transactions posted in the G/L. In SAP, this matching process clears open items in the G/L bank clearing accounts and posts offsetting entries in the main bank account.

There are two methods for bank reconciliation in SAP. The first is the electronic bank statement option. With this option, electronic bank statements are imported into SAP and automatically matched and reconciled. The second option is manual bank statement reconciliation, in which a user inputs each bank statement transaction manually.

Let's begin with a discussion of electronic bank statements.

15.3.1 Electronic Bank Statements

As a tip, if you are just getting started with electronic bank statements, knowing your bank data is just as important as knowing how to use the bank reconciliation features in SAP. Most importantly, become familiar with all the transaction types received in an electronic file from your bank. This is important to your G/L bank clearing account structure, account determinations, and mapping external to internal transactions.

With that said, let's dive into the details of importing an electronic bank statement in SAP. Importing electronic bank statements is usually set up as a schedule job to run daily. You don't have to reconcile bank statements daily, but it is a best practice.

To import a bank statement, follow application menu path ACCOUNTING • FINANCIAL ACCOUNTING • BANKS • INCOMINGS • BANK STATEMENT • FF_5—IMPORT, as shown in Figure 15.17.

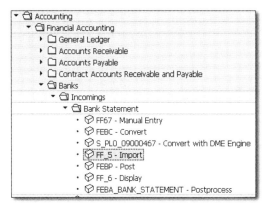

Figure 15.17 Transaction FF_5 Application Menu Path

Double-click FF_5—IMPORT from the menu path shown in Figure 15.17. The BANK STATEMENT: VARIOUS FORMATS (SWIFT, MULTICASH, BAI...) screen will open (Figure 15.18). Numerous selection options and specifications exist on this screen.

In the FILE SPECIFICATIONS portion of the screen, several basic selections must be made, including file format and file location. Of particular note, the IMPORT DATA checkbox must be selected to import the file into the system.

POSTING PARAMETERS options determine if the bank statement creates postings immediately, creates a batch input session, or does not post. In addition, the ONLY BANK ACCOUNTING checkbox, when selected, causes the statement to post to the G/L bank accounts but blocks postings to subledgers.

The CASH MANAGEMENT options are only used if you are using the Cash Management module.

BAI PREPROCESSOR options only exist when the BAI format is specified in the ELECT. BANK STATEMENT FORMAT field. These options allow you to check, convert, and adjust data in the file prior to processing the file for bank reconciliation.

ALGORITHMS allow you to specify or reference document number ranges. When this option is used, all other document numbers are ignored and cannot be used to clear open items.

Finally, OUTPUT CONTROL provides additional output options.

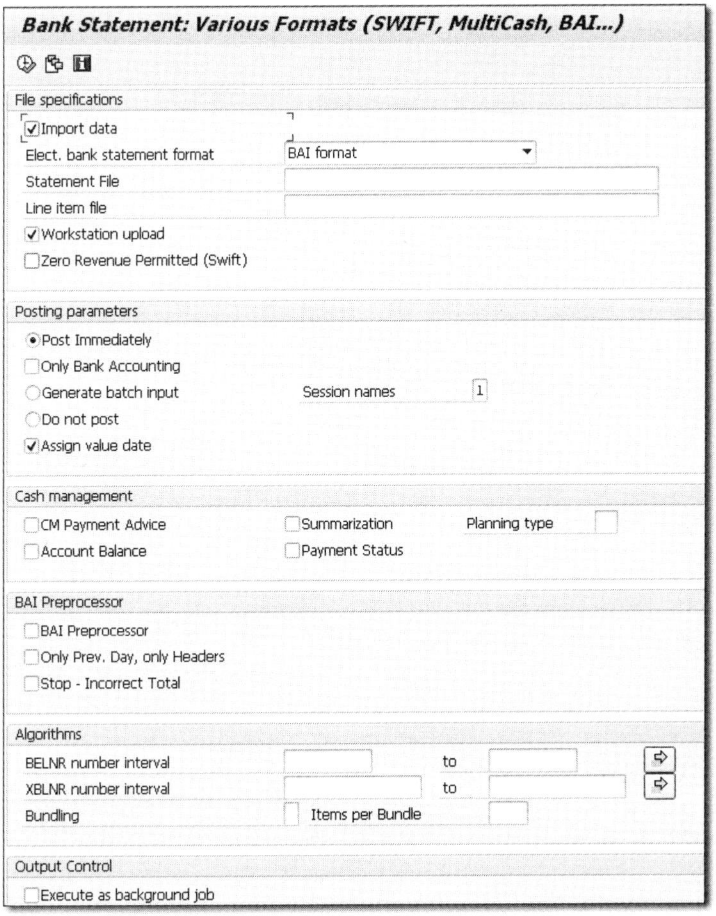

Figure 15.18 Import Electronic Bank Statement

Once all your selections are made as in Figure 15.18, you can save your choices as a variant and use it in a scheduled job.

Now let's walk through the complete import of an electronic bank statement using Transaction FF_5. After specifying the statement file location and making other selections (Figure 15.19), press the EXECUTE icon ⊕.

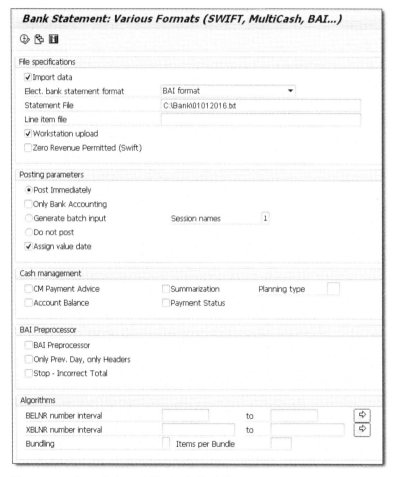

Figure 15.19 Example Import Electronic Bank Statement

After the import process is completed, the bank statement posting log is displayed (Figure 15.20).

Press the BACK icon ☻ to review bank statement statistics (Figure 15.21).

Update Account Statement/Check Deposit Transaction

Bank statement posti
Posting Log

Posting Ar Bank Key Bank name Bank acct St no Shrt Key

MR no	Shrt key	Pst. rule	ExtT	TCode	Itm	Type	PK	Account	Description	AC	Amount	Field
Bank Accounting			BAMER	123456789	10	4106						
1	4106	ZB03	142	FB05	1	ZR	40	105000	CCB-OPERATIN	USD	154.00	
	4106				2			105040	OPERATING MISC DEBTS	USD	154.00	WRBTR
2	4106	ZB03	142	FB05	1	ZR	40	105000	CCB-OPERATIN	USD	12,543.00	
	4106				2			105040	OPERATING MISC DEBTS	USD	12,543.00	WRBTR
3	4106	ZB03	142	FB05	1	ZR	40	105000	CCB-OPERATIN	USD	5,382.00	
	4106				2			105040	OPERATING MISC DEBTS	USD	5,382.00	WRBTR
4	4106	ZB03	142	FB05	1	ZR	40	105000	CCB-OPERATIN	USD	332.67	
	4106				2			105040	OPERATING MISC DEBTS	USD	332.67	WRBTR
5	4106	ZB03	142	FB05	1	ZR	40	105000	CCB-OPERATIN	USD	23,297.25	
	4106				2			105040	OPERATING MISC DEBTS	USD	23,297.25	WRBTR
6	4106	ZB07	142	FB05	1	ZR	40	105000	CCB-OPERATIN	USD	492.20	
	4106				2			105020	OPERATING INCOMING C	USD	492.20	WRBTR
7	4106	ZB07	142	FB05	1	ZR	40	105000	CCB-OPERATIN	USD	141.95	
	4106				2			105020	OPERATING INCOMING C	USD	141.95	WRBTR
8	4106	ZB07	142	FB05	1	ZR	40	105000	CCB-OPERATIN	USD	25.00	
	4106				2			105020	OPERATING INCOMING C	USD	25.00	WRBTR
9	4106	ZB07	142	FB05	1	ZR	40	105000	CCB-OPERATIN	USD	99.00	
	4106				2			105020	OPERATING INCOMING C	USD	99.00	WRBTR
10	4106	ZB07	142	FB05	1	ZR	40	105000	CCB-OPERATIN	USD	302.22	
	4106				2			105020	OPERATING INCOMING C	USD	302.22	WRBTR
11	4106	ZB07	142	FB05	1	ZR	40	105000	CCB-OPERATIN	USD	82.00	
	4106				2			105020	OPERATING INCOMING C	USD	82.00	WRBTR
12	4106	ZB07	142	FB05	1	ZR	40	105000	CCB-OPERATIN	USD	180.00	
	4106				2			105020	OPERATING INCOMING C	USD	180.00	WRBTR
13	4106	ZB07	175	FB05	1	ZR	40	105000	CCB-OPERATIN	USD	1,235.40	
	4106				2			105020	OPERATING INCOMING C	USD	1,235.40	WRBTR
14	4106	ZB07	175	FB05	1	ZR	40	105000	CCB-OPERATIN	USD	178,175.04	
	4106				2			105020	OPERATING INCOMING C	USD	178,175.04	WRBTR
15	4106	ZB07	175	FB05	1	ZR	40	105000	CCB-OPERATIN	USD	141.64	
	4106				2			105020	OPERATING INCOMING C	USD	141.64	WRBTR
16	4106	ZB07	175	FB05	1	ZR	40	105000	CCB-OPERATIN	USD	155.00	
	4106				2			105020	OPERATING INCOMING C	USD	155.00	WRBTR
17	4106	ZB07	175	FB05	1	ZR	40	105000	CCB-OPERATIN	USD	1,039.28	
	4106				2			105020	OPERATING INCOMING C	USD	1,039.28	WRBTR

Figure 15.20 Bank Statement Posting Log

Update Account Statement/Check Deposit Transaction

Bank statement posting
Processing Statistics

Time 18:06:43 Date 02/24/2016
RFEBBU00/C_DBURNS Page 1

Posting Ar	Bank Key	Account Nu	Sessn	Group	FB01	FB05	PmtAcc	No Posting	Error	Total	Total Deb.	Total Cred
Bank Accounting		123456789			0	0	0	0	48	48	9,919,576.71	48,725,642.62
* Bank Accounting					0	0	0	0	48	48	9,919,576.71	48,725,642.62
** Bank Accounting					0	0	0	0	48	48	9,919,576.71	48,725,642.62
Subledger acctng		123456789			0	0	0	48	0	48	9,919,576.71	48,725,642.62
* Subledger acctng					0	0	0	48	0	48	9,919,576.71	48,725,642.62
** Subledger acctng					0	0	0	48	0	48	9,919,576.71	48,725,642.62
***					0	0	0	48	48	96	19,839,153.42	97,451,285.24

Figure 15.21 Bank Statement Statistics

Once the process of importing an electronic bank statement is complete, the next step is the post-processing of bank statement transactions that didn't clear automatically. For details, see Section 15.4.

15.3.2 Manual Bank Statements

For numerous reasons, your company may not opt to receive electronic files from your bank, perhaps due to cost or because an account has a small number of transactions. If this is the case, an alternative is to use manual bank statements. This approach may be used for smaller bank accounts for which the volume of transactions is so low that using electronic bank statements is not justifiable.

To manually enter a bank statement, follow application menu path ACCOUNTING • FINANCIAL ACCOUNTING • BANKS • INCOMINGS • BANK STATEMENT • FF67—MANUAL ENTRY, as shown in Figure 15.22.

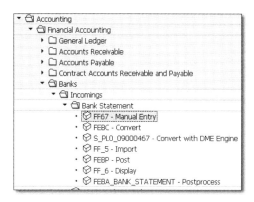

Figure 15.22 Transaction FF67 Application Menu Path

Double-click FF67—MANUAL ENTRY from the menu path shown in Figure 15.22. The PROCESS MANUAL BANK STATEMENT screen will open (Figure 15.23). Numerous selection options and specifications exist on this screen.

At the top of the screen, fields that require entry are COMPANY CODE, HOUSE BANK, ACCOUNT ID, STATEMENT NUMBER, and STATEMENT DATE. Some variation in field control may exist, depending on your screen variant.

In the CONTROL section, enter opening and closing balances to ensure consistency from one statement to the next. The POSTING DATE entered is the posting date used for bank account and subledger transactions created.

The SELECTION OF PAYMENT ADVICES options are relevant if you use payment advices.

FURTHER PROCESSING gives you the option, via the BANK POSTINGS ONLY checkbox, to post to G/L bank accounts only. If this option is selected, subledger postings are blocked.

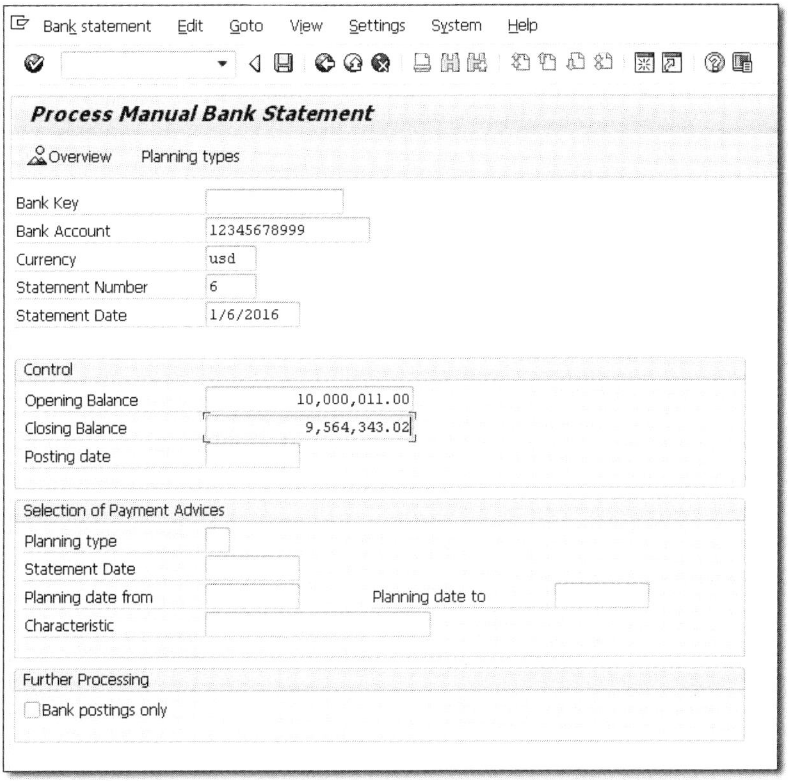

Figure 15.23 Process Manual Bank Statement

Manual bank statements may have little to no applicability in your company. However, for some organizations they are a viable option. There is no doubt that the best option is to use electronic bank statements whenever possible, but if there is a bank account with limited activity or you need a temporary solution while your company restructures its bank accounts, then manual bank statements may be the answer.

15.4   Post Processing of Electronic Bank Statements

When you import an electronic bank statement, SAP attempts to match individual transactions on the bank statement with G/L line items in bank clearing accounts. This matching process takes place based on interpretation algorithms.

The post-processing program is used to check the status of bank statements and manually clear bank transactions that didn't clear automatically. To post-process an electronic bank statement, follow the application menu path ACCOUNTING • FINANCIAL ACCOUNTING • BANKS • INCOMINGS • BANK STATEMENT • FEBA_BANK_STATEMENT - POSTPROCESS, as shown in Figure 15.24.

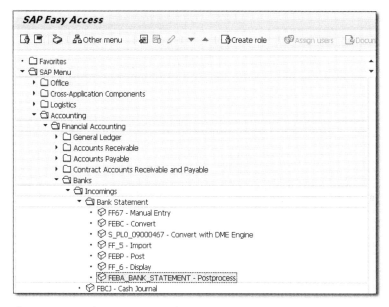

Figure 15.24 Application Menu Path EBS Postprocess

Double-click FEBA_BANK_STATEMENT from the menu path shown in Figure 15.24. The BANK STATEMENT SUBSEQUENT PROCESSING screen will open (Figure 15.25). Numerous selection options and specifications exist on this screen. Let's take a few minutes to discuss some of the key fields on this selection screen.

► APPLICATION: Select ELECTRONIC AND MANUAL BANK STATEMENT from the drop-down list.

► COMPANY CODE: This is a required field

▶ HOUSE BANK: This is a required field

▶ ACCOUNT ID: This is a required field

You can enter either a STATEMENT NUMBER, STATEMENT DATE, or both.

The last field selection we will discuss is the POSTING AREA. If you are set up to clear vendors and customers, there is a selection option in the drop-down menu for subledger accounting. Otherwise, select G/L ACCOUNTING.

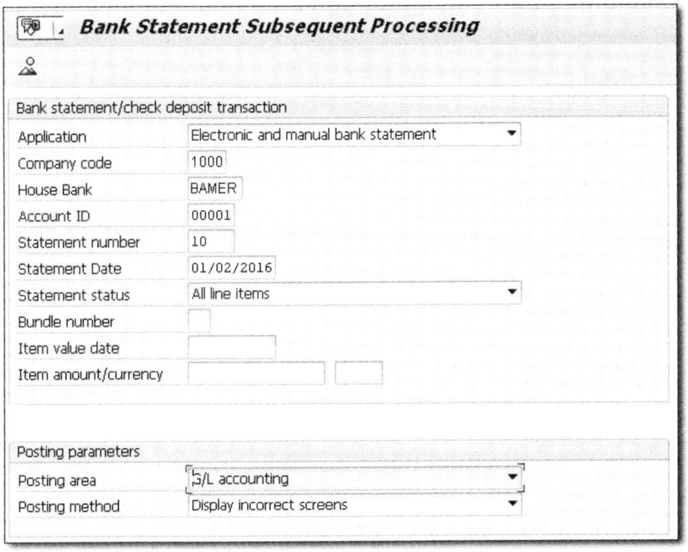

Figure 15.25 Bank Statement Subsequent Processing Screen

With all your field parameters entered, click the STATEMENT OVERVIEW icon 🔼. The BANK STATEMENT OVERVIEW screen will appear (Figure 15.26).

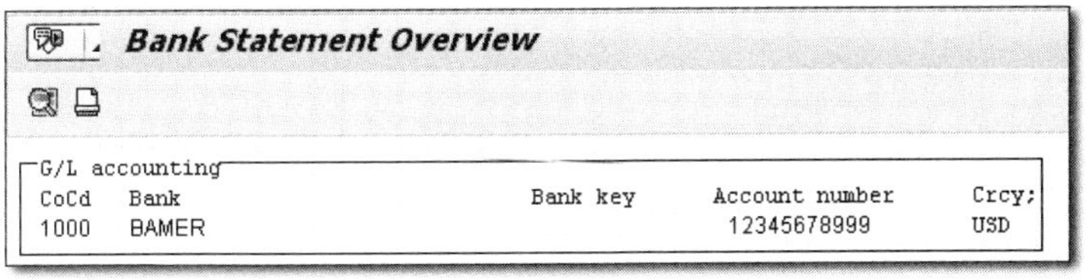

Figure 15.26 Bank Statement Overview Screen

Double-click on the statement line and the BANK STATEMENT OVERVIEW STATE-MENT NUMBER screen appears (Figure 15.27).

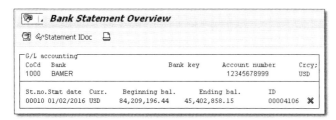

Figure 15.27 Bank Statement Overview Statement Number

Double-click on the statement and the BANK STATEMENT OVERVIEW STATEMENT TRANSACTIONS screen will appear (Figure 15.28). This is where it gets interesting. On this screen, all the individual transactions on the bank statement are listed. Each will have a status of POSTED or TO BE POSTED.

```
 [icon]  .  Bank Statement Overview

   [icon]  &^Document    &^Turnover IDoc    [icon]

  ┌─G/L accounting─────────────────────────────────────────────────┐
   CoCd   Bank                    Bank key      Account number    Crcy;
   1000   BAMER                                  12345678999       USD

   St.no.Stmt date  Curr.   Beginning bal.     Ending bal.      ID
   00010 01/02/2016 USD     84,209,196.44    45,402,858.15     00004106  ✖

   No.   Tran. Value date       Amount  Doc.no.      OnActDocNo
   00001 ZB03 01/02/2016        154.00  2000415911          Posted
   00002 ZB03 01/02/2016     12,543.00                      To be posted
   00003 ZB03 01/02/2016      5,382.00                      To be posted
   00004 ZB03 01/02/2016        332.67                      To be posted
   00005 ZB03 01/02/2016     23,297.25                      To be posted
   00006 ZB07 01/02/2016        492.20                      To be posted
   00007 ZB07 01/02/2016        141.95                      To be posted
   00008 ZB07 01/02/2016         25.00                      To be posted
   00009 ZB07 01/02/2016         99.00                      To be posted
   00010 ZB07 01/02/2016        302.22                      To be posted
   00011 ZB07 01/02/2016         82.00                      To be posted
   00012 ZB07 01/02/2016        180.00                      To be posted
   00013 ZB07 01/02/2016      1,235.40                      To be posted
   00014 ZB07 01/02/2016    178,175.04                      To be posted
   00015 ZB07 01/02/2016        141.64                      To be posted
   00016 ZB07 01/02/2016        155.00                      To be posted
   00017 ZB07 01/02/2016      1,039.28                      To be posted
   00018 ZB07 01/02/2016      3,994.00                      To be posted
   00019 ZB07 01/02/2016     11,961.19                      To be posted
   00020 ZB07 01/02/2016        471.60                      To be posted
   00021 ZB07 01/02/2016         95.25                      To be posted
   00022 ZB07 01/02/2016        103.75                      To be posted
   00023 ZB07 01/02/2016        136.55                      To be posted
   00024 ZB07 01/02/2016        145.90                      To be posted
   00025 ZB07 01/02/2016        267.85                      To be posted
   00026 ZB07 01/02/2016        279.36                      To be posted
   00027 ZB08 01/02/2016    272,105.40                      To be posted
   00028 ZB08 01/02/2016    146,709.87                      To be posted
   00029 ZB12 01/02/2016        150.00                      To be posted
   00030 ZB12 01/02/2016  9,259,378.34                      To be posted
   00031 ZB17 01/02/2016    978,106.53-                     To be posted
   00032 ZB17 01/02/2016        303.33-                     To be posted
   00033 ZB17 01/02/2016    145,392.00-                     To be posted
```

Figure 15.28 Bank Statement Overview Statement Transactions

In this example, we double-click on the second transaction in the amount of $12,543. The BANK TRANSACTION TO BE POSTED screen appears (Figure 15.29).

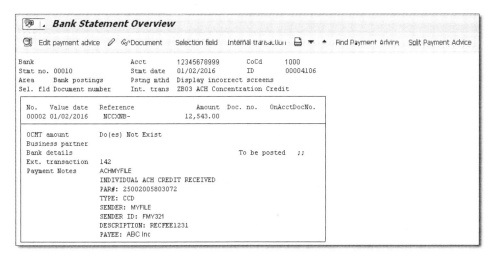

Figure 15.29 Bank Transaction to be Posted

Click on the POST icon ☑. When you do so, the program attempts to find a matching entry in the G/L using Transaction FB05. If it is successful, a document posted message appears, as shown at the bottom of Figure 15.30.

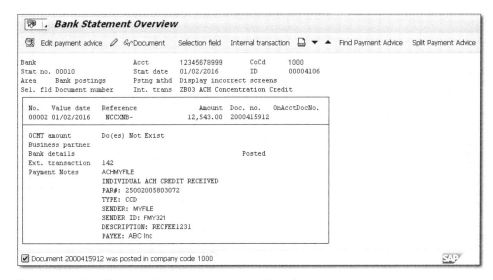

Figure 15.30 Bank Statement Transaction Document Posted

Click the BACK button ❖ to return to the BANK STATEMENT OVERVIEW screen. In this example, you see in Figure 15.31 that our transaction in the amount of $12,543 has a status that changed from TO BE POSTED to POSTED.

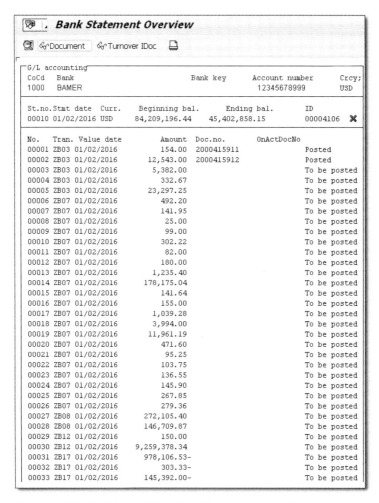

Figure 15.31 Bank Statement Overview After Document Posted

The post-processing of electronic bank statements can take many twists and turns to completely reconciling a statement. Yet, in this section you have seen the essentials needed to get started.

15.5 Summary

This chapter covered bank master data in detail, including house bank accounts and vendor and customer bank master records. The distinction between house banks and other bank master records is simple: house banks are your company's accounts. They are the banks with which your company does business and are used to hold cash, disburse payments, and receive money. Customer and vendor bank accounts, on the other hand, are the bank accounts of your business partners. For those bank accounts that you use to send or receive money, a bank account master record is created and assigned in the business partner master record.

G/L bank accounts and their relationships to bank master data are of particular importance. G/L bank accounts should be set up with a one-to-one relationship with house bank accounts. The house bank account and G/L account are set up with a bidirectional link. In other words, in the house bank account, the G/L account is specified, and in the G/L bank account, the house bank and Account ID are specified.

In banking, clearing accounts are used for bank reconciliation purposes. G/L clearing accounts are used to house transactions that posted in the general ledger, but are not yet reconciled on a bank statement. Therefore, a transaction in a bank clearing account with open status is one that has not been matches with a transaction on the bank statement. A G/L transaction with the cleared status is one that is matched with a bank statement item with an offsetting entry posted to the main bank account.

Creating the G/L bank accounts in a structured fashion is critical to keeping your G/L clean and organized. There is a one-to-one relationship between a House Bank account and a main G/L bank account, and the G/L account should contain a "0" as the last digit. Moreover, G/L bank clearing accounts should be structured with a consistent naming convention utilizing the last digit of the account (i.e., 1–9) to represent transaction type. In this way, posting logic for bank reconciliation is most efficient.

This chapter also covered the bank statement reconciliation process. *Bank reconciliation* is the process of matching of bank statement transactions with transactions in the G/L. In SAP, this matching process clears open items in the G/L bank clearing accounts and posts an offsetting entry to the main G/L bank account.

There are two methods for bank reconciliation in SAP. The first is the electronic bank statement option, using Transaction FF_5. With this option, electronic bank statements are imported into SAP and automatically reconciled. The second option is manual bank statement reconciliation, using Transaction FF65, in which a user inputs each bank statement transaction manually.

Regardless of whether or not you are using SAP bank reconciliation, the G/L account structure should be designed in a manner that allows your company to implement this capability down the road without having to restructure G/L bank accounts. Doing so also paves the way for additional functionality, such as Cash and Liquidity Management.

This concludes the discussion of bank master data and processes. In the next chapter, we will discuss financial close processes.

In this chapter, we cover essential financial close processes for month-end and year-end, including opening and closing periods, carrying balances forward, periodic processing, and more.

16   Financial Close Processes

This chapter covers financial close steps in FI. For details on integrated financial close processes, see Chapter 17.

Financial close is one of the most important business functions in FI. It requires knowledge of internal business processes, relevant SAP transactions, and financial reporting. Special attention is given to the timing of steps executed in the close process. Well-crafted close procedure documentation is your best friend. If your company has not documented its close procedures, you should take the initiative to do so.

SAP developed a tool called the Financial Close Cockpit to monitor, control, and provide greater efficiency when closing. The Financial Close Cockpit is beyond the scope of this chapter, but it is important to be aware of its existence and capabilities.

Whether you use a spreadsheet to track financial close steps or the Financial Close Cockpit, your financial close procedures should list steps and transactions in the order in which they need to be executed. In addition, throughout the close process it is important to track the persons responsible for executing each step and expected completion dates.

For the most part, year-end financial close consists of month-end steps plus additional tasks, such as opening and closing fiscal years and carrying forward G/L balances. You may also be required to create additional master data, such as cost centers.

In the next section, we will begin our financial close discussions on the opening and closing accounting periods in FI.

16.1 Opening and Closing Financial Periods

This section discusses the opening and closing of accounting periods using Transaction OB52. Keep in mind that other modules (e.g., MM) require opening and closing of periods, which use different SAP transaction codes. This scope of this section is limited to FI periods only. For further details on opening and closing periods in other modules, see Chapter 17.

To open and close periods in FI, enter "OB52" in the COMMAND field (as shown in Figure 16.1) and press Enter.

Figure 16.1 OB52 in Command Field

The CHANGE VIEW "POSTING PERIODS: SPECIFY TIME INTERVALS": OVERVIEW screen will open (Figure 16.2). The periods open for postings are the range of periods in the FROM PER.2 and TO PERIOD fields shown on the right-hand side of Figure 16.2. In this example, general users are allowed to post in period 12, 2015.

Change View "Posting Periods: Specify Time Periods": Overview

New Entries

Pstng period variant 0001

Posting Periods: Specify Time Periods

A	From acct	To account	From per.1	Year	To per. 1	Year	From per.2	Year	To per. 2	Year	AuGr
+							1	2016	2	2016	
A	ZZZZZZZZZZ						1	2016	2	2016	
D	ZZZZZZZZZZ						1	2016	2	2016	
K	ZZZZZZZZZZ						1	2016	2	2016	
M	ZZZZZZZZZZ						1	2016	2	2016	
S	ZZZZZZZZZZ						1	2016	2	2016	

Figure 16.2 Change Posting Periods

Sometimes, a person with special privileges (e.g., the accounting director) needs to make accounting entries in a period not open to general users, or there may be a need to post a prior period that was closed or post to a special period (i.e., 13–16). To allow select individuals to perform these tasks, assign them to an authorization group.

Figure 16.3 shows an example of Transaction OB52 with an authorization group specified. This authorization group is entered in the AuGr field. The periods open for posting to individuals assigned to the authorization group are the range of periods in the FROM PER.1 and TO PERIOD fields shown on the left-hand side of Figure 16.3.

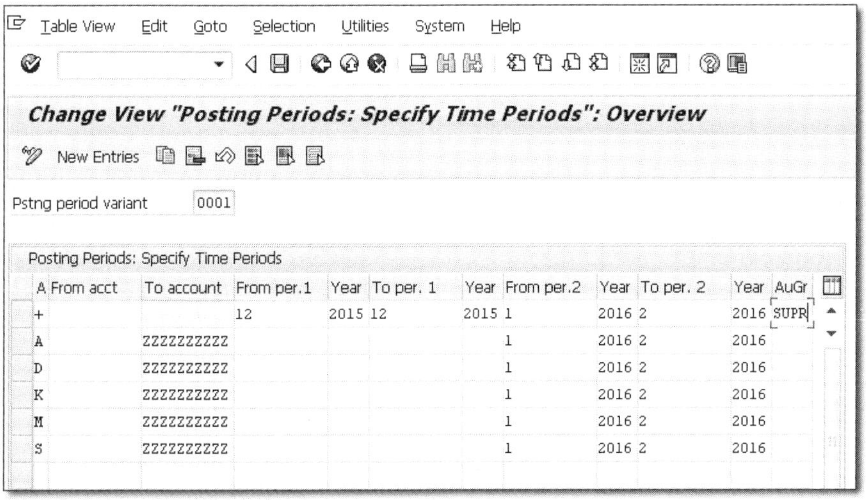

Figure 16.3 Change Posting Periods Screen with Authorization Group

To limit specific users to a particular posting period, an authorization group must be created and the posting period authorization (i.e., authorization object F_BKPF_BUP) added to the group members' security roles.

Transaction OB52 has a masking feature, indicated in column A (second column from the left) in Figure 16.3. This features enables you to designate open periods by account type. The + sign indicates all account types, but it is overridden when more specific account designations are provided.

Available masking options are listed in Table 16.1.

Masking Option	Description
+	Valid for all account types
A	Assets
D	Customers
K	Vendors
M	Materials
S	G/L accounts
V	Contract accounts

Table 16.1 Transaction OB52 Masking Options

The masking feature provides flexibility and control in designating open FI periods by account type.

Now that we have discussed opening and closing financial periods, let's move on to discuss the carryforward of G/L account balances.

16.2   Balance Carryforward

Carrying forward balances to a new fiscal year is a core accounting concept and necessary for year-end close.

When you think of carryforward balances, you probably think automatically of G/L account balances. It's true that G/L account balances are the primary target in the carryforward process, but you also need to perform carryforward functions for local ledgers, special ledgers, and subledgers. In this section, we will begin with a discussion of G/L account balances and then address these other areas.

The primary balance carryforward step is for G/L account balances in the leading ledgers. It is executing using Transaction FAGLGVTR. In the same way, this step needs to be completed for each of your local ledgers. The program used to carryforward G/L balances can be run multiple times but does not normally need to be run more than once per year. After the program is run, postings to the previous fiscal year are automatically carried forward to the new fiscal year.

The process of G/L balance carryforward is twofold: First, balance sheet accounts are summarized with additional account assignments and transferred to the new fiscal year. Second, profit and loss accounts are carried forward to the retained earnings account without additional account assignments. For both, the transaction currencies are not transferred and are totaled in the local currency.

To carry forward G/L balances, use Transaction FAGLGVTR or application menu path ACCOUNTING • FINANCIAL ACCOUNTING • GENERAL LEDGER • PERIODIC PROCESSING • CLOSING • CARRYING FORWARD • FAGLGVTR – BALANCE CARRYFORWARD (NEW), as shown in Figure 16.4.

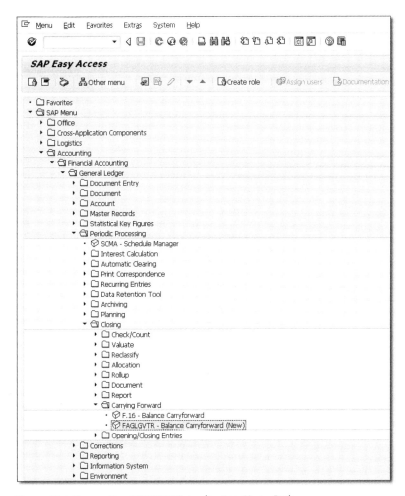

Figure 16.4 Transaction FAGLGVTR Application Menu Path

Double-click on FAGLGVTR—BALANCE CARRYFORWARD (NEW) from the menu path shown in Figure 16.4 and the BALANCE CARRYFORWARD screen will open (Figure 16.5). Here, enter values in the LEDGER, COMPANY CODE, and CARRY FORWARD TO FISCAL YEAR fields. Notice in the PROCESSING OPTIONS section of the screen the option to run the program in test mode. In this example, we also selected options in the LIST OUTPUT section at the bottom of Figure 16.5 to output results and profit and loss balance transfers to retained earnings.

Note that the screen selection permits the entry of a range of company codes, but only one ledger. Therefore, this program has to be run separately for each ledger.

With all field selections made, click the EXECUTE icon ⊕.

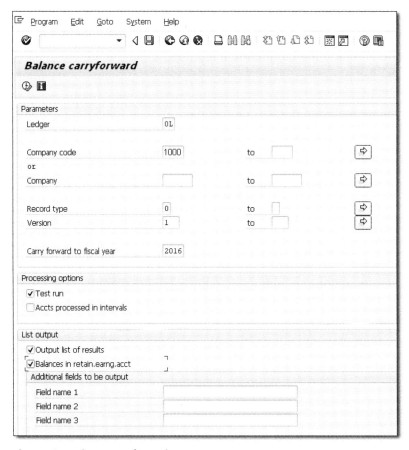

Figure 16.5 Balance Carryforward

The output screen will open (Figure 16.6).

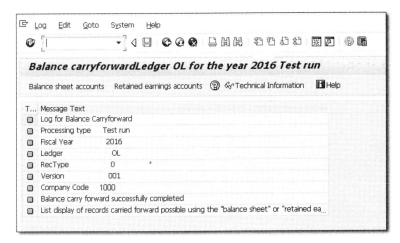

Figure 16.6 Balance Carryforward Output

Click on the BALANCE SHEET ACCOUNTS button, and the DISPLAY OF BALANCE SHEET ACCOUNTS screen will open (Figure 16.7). This screen shows individual balance sheet account balances, summarized by additional account assignment elements, being carried forward to the new fiscal year.

Year	CoCd	R	Ver	Account	Crcy	BUn	Trans.cur.	Co.cd.curr	Crcy2	Quantity
2016	1000	0	1	121000	USD		20,000.00	20,000.00	USD	
2016	1000	0	1	211000	USD		41,000.00-	41,000.00-	USD	
*					USD		21,000.00-	21,000.00-	USD	

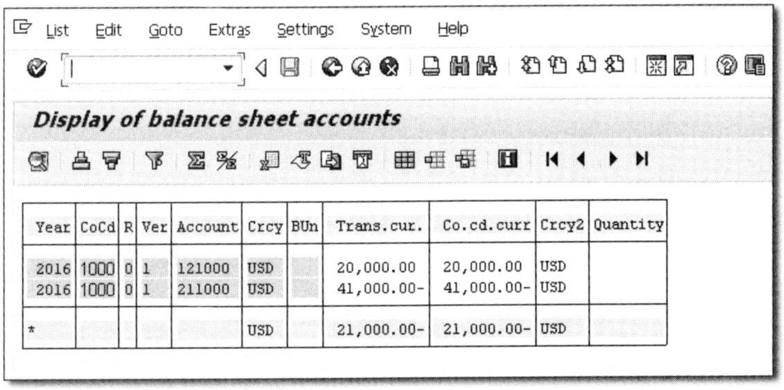

Figure 16.7 Display of Balance Sheet Accounts

Click on the BACK button ⬅ to return to the output screen (Figure 16.6). Click on the RETAINED EARNINGS ACCOUNTS button, and the DISPLAY OF RETAINED EARNINGS ACCOUNTS screen will open (Figure 16.8). This screen shows individual profit and loss account balances to be carried forward to the new fiscal year.

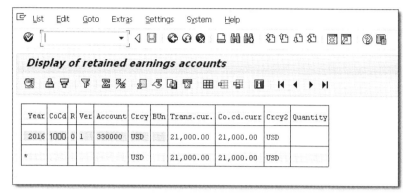

Figure 16.8 Display of Retained Earnings Accounts

In addition to Transaction FAGLGVTR, there are some other balance carryforward transactions for Special Purpose Ledger, AP, AR, and Classic G/L. A list of these transactions is provided below.

- **Transaction GVTR**
  This transaction is used to carryforward balances in the Special Purpose Ledger.

- **Transaction F.07**
  This transaction is used to carryforward subledger balances in A/R and A/P.

- **Transaction F.16**
  This transaction is used to carryforward G/L balances in Classic G/L (versus New G/L).

Now that you have learned about carrying forward G/L account balances in the G/L, let's discuss financial close steps for fixed assets.

16.3   Fixed Assets

Whenever you have subledgers, there are financial close activities that have to take place. For both vendor and customers, you carryforward subledger balances using Transaction F.16 at year-end. At month-end, you also run dunning, the automated payment program, etc., in A/P. For A/R you execute billing and customer statements.

Asset Accounting (FI-AA) is also a subledger. As such, it has unique steps for financial close. For FI-AA at year-end, there are two primary steps that must be performed. The first is to change the fiscal year using Transaction AJRW. This is a technical step required to carry forward assets into a new fiscal year.

To carry forward fixed assets, use Transaction AJRW or application menu path ACCOUNTING • FINANCIAL ACCOUNTING • FIXED ASSETS • PERIODIC PROCESSING • AJRW—FISCAL YEAR CHANGE, as shown in Figure 16.9.

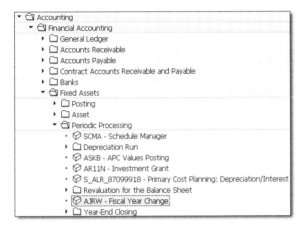

Figure 16.9 Transaction AJRW Application Menu Path

Double-click AJRW—FISCAL YEAR CHANGE from the menu path shown in Figure 16.9 and the ASSET FISCAL YEAR CHANGE screen will open (Figure 16.10). On this screen, enter values in the COMPANY CODE(S) and NEW FISCAL YEAR fields. There is also a checkbox for TEST RUN, giving you the ability to execute this program in test mode.

With all field selections made, click the EXECUTE icon ⊕.

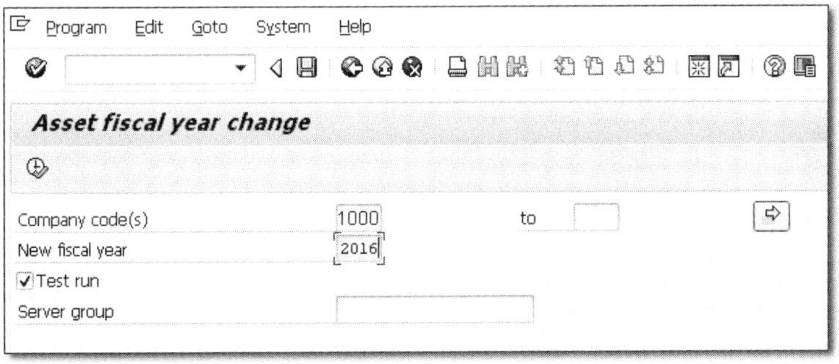

Figure 16.10 Asset Fiscal Year Change

The ASSET FISCAL YEAR CHANGE output screen will open (Figure 16.11). If the STATUS column shows a green light, it indicates that the test run is successful and the fixed assets can be carried forward into the new fiscal year specified.

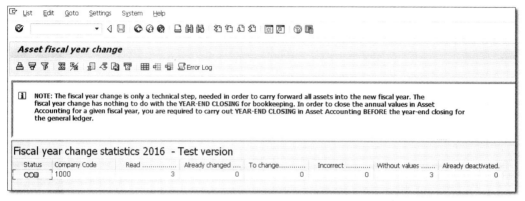

Figure 16.11 Asset Fiscal Year Change Output

While Transaction AJRW can be run in the foreground in test mode, in production mode it must be run in the background. This is also true of the next step in FI-AA: Transaction AJAB.

The second step for FI-AA at year-end is to change the fiscal year using Transaction AJAB or application menu path ACCOUNTING • FINANCIAL ACCOUNTING • FIXED ASSETS • PERIODIC PROCESSING • YEAR-END CLOSING • AJAB—EXECUTE, as shown in Figure 16.12.

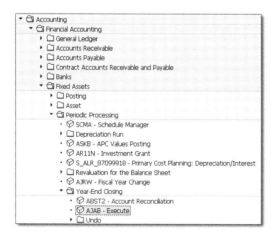

Figure 16.12 Transaction AJAB Application Menu Path

Double-click AJAB—EXECUTE from the menu path shown in Figure 16.12 and the YEAR-END CLOSING ASSET ACCOUNTING screen will open (Figure 16.13). On this screen, enter values in the COMPANY CODE and FISCAL YEAR TO BE CLOSED fields. You can also execute this program in test mode.

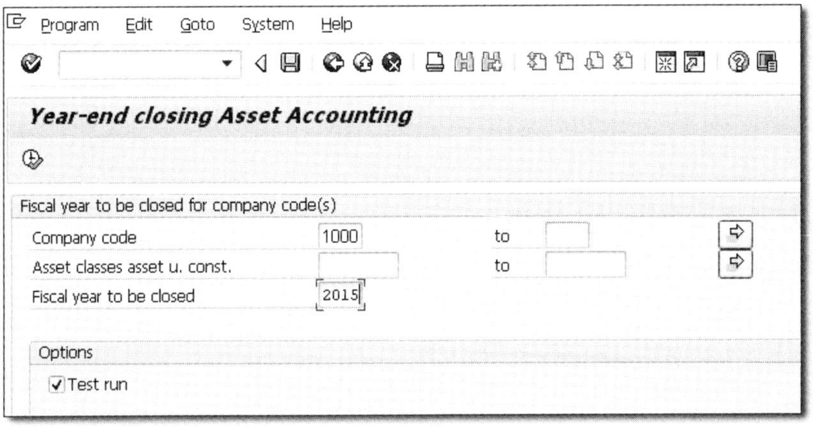

Figure 16.13 Year-End Closing Asset Accounting

Transaction AJAB checks that there are no assets that have been posted (i.e., have an acquisition date) but not capitalized (i.e., no capitalization date). These assets are captured as errors when the program runs. This check does not make sense for assets under construction (AuC), and therefore you have the ability to specify AuC asset classes in the ASSET CLASSES ASSET U. CONST screen selection to bypass the check and keep your error log clean.

You can execute Transaction AFAB in the foreground in test mode. As previously mentioned, when run in production mode, Transaction AFAB must be run as a background job. Enter your field values as in Figure 16.13, save as a variant, and work with your SAP Basis Administrator to schedule the job to run automatically at each year end.

Now that we've covered fixed asset close processes, let's look at periodic processing functions in the next section.

16.4   Periodic Processing

Periodic processing is a classification of transactions that are executed at regular intervals. Some of them may be executed more frequently than at month end or year end, but they are included as closing steps because they are essential to producing financial statements.

There are numerous transactions considered to be periodic processing tasks. Which ones you need to execute in financial close is dependent upon your business processes and the SAP modules implemented to support your business. The following are some of the more common transactions; this is not a complete list, but provides a good representation.

▸ **Recurring entries**
  Transaction F.14 creates financial documents from recurring entry documents. Recurring entry documents can be created for financial transactions with a fixed amount, interval (e.g., monthly), and life (e.g., twenty-four months).

▸ **Dunning**
  Transaction F150 creates dunning notices to send customers for overdue payments and updates customer master data with the dunning level and a last dunned date.

▸ **Payments**
  Transaction F110 issues vendor payments in mass. It creates the payment medium necessary for monetary transfer and the financial postings necessary to update the G/L and subledgers. For details on running Transaction F110, see Chapter 7.

▸ **Depreciation**
  Transaction AFAB creates depreciation postings. Fixed asset net book values are updated and accounting entries are made to accumulated depreciation and depreciation expense accounts.

▸ **Interest calculations**
  There are several types of interest calculations. Transaction F.52 is used to calculate interest on G/L balances. Transaction FINT is used for calculating interest in arrears for overdue customer accounts. Transaction FINTAP is used for vendor interest calculation. Other interest calculation transaction codes also exist for interest in arrears.

In addition to the transactions listed in the preceding list, periodic processing steps may include transactions for automatic clearing, printing correspondence, currency translation and valuation, manual accruals, reverse accruals, and more.

Now that you have an understanding of what periodic processes are, let's walk through an example for recurring entries.

In Chapter 3, the creation of a recurring document is demonstrated. As discussed in that chapter, when a recurring document is saved, no accounting entries are created. It is only when the recurring entry program is run that accounting documents are posted and G/L balances updated.

To create accounting documents from recurring entry reference documents, use Transaction F.14 or application menu path ACCOUNTING • FINANCIAL ACCOUNTING • GENERAL LEDGER • PERIODIC PROCESSING • RECURRING ENTRIES • F.14 — EXECUTE, as shown in Figure 16.14.

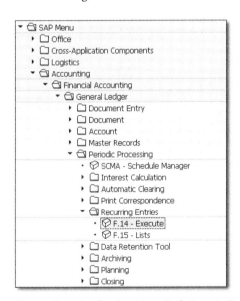

Figure 16.14 Application Menu Path Execute Recurring Entries

Double-click on F.14 - EXECUTE from the menu path shown in Figure 16.14 and the CREATE POSTING DOCUMENTS FROM RECURRING DOCUMENTS screen will open (Figure 16.15).

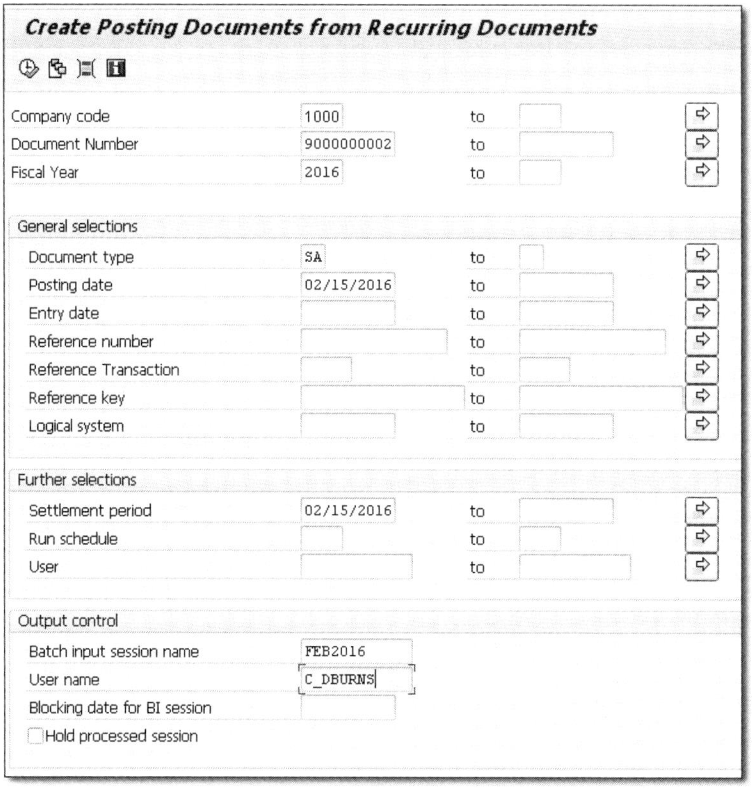

Figure 16.15 Create Posting Documents from Recurring Documents

Make sure to fill all required fields, such as Company code, Document Number (this is the reference document number), Fiscal Year, and Batch input session name. You can also enter additional field values in the General selections portion of the screen to narrow your selection of recurring documents.

The Settlement period field is particularly important. Within the date range provided, it must contain the date on which the next recurring entry is scheduled. If you are unsure, view the recurring entry document in your reference document using Transaction FBD3.

With all field values entered, press the Execute icon ⊕. A message will appear that a session was created (Figure 16.16).

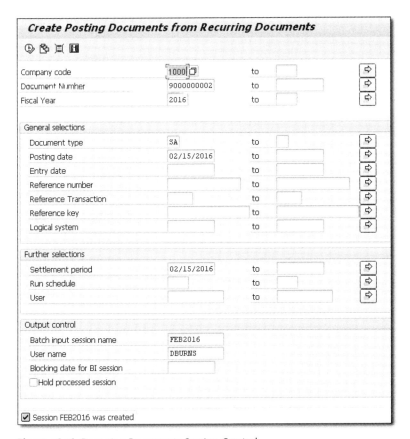

Figure 16.16 Recurring Documents Session Created

To view your session, use Transaction SM35. The BATCH INPUT: SESSION OVER-VIEW screen will appear (Figure 16.17).

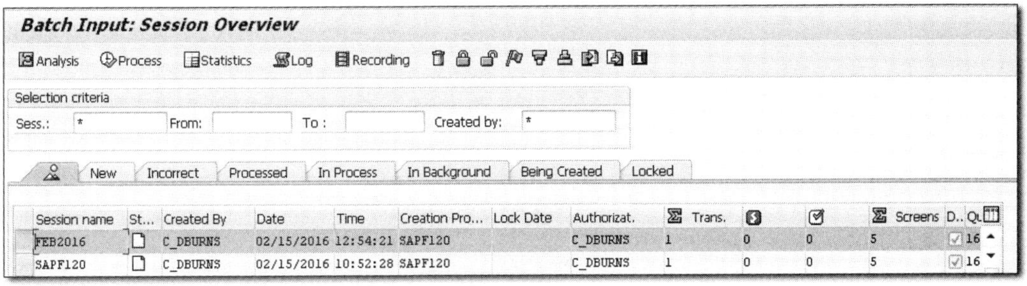

Figure 16.17 Batch Input Session Overview Screen

Highlight your session name and click the PROCESS button. The PROCESS SESSION dialog box will appear (Figure 16.18).

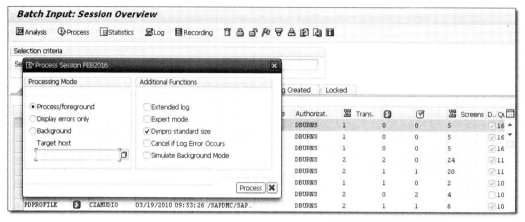

Figure 16.18 Process Session Screen

Select PROCESS/FOREGROUND to watch your accounting document as it's created. Click the PROCESS button. The REALIZE RECURRING ENRY: HEADER DATA screen will appear (Figure 16.19).

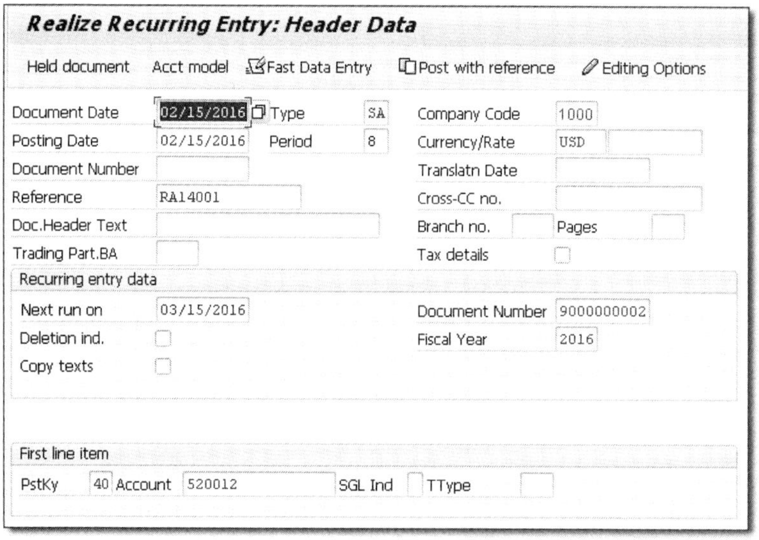

Figure 16.19 Realize Recurring Entry Header Screen

Press ⟨Enter⟩ through the screens until your document is posted.

This concludes our discussion of periodic processes. As you can see, there are numerous types of periodic processes utilized during month-end and year-end close. It important to know your company's business processes to understand which periodic processing transaction codes to use.

16.5 Foreign Currency Valuations

In this section, we will discuss foreign currency valuation at a high level. To execute this process, several configuration steps are required. This book is not a configuration guide, but you should be aware of this configuration since you depend on it to execute foreign currency valuation.

In configuration, a *valuation method* must be defined. In the valuation method, the *valuation procedure* must be specified. For example, one type of valuation procedure is the *lowest value principle*. In the valuation method, specifications are also provided that determine how exchange rate differences should be posted and the basis for determining the exchange rate type used. In addition to defining the valuation method in configuration, you also define *valuation areas*, *accounting principles*, and specify *account determinations*.

In a nutshell, foreign currency valuation is needed to produce financial statements. The ability to valuate account balances in your reporting currency is provided with Transaction FAGL_FC_VAL (or Transaction F.05 if you are using the classic G/L). This step is relevant to G/L accounts managed in foreign currency and open items that were posted in foreign currency. You can perform the valuation in local currency or parallel currency. The result of the valuations can be stored per valuated document and posted to adjustment accounts and P&L accounts.

You may have G/L accounts managed in foreign currency, for example, when you process payments in foreign currency. In this case, a G/L account can only be posted in this foreign currency and the transaction figures and the account balance are kept in the foreign currency and the local currency. In such a case, G/L accounts are not open item managed.

There are a couple different ways in which valuation take place. For open items in customer, vendor, and G/L accounts, the items are read as of specified key date and balanced by account or group and currency. For G/L account balances, reconciliation accounts and accounts managed on an open item basis are not valuated, and P&L accounts are only valuated as required.

Documents or balances are balanced by currency and account. The exchange rate type for the valuation is determined from this balance. Valuation differences are posted as determined by the valuation area configured and selected. Postings for accounts managed on an open item basis in the subledger and the general ledger are posted to an adjustment account and a P&L account. Postings for G/L accounts not managed on an open item basis are posted to adjustment accounts or by account determination.

16.6   GR/IR Clearing

The next topic we'll discuss is the GR/IR clearing function. This topic is also discussed in Chapter 17. The content here, however, is more focused on FI, whereas Chapter 17 discusses GR/IR clearing from the broader perspective of integrated financial close.

GR/IR clearing computes price variances between GR and IR and allocates variances to inventory, price differences, or the assignment object based on the valuation procedure in the material master and the settings in the PO line item. The values are stored in a G/L GR/IR clearing account and settled periodically using the GR/IR clearing function.

GR/IR account maintenance is a process that should be performed regularly, although most consider it as strictly a month-end function. The system matches GRs with IRs based on the PO number, PO item, type of PO, indicator for invoice verification, and material or delivery costs.

There are several tools available for GR/IR clearing account analysis. The first is Transaction F.19. This can be found using application menu path Accounting • Financial Accounting • General Ledger• Periodic Processing • Closing • Reclassify • F.19 – GR/IR Clearing, as shown in Figure 16.20.

Double-click on Transaction F.19 and the Analyze GR/IR Clearing Accounts and Display Acquisitions Tax screen appears (Figure 16.21).

Figure 16.20 Application Menu Path Transaction F.19 GR/IR Clearing

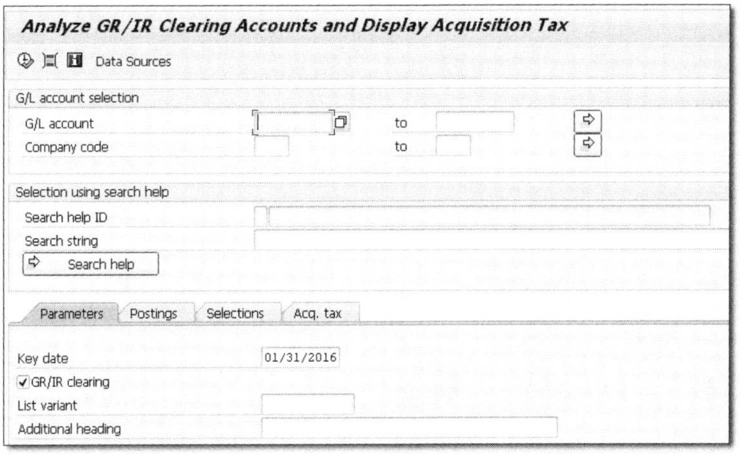

Figure 16.21 Analyze GR/IR Clearing Account Selection Screen

This program is used to analyze GR/IR clearing accounts at a specified key date. It can also be used to generate adjustment postings which are needed to display the following business transactions in the balance sheet:

- ▸ Goods delivered, but not invoiced
- ▸ Goods invoiced, but not delivered

When Transaction F.19 is executed, it selects all items in GR/IR clearing accounts that are open at the specified key date. If the open items per purchase order number and items in local currency do not balance to zero, adjustment postings are created. A credit balance in the GR/IR account reflects PO items that are delivered, but not invoiced. A debit balance reflects items that are invoiced, but not delivered.

Keep in mind that the adjustments to GR/IR are necessary for reporting, but subsequent purchasing activity will likely take place to net GR/IR line items to zero. Therefore, adjustment postings are intended to be reversed at a future date. All postings are reversed at the specified reverse posting date entered on the Postings tab, as shown in Figure 16.22. If no date is entered, the program reverses the postings on the day after the key date.

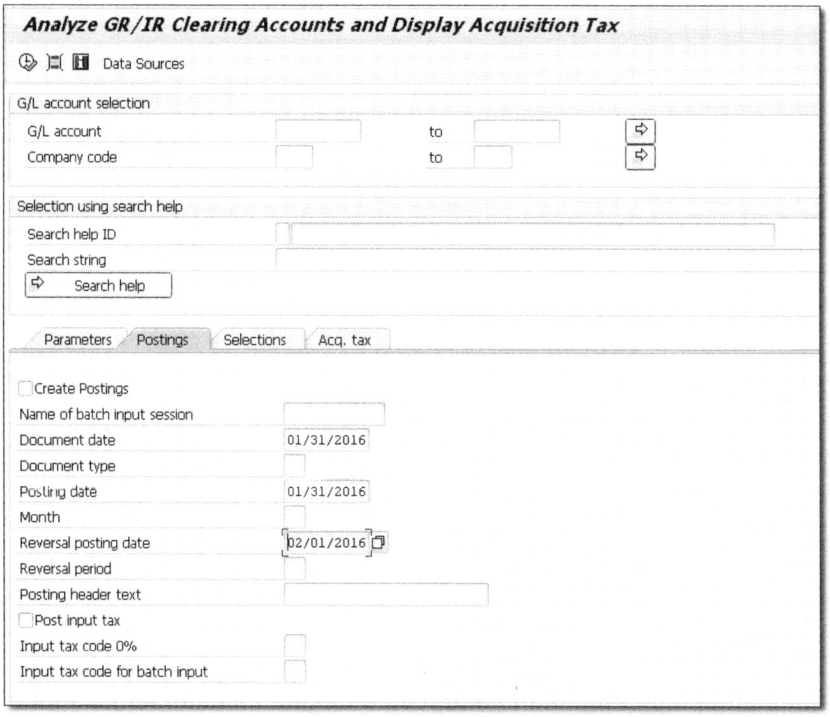

Figure 16.22 Analyze GRIR Clearing Accounts Postings Tab

Another tool in FI for GR/IR account maintenance is Transaction F.13. This can be found using application menu path ACCOUNTING • FINANCIAL ACCOUNTING • GENERAL LEDGER • PERIODIC PROCESSING • AUTOMATIC CLEARING • F.13 – WITHOUT SPECIFICATION OF CLEARING CURRENCY, as shown in Figure 16.23.

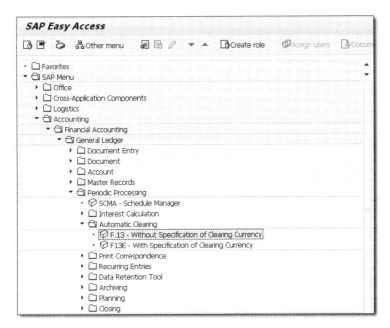

Figure 16.23 Automatic GRIR Account Clearing

Double-click on Transaction F.13 and the AUTOMATIC CLEARING screen appears (Figure 16.24).

Transaction F.13 is not used exclusively for GR/IR clearing. It is also used to clear open items in customer, vendor and G/L accounts. The logic, however, is the same for clearing GR/IR accounts. For GR/IR accounts, the program logic attempts to match documents that can be cleared by and omit documents that cannot.

There is one particular point to emphasize with GR/IR matching. There is a GR/IR ACCOUNT SPECIAL PROCESS checkbox (Figure 16.24) you can select. This special process is used when the assignment of goods receipts to the corresponding invoice receipts is insufficient, based on the purchase order number and purchase order item. This indicator then not only matches GR/IR items by PO number and the PO item, but also using the material document if a goods receipt-related invoice verification is defined in the purchase order item.

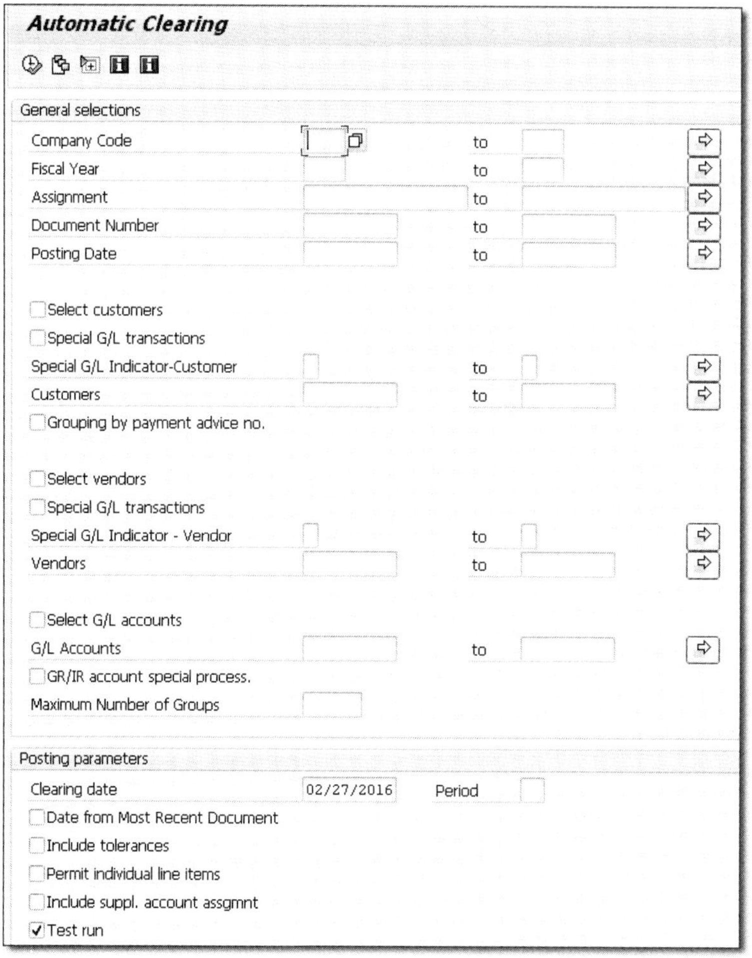

Figure 16.24 Automatic GRIR Account Clearing Selection Screen

16.7 Depreciation

Depreciation is covered in detail in Chapter 13. Rather than repeat the information already contained in that chapter, we'll summarize a few of the key points here.

Depreciation of an asset is typically referred to as *asset consumption*. It decreases the value of an asset and allocates costs of an asset to periods in which it is used.

The primary output of an SAP depreciation run is a summary level document with accounting entries that include credits to accumulated depreciation G/L accounts (on the balance sheet) and debits to asset expense G/L accounts (on the profit and loss statement).

Executing depreciation is an important step in financial close. It is done using Transaction code Transaction AFAB or application menu path ACCOUNTING • FINANCIAL ACCOUNTING • FIXED ASSETS • PERIODIC PROCESSING • AFAB—EXECUTE, as shown in Figure 16.25.

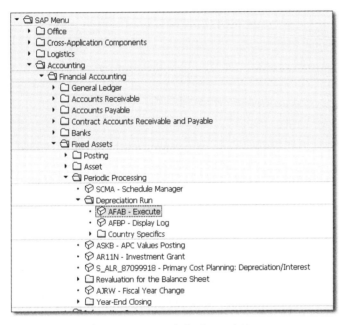

Figure 16.25 Application Menu Path for Depreciation

It is always a good idea to run depreciation in test mode first. To view the results of a depreciation run, use Transaction AFBP.

16.8 Summary

This chapter covered essential transactions in the month-end and year-end close processes. Financial close involves much more than the system mechanics of closing FI in SAP. Several manual steps, analyses, and accounting corrections need to be made to produce clean and accurate financial statements. Having a complete and organized process for closing the books is vital.

This chapter began with a discussion of opening and closing FI periods using Transaction OB52. This transaction is the control center to ensure general users are restricted to posting in a particular accounting period. Furthermore, this transaction provides flexibility in allowing you to specify open periods by account type. Transaction OB52 also permits the use of authorization groups which enables a special user (e.g., the accounting director) to make entries in periods not open to general users.

G/L account balance carryforward is another important financial close process and is the critical step in year-end close. Transaction FAGLGVTR is the primary transaction in New G/L used to carry forward G/L balances. However, if you use a Special Ledger, you will also need to execute Transaction GVTR to carry forward Special Ledger balances. This chapter also covered the carryforward of subledgers, including vendors and customers.

Fixed assets is a subledger that needs special consideration. Depreciation is a process step in both month-end and year-end close. During year-end close, two transactions must be executed. The first, Transaction AJRW, is a technical step to carryforward fixed assets into the new fiscal year. The second, Transaction AJAB, changes the fiscal year in FI-AA.

There are also several different type of periodic processes that were discussed. This category includes numerous transactions, such as recurring entries. Which ones you need to execute as a part of financial close is dependent upon your business processes and the SAP modules implemented to support your business. They include such functions as recurring entries, dunning, outgoing payments, depreciation, interest calculations, and more. In this chapter, an example of a recurring entry is demonstrated.

This concludes our discussion of month-end and year-end close procedures in FI. Closing the books is not isolated to SAP FI. Any integrated process that crosses SAP modules may require action, due to financial integration. In the next chapter, we build on the financial close processes discussed in this chapter by addressing integrated financial close, for which specific steps are needed in modules other than FI.

In this chapter, we cover integrated financial close processes. FI practitioners have to be able to step out of FI to understand integrated business scenarios and their dependencies in the close process.

17   Integrated Financial Close in SAP ERP

Financial close at month-end and year-end does not happen in a vacuum. Coordinated efforts are required across teams that manage sales, production, logistics, accounting, and more. Because finance and accounting departments are the ones primarily responsible for financial close, they need to understand not only their own close processes, but also integrated team close activities across business processes.

Understanding the broad reach of month-end and year-end close is important to a timely and coordinated financial close. Close steps need to be sequenced, and it is important to understand dependencies between close activities. Moreover, finance and accounting are on the hook if financial close is not executed in a timely fashion. Therefore, an accounting department's ability to coordinating close activities with other teams is important for achieving the company's goals.

This chapter focuses on a limited number of integrated financial close steps in Controlling (CO), Sales and Distributions (SD), and Materials Management (MM). It is not intended to provide a complete spectrum of close activities in these modules, but rather emphasizes the importance of understanding the role of integration in the financial close process

Let's begin with a discussion of financial close in the CO module.

17.1 Integrated Financial Close and Cost Accounting

Cost accounting, often referred to as *management accounting*, is managed in the CO module. CO provides an internal view of financial information and numerous capabilities, including profitability analysis, cost assessments and allocations, planning, and much more. There are several books and resource materials available on CO that you can reference to learn more about these topics.

The primary focus of this section is CO period locks which is essentially the CO equivalent of opening and closing periods.

17.1.1 CO Period Locks

Period control in CO is managed through the period lock function. CO period control is unique in that it can be set by period and transaction type. Most companies do not use all the CO transaction types, so it is important to note in addressing this topic that you need to become familiar with the CO transaction types used in your organization.

To change CO period locks, use Transaction OKP1 or application menu path ACCOUNTING • CONTROLLING • COST ELEMENT ACCOUNTING • ENVIRONMENT • PERIOD LOCK • OKP1—CHANGE, as shown in Figure 17.1.

Double-click OKP1—CHANGE from the menu path shown in Figure 17.1 and the CHANGE PERIOD LOCK: INITIAL SCREEN screen will open (Figure 17.2). On this screen, you must enter a CONTROLLING AREA, FISCAL YEAR, and VERSION.

The VERSION field deserves further explanation. There is one specific version for actual and planned costs (i.e., version 0) in each controlling area. This version is automatically created when you set up a controlling area. In addition to version 0, you can create any number of extra planning versions in which you can enter planning figures. However, when posting actual costs, there is no option to enter a version. The actual values are automatically posted to version 0.

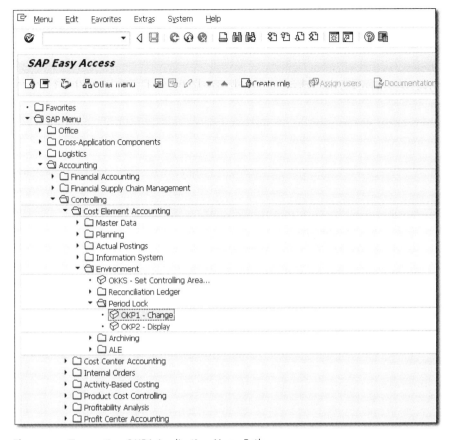

Figure 17.1 Transaction OKP1 Application Menu Path

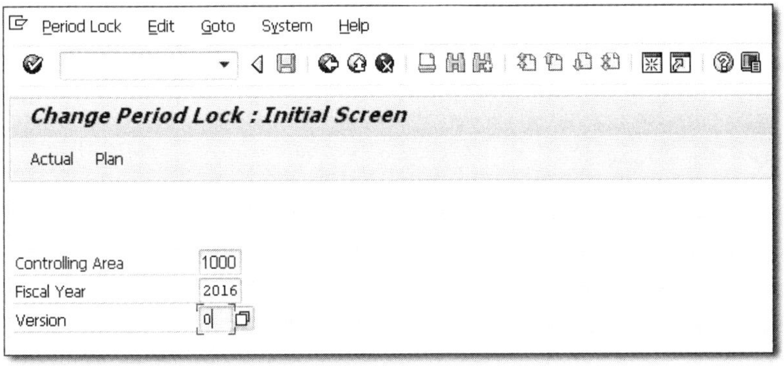

Figure 17.2 Change Period Lock: Initial Screen

With all the field values entered as in Figure 17.2, click the ACTUAL button in the top left of the screen. The CHANGE ACTUAL PERIOD LOCK: EDIT screen will open (Figure 17.3).

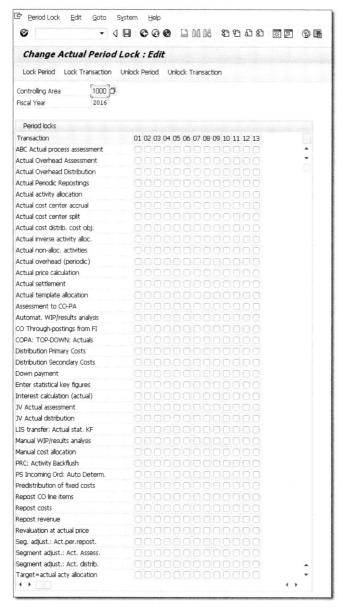

Figure 17.3 Change Actual Period Lock: Edit

CO periods can be locked by transaction, by period, or by individual transaction and period. Figure 17.4 shows an example of a lock by period, meaning that a specific period (i.e., period 01) is locked for all transaction types.

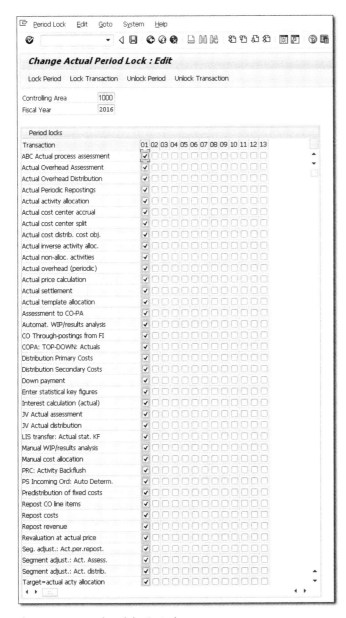

Figure 17.4 Period Lock by Period

Figure 17.5 shows an example period lock by transaction, meaning that a transaction (e.g., ABC ACTUAL PROCESS ASSESSMENT) is locked for all periods.

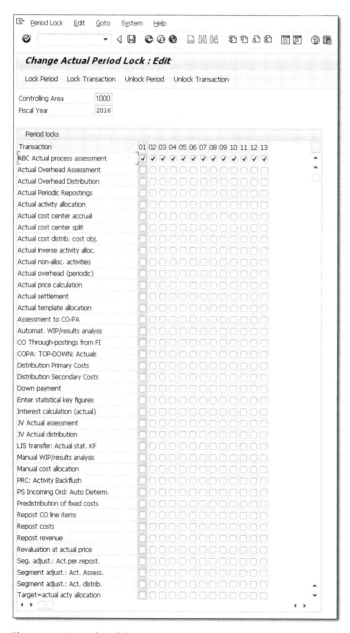

Figure 17.5 Period Lock by Transaction

Figure 17.6 shows an example of a period lock by transaction and period, meaning that specific periods are locked (e.g., periods 01–11) for a specific transaction (e.g., ABC ACTUAL PROCESS ASSESSMENT) while other periods (e.g., periods 12–16) remain open.

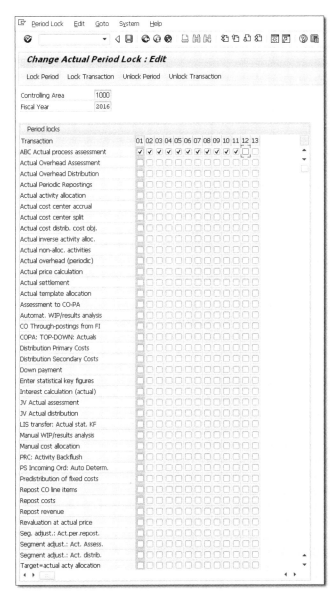

Figure 17.6 Period Lock by Transaction and Period

In this section you learned the importance of locking periods in CO. Using Transaction OB52 to open and close FI periods is not sufficient if you use CO. Period maintenance in CO is required. Make it a regular part of your close procedures to open/close CO periods in coordination with FI periods.

Now that you have a detailed understanding of CO period locks, let's address some other close tasks in CO, at a high level. As mentioned previously, there are many books and reference materials specialized on SAP CO, which you use if you need more detail on these topics.

17.1.2 Other CO Close Activities

In CO, there are several different period-end closing functions that can be executed. These transactions are spread across several submodules within CO, including Cost Element Accounting, Cost Center Accounting, Internal Orders, Activity-Based Costing, Product Cost Controlling, and Profitability Analysis.

As a caveat, it should be understood that the CO topics discussed in this section aren't exclusively considered financial close tasks. In fact, many CO transactions are executed many times throughout any given month. We emphasize them here simply because the timing of their execution at financial close is important to consider.

One of the most common themes in CO is the reposting of revenues and expenses. This activity includes the manual reposting of costs and revenues, reposting line items, and activity allocations. If your company uses the reposting, allocation, and assessment functions in CO, you should make an extra effort to become familiar with their capabilities and transaction codes. Even if you are not the person responsible for executing CO transactions, you should be aware of when they are executed, by whom, and the expected impact to FI.

There are several types of cost allocations, including overhead allocations, distributions, and assessments. If your company uses these CO transactions, it is important to know the differences and how to troubleshoot errors when the financial result is not what's expected. Build them into your close procedures and ensure that the timing of their execution is carefully coordinated with other close activities.

The main point to understand is that repostings, cost allocations, etc., need to be executed shortly before financial close is finalized. The timing is critical to ensure your internal and external financial reports accurately reflect the activity for the reporting period.

Another important concept we will briefly touch on is CO *settlements*. The concept is relatively straightforward. When financial transactions are posted, a cost collecting object can be used to accumulate the costs, which at a later point in time will be settled to a final receiver. For example, an internal order (IO) is a short-lived cost collector, whose costs will eventually be settled to a receiver, such as a material or cost center. Settlements can be executed for individual IOs using Transaction KO88 or collectively using Transaction KO8G.

The concept of settlements goes beyond CO. Some other examples of SAP objects that collect costs for settlement are WBS elements and Plant Maintenance orders. Furthermore, certain sales orders may need to be settled to CO-PA. It is important to gain a full understanding of all your business processes to know the applicability of settlements across the SAP modules implemented at your company. There may be dependencies, so the timing of settlements across the modules needs to be coordinated to coincide with financial close and the production of your financial statements.

This concludes our discussion of CO related financial close activities. In the next section, we will discuss integrated close and the MM module.

17.2 Integrated Financial Close and Materials Management

There are several financial close-related activities in Materials Management module. We begin with a discussion of period control.

17.2.1 MM Period Maintenance

We've already seen that separate control transactions exist in FI (i.e. Transaction OB52) and CO (Transaction OKP1). Now we'll introduce yet another, this one existing in MM.

At this point you may be asking yourself, why does period control have to be managed separately in different modules? The simple answer is that each module was created separately with a certain business function in mind. Wherever transactions are created that have a financial impact, you need the ability to control and restrict financial activity.

Now let's discuss the specifics of period control in MM. To open a new period, use Transaction MMPV or application menu path LOGISTICS • MATERIALS MANAGEMENT • PURCHASING • MASTER DATA • SUBSEQUENT SETTLEMENT • VENDOR REBATE ARRANGEMENTS • ENVIRONMENT • CONDITION/ARRANGEMENT • ENVIRONMENT • MATERIAL • OTHER • MMPV—CLOSE PERIOD, as shown in Figure 17.7.

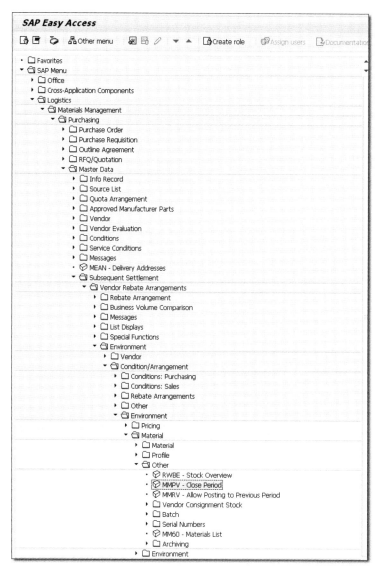

Figure 17.7 Transaction MMPV Application Menu Path

Double-click MMPV—CLOSE PERIOD from the menu path shown in Figure 17.7 and the CLOSE PERIOD FOR MATERIAL MASTER RECO RDS screen will open (Figure 17.8). On this screen, enter values in the COMPANY CODE, PERIOD, and FISCAL YEAR fields. Notice that selection buttons exist for the following:

▶ CHECK AND CLOSE PERIOD

▶ CHECK PERIOD ONLY

▶ CLOSE PERIOD ONLY

Checkboxes also exist for the following:

▶ ALLOW NEGATIVE QUANTITIES IN PREVIOUS PERIOD

▶ ALLOW NEGATIVE VALUES IN THE PREVIOUS PERIOD

If negative quantities or values exist and the respective checkbox is not selected, the period check will fail and changing the period will not be permitted.

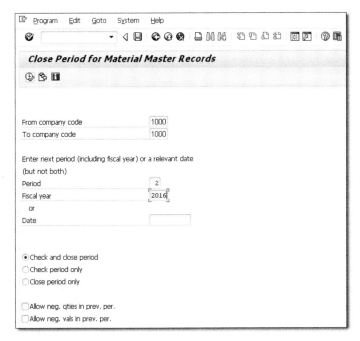

Figure 17.8 Close Period for Material Master Records

To display the current open MM period and to allow posting to the prior period, use Transaction MMRV or application menu path LOGISTICS • MATERIALS

Management • Purchasing • Master Data • Subsequent Settlement • Vendor Rebate Arrangements • Environment • Condition/Arrangement • Environment • Material • Other • MMRV—Allow Posting to Previous Period, as shown in Figure 17.9.

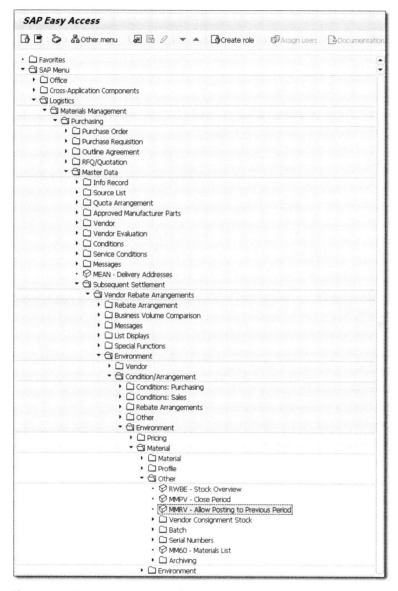

Figure 17.9 Transaction MMRV Application Menu Path

Double-click MMRV—Allow Posting to Previous Period from the menu path shown in Figure 17.9 and the initial screen in which to select a company code will open (Figure 17.10).

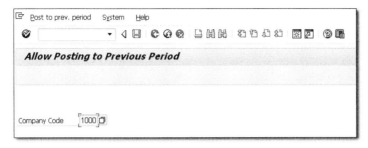

Figure 17.10 Company Code Selection Screen

Enter a company code and press ⌊Enter⌋. The Allow Posting to Previous Period screen will open (Figure 17.11). Notice that the current period, previous period, and last period in the previous year are listed. In addition, the Post to Previous Period section has two checkboxes. The first, Allow posting to Previous Per. allows postings to the previous MM period. By default, this option is selected, unless the second checkbox is chosen: Disallow Backposting Generally. This second checkbox prevents postings to the prior period and prevents the first checkbox (i.e., Allow Posting to Previous Per.) from being set automatically during period close.

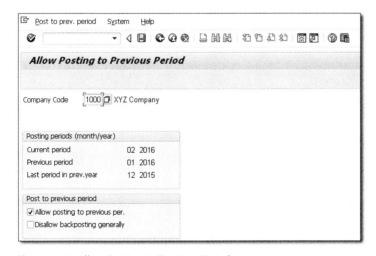

Figure 17.11 Allow Posting to Previous Period

As you can see, changing periods in MM is required. Opening and closing FI periods using Transaction OB52 is not sufficient if you use MM. Make it a regular part of your close procedures to open/close MM periods along with the FI periods.

Now that you know how to manage period control in MM, we'll move on to some other MM activities important to integrated financial close.

17.2.2   Other MM Close Activities

A review of open purchase orders (POs) and purchase requisitions (PRs) is a good business practice. These documents need to regularly be reviewed, edited, or cancelled as the need arises. This activity should not be restricted to month-end and year-end, but it does become more important as you consider closing the books.

Follow-on transactions to open POs should also be reviewed. Are there goods receipts that have not been processed? Have invoices been received that have not been processed? Again, these steps are not strictly month-end and year-end processes steps, but just good business practices. Entering outstanding receipts and invoices in a timely fashion keeps the statuses of POs and PRs current and ensures that any financial impact is reflected in FI prior to closing the books.

Now let's discuss a few MM integration points that can have a substantial financial impact. These include the creation of A/P invoices through Logistics Invoice Verification (LIV) and the matching of goods receipts (GR) with invoice receipts (IR).

First, let's discuss A/P invoices. It is important to make sure your company has good business processes in place to enter vendor invoices into A/P. . Processing invoice receipts in a timely fashion has a downstream impact. It produces A/P invoices in FI that are paid using the automatic payment program (Transaction F110). Coordination between the FI and Logistics teams is important during month end and year end to ensure all invoice receipts are entered and paid.

The next topic we'll discuss is the GR/IR clearing function, which computes price variances between GR and IR and allocates variances to inventory, price differences, or the assignment object based on the valuation procedure in the material master and the settings in the purchase order line item. The values are stored in a G/L GR/IR clearing account and settled periodically using the GR/IR clearing function.

GR/IR account maintenance is a process that should be performed regularly, especially at month-end and year-end close. The system matches GRs with IRs based on the following information:

- Purchase order
- Purchase order item
- Type of purchase order item (e.g., standard PO, service PO)
- Indicator for invoice verification (e.g., goods receipt-based invoice verification)
- Material or delivery costs

Variances are calculated by comparing each GR with its associated IR. IRs are recorded as a debit in the GR/IR clearing account, whereas GRs are recorded as credits. Price variances are computed using the lower of the goods receipt quantity or the invoice receipt quantity. Because price variances are quantity based, it is possible to settle variances for partial deliveries and partial invoices.

There are several tools available for GR/IR maintenance:

- **Transaction MB5S—List of GR/IR Balances**
  This report compares the GR quantities and values relating to a PO with the invoice quantities and values for the same PO. The report is used to check goods and invoice receipts when the purchasing documents show some discrepancy.

- **Transaction MR11—Maintain GR/IR Clearing Account**
  For differences between GR and IR with reference to a PO, entries in the GR/IR clearing account need to be cleared manually using Transaction MR11. There are many reasons that such a difference may occur. For example, an invoice may have been posted through A/P instead of in procurement. Another example occurs if goods were received and returned for poor quality, but the vendor was accidently paid.

- **FI Clearing Transactions**
  When GR=IR, both are still maintained in the G/L clearing account as open items until they are cleared. To clear open G/L items, FI transactions can be used, such as Transactions F.13 and F13E. Once these GR and IR items are matched using a clearing program, individual line item statuses are changed from open status to cleared.

This concludes our discussion of MM. Next, let's move on to our final topic on integrated financial close: the Sales and Distribution (DS) module.

17.3   Integrated Financial Close and Sales and Distribution

Closing activities in the SD module are important for reporting sales and revenue. In some cases, billing documents do not post to costing-based CO-PA for the made-to-order scenario. In such a case, you need to settle to CO-PA using Transaction VA88.

In addition, other SD activities relevant to month-end and year-end close include the following:

▶ **Review open sales orders**
This is important to ensure that any sales cancellations, returns, or other follow-on functions have been entered into the system. Every effort should be made to ensure that sales orders reflect their current status.

▶ **Execute billing**
Using Transaction VF01, a billing run should be executed for relevant orders. This ensures that customer invoices are created and that sales order statuses are up-to-date and accurate at month-end and year-end close.

▶ **Open receivables**
A review of open and overdue receivables is important for collections and cash forecasting. In Chapter 16, we discussed dunning. Make every effort to collect outstanding receivables and past due invoices prior to month-end and year-end close.

17.4   Summary

Financial close is not isolated to FI. Many essential month-end and year-end close activities take place in FI, but SAP is an integrated system, which means that business processes cross modules and have dependencies. This chapter focused on some of the key FI financial close integration points with MM, SD, and CO.

Finance and accounting departments are usually the ones primarily responsible for financial close tasks, but FI practitioners have to be able to step out of FI to understand integrated business scenarios and their dependencies in the close process. At a minimum, you need to be prepared to coordinate with logistics, sales, cost accounting, and other teams to ensure a smooth financial close.

In this chapter, we discussed period maintenance in MM and CO. Details of period maintenance in FI are covered in Chapter 16. Separate transaction codes exist in CO and MM for opening and closing periods. In MM, Transaction MMPV is used. In CO, the period maintenance transaction is OKP1. These transaction codes each operate differently.

In addition to period maintenance, integrated close requires careful attention to transactions originating outside FI that have a financial impact. The specific non-FI document related close tasks that need to be considered depends upon your business processes and the SAP modules implemented.

Another common theme throughout integrated close is the need for document review, processing, reconciliation, and adjustments. For example, in both SD and MM, processes need to be in place to ensure the timeliness of posting follow-on documents. The accuracy of financial information and the status of SD and MM documents is dependent on the timely entry of documents.

We covered a lot of territory in this chapter. The big takeaway, however, is that as a financial professional, you need to completely understand your business processes. Many process steps take place outside of FI, yet have a financial impact. As a result, the company depends on your expertise execute an accurate and timely financial close process.

Appendices

A   The New General Ledger

The content of this book, in its entirety, was written and presented with the New G/L. However, there are still many SAP customers using the classic G/L. This appendix will provide supplemental details about the New G/L for informational purposes rather than to demonstrate functionality or teach configuration.

There is so much new functionality available in the New G/L that there is no way a single chapter can do it justice. Therefore, only a subset of critical capabilities is presented in this appendix. Several books and reference materials exist on the topic that you should read to obtain a greater understanding.

Unlike the chapters in this book, this appendix is not written from a transactional point of view. It is intended to provide supplemental information to enhance your understanding of the New G/L and its unique capabilities. Configuring FI is beyond the scope of this book, but discussing some configuration concepts is necessary to assist in your understanding of the topic.

If you are installing SAP for the first time, the New G/L will be automatically activated. If your company is still on classic G/L and intends to upgrade to the New G/L, you will need to launch a migration project. The content in this appendix will assist you with your preparations for both these situations: If you are already using the New G/L, it will help you better understand its capabilities, and if you are migrating to the New G/L from the classic G/L, it will help you in making design decisions.

The *New G/L* is described as an enhanced version of the classic G/L, with greater flexibility and extensibility. A major accomplishment of the New G/L was to incorporate some functionality that resided outside the G/L, including profit center accounting (PCA), recon ledger, and special purpose ledger (SPL). In doing so, the New G/L has also significantly reduced the time and effort required to close the books at period and year end.

In this section, we will begin with a discussion on the flexibility and extensibility of New G/L. After that, we will discuss the key features of New G/L, including the following:

- ▶ Parallel Ledgers
- ▶ Document Splitting
- ▶ Segments
- ▶ Profit Center Accounting

A.1   Flexibility and Extensibility

To fully grasp how the New G/L is more flexible and extensible, you first need to understand some of the limitations of the classic G/L, such as the following:

- No parallel ledgers. In the classic G/L, SPL can be used to add additional dimensions to meet reporting requirements, and parallel accounting can be accomplished through the creation of additional G/L accounts.

- No real-time reconciliation between Management Accounting and FI. Reconciliation was accomplished through a reconciliation ledger.

- No ability to extend data structure with customer fields.

- No segment reporting capability. In other words, you cannot subdivide classic G/L balances by other characteristics to produce full financial statements.

This list is by no means a complete account of the limitations of the classic G/L. Removing all of these limitations was the catalyst for the New G/L design. With that said, *flexibility* and *extensibility* of the New G/L specifically refer to the ability to perform financial reporting from a central source, with the ability to extend the totals table (i.e., table FAGLFLEXT) and produce financial statements by multiple dimensions. New G/L also provides another set of tables (i.e., table FMGLFLEX*) for use in the public sector.

In the past, multiple totals tables were needed (e.g., tables GLT0, GLPCT). SAP has consolidated the multiple totals tables into a single totals table (i.e., table FAGL-FLEXT) in New GL. Having one summary table with multiple dimensions and the ability to add customer fields provides flexibility unprecedented in FI.

In addition to the new totals table, table FAGLFLEXT, New G/L also has new line item tables: table FAGLFLEXA for actual line items and table FAGLFLEXP for planned line items.

With regards to New G/L, the term *extensibility* more specifically refers to an extended data structure. This means that you can activate additional fields, such as segment, or create your own.

Let's take a look at the activation of New G/L.

A.2   Activation of the New G/L

To activate the New G/L, follow the IMG menu path FINANCIAL ACCOUNTING •
FINANCIAL ACCOUNTING GLOBAL SETTINGS • ACTIVATE NEW GENERAL LEDGER
ACCOUNTING, as seen in Figure A.1.

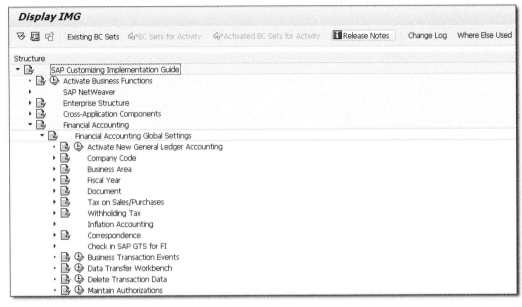

Figure A.1 IMG Menu Path Activate New G/L

Double-click on the ACTIVATE NEW GENERAL LEDGER ACCOUNTING node. The
CHANGE VIEW "ACTIVATION OF NEW GENERAL LEDGER ACCOUNTING": DETAILS
screen will appear (Figure A.2).

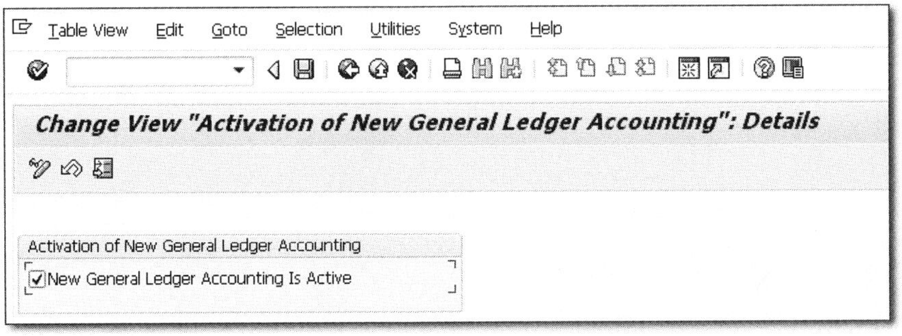

Figure A.2 Activate New G/L Screen

The check-box for NEW GENERAL LEDGER ACCOUNTING IS ACTIVE is basically an on/off switch. By activating the New G/L, the functions for it become available, including the activation of the New G/L tables. In addition, in the IMG the previous FINANCIAL ACCOUNTING menu is replaced by the FINANCIAL ACCOUNTING (NEW) menu (Figure A.3). This is where you configure the New G/L.

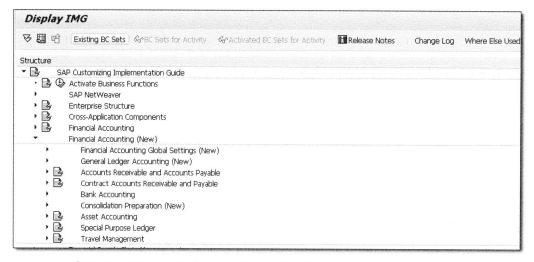

Figure A.3 IMG Menu Path Financial Accounting (New)

If you already use the classic G/L in your production system, the transition to the New G/L involves more than just flipping the switch. You need to perform the migration of your G/L data before you activate the New G/L. Migration is only possible as part of a project in collaboration with the SAP G/L Migration Service.

Now that you have learned about the flexibility, extensibility, and activation of the New G/L, let's discuss the concepts of ledgers and parallel ledgers. Going into this topic, you should fully understand what a ledger is: SAP defines a *ledger* as a section of a database table that only contains those dimensions of the totals table that the ledger is based on and that are required for reporting.

A.3   Ledgers

To begin, let's talk in more depth about the ledger concept. SAP was built with individual and separate ledgers that each served a different purpose and spanned across multiple modules. These ledgers include the classic G/L ledger for external and legal financial reporting, the CO-to-FI Reconciliation ledger, a Cost of Goods Sold (COGS) or Cost of Sales ledger, a Profit Center Accounting ledger, and Special Purpose ledgers. As you can imagine, this approach presented numerous challenges in reconciling the ledgers and pulling together pieces of data for financial reporting. In the New G/L, these ledgers can be combined.

A.3.1 Assigning Scenarios to Ledgers

In the New G/L, scenarios are assigned to ledgers, which in turn determine which fields are updated in the ledger when postings are made.

To assign scenarios to ledgers, follow the IMG menu path FINANCIAL ACCOUNTING (NEW) • FINANCIAL ACCOUNTING GLOBAL SETTINGS (NEW) • LEDGERS • LEDGER • ASSIGN SCENARIOS AND CUSTOMER FIELDS TO LEDGERS, as seen in Figure A.4.

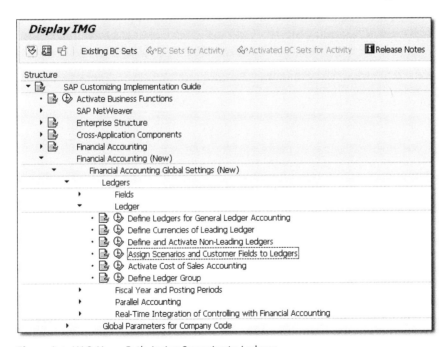

Figure A.4 IMG Menu Path Assign Scenarios to Ledgers

Click on the ASSIGN SCENARIOS AND CUSTOMER FIELDS TO LEDGERS node. The NEW ENTRIES: OVERVIEW OF ADDED ENTRIES screen appears (Figure A.5). From this screen you can use the DIALOGUE STRUCTURE on the left of the screen to navigate to the specific scenarios assigned to a ledger.

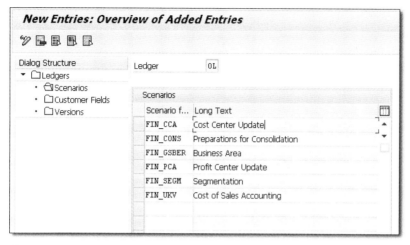

Figure A.5 Assign Scenarios to Ledgers Screen

The New G/L provides six standard scenarios:

▶ Business Area Scenario — Sender Business Area and Receiver Business Area

▶ Profit Center Update Scenario — Profit Center and Partner Profit Center

▶ Segmentation Scenario — Segment, Partner Segment, and Profit Center

▶ Preparation for Consolidation Scenario — Consolidation Transaction Type and Trading Partner

▶ Cost of Sales Accounting Scenario — Sender Functional Area and Receiver Functional Area

▶ Cost Center Update Scenario — Sender Cost Center and Receiver Cost Center

Customer-specific scenarios cannot be created, but custom fields can be required when assigning scenarios to a ledger. All six scenarios can be assigned to a ledger.

A.3.2 Parallel Ledgers

Companies need parallel accounting to reflect accounting valuations according to country-specific accounting principles and legal requirements. Global companies need the ability to meet International Accounting Standards (IAS) simultaneously in the global environment, and New G/L provides the capability of doing so with parallel ledgers.

Of course, the accounting principles followed in the country of incorporation dictates group reporting valuations, but local valuations and accounting principles still need to be reflected for each country in which you do business. This is the essence of parallel accounting: It enables you to provide accounting valuations and closing functions for each company code according to the accounting principles of the company as a whole, as well as doing so according to local accounting principles and regulatory requirements. Therefore, parallel accounting allows you to capture and report accounting principles for the group as a whole, as well as local accounting principles.

At this point, it is important to mention that a commonly accepted approach to implementing parallel accounting exited in the classic G/L. This approach involved creating additional G/L accounts, in which case parallel ledgers are not needed. This is the old method of parallel accounting and no longer preferred. With this method, one joint account was needed for postings for both accounting principles. In addition, specific area accounts are used for each accounting principle.

With the New G/L, you have the ability to post data to all ledgers, to a specified selection of ledgers, or to a single ledger.

In the New G/L, one leading ledger is created and multiple local ledgers can be activated. It is important to understand the difference between the leading ledger and local ledgers. When the New G/L is configured, exactly one leading ledger is defined. This leading ledger contains the data required for consolidated financial statements. It is fully integrated with the subsidiary ledgers and updated in all company codes. In other words, the leading ledger is automatically assigned to all company codes. Nonleading ledgers, on the other hand, are specific to one accounting principle and must be assigned to company codes individually.

Each parallel ledger serves a different purpose in that it is used to account for different country-specific legal and accounting reporting requirements. For example, the leading ledger might manage the G/L according to International Financial

Reporting Standards (IFRS), while a nonleading ledger may designated for US Generally Accepted Accounting Principles (GAAP).

This concludes our discussion of parallel ledgers. In the next section, we will move our discussion to document splitting.

To make sure you thoroughly understand this concept, let's walk through an example of how this is setup. First, you have to define your ledgers in the New G/L. To do so, follow IMG menu path FINANCIAL ACCOUNTING (NEW) • FINANCIAL ACCOUNTING GLOBAL SETTINGS (NEW) • LEDGERS • LEDGER • DEFINE LEDGERS FOR GENERAL LEDGER ACCOUNTING, as seen in Figure A.6.

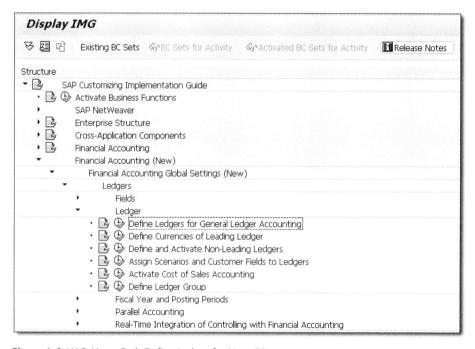

Figure A.6 IMG Menu Path Define Ledger for New G/L

Click on the DEFINE LEDGERS FOR GENERAL LEDGER ACCOUNTING node. The CHANGE VIEW "DEFINE LEDGERS IN GENERAL LEDGER ACCOUNTING": OVERVIEW screen appears (Figure A.7). Notice that a leading ledger and totals tables are specified.

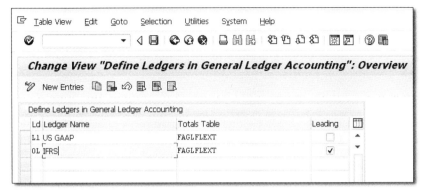

Figure A.7 Define Ledgers in New G/L Accounting Screen

Once the ledgers are defined, accounting principles can be defined and assigned. To do so, follow IMG menu path Financial Accounting (New) • Financial Accounting Global Settings (New) • Ledgers • Parallel Accounting, as seen in Figure A.8.

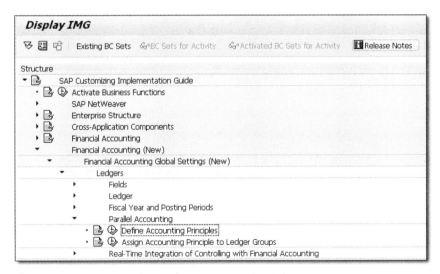

Figure A.8 IMG Menu Path to Define Accounting Principles

Click on the Define Accounting Principles node. The Change View "Accounting Principles": Overview screen appears (Figure A.9).

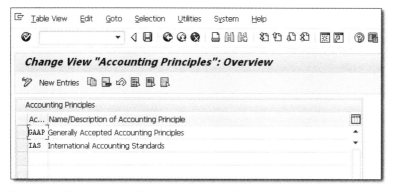

Figure A.9 Change Accounting Principles Overview Screen

The last step is to assign an accounting principle to a target ledger. From Figure A.8, click Assign Accounting Principle to Ledger Groups. The Change View "Assignment of Accounting Principle to target Ledger Group screen appears (Figure A.10).

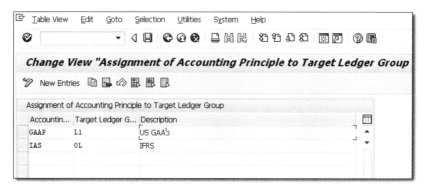

Figure A.10 Assign Accounting Principle to Target Ledger Screen

This concludes our discussion of parallel ledgers. In the next section the topic of document splitting is presented.

A.4   Document Splitting

Document splitting is the ability to split document line items according to specified dimensions, such as segment, business area, or profit center. With real-time document splitting, balance sheets can be created for each dimension.

There are three types of document splitting:

▸ **Active splitting**
The splitting of account assignments based on configuration settings. In essence, this method of splitting utilizes designated "sender" lines as the source of account assignments and "receiver" lines as the recipient for the account assignment.

▸ **Passive splitting**
The automatic inheritance of splitting assignment based on clearing documents and invoice reference documents.

▸ **Zero balancing**
This form of splitting involves the automatic generation of additional line item items to ensure that the specified dimension balances to zero in each transaction. An activation flag is set in configuration for each dimension for which to perform zero balancing.

Active document splitting is used to automatically split line items from sender line items to receiver lines for selected dimensions. For example, expense line items with the segment dimension can be sender lines with the payable line as a receiver. The net effect can be a zero balancing of line items in a financial document by the dimensions specified, and balance sheets can be created for these dimensions. In addition, document splitting enables the system to create additional clearing lines.

Now that you have learned the basics of document splitting, let's see an example of active document splitting in which a vendor invoice is entered with the values listed in Table A.1.

Debit/Credit	Account	Segment	Amount
Credit	Vendor	Blank	1000
Debit	Expense	1001	200
Debit	Expense	1002	800

Table A.1 Example Vendor Invoice Data

Document splitting then creates the a document in the G/L view (Table A.2), actively splitting the vendor lines according to the segment dimension specified in the expense line items.

Debit/Credit	Account	Segment	Amount
Credit	Vendor	1001	200
Credit	Vendor	1002	800
Debit	Expense	1001	200
Debit	Expense	1002	800

Table A.2 Example G/L View Document

The example in Table A.2 shows an active splitting controlled by configuration. Passive document splitting, on the other hand, is not controlled by configuration. Passive splitting takes place for transactions that include clearing and transactions in which an invoice is referenced—for example, an outgoing payment.

Building on the prior example of actively splitting a vendor invoice, Table A.3 shows the passive splitting of the segment dimension on cash when the outgoing payment is made.

Debit/Credit	Account	Segment	Amount
Debit	Vendor	1001	200
Debit	Vendor	1002	800
Credit	Cash/Bank	1001	200
Credit	Cash/Bank	1002	800

Table A.3 Passive Splitting Example

With the outgoing payment, the cash/bank document line items passively inherit the segment dimension according to the values in the vendor line items.

By using document splitting with zero balancing enabled per dimension, complete financial statements can be produced at any time for any of the following dimensions:

▸ Customer-defined fields
▸ Segments
▸ Profit centers
▸ Funds
▸ Business areas

Document splitting in the New G/L is a significant improvement over the classic G/L. It provides additional reporting capability. Setting it up, however, can be time-consuming. To do so properly requires thorough analysis of your business processes and typically requires the introduction of several new FI document types.

Without getting into the configuration details, document splitting is based on the assignment of document types to business transactions and business transaction variants, as well as the assignment of G/L accounts to item categories. In turn, item categories are used to define document splitting rules, which determine the document line items to split and how. These document splitting rules are assigned to a document splitting method.

The logic of document splitting can be broken down into the following rules:

1. When posting, the system validates that the item categories (i.e., G/L accounts) are permitted. The link to item categories is made from the document type and the business transaction.

2. For clearing and reference transactions (e.g., outgoing payments), the system applies passive document splitting. With passive document splitting, the system transfers account assignments for the line items being created.

3. The system applies the document splitting rule for the document being posted. This is referred to as *active document splitting*.

4. Enhancement logic, if activated, will provide account assignments for individual line items for which no account assignments could be determined (e.g., tax).

5. The system validates the document splitting characteristics. This ensures that the document type logically matches the business transaction to be updated.

6. The system creates a zero balance setting for each document. In other words, if the document cannot balance to zero according to the splitting dimensions specified, the system creates additional clearing items to make it balance to zero. This is necessary for creating balance sheets.

This concludes our discussion of document splitting. In the next section, we will discuss segment dimension.

A.5   Segments

With New G/L, SAP added the segment dimension. SAP defines a *segment* as a division of a company for which you can create financial statements for external reporting.

Why is this important? IFRS requires an entity to report financial data about its reportable segments, which are operating segments or aggregations of operating segments that meet any of the following criteria:

▸ Its reported revenue, from both external customers and intersegment sales or transfers, is 10 percent or more of the combined revenue, internal and external, of all operating segments.

▸ The absolute measure of its reported profit or loss is 10 percent or more of the greater, in absolute amount, of (i) the combined reported profit of all operating segments that did not report a loss, and (ii) the combined reported loss of all operating segments that reported a loss or, its assets are 10 percent or more of the combined assets of all operating segments.

You should also be familiar with GAAP or other local accounting rules for segment reporting.

Segments are defined in SAP configuration. SEGMENT is a ten-character field with a fifty-character DESCRIPTION field. It has no other fields, parameters, or control settings. Document splitting is required to produce financial statements by segment. In addition, the zero balance setting needs to be made for the segment characteristic.

You have now learned what the SEGMENT field is and why it is important, but the next important question is: How is it entered into a financial transaction? There are three different methods:

▸ Enter a segment in the master record of a profit center and therefore have the segment derived based on its association with the profit center master record.

▸ Manually enter the segment during posting (only possible for transactions in FI).

▸ Use a customer enhancement to set up your own rules for deriving the segment during posting.

As previously mentioned, segments are defined in the IMG. Let's take a look at an example of a segment that has been configured and assigned to a profit center.

To define the enterprise structure for FI, follow the IMG menu path ENTERPRISE STRUCTURE • DEFINITION • FINANCIAL ACCOUNTING • DEFINE SEGMENT, as shown in Figure A.11.

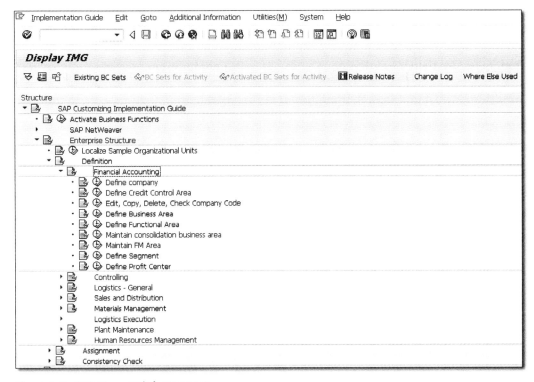

Figure A.11 IMG Menu Path for Segment

Click the EXECUTE icon. The DISPLAY VIEW "SEGMENTS FOR SEGMENT REPORTING": OVERVIEW screen will open (Figure A.12).

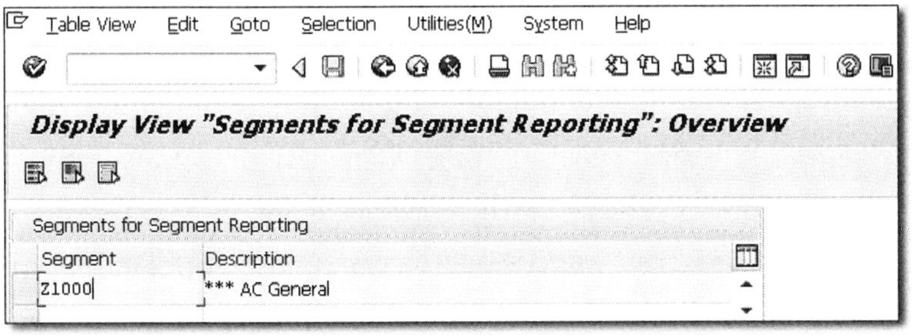

Figure A.12 Segments Display View

Once created, a segment can be assigned to a profit center, as shown in Figure A.13.

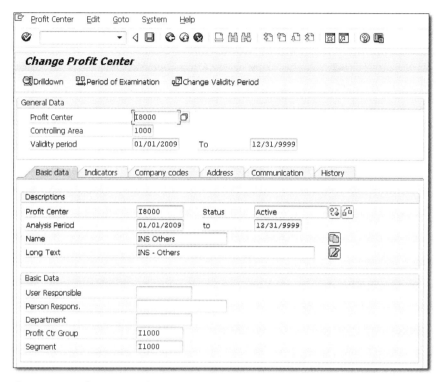

Figure A.13 Profit Center with Segment Assigned

This concludes our discussion of segments. In the next section, we will look into profit center accounting.

A.6 Profit Center Accounting

One of the key features of New G/L is the merging of Profit Center Accounting (PCA) into the G/L. In the classic PCA, a separate document is posted into PCA (ledger 8A). With New G/L, there is no need for a separate document, because the profit center is another dimension on the line item that can be reported from New G/L.

The classic PCA had limitations for non-cost-element P&L line items and balance sheet line items. The system could not derive a profit center in real time because they are not posted to a cost object (e.g., cost center).

In New G/L, financial statements can be produced directly out of the G/L. New functionality exists to default a profit center into a financial line item when no cost element exists. To do so, a default profit center has to be assigned for balance sheet account ranges using Transaction 3KEH.

To setup Transaction 3KEH, following the IMG menu path CONTROLLING • PROFIT CENTER ACCOUNTING • ACTUAL POSTINGS • CHOOSE ADDITIONAL BALANCE SHEET AND P&L ACCOUNTS • CHOOSE ACCOUNTS, as seen in Figure A.14.

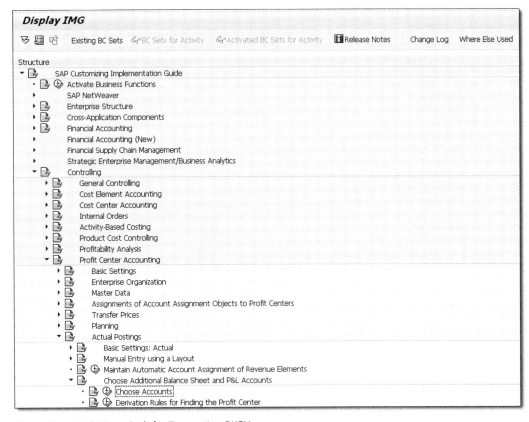

Figure A.14 IMG Menu Path for Transaction 3KEH

Click on the CHOOSE ACCOUNTS node. The CHANGE VIEW "EC-PCA: ADDITIONAL BALANCE SHEET AND PROFIT + LOSS ACCOUNTS screen appears (Figure A.15). In this example, a default profit center has been assigned to a range or balance sheet accounts.

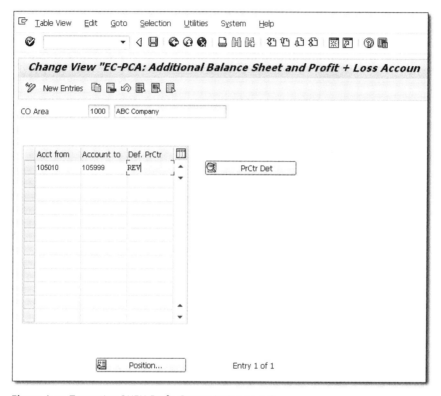

Figure A.15 Transation 3KEH Profit Center Assignment Screen

This concludes our discussion of PCA in the New G/L. Keep in mind that with the introduction of PCA into New G/L, the old PCA tables are no longer used. These include the totals table (i.e., table GLPCT), the line item table (i.e., table GLPCA), and the planned line items table (i.e., table GLPCP).

A.7 Summary

New G/L is described as enhanced G/L with greater flexibility and extensibility. In the past, multiple totals tables were needed, but with New G/L SAP has consolidated the multiple totals tables into a single totals table (i.e., table `FAGLFLEXT`). Having one summary table with multiple dimensions and the ability to add customer fields provides flexibility that did not exist in the classic G/L. Along with that flexibility came enhanced reporting and the ability to produce a financial statement at a level lower than the company code.

The key features of the New G/L covered in this appendix include parallel ledgers, document splitting, segments, and profit center accounting.

Parallel ledgers in the New G/L enable accounting valuations at a group level and according to country-specific accounting principles and legal requirements. With parallel ledgers, when posting financial transactions, you have the ability to post data to all ledgers, to a specified selection of ledgers, or to a single ledger.

When the New G/L is configured, a leading ledger is specified. This leading ledger contains the data required for consolidated financial statements. It is fully integrated with the subsidiary ledgers and updated in all company codes. Nonleading ledgers, on the other hand, are specific to one accounting principle and must be assigned to company codes individually.

Another concept introduced in the New G/L is document splitting, the ability to split document line items according to specified dimensions (e.g., segment). With real-time document splitting and zero balancing, balance sheets can be created for each dimension.

The twenty-first century has seen widespread adoption of accounting standards for segment reporting, and New G/L added the segment dimension. SAP defines a segment as a division of a company for which you can create financial statements for external reporting.

Segments are defined in SAP configuration. SEGMENT is a ten-character field with a fifty-character DESCRIPTION field. It has no other fields, parameters, or control settings. Document splitting is required to produce financial statements by segment. In addition, the zero balance setting needs to be made for the segment characteristic. Within an FI transaction, the segment can be entered manually, derived from its assignment to a profit center, or set up to derive with your own rules using a customer enhancement.

The last topic we discussed in this appendix was PCA. New G/L merges PCA into the G/L. The classic PCA had several limitations, including the need to create a separate document in PCA and the inability to derive a profit center into non-cost-element P&L line items and balance sheet line items. With the New G/L, these limitations are overcome, and financial statements using the profit center dimension can be produced directly out of the G/L. New functionality exists to default a profit center into a financial line item when no cost element exists or cost object exists.

B Important Tables in Financial Accounting

In this appendix you will find a list of all the important tables in FI.

Table	Description
ANAR	Asset Types
ANAT	Asset type text
ANEK	Document Header Asset Posting
ANEKPV	Line Item View for AuC Settlement
ANEP	Asset Line Items
ANEV	Asset downpymt settlement
ANKA	Asset classes: general data
ANKB	Asset class: depreciation area
ANKP	Asset classes: Fld Cont Dpndnt on Chart of Depreciation
ANKT	Asset classes: Description
ANKV	Asset classes: insurance types
ANLA	Asset Master Record Segment
ANLB	Depreciation terms
ANLBZA	Time-Dependent Depreciation Terms
ANLBZW	Asset-specific base values
ANLC	Asset Value Fields
ANLH	Main asset number
ANLP	Asset Periodic Values
ANLT	Asset Texts
ANLV	Insurance data
ANLX	Asset Master Record Segment
ANLZ	Time-Dependent Asset Allocations
BKPF	Accounting Document Header
BNKA	Bank Master Record
BSAD	Accounting: Secondary Index for Customers (Cleared Items)
BSAK	Accounting: Secondary Index for Vendors (Cleared Items)
BSAS	Accounting: Secondary Index for G/L Accounts (Cleared Items

Table	Description
BSEC	One-Time Account Data Document Segment
BSEG	Accounting Document Segment
BSEGC	Document: Data on Payment Card Payments
BSET	Tax Data Document Segment
BSID	Accounting: Secondary Index for Customers
BSIK	Accounting: Secondary Index for Vendors
BSIM	Secondary Index, Documents for Material
BSIP	Index for Vendor Validation of Double Documents
BSIS	Accounting: Secondary Index for G/L Accounts (Cleared Items
CEPC	Profit Center Master Data
CEPCT	Profit Center Master Data Text
FEBCL	Clearing data for an electronic bank state
FEBEP	Electronic Bank Statement Line Items
FEBEXTTRN	External transaction code text definition
FEBKO	Electronic Bank Statement Header Records
GLFLEXA	Flexible general ledger: Actual line items
GLFLEXP	Flexible G/L: Plan line items
GLFLEXT	Flexible G/L: Totals
GLSO1	FI-SL Line Item Table with Objects for GLT01
GLSO2	FI-SL Table with Objects, Structure corresponds to GLS2
GLSO3	FI-SL LI Table with Objects for GLTO3
GLT0	G/L account master record transaction figures
GLT1	Local General Ledger Summary Table
GLT2	Consolidation totals table
GLT3	Summary Data Preparations for Consolidatio
GLTO1	FI-SL Table with Objects, Structure Corresponds to GLT1
GLTO2	FI-SL Table with Objects, Structure Corresponds to GLT2
GLTO3	FISL Table with Objects, Amounts and Quantities in Format P9
KNA1	General Data in Customer Master
KNAS	Customer master (VAT registration numbers general section)
KNAT	Customer Master Record (Tax Groupings)

Table	Description
KNB1	Customer Master (Company Code)
KNB4	Customer Payment History
KNB5	Customer master (dunning data)
KNBK	Customer Master (Bank Details)
KNBW	Customer master record (withholding tax types)
KNC1	Customer master (transaction figures)
KNC3	Customer master (special G/L transaction figures)
KNEA	Assign Bank Details and Payment Methods to Revenue Type
KNKA	Customer master credit management: Central data
KNKK	Customer master credit management: Control area data
KNKKF1	Credit Management: FI Status Data
KNKKF2	Credit Management: Open Items by Days in Arrears
KNVI	Customer Master Tax Indicator
KNVK	Customer Master Contact Partner
KNVP	Customer Master Partner Functions
KNVV	Customer Master Sales Data
KNZA	Permitted Alternative Payer
LFA1	Vendor Master (General Section)
LFAS	Vendor master (VAT registration numbers general section)
LFAT	Vendor master record (tax groupings)
LFB1	Vendor Master (Company Code)
LFB5	Vendor master (dunning data)
LFBK	Vendor Master (Bank Details)
LFBW	Vendor master record (withholding tax types)
LFC1	Vendor master (transaction figures)
LFC3	Vendor master (special G/L transaction figures)
LFM1	Vendor master record purchasing organization
LFM2	Vendor Master Record: Purchasing Data
LFZA	Permitted Alternative Payee
PAYR	Payment Medium File
REGUH	Settlement data from payment program

Table	Description
SKA1	G/L Account Master (Chart of Accounts)
SKAS	G/L account master (chart of accounts: key word list)
SKAT	G/L Account Master Record (Chart of Accounts: Description)
SKB1	G/L account master (company code)
SKM1	Sample G/L accounts
SKMT	Sample Account Names
T012	House Banks
T012K	House Bank Accounts
T012T	House Bank Names

C   The Author

David Burns has more than 25 years of experience as a solution architect, consultant, author, and project manager. David regularly consults with leading public and private enterprises on the implementation and support of SAP and other enterprise applications. He advises on infrastructure and application selection, and provides expertise in finance, accounting, project and program management, and strategic planning.

Over the past two years, David has also been a contributing writer to SAP Experts, and was featured in the 2015 Q1 edition of insiderPROFILES magazine.

Index

- ▶ Learn what SAP S/4HANA Finance is—and what it can do for you

- ▶ Understand the technical foundation of SAP S/4HANA

- ▶ Explore your SAP S/4HANA Finance deployment options: on-premise, cloud, and hybrid

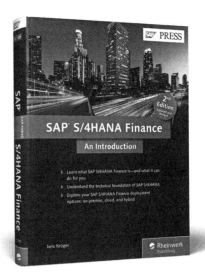

Jens Krüger

SAP S/4HANA Finance

An Introduction

It's time you got to know SAP S/4HANA Finance. Learn what SAP S/4HANA Finance can do, what it offers your organization, and how it fits into the SAP S/4HANA landscape. Explore critical SAP S/4HANA Finance functionality, from cash management to profitability analysis, and consider your deployment options. Now's your chance to lay the groundwork for your SAP S/4HANA Finance future.

411 pages, 2nd edition, pub. 02/2016
E-Book: $59.99 | **Print:** $69.95 | **Bundle:** $79.99

www.sap-press.com/4122

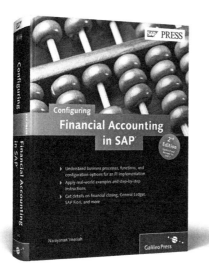

- ▶ Understand business processes, functions, and configuration options for an FI implementation

- ▶ Apply real-world examples and step-by-step instructions

- ▶ Get details on financial closing, General Ledger, SAP Fiori, and more

Narayanan Veeriah

Configuring Financial Accounting in SAP

Are you FI savvy? From intricate system configuration to far-reaching mobile apps, even the simplest Financial Accounting implementations are complex. Master the processes, subcomponents, and tools you need to align your FI system with unique business requirements. Get the tips and tricks to handle global settings configuration, SAP ERP integration, and General Ledger use with ease!

907 pages, 2nd edition, pub. 11/2014
E-Book: $69.99 | **Print:** $79.95 | **Bundle:** $89.99

www.sap-press.com/3665

www.sap-press.com

- ▶ Work with the many features and functionalities of the Controlling component

- ▶ Enhance your Controlling capabilities with integrated process flows, cost planning, SAP HANA, and more

- ▶ Up to date for EHPs 6 and 7

Janet Salmon

Controlling with SAP: Practical Guide

Let this practical guide to the Controlling module make your to-do list easier! From transactions to reporting, learn how to trace every last penny using the Controlling functions. Manage master data, set up planning and budgeting work, conduct actual postings, and execute a proper period close more efficiently. Get details about well-known CO capabilities and new technologies integrated with the component.

700 pages, 2nd edition, pub. 09/2014

E-Book: $59.99 | **Print:** $69.95 | **Bundle:** $79.99

www.sap-press.com/3625

▶ Configure the CO module to meet your business needs

▶ Improve interaction between CO and other modules

▶ Learn how SAP HANA impacts your financials processes

Kathrin Schmalzing

Configuring Controlling in SAP ERP

Configure SAP ERP Controlling to reflect each organization's unique processes! First create organizational objects like company codes and cost centers and assign them to each other. Then follow step-by-step instructions for managing master data, planning, reporting, and actual postings for Cost Element Accounting, Internal Orders, Profitability Analysis, and more. Take control of CO!

526 pages, pub. 02/2016

E-Book: $69.99 | **Print:** $79.95 | **Bundle:** $89.99

www.sap-press.com/3887

Interested in reading more?

Please visit our website for all new
book and e-book releases from SAP PRESS.

www.sap-press.com